Lecture Notes in Computer Science

Edited by G. Goos and J. Hartmanis

348

P. Deransart B. Lorho
J. Małuszyński (Eds.)

Programming
Languages Implementation
and Logic Programming

International Workshop PLILP '88
Orléans, France, May 16–18, 1988
Proceedings

Springer-Verlag

Berlin Heidelberg New York London Paris Tokyo

Editors

Pierre Deransart
INRIA-Rocquencourt, Domaine de Voluceau
B.P. 105, F-78153 Le Chesnay Cedex, France

Bernard Lorho
Université d'Orléans, Faculté des Sciences
Laboratoire d'Informatique Fondamentale (LIFO)
B.P. 6759, F-45067 Orléans Cedex 2, France

Jan Maluszyński
Department of Computer and Information Science
Linköping University
S-58183 Linköping, Sweden

CR Subject Classification (1987): F.4.1–2, D.3.1, D.3.4, F.3.3, I.2.3

ISBN 3-540-50820-1 Springer-Verlag Berlin Heidelberg New York
ISBN 0-387-50820-1 Springer-Verlag New York Berlin Heidelberg

Printing and binding: Druckhaus Beltz, Hemsbach/Bergstr.
2145/3140-543210 – Printed on acid-free paper

PREFACE

PLILP '88, the first international Workshop on Programming Languages Implementation and Logic Programming, was held from May 16 to May 18, 1988 in Orléans. PLILP '88 has been organized by the Laboratoire d'Informatique Fondamentale d'Orléans (LIFO-Université d'Orléans) and Institut National d'Informatique et d'Automatique (INRIA-Rocquencourt).

The aim of the workshop was to discuss whether research on the implementation of programming languages and research on logic programming can mutually benefit from each other's results.The intention was to bring together researchers from both fields, especially those working in the area of their intersection.

Problems such as formal specification of compilers and syntax-based editors, program analysis and program optimization have been traditionally studied by implementors of algorithmic languages and have resulted in a number of well-established notions, formalisms and techniques. At the same time, an increasing number of people use logic programming as a way of specifying compilers or other programming environment tools, taking advantage of the relatively high level of logic programming and the growing efficiency of Prolog implementations.

On the other hand, research on logic programming raises the questions of analysis of logic programs and their optimization. These are motivated primarily by compiler construction for logic programs, by studies on the methodology of logic programming and by the attempts to amalgamate logic programming and functional programming.

Research in the field of logic programming, including its applications to the implementation of other programming languages, may or may not refer to the well-known results of the other field. In the first case the field of logic programming may benefit from these results. For example application of LR parsing techniques may contribute to a more efficient implementation of definite clause grammars. On the other hand, techniques of logic programming may contribute to the development of the other field. As an example, one may consider the use of logic programs for compiler specification.

The purpose of the workshop was to review the techniques developed in one (or both) of the fields which could also be of some help in the other one and to facilitate the transfer of expertise. It seems important to compare notions used in both fields : pointing out similarities between them may prevent rediscovering results already known, while studying the differences may contribute to the transfer of technology.

The workshop consisted of a series of invited talks and a panel discussion. This book presents some of the most significant talks.

We gratefully acknowledge the financial support provided by the following institutions :
- INRIA,
- Université d'Orléans,
- GRECO de Programmation et Outils pour l'Intelligence Artificielle du CNRS.

Le Chesnay, Orléans, Linköping
December 1988

Pierre Deransart
Bernard Lorho
Jan Maluszynski

Table of Contents

Attribute Grammars in Logic Programming

Logic Programming for Programming Environments

Static Analysis Of
Functional Programs With Logical Variables*

Gary Lindstrom
Department of Computer Science
University of Utah
Salt Lake City, Utah 84112 USA

Abstract

It has recently been discovered by several researchers that logical variables, even under unconditional unification, can significantly increase the expressive power of functional programming languages. Capabilities added under this extension include (i) support for use before binding of variables, e.g. in constructing functionally attributed parse trees; (ii) computation by constraint intersection, e.g. polymorphic type checking; (iii) "micro object" support for object oriented programming, e.g. for direct message delivery, and (iv) monotonic refinement of complex data structures, e.g. function evaluation by graph reduction.

In contrast to the fundamental producer-consumer orientation of pure functional programming, there is no single "producer" of the value of a logical variable. All efficient implementations of pure functional programming rely on direct access to value sources, and exploit the resulting uni-directional information flow (e.g. by dataflow, demand propagation, or normal order graph reduction). One may therefore ask whether these implementation techniques can be augmented to accommodate the "isotropic" information flow associated with logical variables. In a previous paper we showed that the answer is largely affirmative for fine grain (S, K, I) combinator reduction implementations. We now outline an approach that adapts this technique to larger granularity combinators through a static analysis technique that estimates both operator strictness (graph partitioning into co-evaluation equivalence classes) and mode effects on logical variables (e.g. "read-only" occurrences). Many advantages are achieved, but the impossibility of comprehensive flow analysis means that the resulting large grain combinators cannot comprise exclusively sequential code.

*This research was supported in part by grant CCR-8704778 from the National Science Foundation, and by an unrestricted gift to the University of Utah from Telefonaktiebolaget LM Ericsson, Stockholm, Sweden.

1 Functional Programming With Logical Variables

1.1 What Do Logical Variables Add?

Functional and logic programming languages share common roots as declarative programming methodologies, but exhibit several distinguishing characteristics as well. Functional programming relies heavily on algebraic concepts, with a strong emphasis on combining forms, facilitated by higher order functionals and Curried notation. However, the pervasive producer-consumer orientation of functional programming dictates that all variables must be bound at the place of their introduction.

In contrast, logic programming offers the notions of *logical variables* and delayed binding via *unification*. Together, these serve several important purposes in languages such as Prolog:

1. Use of logical variables as "output" parameters in goals;

2. Construction of data structures supporting use before definition;

3. Pattern driven clause selection in procedures, and

4. Inter-process synchronization and communication (in committed choice dialects).

We argue that unification failure and nondeterminism (OR-parallelism or backtracking), while undeniably important concepts, are *not* inherent in the semantics of logical variables. Indeed, it has often been observed that logical variables formalize the mathematician's concept of "variables" — and good mathematical exposition strives to be deterministic!

Recently several researchers have discovered that logical variables, even if restricted to unconditional unification, can add significant power to functional programming languages. Capabilities facilitated by this extension include:

1. Solution of cyclic networks of equations, constructed through use before binding of variables, e.g. in functionally attributed parse trees [21];

2. Computation by constraint intersection, e.g. polymorphic type checking [33];

3. "Micro object" support for object oriented programming, e.g. for direct message delivery [29], and

4. Monotonic refinement of shared data structures, e.g. function evaluation by graph reduction [37,38].

These new capabilities rely on deferred specification of the "producer" (indeed, *producers*) of a binding, resulting in unpredictable information flow directionality throughout function graphs [39]. All efficient implementations of functional programming exploit uni-directional information flow, e.g. dataflow, demand propagation, or normal order graph reduction. One may therefore ask whether these implementation techniques can be adapted to accommodate the "isotropic" flow of information associated with logical variables. In a previous paper we showed that the answer is largely affirmative for fine-grain (S, K, I) combinator reduction implementations. We now outline an approach that adapts this technique to larger granularity combinators through a static analysis technique that estimates both operator strictness (graph partitioning into co-evaluation equivalence classes) and mode effects on logical variables (e.g. "read-only" occurrences).

1.2 Semantic Requirements

We propose the following informal criteria in judging the adequacy of a logical variable extension to a normal order (lazy) functional language:

1. Retention of normal order semantics for function and constructor application;

2. Continued availability of higher order functions (albeit with some restrictions on the role of functions as unifiable objects);

3. Binding of logical variables through a narrowing-like extension to unification, whereby expressions to be unified are evaluated lazily until "syntactic" unification obtains (or fails);

4. Determinate (repeatably unique) results, even under parallel evaluation, while:

5. Continuing to exploit information directionality wherever possible, e.g. as an evaluation strategy for purely functional subexpressions.

1.3 Sample Languages

Many languages combining functional and logic programming have been proposed, with varying levels of semantic and implementational ambition [11]. However, most do not match our criteria, often by being more liberal in some areas (e.g. supporting conditional unification), and more conservative in others (e.g. presuming only sequential evaluation). The closest examples are:

- Id Nouveau [2,35,36], which uses write-once *I-structures* as a form of logical variables in a dataflow framework;

- Kieburtz's F+L [24,25], employing equational clauses within function definitions to solve for logical variable bindings, and

- FGL+LV [27] and SASL+LV [3], two experimental languages that have preceded the work reported here.

Danforth has critically examined this language design area as a whole [9].

2 A Simple Language

2.1 SFLV

We now introduce SFLV, a simple language representative of the class of languages of interest here.[1] SFLV resembles a subset of SASL [42], with the following distinctions:

---

[1]SFLV is essentially SASL+LV [3], with unification moved from actual/formal parameter matching to equational clauses. This new form is more general, and we judge it to be more intuitive. SASL+LV, in turn, is a more complete version of the "gedanken" language FGL+LV, couched in SASL syntax.

```
diff x y =
    u : w
        assuming
            x = u : v,
            y = v : w;

diff ((1 : 2 : a) : a) ((3 : 4 : 5 : nil) : nil)
```

Figure 1: Sample SFLV source program.

```
datatype
        pgm =
                program             of func list * expr
and
        expr =
                assuming            of expr * eqn list |
                appl                of expr * expr |
                ename               of string |
                intconst            of int |
                boolconst           of bool |
                nilconst
and
        func =
                function            of string * string list * expr
and
        eqn =
                unify               of expr * expr;
```

Figure 2: Abstract syntax of SFLV.

- *Functional programming aspects:*
  - A program is a sequence of non-nested ("lambda lifted" [20]) functions, followed by an expression to be evaluated.
  - Functions are Curried as in SASL, but formal parameters are restricted to individual identifiers (no patterns).

- *Logical programming aspects:*
  - All identifiers denote logical variables, except formal parameters and function names.
  - Expressions may be qualified by a sequence of equations, with the keyword assuming generalizing the role of where in SASL.

Fig. 1 depicts the familiar Prolog difference list example in SFLV (the right associative infix operator : denotes pair construction; the result of this program is ((1 : 2 : 3 : 4 : 5 : nil) : nil)). An abstract syntax for SFLV is specified in Fig. 2, using Standard ML [34] datatype definitions; Fig. 3 shows the diff example represented in this abstract syntax.

```
program(
  [function("diff", ["x", "y"],
    assuming(
      appl(appl(ename ":", ename "u"), ename "w"),
      [unify(
        ename "x",
        appl(appl(ename ":", ename "u"), ename "v")),
      unify(
        ename "y",
        appl(appl(ename ":", ename "v"), ename "w"))]))],
  appl(appl(ename "diff",
    appl(appl(ename ":",
      appl(appl(ename ":", intconst 1),
        appl(appl(ename ":", intconst 2), ename "a"))), ename "a")),
    appl(appl(ename ":",
      appl(appl(ename ":", intconst 3),
        appl(appl(ename ":", intconst 4),
          appl(appl(ename ":", intconst 5), nilconst)))),
      nilconst)));
```

Figure 3: Abstract syntax of sample SFLV source program.

2.2 Informal Semantics of SFLV

SFLV has conventional normal order semantics, extended to deal with logical variables and equations. The semantics of these two extensions are informally specified as follows:

- *Equations:* Consider the meaning of an expression assuming(exp, [eqn1, ..., eqnk]):
  1. *Strictness:* The expression's value is that of exp, provided that simultaneous solutions can be found for the equations eqn1, ..., eqnk. Otherwise, the expression evaluates to error. Typically, exp depends in part on logical variables that receive bindings through the solution of equations eqn1, ..., eqnk.
  2. *Solving:* An equation unify(exp1, exp2) is solved by unifying exp1 and exp2. This is accomplished by evaluating exp1 and exp2 collaterally until they unify or the attempt to unify them fails. The unification strategy is governed by lazily applied recursive rules, as outlined in [28].

- *Logical variables:*
  1. *Binding:* A logical variable can become bound when it occurs as an operand to a unification operation, in the customary manner.
  2. *Coercion to a pair:* Alternatively, a logical variable can become bound to a pair u : v of newly created logical variables when it occurs as the argument to a pair selector hd or tl. This recently adopted policy facilitates optimization techniques such as open coded unification (discussed in Section 5).[2]

---

[2]Since unification failure is fatal in SFLV, and speculative computation is not allowed, this binding eagerness is semantically benign.

3. *Read-only accesses:* An expression is considered to be a *read-only* (atomic) expression if it occurs as an argument required to be an atomic value (e.g. as an arithmetic operand). If this expression yields a logical variable, no operational effect results until that variable becomes bound (by a unification action elsewhere). Note that many operators are transparent to logical variables as operands, e.g. then/else arms of conditionals, arguments to the pair constructor :, actual parameters to programmer defined functions, etc.

An approach to formalizing this semantics denotationally is sketched for FGL+LV in [27]. Overall determinacy is retained, despite indeterminate binding refinement sequences for logical variables. The reliance on normal order evaluation during unification, plus strictness on unification success in expressions containing equations, guarantee another desirable effect, termed *definiteness* [27]:

1. If the overall result of a computation depends on an expression involving conflicting unifications, that error condition will necessarily be discovered and reported as an **error** value, even in parallel or distributed implementations.

2. Conversely, no conflicting unifications can occur that are not crucial to the computation of the desired overall result.

There are, however, some semantic "costs" associated with this extension.

1. *Loss of referential transparency:* Logical variables have a unique identity property that contravenes referential transparency. Consider, for example, the function f x = y. Each application of f delivers a new logical variable; it is incorrect, therefore, to infer by referential transparency that assuming u = f 1, v = f 1 implies u = v.

2. *Reliance on normal order:* In traditional functional languages, normal order evaluation avoids divergence by evaluating ⊥-denoting expressions only as necessary. In SFLV, there is another danger to over-evaluation: **error** values needlessly arising from aggressively applied unifications. As an example, consider if b then f x else g x, where x is a logical variable, f binds x to 1, and g binds x to 2. If both arms of the conditional are evaluated eagerly, a needless unification conflict will result.

3. *Mandatory multi-tasking:* Since the binding order of logical variables is in general unpredictable (our efforts in this paper notwithstanding), a read-only access of an unbound logical variable must suspend awaiting the variable's binding. Since such accesses can occur within unify operations, this implies that unification actions cannot be sequentially scheduled *a priori*. Hence parallel, or at least pseudo-parallel (multi-tasked) evaluation is more than an acceleration technique: it is a *semantic necessity*.

2.3 Combinator Implementation

An implementation of SFLV (actually, its precursor language SASL+LV) by means of S, K, I combinators is described in [3]. Only four new combinators are required. The implementation is upward compatible in the sense that previously existing combinators are not redefined. However, as noted above, read-only variable usage in SFLV programs requires a "multi-tasking" extension of the customary stack-based evaluation method. Mechanisms are presented in [3] for managing this multi-tasking on both single and multi-processor systems.

This implementation, as does any S, K, I combinator graph reduction scheme, offers many advantages, including:

1. Normal order semantics achieved by a simple leftmost, outermost reduction strategy (within tasks);

2. Full support for higher order functions (including Currying);

3. Avoidance of recomputation, through sharing of partially evaluated expressions [1];

4. A small but powerful set of object code operators, and

5. Simplified heap management (dealing only with acyclic networks of binary nodes).

However, the S, K, I approach suffers from inefficiencies due to storage churning and redundant type and evaluation status testing. Many of the advantages of combinator graph reduction can be obtained more efficiently by compiling subgraphs into *basic blocks* of conventional imperative code [12,14,18,19]. Despite this aggregation, these subgraphs continue to be combinators in the formal sense, due to their functionality and the absence of environment data structures. These blocks also typically achieve thorough type checking on arguments at their boundaries, so that the compiled code within a block can execute in a sequential "burst" once the block's "firing conditions" are met.

3 Static Analysis

3.1 Strictness and Mode Analysis

Implementations of functional and logic programming systems can each benefit from optimizations facilitated by static (i.e. compile time) analysis.

1. In normal order functional programming systems, *strictness analysis* groups operators on the basis of co-evaluation equivalence, and

2. In logic programming systems, *mode analysis* categorizes goal arguments on the basis of prior instantiation status (e.g. *input, output,* or *unknown*) [10].

3.2 Strictness Analysis Techniques

Several techniques for mapping functional programs into large grain combinators have been investigated. As noted above, the most systematic of these rely on strictness analysis to group operators that can always be evaluated together [5,6,7,8,15,16,17,23,26,44,46]. Our strictness analysis method, reported elsewhere [13,30,31,32,47], is now briefly summarized.

3.3 Simplified Domain of Static Analysis

Our analysis is performed over a domain D of demand and type indicators, including the following primitive elements:[3]

- $\perp$: indicating, as usual, a total lack of information;

- d: indicating commitment to at least one level of normal order evaluation (e.g. to an atom or pair, possibly with unevaluated components);

- a: indicating commitment to exhaustive evaluation, with anticipation of an atomic result, and

- $\top$: indicating an atom vs. pair type clash.

D is then recursively closed with all pairs $[x, y]$ where $x, y \in D$. The ordering $\sqsubseteq$ on this domain is:

$$\perp \sqsubseteq d \sqsubseteq a$$

$$d \sqsubseteq [x, y], \forall x, y$$

$$[x, y] \sqsubseteq [u, v], \forall x \sqsubseteq u, \forall y \sqsubseteq v$$

$$x \sqsubseteq \top, \forall x$$

We extend D to $complete(D)$ including all chain limits; this makes D a (pointed) complete partial order. Reference [30] demonstrates how sup ($\sqcup$) and inf ($\sqcap$) operations on this domain model combined evaluation effects on common subexpressions (CSE's) that are *unconditionally* and *conditionally* shared, respectively. We point out a few illustrative cases: unconditional CSE's: $\sqcup(a, [d, \perp]) = \top$; $\sqcup([d, a], [a, d]) = [a, a]$; $\sqcup(d, [a, d]) = [a, d]$; conditional CSE's: $\sqcap(a, [a, a]) = d$; $\sqcap([a, d], [\perp, a]) = [\perp, d]$; $\sqcap([\top, [a, d]], [d, a]) = [d, d]$.

3.4 Augmented Domain

Domain D is sufficient for studying the effect of *individual* sources of demand (e.g. demand at function application). However, this is inadequate for the compilation of entire programs, where repeated analyses would be required with new sites of hypothesized demand to resolve all $\perp$ annotations. Consequently, we augment D with block numbers at each level of evaluation, permitting "wholesale" analysis of an entire program:

$$D = complete(\{d_i, a_i, \top_i\} \cup [u, v]_i, u, v \in D, i \in \mathcal{N})$$

where $\mathcal{N}$ is the set of natural numbers. For each i, all operators yielding values with annotations α_j for $j \equiv i$ (see below) will be compiled into the same basic block. The absence of $\perp$ indicates that if an expression is *ever* evaluated, it will be evaluated with strength at least d. Thus arcs in program graph are initially annotated with d_i for distinct $i \in \mathcal{N}$; these serve as $\perp$-analogs. Three relations involving $\mathcal{N}$ are defined:

- *equivalence* ($i \equiv j$), a binary relation expressing operator grouping by strictness; initially no element of $\mathcal{N}$ is equivalent to any other.

---

[3]For simplicity, we omit here indicators of persistent, or applicative order demand [32].

- *dominance* $(i \angle j)$, a binary relation expressing block nesting; initially dominance is simply syntactic by path domination $(i \angle j$ iff all paths from an arc annotated with β_j to the function result arc include an arc with annotation α_i). Dominance is (i) reflexive; (ii) transitive; (iii) antisymmetric $(i \angle j \wedge j \angle i \Leftrightarrow i \equiv j)$, and (iv) consistent with respect to equivalence $(i \angle j \wedge (m \equiv i) \wedge (n \equiv j) \Rightarrow m \angle n)$.

- *disjunction* $(i = j \vee k)$, a ternary relation, representing conditional evaluation effects, i.e. if $\mathbf{v} = \mathbf{cond(p, t, e)}$, and the annotations of v, t, and e are α_i, β_j, and γ_k, respectively, then $i = j \vee k$. Disjunction is made consistent with respect to equivalence.

Ordering in our augmented D is sensitive to both *structural refinement* (indicating more type information), and *block number reoccurrence* (indicating more strictness). Thus $d_0 \sqsubseteq [d_1, a_2]_0 \sqsubseteq [d_0, a_2]_0 \sqsubseteq [d_0, a_0]_0$.

It is also useful to define a relation $\le$ on D, capturing type information only (ignoring the strictness information conveyed by block number subscripts). Let α and β, respectively, be α_i and β_j with all block number subscripts removed. Then $\alpha_i \le \beta_j$ iff $\alpha \sqsubseteq \beta$, where $\sqsubseteq$ in this case refers to the ordering on the simple domain described in Section 3.2.

3.5 Rules

Let u be an arc in a function graph; the annotation of u is denoted $\chi(\mathbf{u})$. These annotations monotonically increase in D during static analysis. The effect of each operator over D is defined by a set of rules indicating typing and evaluation causality (strictness). These rules operate in the *demand-* (i.e. *anti-data*)-flow direction (some rules for propagation in the data-flow direction are included here as well.) For example, suppose u $=$ ident(v), with $\chi(\mathbf{u}) = \alpha_i$, and $\chi(\mathbf{v}) = \beta_j$. Then the rule for ident constrains $\chi(\mathbf{v})$ to be strengthened, if necessary, so that $\alpha_i \sqsubseteq \chi(\mathbf{v})$. As a "side effect", it is therefore mandated that $i \equiv j$, i.e. the ident operator should not constitute a strictness subgraph boundary.

Mandating $\alpha_i \le \beta_j$ means "refine β_j so that its type-only image β is no less than the type-only image α of α_i." This may be accomplished by making β_j sufficiently more type specific, while introducing new "don't care" block numbers as necessary. Example: if $\beta_j = d_3$ and we mandate $[a_0, d_1]_2 \le \beta_j$, then β_j might be refined to $[a_4, d_5]_3$, where 4 and 5 are new block numbers.

Rules for all other operators are defined in similar terms. Of particular interest are:

- the pair constructor :, which maintains block boundaries, reflecting laziness;

- cond, where strict atomic demand is propagated to the predicate, but disjunctive replicas (isomorphic images with new block numbers) of the demand pattern are propagated to the then/else arguments, and

- the value sharing CSE operator (u1, ..., un) $=$ fork(v), where equivalence, dominance, and disjunction all combine to propagate strictness and type information through CSE's in a safe but thorough way (see Section 4.3).

Our rules are all monotonic and continuous over D; hence fixpoint solutions for program annotations always exist. However, given the infinite height of the domain, only finite approximations can be computed in general [22]. Nevertheless, since such approximations are conservative, they never err by licensing overly aggressive evaluation.

4 Static Analysis of SFLV

4.1 Objectives

We turn now to the issue of principal concern here: how to extend static analysis to determine modes and types of logical variables, as well as strictness analysis on functional expressions. The following goals are proposed for the adequacy of this combined analysis:

1. *Correctness:* Optimizations resulting from the analysis should be semantically transparent. Over-evaluation in violation of normal order semantics must, of course, be avoided. In addition, basic block firing conditions, extended to deal with logical variables, should not introduce any risk of evaluation deadlock through excessive synchronization (under-evaluation).

2. *Open coding:* Given adequate type and evaluation status information, unification operations should be statically expanded to permit direct testing and/or binding of operands without run time recursion.

3. *Localization of task boundaries:* The situations where *bona fide* atomic operands are needed, but unbound logical variables may transiently result (see Section 6.2), should be limited to specific operators equipped to provide the necessary enqueueing and notification services.

4. *Simple run-time control:* Demand and type patterns (annotations from D) should be static analysis devices only, and should not be explicitly utilized as run time data structures.

5. *Extensibility to conditional unification:* The approach should be suitable as a platform for later extension to deal with failing unifications, e.g. in a committed choice dialect [41].

4.2 Extended Domain

The extension to D required to accommodate logical variables is surprisingly simple. We "split" the atomic result indicator a_i into two cases:

- $a_{g,i}$, indicating a result which can only manifest as a ground atomic value, i.e. where a logical variable *cannot* occur (this is the indicator a of our original domain D), and

- $a_{c,i}$, indicating an atomic value which may *initially* manifest as a logical variable.

The subscripts c and g are meant to connote *constrainable* and *ground* usages, respectively. We revise the interpretation of the previous elements of D as follows (T_i is unchanged):

- d_i indicates a value which may manifest as an atom, pair, or logical variable, and

- $[\alpha_j, \beta_k]_i$ indicates a value which may manifest as a pair or a logical variable.

Note that $[u, v]_{c,i}$ vs. $[u, v]_{g,i}$ annotation on pairs is superfluous, since hd and tl automatically coerce unbound logical variables to pairs.

Our intended meanings for $a_{c,i}$ and $a_{g,i}$ reveal their correct ordering in D:

$$d_i \sqsubseteq a_{c,i} \sqsubseteq a_{g,i}.$$

This ordering ensures that if an operator such as + is known to produce an atomic value (and cannot produce a logical variable), then the annotation on its output arc will be $a_{g,i}$, even if some usage of that value (e.g. as an input to a unify operation) also constrains it to be at least $a_{c,i}$ (or d_i).[4]

It will be useful at times to map elements in D involving $a_{g,i}$ occurrences to "weaker" counterparts involving only $a_{c,i}$ occurrences. Thus we define a function $\lambda : D \rightarrow D$ for this purpose: $\lambda(a_{g,i}) = a_{c,i}$, $\lambda([\alpha_i, \beta_j]_k) = [\lambda(\alpha_i), \lambda(\beta_j)]_k$, and $\lambda(\alpha_i) = \alpha_i$ for all other $\alpha_i \in D$.

4.3 New Rules

We must now provide static analysis rules over D for unify, our only new operator, as well as update our old rules to reflect the refinement of a_i into $a_{c,i}$ and $a_{g,i}$. Consider a = unify(b, c), with $\chi(\mathbf{a}) = \alpha_i$, $\chi(\mathbf{b}) = \beta_j$, and $\chi(\mathbf{c}) = \gamma_k$. The following static analysis rules apply (expressed for $\chi(\mathbf{b})$ in terms of $\chi(\mathbf{a})$ and $\chi(\mathbf{c})$; symmetric rules apply to $\chi(\mathbf{c})$ in terms of $\chi(\mathbf{a})$ and $\chi(\mathbf{b})$):

- $d_i \sqsubseteq \chi(\mathbf{b})$: unify is strict on its arguments (to one level of evaluation).

- $\lambda(\gamma_k) \sqsubseteq \chi(\mathbf{b})$: type and strictness information are shared between the arguments of unify, but with ground occurrences of atoms converted to constrainable occurrences. The symmetric application of this rule means that this sharing results in a *sup* effect (modulo the effect of λ).

The rules for other operators are unchanged, except that all explicit occurrences of a_i are replaced as follows:

- Atom annotations associated with operator *output* arcs are replaced with $a_{g,i}$, while

- Atom annotations associated with operator *input* arcs are replaced with $a_{c,i}$.

For example, consider an increment operator u = add1(v), with $\chi(\mathbf{u}) = \alpha_i$, and $\chi(\mathbf{v}) = \beta_j$. The static evaluation rules for add1 are then:

- *Downward propagation of type and strictness:* $a_{g,i} \sqsubseteq \chi(\mathbf{u})$: an atomic value will surely be delivered for u (i.e. not a logical variable), and

- *Upward propagation of type:* $a_{c,i} \sqsubseteq \chi(\mathbf{v})$: the operand v may deliver a logical variable (presumably as an intermediate stage to ultimately delivering an atomic value). Moreover, $j \equiv i$ (per Section 3.5), i.e. add1 is strict on its operand.

---

[4] The indicators $a_{c,i}$ and $a_{g,i}$ are an outgrowth of the demand indicators d_c and d_v, as defined in [27]. However, we have come to realize that the ordering $d_v \sqsubseteq d_c$ in this earlier work was incorrect. Moreover, only atoms now receive this discrimination, and the notation v has been changed to g to emphasize *groundness*.

These rules for $a_{c,i}$ and $a_{g,i}$ have an important property: a ground annotation $a_{g,i}$ is introduced only when the *source* of a value indicates at compile time that the value will be produced directly as an atom, without passing through a logical variable "larval stage." This means, for example, that atomic annotations on the output arcs of CSE's can only be of the $a_{c,i}$ variety, unless the input arc of the CSE bears an $a_{g,i}$ annotation. This will be very important in obtaining correct basic block firing conditions, as described in Section 6.1.

We offer two examples of previous rules that carry over unchanged:

- *Pair selectors:* Consider u = hd(v), with $\chi(u) = \alpha_i$, and $\chi(v) = \beta_j$. The following static analysis rules apply:

  1. *Downward propagation of type and head strictness:* $[\alpha_i, d_k]_i \sqsubseteq \chi(v)$, for new block number k.

  2. *Upward propagation of type:* if $[\gamma_l, \delta_m]_j \sqsubseteq \chi(v)$, then $\gamma_l \sqsubseteq \chi(u)$.

- *CSE's:* Consider (u, v) = fork(w), with $\chi(u) = \alpha_i$, $\chi(v) = \beta_j$, and $\chi(w) = \gamma_k$.[5] The following static analysis rules apply:

  1. *Downward propagation of type:* $\sqcap(\alpha_i, \beta_j) \le \chi(w)$.

  2. *Disjunctive strictness:* if $m = i \vee j$ for some m, then $k \equiv m$. This will arise when w is an expression shared across matching conditional arms; their consensus (inf) annotation is then made unconditional.

  3. *Dominance:* if $i \mathcal{L} j$, then $\alpha_i \sqsubseteq \chi(w)$. This occurs when block i dominates block j, i.e. if block j is nested inside block i. In this case, operand w is moved into the outer block i. Note that $(i \equiv j) \Leftrightarrow i \mathcal{L} j \wedge j \mathcal{L} i$ by antisymmetry; hence this rule is applied symmetrically when $i \equiv j$, resulting in a *sup* constraint on $\chi(w)$.

  4. *Upward propagation of type:* $\gamma_k \le \chi(u) \wedge \gamma_k \le \chi(v)$.

For structured annotations, these rules are recursively applied componentwise. We note that the problem of computing fixpoints over this extended domain is no different in character than that for the unextended domain.

5 Example

We now illustrate the use of SFLV and our static analysis technique on a simple function **area**, shown in Fig. 4. This function computes the area of a square, given *either* the (integer) length of a side, or its perimeter (or both). As a side effect, *both* the side and perimeter are computed as necessary, and checked for consistency.

The resulting analysis is shown in Fig. 5. Block 0 dominates all other blocks, and $0 = 1 \vee 2$. This analysis reveals much useful structure in **area**:

1. *Block structure:* The function **area** is strict on all its **unify** operators.

---

[5]For simplicity, we consider here only binary **fork** operators. Rules for the full n-ary case are presented in [47].

```
fun area ps =
    side * side
        assuming
            ps = perimeter : side,
            perimeter = 4 * side,
            side = perimeter / 4
```

Figure 4: Sample function graph.

2. *Strictness on* ps: The formal parameter ps is required to be a pair of atoms or logical variables. However, **area** need not rely on that pair being externally produced; instead, it stands ready to bind ps to a pair of logical variables, if necessary.

3. *Open coding:* The annotation $[a_{c,3}, a_{c,4}]_0$ on ps indicates that when block 0 fires (see Section 6.1), that arc will necessarily have a value equal to a pair of values, each of which will be an atom or a logical variable (unbound). This means that the equation ps = perimeter : side can be transformed at compile time to the pair of equations hd(ps) = perimeter and tl(ps) = side (not shown in Fig. 5). This provides the very useful optimization of eliminating the run-time recursive expansion of unify(ps, perimeter : side) (e.g. as optimized in the Warren Abstract Machine for Prolog [45]).

6   Operational Semantics

6.1   Firing Conditions At Block Boundaries

Once statically analyzed, a SFLV program can be compiled into large grain combinators, as per [31]. As before, a block becomes executable when each of its entering arcs bears a value meeting or exceeding its associated annotation. If the annotation is:

- d_i, the value must be a logical variable, atom, or pair;

- $a_{c,i}$, the value must be a logical variable or atom;

- $a_{g,i}$, the value must be an atom;

- $[\alpha_i, \beta_j]_k$, the value must be a logical variable or a pair:
  - If the value is a logical variable u, then u is bound to a pair of newly created logical variables $[v, w]$, and we recursively match v with α_i, and w with β_j;
  - If the value is already a pair $[u, v]$, then we recursively match u with α_i, and v with β_j.

When all the annotations on arcs entering a block are fulfilled by the values delivered, the block "fires". As in [31], the operations within the block may be compiled under the invariant that each arc, when accessed, will necessarily bear a concrete value consistent with its associated static annotation.

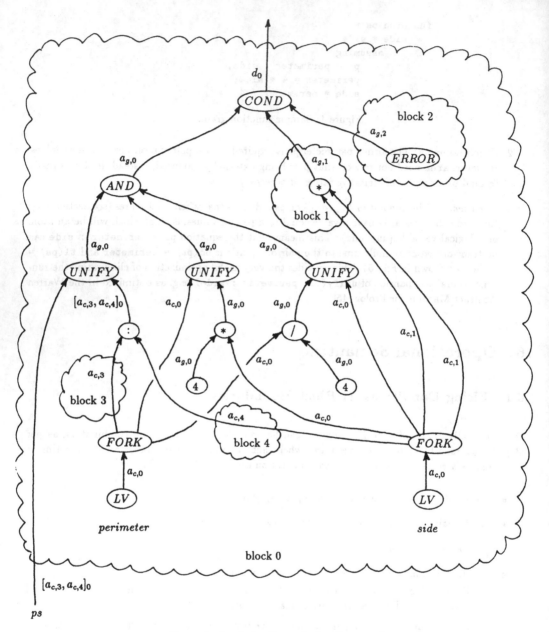

Figure 5: Analysis of sample function graph.

6.2 Interpreting $a_{c,i}$ To $a_{g,i}$ Transitions

As illustrated by the * and / operators of Fig. 5, and the add1 example of Section 4.3, some operators may not fire until they receive atomic arguments. This constitutes a read-only usage of that argument value, and will give rise to an evaluation delay if a logical variable is delivered. Such arcs, representing $a_{c,i}$ to $a_{g,i}$ transitions, are compiled with read-only identity operators inserted. The read-only operator, if presented with a logical variable, will suspend pending the binding of that logical variable to an atomic value.

The following considerations must be observed in compilation:

1. *Multi-track code:* The operators within each strictness group are compiled to a basic block of imperative code. Each basic block consists of one or more sequential *tracks.*

2. *Track boundaries:* Each read-only operator constitutes a possible interruption in the sequential flow of code execution within a basic block. Note that the execution of the block as a whole cannot suspend, for the needed logical variable binding may only occur as a side-effect of another track in the same block. Instead, execution must continue with another track of operators not dependent on the missing atomic value.

3. *Track continuation:* When a read-only operator is notified of a needed atomic value, the track which it heads can be continued. Where tracks merge (i.e. at n-ary operators, for $n \geq 2$), barrier synchronization must be employed to determine when all merging tracks have delivered values, and the operator can be applied. The queueing and notification techniques used in our S, K, I implementation serve as a model [3].

7 Future Work

We have reported here only a preliminary sketch of a novel application of static analysis. Much further work remains, including:

- *Track compilation:* Precise specification of the multi-track series-parallel code for combinators, building on the crude sketch in Section 6.2.

- *Implementation:* Implementation of the analysis method, including full integration with other embellishments of the basic method, including representations of persistent (call by value, or "applicative order") demand [32].

- *Parallel evaluation:* A prototype implementation of SFLV in S, K, I combinators has been completed, running both on a single processor, and on an 18-node BBN Butterfly multiprocessor. It will form the basis for a new implementation using large grain combinators, based on the analysis techniques outlined here.

- *Application studies:* The utility of SFLV must be assessed in one or more application areas of recognized importance. One candidate is hardware description [40], where higher order functions (for module composition), lazily evaluated streams (for feedback relationships), and logical variables (for buses and pass transistors) all have clear utility.

- *Committed choice:* An extension of SFLV to deal with unification failures has been designed and added to our prototype implementation [4]. This extension builds on the ideas in committed choice logic programming languages [41,43]. The impact of committed choice indeterminacy on the analysis method reported here must be investigated to determine if similar implementation economies can result.

References

[1] Arvind, Vinod Kathail, and Keshav Pingali. Sharing of Computation in Functional Language Implementations. In *Proceedings of International Workshop on High-level Computer Architecture*, Los Angeles, May 21-25 1984.

[2] Arvind, R. S. Nikhil, and K. K. Pingali. I-Structures: Data Structures for Parallel Computing. In Joseph H. Fasel and Robert M. Keller, editors, *Graph Reduction: Proceedings of a Workshop*, pages 336–369, Springer-Verlag, 1987. Lecture Notes in Computer Science No. 279.

[3] Göran Båge and Gary Lindstrom. *Combinator Evaluation of Functional Programs with Logical Variables.* Technical Report UUCS-87-027, Department of Computer Science, University of Utah, October 1987.

[4] Göran Båge and Gary Lindstrom. Committed Choice Functional Programming. In *Proc. International Conference on Fifth Generation Computer Systems*, Institute for New Generation Computer Technology (ICOT), Tokyo, November 1988.

[5] Adrienne Bloss and Paul Hudak. Variations on Strictness Analysis. In *Conference on Lisp and Functional Programming*, pages 132–142, ACM, Cambridge, Massachusetts, August 1986.

[6] G. L. Burn, C. L. Hankin, and S. Abramsky. Theory and practice of strictness analysis for higher order functions. April 1985. Dept. of Computing, Imperial College of Science and Technology.

[7] C. Clack and S. L. Peyton Jones. Generating parallelism from strictness analysis. In *Prof. Conf. on Func. Prog. Lang. and Comp. Arch.*, IFIP, Nancy, France, September 1985. Lecture Notes in Computer Science, number 201.

[8] C. Clack and S. L. Peyton Jones. Strictness Analysis - A Practical Approach. In *Proc. Conf. on Functional Programming Languages and Computer Architectures*, pages 35–49, Springer Verlag, 1985. Lecture Notes in Computer Science, number 201.

[9] S. H. Danforth. *Logical Variables for a Functional Language.* Technical Report PP-120-85, Microelectronics and Computer Technology Corp., 1985.

[10] Saumya K. Debray and David S. Warren. Automatic Mode Inference for Prolog Programs. In Robert M. Keller, editor, *Symposium on Logic Programming*, pages 78–88, IEEE Computer Society, Salt Lake City, September 1986.

[11] D. DeGroot and G. Lindstrom. *Logic Programming: Functions, Relations and Equations.* Prentice-Hall, Englewood Cliffs, NJ, 1986. $39.95; reviews in *Computing Reviews* Aug. 1987, no. 8708-0643; SIGART Newsletter, July 1987, no. 101.

[12] Jon Fairbairn and Stuart Wray. TIM: A Simple, Lazy Abstract Machine to Execute Combinators. In *Proc. Conf. on Functional Programming Languages and Computer Architectures*, pages 34–45, Springer Verlag, 1987. Lecture Notes in Computer Science, number 274.

[13] Lal George. *Efficient Normal Order Evaluation Through Strictness Information*. MS thesis, University of Utah, March 1987.

[14] B. Goldberg and P. Hudak. Serial Combinators: Optimal Grains of Parallelism. In *Proc. Conf. on Functional Programming Languages and Computer Architectures*, pages 382–399, Springer Verlag, Nancy, France, 1985. Lecture Notes in Computer Science, number 201.

[15] Cordelia V. Hall and David S. Wise. *Compiling Strictness Into Streams*. Technical Report 209, Indiana Univ., December 1986.

[16] P. Hudak and J. Young. A set-theoretic characterization of function strictness in the lambda calculus. In *Proc. Workshop on Implementations of Functional Languages*, Chalmers Univ., Aspenas, Sweden, February 1985.

[17] J. Hughes. Strictness detection in non-flat domains. 1985. Programming Research Group, Oxford.

[18] John Hughes. Super Combinators: a New Implementation Method for Applicative Languages. In *Proc. Symp. on Lisp and Func. Pgmming. and Computer Architectures*, pages 1–10, ACM, Pittsburgh, Pa., 1982.

[19] T. Johnsson. Efficient compilation of lazy evaluation. In *Proc. Symp. on Compiler Const.*, ACM SIGPLAN, Montreal, 1984.

[20] T. Johnsson. Lambda Lifting: Transforming Programs to Recursive Equations. In J.-P. Jouannaud, editor, *Proc. Symp. on Functional Programming Languages and Computer Architectures*, pages 190–203, Springer-Verlag, 1985.

[21] R. M. Keller and G. Lindstrom. Applications of Feedback in Functional Programming. In *Proc. Conf. on Functional Programming Languages and Computer Architecture*, pages 123–130, Portsmouth, NH, October 1981. Appeared in preliminary form as Invited Paper, Symposium on Functional Languages and Computer Architecture, Laboratory on Programming Methodology, Department of Computer Sciences, Chalmers University of Technology, Goteborg, Sweden, June 1981.

[22] R. B. Kieburtz. Abstract Interpretations Over Infinite Domains Cannot Terminate Uniformly. February 17, 1986. Unpublished note, Dept. of Computer Science, Oregon Graduate Center.

[23] R. B. Kieburtz and M. Napierala. A Studied Laziness – Strictness Analysis With Structured Data Types. 1985. Extended abstract, Oregon Graduate Center.

[24] Richard B. Kieburtz. Functions + Logic in Theory and Practice. February 25, 1987. 21 pp. unpublished paper.

[25] Richard B. Kieburtz. Semantics of a Functions + Logic Language. September 3, 1986. 17 pp. unpublished paper.

[26] T.-M. Kuo and P. Mishra. On Strictness and its Analysis. In *Proc. Symp. on Princ. of Pgmming. Lang.*, ACM, Munich, West Germany, March 1987.

[27] G. Lindstrom. Functional Programming and the Logical Variable. In *Proc. Symp. on Princ. of Pgmming. Lang.*, pages 266–280, ACM, New Orleans, January 1985. Also available as INRIA Rapport de Recherche No. 357.

[28] G. Lindstrom. Implementing Logical Variables on a Graph Reduction Architecture. In R. M. Keller and J. Fasel, editors, *Proc. Santa Fe Workshop on Graph Reduction*, pages 382–400, Springer-Verlag, 1987. Lecture Notes in Computer Science 279.

[29] G. Lindstrom. Notes on Object Oriented Programming in FGL+LV. March 20, 1985. Unpublished working document.

[30] G. Lindstrom. Static Evaluation of Functional Programs. In *Proc. Symposium on Compiler Construction*, pages 196–206, ACM SIGPLAN, Palo Alto, CA, June 1986.

[31] G. Lindstrom, L. George, and D. Yeh. Generating Efficient Code from Strictness Annotations. In *TAPSOFT'87: Proc. Second International Joint Conference on Theory and Practice of Software Development*, pages 140–154, Pisa, Italy, March 1987. Springer Lecture Notes in Computer Science No. 250.

[32] Gary Lindstrom, Lal George, and Dowming Yeh. Compiling Normal Order to Fair and Incremental Persistence. August 1987. Technical summary; 12 pp.

[33] R. Milner. A Theory of Type Polymorphism. *J. of Comp. and Sys. Sci.*, 17(3):348–375, 1978.

[34] Robin Milner. *The Standard ML Core Language (Revised)*. LFCS Report ECS-LFCS-86-2, Dept. of Computer Science, Univ. of Edinburgh, Scotland, March 1986. Part I of *Standard ML*, by Robert Harper, David MacQueen and Robin Milner.

[35] R. S. Nikhil. *Id World Reference Manual (for Lisp Machines)*. Technical Report Computation Structures Group Memo, MIT Laboratory for Computer Science, April 24, 1987.

[36] R. S. Nikhil, K. Pingali, and Arvind. *Id Nouveau*. Technical Report Computation Structures Group Memo 265, MIT Laboratory for Computer Science, July 1986.

[37] Keshav K. Pingali. *Demand-Driven Evaluation on Dataflow Machines*. PhD thesis, Mass. Inst. of Tech., Cambridge, Mass., May 1986.

[38] Keshav K. Pingali. Lazy Evaluation and the Logical Variable. In *Proc. Inst. on Declarative Programming*, Univ. of Texas, Austin, Texas, August 24-29, 1987.

[39] U.S. Reddy. On the Relationship Between Functional and Logic Languages. In D. DeGroot and G. Lindstrom, editors, *Logic Programming: Functions, Relations, and Equations*, Prentice Hall, 1986.

[40] Mary Sheeran. Designing Regular Array Architectures Using Higher Order Functions. In *Proc. Conf. on Functional Programming Languages and Computer Architectures*, pages 220–237, Springer Verlag, Nancy, France, 1985. Lecture Notes in Computer Science, number 201.

[41] Stephen Taylor, Shmuel Safra, and Ehud Shapiro. A Parallel Implementation of Flat Concurrent Prolog. *International Journal of Parallel Programming*, 15(3):245–275, June 1986.

[42] D. A. Turner. A New Implementation Technique for Applicative Languages. *Software Practice and Experience*, 9:31–49, 1979.

[43] K. Ueda. *Guarded Horn Clauses: A Parallel Logic Programming Language with the Concept of a Guard*. Technical Report TR-208, ICOT, Tokyo, 1986.

[44] Phil Wadler. Strictness analysis on non-flat domains (by abstract interpretation over finite domains). November 10, 1985. Unpublished note, Programming Research Group, Oxford Univ.

19

[45] D. H. D. Warren. *An Abstract Prolog Instruction Set.* SRI Project 4776 Technical Note 309, SRI International, Menlo Park, Calif., October 1983.

[46] S. C. Wray. A new strictness detection algorithm. In *Proc. Workshop on Implementations of Functional Languages*, Chalmers Univ., Aspenas, Sweden, February 1985.

[47] Dowming Yeh. *Static Evaluation of a Functional Language Through Strictness Analysis.* MS thesis, University of Utah, September 1987.

Towards a Clean Amalgamation of Logic Programs with External Procedures [1]

Staffan Bonnier, Jan Małuszyński
Department of Computer and Information Science,
Linköping University,
S-581 83 Linköping, Sweden

Abstract :

The paper presents a clean approach to the amalgamation of logic programming with external functional procedures. Both the logical semantics and the operational semantics of the amalgamated language are outlined. The operational semantics is based on an incomplete $\mathcal{E}$-unification algorithm which we call S-unification. It is suggested to use abstract interpretation techniques in order to identify classes of goals for which the approach is complete. For this purpose a domain of abstract substitutions is defined, and an abstract unification algorithm used for a compile-time check is developed.

1 Introduction

This paper presents a systematic approach to the problem of amalgamating logic programs with external procedures. The motivation for this is twofold:

- To allow for re-using of existing (possibly imperative) software while still preserving the declarative nature or the top-level logic programs.

- To allow for use of functions in logic programming whenever it is more natural than expressing a function as a relation.

In recent years there have been a number of suggestions concerning combination of functional and logic programming in a single framework (see e.g. [6] or [3] for a survey). The approaches can be classified as:

- Integrating existing programming languages and logic programs (well-known examples of this type are LOGLISP [21], QLOG [14], POPLOG [18] and APPLOG [5]).

- Construction of new languages which allow one to define functions and relations and to combine functional and relational definitions. (well-known examples are EQLOG [8], LEAF [2] and FUNLOG [22]).

---

[1] This paper was originally published in the ICLP proceedings, copyright 1988 by the MIT Press

The main objective within the first approach is often to give access from logic programs to specific features of the underlying programming language, or programming environment. This aspect is usually more important than concern about the declarative semantics of the amalgamation. It may be rather difficult to give such a semantics if low-level features of the underlying system are accessible in the resulting language. On the other hand, within the second approach the objective is often to have a clean logical semantics.

This paper combines the objectives of both approaches by limiting their generality. The assumption is that the language of external procedures is given, but we are not specific about its definition, so that our approach could be applied for any language. The task is to integrate the external procedures with logic programs in such a way that the amalgamation has a clean logical semantics and a reasonably efficient operational semantics, as complete as possible.

The basis for the construction of an interface between the two different systems is the assumption that terms are their common data structure. A call of a functional procedure is itself a term. Since its execution is assumed to return a term, we can view the underlying programming system as a term rewriting system. This permits the use of the theory of logic programming with equality (see e.g. [11]) to give a clean declarative semantics of the amalgamated language, and for application of $\mathcal{E}$-unification in its interpreter. However, since we are not specific about the language of the functional procedures, we have no access to the rewrite rules used by the system, and we cannot use them for construction of $\mathcal{E}$-unifiers. Our solution to this problem is an incomplete $\mathcal{E}$-unification algorithm, called S-unification, outlined first in [16]. It has the property that whenever it succeeds, the result is a complete set of $\mathcal{E}$-unifiers of the arguments (which due to our restrictions is a singleton). It may also fail or report that it is unable to solve the problem of $\mathcal{E}$-unification for the given arguments. If the algorithm fails the actual arguments have no $\mathcal{E}$-unifier. In [15] we give a formal presentation of the S-unification algorithm and we prove its properties stated above.

This paper uses the results to develop a sufficient condition for the safe use of amalgamated programs. A compile-time check is presented which for a given amalgamated program P and a class of goals can show that the execution of P with any goal of the class will not abort due to the "don't know" outcome of S-unification.

2 The Language

The main feature of the syntax is the partition of functors and predicate symbols into internal and external symbols. The role of the external symbols is to denote the external procedures to be used in logic programs. The alphabet is, as usual, the union ot three different sets of symbols:

- Σ, the set of *function symbols* (or *functors*).

- Π, the set of *predicate symbols*.

- *VAR*, the set of *variables*.

To each function symbol and predicate symbol we assign an *arity*. Σ partitions into two disjoint sets: one of *internal functors* (or *constructors*) and one of *external functors*. Similarly Π partitions into the three sets of *internal predicate symbols, external predicate symbols* and $\{=\}$ where $=$ is a distinguished *equality symbol* of arity two. The terms are built in the standard way over VAR and Σ. Terms built only from variables and constructors are called *structures*. The *atoms* are constructed by filling the argument places of the predicate symbols with terms. In particular, the atoms constructed from $=$ are called *equations*. By a *program clause* we mean a construction of the form $H : -B_1 \ldots B_n$ where H, called the *head* of the clause, is an atom built from an internal predicate symbol, and $B_1 \ldots B_n$ is a possibly empty sequence of atoms, called the *body* of the clause. By a *goal clause* we mean a program clause with no head. Finally we define an (amalgamated) *program* to be a finite set of program clauses.

3 The Logical Semantics

Our main idea is to allow the use of functional procedures written in *any* language (be it assembler or be it ML) in logic programs. However, in order to assign a clean formal semantics as well as an operational semantics to the amalgamated programs, some restrictions on the permitted procedures are needed. First of all we restrict ourselves to procedures working on ground (i.e. variable free) terms. It is assumed that whenever a functional procedure is called with all its arguments instantiated to ground terms of the appropriate sort, it terminates and returns a ground term as result. In order for this term to be completely reduced, we also require it to be a structure. In the sequel we distinguish a special class of functional procedures which return truth values (succeed or fail). They will be called *tests*. Each external functor f is the name of one non-test procedure with n arguments, where n is the arity of f. Similarly the external predicate symbols are names of test procedures. Hence $s(t_1 \ldots t_n)$ denotes the application of the procedure named by s to the terms $t_1 \ldots t_n$, while $s(t_1 \ldots t_n)\downarrow$ denotes the result of its evaluation. The restriction of $\downarrow$ to non-test procedures will be denoted by $\downarrow_f$ and its restriction to test procedures will be denoted by $\downarrow_t$. In the rest of the paper we will consider the extension of $\downarrow_f$ to *all* ground terms, including structures: For every n-ary constructor c and ground terms $t_1 \ldots t_n$, $c(t_1 \ldots t_n)\downarrow_f$ is defined to be $c(t_1\downarrow_f \ldots t_n\downarrow_f)$. Two ground terms t_1 and t_2 are considered to be *equivalent*, denoted by $t_1 \sim t_2$, iff $t_1\downarrow_f = t_2\downarrow_f$. As a further restriction on the non-test procedures, we require that $\sim$ is a congruence relation, that is, for each n-ary functor f, $f(t_1 \ldots t_n) \sim f(t_1' \ldots t_n')$ whenever $t_i \sim t_i'$ for $1 \leq i \leq n$. From a computational point of view, this means that the result obtained by evaluating a term does not change if its subterms are reduced first. Similarly we require that the relations computed by the test procedures respect $\sim$, i.e. whenever $t_i \sim t_i'$ for $1 \le i \le n$ and p is an external predicate symbol, $p(t_1 \ldots t_n)\downarrow_t$ succeeds iff $p(t_1' \ldots t_n')\downarrow_t$ succeeds. Now the standard construction may be used to obtain the least (or *initial*) model for each amalgamated program P (see e.g. [9]):

First divide the ground term algebra by $\sim$ (to obtain a model for the non-test procedures) and then extend this quotient to the least model for the sentences in P which interprets $=$ as the identity relation and which, for each external predicate symbol p, satisfies $p(t_1 \ldots t_n)$ iff $p(t_1 \ldots t_n)\downarrow_t$ succeeds.

4 S-unification

This section is primarily concerned with equation solving or $\mathcal{E}$-*unifica-tion* in the presence of a set $\mathcal{E}$ of equations. For this purpose we develop an incomplete $\mathcal{E}$-unification algorithm, called S-unification.

4.1 $\mathcal{E}$-unification

Let $\mathcal{E}$ be a set of equations. The least congruence on terms (equational theory) generated by $\mathcal{E}$ is denoted by $=_{\mathcal{E}}$. By an $\mathcal{E}$-*unifier* of two terms t_1 and t_2 we mean a substitution σ such that $t_1\sigma =_{\mathcal{E}} t_2\sigma$. A set S of $\mathcal{E}$-unifiers of t_1 and t_2 is *complete* iff every $\mathcal{E}$-unifier σ of t_1 and t_2 factors into $\sigma =_{\mathcal{E}} \theta\gamma$ for some substitutions $\theta \in S$ and γ. Here $=_{\mathcal{E}}$ is defined for substitutions σ_1 and σ_2 by $\sigma_1 =_{\mathcal{E}} \sigma_2$ iff $x\sigma_1 =_{\mathcal{E}} x\sigma_2$ for each $x \in VAR$. Traditionally the problem of $\mathcal{E}$-unification is solved by transforming the (finite set of) equations defining the functions into *rewrite rules*. By applying a technique called *narrowing* [10] or some variant thereof, it is then sometimes possible to construct a complete set of $\mathcal{E}$-unifiers for the given terms, or to decide that the terms are not $\mathcal{E}$-unifiable. Due to the restrictions presented in section 3, the functions computed by the non-test procedures may be thought of as being defined by the following set of equations:

$$\mathcal{E} = \{t_1 = t_2 \mid t_1\gamma \sim t_2\gamma \text{ for } every \text{ grounding substitution } \gamma \text{ of } t_1, t_2\}$$

Clearly, in our case we only have access to an infinite set of ground equations, and it is therefore impossible to give a general algorithm, which enumerates a complete set of $\mathcal{E}$-unifiers of two terms. Our approach is instead to carefully select some cases when it is possible to construct a complete *singleton* of $\mathcal{E}$-unifiers for the given terms, or to decide that no $\mathcal{E}$-unifier of the terms can exist. The incomplete $\mathcal{E}$-unification algorithm obtained in this way will be called S(tructure oriented) unification.

4.2 The Disagreement set

The *reduced form* of a term t is the term obtained by substituting each ground subterm u of t by $u\downarrow_f$. If for example c and the numerals are constructors, x is a variable and $+$ is an external functor with its usual interpretation, then the reduced form of $c(x, (2 + 5) + x)$ is $c(x, 7 + x)$.

Let t_1 and t_2 be terms and let r_1 and r_2 be their respective reduced forms. We define the *disagreement set* of t_1 and t_2, denoted by $\mathcal{D}(t_1, t_2)$, to be the least set which satisfies the following three conditions:

1. If the top symbol of r_1 and r_2 differs, then $\{r_1, r_2\} \in \mathcal{D}(t_1, t_2)$.

2. If r_1 and r_2 are distinct but have the same external functor as top symbol, then $\{r_1, r_2\} \in \mathcal{D}(t_1, t_2)$.

3. If $r_1 = c(u_1 \ldots u_n)$ and $r_2 = c(u'_1 \ldots u'_n)$ where c is a constructor, then $\mathcal{D}(u_i, u'_i) \subseteq \mathcal{D}(t_1, t_2)$ for $1 \leq i \leq n$.

Example :

Let $t_1 = c(x * x, c(2 + 2, x + 2))$ and $t_2 = c(y * y, c(7 - 2, x + 2))$ where c and the numerals are constructors, $x, y \in VAR$ and $+, -$ and $*$ are external functors with their usual interpretations. The reduced forms of t_1 and t_2 are $c(x * x, c(4, x + 2))$ and $c(y * y, c(5, x + 2))$ respectively. By two applications of 3 we see that $\mathcal{D}(t_1, t_2) = \mathcal{D}(x * x, y * y) \cup \mathcal{D}(4, 5) \cup \mathcal{D}(x + 2, x + 2)$. From 2 then follows that $\{x * x, y * y\} \in \mathcal{D}(t_1, t_2)$, and from 1 it follows that $\{4, 5\} \in \mathcal{D}(t_1, t_2)$. Hence $\mathcal{D}(t_1, t_2) = \{\{x * x, y * y\}, \{4, 5\}\}$.
□

It is not hard to see that the condition: $\forall \{u_1, u_2\} \in \mathcal{D}(t_1, t_2) : u_1 \sigma =_{\mathcal{E}} u_2 \sigma$, is both necessary and sufficient for σ to be an $\mathcal{E}$-unifier of t_1 and t_2. Note that this would no longer be true if we choose to skip condition 2 in the definition of the disagreement set, and instead handled external functors as constructors (this is done in e.g. [22]). As an example, $\{x \leftarrow -y\}$ is an $\mathcal{E}$-unifier of $x * x$ and $y * y$ but is *not* an $\mathcal{E}$-unifier of x and y, although $\mathcal{D}(x * x, y * y)$ would be $\{\{x, y\}\}$ with the altered definition. If we skipped 2 we would therefore wind up with an algorithm which sometimes produced an *incomplete* set of $\mathcal{E}$-unifiers for the given terms, and hence we would not achieve our goal. Our next step is to analyze $\mathcal{D}(t_1, t_2)$, and by means of this analysis formulate three different conditions: The first condition tells us how any $\mathcal{E}$-unifier of t_1 and t_2 necessarily must bind the variables, and the following two conditions ensures that it is safe to fail:

- If $\{x, u\} \in \mathcal{D}(t_1, t_2)$ where x is a variable which does not occur in u, then any $\mathcal{E}$-unifier of t_1 and t_2 must bind x to a a term equivalent to an instance of u. We therefore name the fact that x is a variable which does not occur in u by $Substcond(x, u)$.

- If $\{u_1, u_2\} \in \mathcal{D}(t_1, t_2)$ and u_1, u_2 both have constructors as top symbols, then no $\mathcal{E}$-unifier of u_1 and u_2 can exist, since these constructors must be distinct, and hence the above condition implies that no $\mathcal{E}$-unifier of t_1 and t_2 exists. We call the existence of such an element in $\mathcal{D}(t_1, t_2)$ by $Failcond_1(\mathcal{D}(t_1, t_2))$.

- If $\{x, u\} \in \mathcal{D}(t_1, t_2)$, $x \in VAR$ and x has at least one occurrence in u, which is outside every subterm of u having an external functor as top symbol, then no $\mathcal{E}$-unifier of u_1 and u_2 can exist, and consequently no such exists for t_1 and t_2 either. This case, which we call $Failcond_2(\mathcal{D}(t_1, t_2))$, corresponds to the usual occur-check failure.

Note that the fact that x occurs in u is *not* sufficient for x and u not to be $\mathcal{E}$-unifiable, even if the top symbol of u is a constructor. Consider for example the case where c is a constructor, f is an external functor and t is a ground term such that $f(c(t))\downarrow_f = t$, then $\{x \leftarrow c(t)\}$ is an $\mathcal{E}$-unifier of x and $c(f(x))$.

4.3 Unification

Next we present the S-unification algorithm. The algorithm may *succeed* and return a substitution as result, it may *fail*, or it may give an *error message*:

$$S\text{-unify}(t_1, t_2) :$$
begin
$\quad \sigma := \epsilon;$
$\quad \mathcal{D} := \mathcal{D}(t_1, t_2);$
$\quad$**while** $\mathcal{D} \neq \emptyset$ **do**
$\quad\quad$**if** $Failcond_1(\mathcal{D})$ **or** $Failcond_2(\mathcal{D})$
$\quad\quad$**then** $FAIL$
$\quad\quad$**else if** $\exists\{x, u\} \in \mathcal{D} : Substcond(x, u)$
$\quad\quad\quad$**then begin**
$\quad\quad\quad\quad\quad \sigma := \sigma\{x \leftarrow u\};$
$\quad\quad\quad\quad\quad \mathcal{D} := \mathcal{D}(t_1\sigma, t_2\sigma);$
$\quad\quad\quad$**end**
$\quad\quad\quad$**else** $ERROR$
$\quad$**else return** σ
end.

An error message indicates that the terms are not sufficiently instantiated, and hence that the algorithm can not decide whether they are $\mathcal{E}$-unifiable. We do however have the following result [15]:

Theorem :

For any terms t_1 and t_2, S-unify(t_1, t_2) terminates. Moreover:

1. If S-unify(t_1, t_2) succeeds and returns σ, then $\{\sigma\}$ is a complete set of $\mathcal{E}$-unifiers of t_1 and t_2.

2. If S-unify(t_1, t_2) fails, then t_1 and t_2 have no $\mathcal{E}$-unifier.

$\square$

It should be mentioned that the S-unification algorithm reduces to Robinsons unification algorithm [20] whenever it is called with both its arguments instantiated to structures.

Example :

Let $t_1 = s(x * x, t)$ and $t_2 = s(x, x)$, where s and the numerals are constructors, $x \in VAR$ and $*$ is an external functor with its usual interpretation. S-unify(t_1, t_2) will succeed and return $\{x \leftarrow t\}$ iff t is 0 or 1, it will fail iff t is any other numeral, and it will give an error message iff t is nonground.
□

5 The Operational Semantics

In this section an interpreter for the amalgamated language is outlined, and some simple examples of amalgamated programs are presented. Troughout this and the following section, internal predicate symbols will be treated as constructors.

5.1 The Interpreter

We start out from a standard Prolog interpreter with its left-to-right computation rule, and exchange its purely syntactic unification for S-unification. Hence the operational semantics of a program P, which defines how an answer substitution is to be computed from a goal clause, may be given in terms of the least relation $\mathcal{O}_P$ between goal clauses and substitutions, satisfying:

- □ $\mathcal{O}_P \epsilon$, where □ is the empty goal.

- If S-unify(t_1, t_2) succeeds and returns σ, then $: - t_1 = t_2 \mathcal{O}_P \sigma$.

- If p is an external predicate symbol and $t_1 \ldots t_n$ are ground terms such that $p(t_1 \ldots t_n)\downarrow_t$ succeeds, then $: - p(t_1 \ldots t_n) \mathcal{O}_P \epsilon$.

- If A is an atom which is built from an internal predicate symbol, $H : - B_1 \ldots B_n$ is a (renamed) clause from P such that S-unify(A, H) succeeds and returns σ_1, and $: - (B_1 \ldots B_n)\sigma_1 \mathcal{O}_P \sigma_2$, then $: - A \mathcal{O}_P (\sigma_1 \sigma_2 \mid \mathcal{V}(A))$, where the last expression denotes the restriction of $\sigma_1 \sigma_2$ to the variables occuring in A.

- If $: - B_1 \ldots B_i \mathcal{O}_P \sigma_1$ and $: - (B_{i+1} \ldots B_n)\sigma_1 \mathcal{O}_P \sigma_2$ where $i \leq n$, then $: - B_1 \ldots B_n \mathcal{O}_P \sigma_1 \sigma_2$.

5.2 Admitted Goals of a Program

If, during the execution of a program P with a goal G, no runtime error caused by S-unification occurs, and no attempt is made to call a test procedure with nonground arguments, then it is not possible at this execution to distinguish our interpreter from SLD-resolution combined with a complete $\mathcal{E}$-unification algorithm. From the fact that such a combination is a complete deduction system for Horn clause logic with equality [11], we may then conclude that we for each program have a class of goals for which our interpreter is complete. If P is a program and G is such a goal, we say that P *admits* G. More precisely, let A be a body atom of P or G, and let $C_G(A)$ be the set of *call instantiations* of A, i.e. the set of all possible instantiations of A whenever A becomes the actual subgoal during the processing of G. Now P admits G iff, for each body atom A of P and G, and $\sigma \in C_G(A)$, the following three conditions are satisfied:

- If $A = (t_1 = t_2)$, then S-unify$(t_1\sigma, t_2\sigma)$ does not give an error message.

- If $A = p(t_1 \ldots t_n)$ where p is an external predicate symbol, then $t_i\sigma$ is ground for $1 \leq i \leq n$.

- If A is built from an internal predicate symbol and $H : - B_1 \ldots B_n$ is any (renamed) clause from P, then S-unify$(A\sigma, H)$ does not give an error message.

5.3 Examples

Next we present two simple examples of amalgamated programs:

Example 1 :

Suppose $+$ and $-$ are external functors, and let $\leq$ be an external predicate symbol, all with their standard interpretations. The predicate *leq* has the same logical semantics as $\leq$ on nonnegative integers, but may be called with its first argument uninstantiated:

$$leq(0, x).$$
$$leq(y + 1, x) : - 1 \leq x, leq(y, x - 1).$$

Hence $: - leq(x, 2)$ would yield the enumeration $x = 0, x = 1$ and $x = 2$. However, the program does not admit goals of the form $: - leq(n, m)$ where n and m are integers, since S-unification of $leq(n, m)$ and $leq(y + 1, x)$ would give $ERROR$ as result. Neither does it admit goals where the second argument is uninstantiated, due to the symbol $\leq$ occuring in the second clause.
□

Example 2 :

By a *partition* of a nonnegative integer n, we mean a sequence of positive integers which sums up to n. The following program, which uses Prologs standard notation for lists, enumerates all partitions of a given integer:

$$part([], 0).$$
$$part([h \mid t], x) : - leq(h, x), h \neq 0, part(t, x - h).$$

The program uses *leq* from the previous example and the external predicate symbol $\neq$ with its obvious interpretation. As an example, the goal : $- \, part(x, 2)$ would yield the following enumeration: $x = [1, 1]$, $x = [2]$.
□

6 Static Analysis of Amalgamated Programs

This section outlines a technique for static analysis of amalgamated programs. The problem is whether a given program admits a given class of goals. This problem is undecidable. This can be proved by reducing it to the halting problem of Turing machines, in a similar way as it was done in [7] for the occur-check problem. Therefore a sufficient condition is suggested, which results in a relatively simple check procedure. The approach is similar to that of abstract interpretation, see e.g. [17], [13], [4], [19]. For the infinite domain of terms, a finite set $\mathcal{K}$ of subdomains is defined. Its elements, called *kinds* are the following:

- **e**, denoting the empty set.

- **v**, denoting the set of variables.

- **g**, denoting the set of all ground terms.

- **s**, denoting the set of all terms having a structure as reduced form.

- **t**, denoting the set of all terms.

The concretization function Δ on $\mathcal{K}$ associates with each kind the corresponding set of terms. By the assumption that the external procedures always terminate and return a structure, $\mathcal{K}$ forms a lattice under the ordering: $k_1 \le k_2$ iff $\Delta(k_1) \subseteq \Delta(k_2)$. An *abstract substitution* π, characterizes a set of substitutions $\mathcal{S}(\pi)$ by specifying:

- D_π : a finite set of variables, the *domain* of π.

- $\kappa_\pi : D_\pi \mapsto \mathcal{K}$: the *kind assignment* which specifies the kind of terms which are allowed to be assigned to the variables, i.e. for every $x \in D_\pi$ and $\sigma \in \mathcal{S}(\pi)$, $x\sigma \in \Delta(\kappa_\pi(x))$.

- $\alpha_\pi \subseteq D_\pi \times D_\pi$: the *aliasing relation*; $x\alpha_\pi y$ iff there is a substitution σ in $\mathcal{S}(\pi)$ such that $x\sigma$ and $y\sigma$ have a common variable.

For an abstract substitution π, κ_π is extended to terms having all their variables in D_π by:

- If t is a constant, then $\kappa_\pi(t) = \mathbf{g}$.

- If t is a variable x, then $\kappa_\pi(t) = \kappa_\pi(x)$.

- If $t = c(t_1 \ldots t_n)$ where c is a constructor, then
  $\kappa_\pi(t) = \vee\{\mathbf{g}, \kappa_\pi(t_1) \ldots \kappa_\pi(t_n)\}$.

- If $t = f(t_1 \ldots t_n)$ where f is an external functor, then $\kappa_\pi(t) = \mathbf{g}$ if $\kappa_\pi(t_i) = \mathbf{g}$ for $1 \le i \le n$. Otherwise $\kappa_\pi(t) = \mathbf{t}$.

It is assumed that the classes of goals checked for admission are characterized by abstract substitutions. Thus, the starting point for the static analysis is a program P, a goal $G =: - B_1 \ldots B_n$ and an abstract substitution π_0 defined on the variables of B_1. π_0 specifies all bindings of the variables of B_1 which are allowed at the invocation time, i.e. when the execution of B_1 starts. Assume now that an abstract substitution is given not only for B_1 but also for $B_2 \ldots B_n$ and for every body literal of P. The abstract substitution π_L assigned to a literal L is said to be a *correct annotation* for P, G and π_0 iff for every $\sigma \in S(\pi_0)$ and at every invocation of L during the execution of $: - B_1\sigma \ldots B_n$, the binding of the variables of L are in $S(\pi_L)$. Correct annotations will be generated by abstract interpretation, but this is outside the scope of this paper. Here we confine ourselves with the definition of an abstract unification algorithm, A-unify, which will be used for checking admissibility of goals. The algorithm applies to two terms t_1 and t_2 and an abstract substitution π. Our design objective for A-unify is that it should be able to recognize whenever there exists a substitution $\sigma \in S(\pi)$ for which S-unify$(t_1\sigma, t_2\sigma)$ yields $ERROR$ as result. The algorithm starts by constructing the disagreement set $\mathcal{D}(t_1, t_2)$. In this way it does exactly the same job as S-unify would have done for any terms $t_1\sigma$ and $t_2\sigma$ with $\sigma \in S(\pi)$. First we note that if $Failcond_1(u_1, u_2)$ or $Failcond_2(u_1, u_2)$ applies for some $\{u_1, u_2\} \in \mathcal{D}(t_1, t_2)$, then no instance of t_1 and t_2 will S-unify, and hence A-unify may safely fail. However, now $\mathcal{D}(t_1, t_2)$ contains pairs of *sets* of terms rather than pairs of terms. Therefore the analysis of $\mathcal{D}(t_1, t_2)$ has to be done in a quite different way than for S-unification. Our intention is to pick elements $\{u_1, u_2\}$ from $\mathcal{D}(t_1, t_2)$ which are *safe* in the sense that for *no* σ in $S(\pi)$, S-unify$(u_1\sigma, u_2\sigma)$ gives an error message. It is not hard to see that each of the following two conditions, which we call $Substcond_1(u_1, u_2, \pi)$ and $Substcond_2(u_1, u_2, \pi)$ respectively, are sufficient for this to be true:

- One of u_1 and u_2 is a variable x, i.e. $\{u_1, u_2\} = \{x, u\}$, $\kappa_\pi(x) = \mathbf{v}$ and for no variable y that occurs in u, $x\alpha_\pi y$.

- $\kappa_\pi(u_1), \kappa_\pi(u_2) \in \{\mathbf{g}, \mathbf{v}, \mathbf{s}\}$.

Now, if none of the failconditions apply we assume that u_1 and u_2 are instantiated by a $\sigma \in S(\pi)$ in such a way that S-unify$(u_1\sigma, u_2\sigma)$ succeeds with a substitution θ as result. Of course this assumption may be wrong. We do know however that S-unify$(u_1\sigma, u_2\sigma)$ will not give an error message. Our next step is then to simulate the composition of $t_1\sigma$ and $t_2\sigma$ with θ. This is done by the construction of two new terms, denoted $t_1 + \{u_1, u_2\}$ and $t_2 + \{u_1, u_2\}$, and a new abstract substitution, denoted $\pi + \{u_1, u_2\}$:

- If one of u_1 and u_2 is a variable x, so that $\{u_1, u_2\} = \{x, u\}$, then $t_i + \{u_1, u_2\} = t_i\{x \leftarrow u\}$ for $i = 1, 2$, and $D_{\pi + \{u_1, u_2\}} = D_\pi - \{x\}$.

- If both u_1 and u_2 are nonvariable terms, then $t_i + \{u_1, u_2\} = t_i$ for $i = 1, 2$, and $D_{\pi + \{u_1, u_2\}} = D_\pi$.

In order to construct $\kappa_{\pi + \{u_1, u_2\}}$ and $\alpha_{\pi + \{u_1, u_2\}}$, three different conditions are defined. A variable x in D_π may or may not satisfy some of them:

1. For no variable y that occurs in u_1 or u_2, $x \alpha_\pi y$ holds.

2. $\kappa_\pi(u_1) = \mathbf{v}$ and x occurs in u_2.

3. x occurs in u_1 or u_2 and at least one of $\kappa_\pi(u_1)$ and $\kappa_\pi(u_2)$ is $\mathbf{g}$.

Now $\kappa_{\pi + \{u_1, u_2\}}(x)$ is defined for each $x \in D_{\pi + \{u_1, u_2\}}$ by:

- If condition 1 or 2 holds for x, then $\kappa_{\pi + \{u_1, u_2\}}(x) = \kappa_\pi(x)$.

- If condition 3 holds for x, then $\kappa_{\pi + \{u_1, u_2\}}(x) = \mathbf{g}$.

- If none of conditions 1 to 3 holds for x, then $\kappa_{\pi + \{u_1, u_2\}}(x) = \kappa_\pi(x) \vee \kappa_\pi(u_1) \vee \kappa_\pi(u_2)$.

Finally, we let S be the subset of $D_{\pi + \{u_1, u_2\}}$, consisting of all variables x such that $\kappa_{\pi + \{u_1, u_2\}}(x)$ is $\mathbf{v}, \mathbf{s}$ or $\mathbf{t}$. $\alpha_{\pi + \{u_1, u_2\}}$ is defined to be the least equivalence relation on S which satisfies:

- If $x \alpha_\pi y$ then $x \alpha_{\pi + \{u_1, u_2\}} y$.

- If x satisfies condition 2, then $x \alpha_{\pi + \{u_1, u_2\}} u_1$.

- If none of conditions 1 to 3 holds for x, and y occurs in u_1 or u_2, then $x \alpha_{\pi + \{u_1, u_2\}} y$.

Now the A-unification algorithm may be defined. However, we can not have $\mathcal{D}(t_1, t_2) = \emptyset$ as termination condition: If $\kappa_\pi(u_1) = \kappa_\pi(u_2) = \mathbf{g}$ holds for each $\{u_1, u_2\} \in \mathcal{D}(t_1, t_2)$ and $\mathcal{D}(t_1, t_2) \neq \emptyset$, then $Substcond_2$ will apply and $\mathcal{D}(t_1, t_2)$ will remain unchanged at the next iteration, i.e. we will wind up in an infinite loop. Therefore we define a termination condition $Stopcond$, which when applied to $\mathcal{D}(t_1, t_2)$ and π holds iff $\kappa_\pi(u_1) = \kappa_\pi(u_2) = \mathbf{g}$ holds for each $\{u_1, u_2\} \in \mathcal{D}(t_1, t_2)$, and $Failcond_i(\mathcal{D}(t_1, t_2))$ does not apply for $i = 1, 2$. It is not hard to see that this is a safe termination condition for A-unify, i.e. for no $\sigma \in \mathcal{S}(\pi)$ S-unify$(t_1 \sigma, t_2 \sigma) = ERROR$.

A-unify(t_1, t_2, π) :
begin
$\quad t_1' := t_1;$
$\quad t_2' := t_2;$
$\quad \pi' := \pi;$
$\quad \mathcal{D} := \mathcal{D}(t_1', t_2');$
$\quad$ **while not** $Stopcond(\mathcal{D}, \pi')$ **do**
$\qquad$ **if** $Failcond_1(\mathcal{D})$ **or** $Failcond_2(\mathcal{D})$
$\qquad$ **then** $FAIL$
$\qquad$ **else if** $\exists \{u_1, u_2\} \in \mathcal{D} : Substcond_1(u_1, u_2, \pi')$ **or**
$\qquad\qquad\qquad\qquad\qquad\qquad Substcond_2(u_1, u_2, \pi')$
$\qquad\quad$ **then begin**
$\qquad\qquad\quad t_1' := t_1' + \{u_1, u_2\};$
$\qquad\qquad\quad t_2' := t_2' + \{u_1, u_2\};$
$\qquad\qquad\quad \pi' := \pi' + \{u_1, u_2\};$
$\qquad\qquad\quad \mathcal{D} := \mathcal{D}(t_1', t_2');$
$\qquad\quad$ **end**
$\qquad$ **else** $ERROR$
end.

For the A-unification algorithm we have the following theorem:

Theorem :

For any abstract substitution π, and terms t_1, t_2 with all their variables in D_π, A-unify(t_1, t_2, π) terminates. Moreover:

1. If A-unify(t_1, t_2, π) fails, then S-unify$(t_1\sigma, t_2\sigma)$ fails for each $\sigma \in \mathcal{S}(\pi)$.

2. If, for some $\sigma \in \mathcal{S}(\pi)$, S-unify$(t_1\sigma, t_2\sigma) = ERROR$, then A-unify$(t_1, t_2, \pi) = ERROR$.

□

For a program P and goal G which are correctly annotated w r t the abstract substitution π_0 it is now straight forward to check the three conditions given in 5.2, by using A-unification and the abstract substitutions instead of S-unification. In this way we have a sufficient check for P to admit the class of goals defined by G and π_0.

7 Conclusion

The paper presents an approach to amalgamation of logic programs with external functional procedures. The amalgamation has a well defined logical semantics, and an operational semantics complete for certain classes of goals. A sufficient check, identifying classes of goals for which the approach is complete, is also developed.

An idea close to S-unification appeared independently in Le Fun [1] but in a purely operational setting. The idea of residuations used in Le Fun, and the idea of delays used in CLP [12] are implicitly present also in our description, but only in the limits of one unification: notice that our abstract presentation of the algorithm concerns selection of certain pairs in the disagreement sets. A more realistic version should probably use left-to-right selection with residuations. Extending this technique beyond the scope of one unification is also possible, but a more elegant solution would be some kind of static analysis of the program leading to some program transformation.

The logical semantics of the language is based on well-known results presented in many papers, e.g. [9], [11]. However, our objectives are different. EQLOG attempts to exploit the narrowing technique, but we cannot do that since our functional procedures are black boxes. Therefore our approach is inherently incomplete. Since the language of functional procedures is left unspecified, we deal as a matter of fact with a family of logic programming languages. In that sense there is a similarity to the CLP family of languages. However, in contrast to the CLP project we do not plan to use additional information about the domains in the interpreter. Thus our approach is "less complete" but applies to any domain. The future work includes the following topics:

- Efficient algorithms for S-unification.

- Methods for static analysis of amalgamated programs, including automatic generation of annotations and program transformation for improving admissibilty of goals.

- Relaxation of the restrictions on the external procedures, e.g. considering lazy evaluation.

- Application of the idea of S-unification to higher-order procedures.

- Amalgamated programs with negation.

Acknowledgements :

This work was supported by STU, the Swedish National Board for Technical Development.

References

[1] H. Aït-Kaci, P. Lincoln and R. Nasr, Le Fun: Logic, Equations and Functions, in: *Proc. 1987 Symposium on Logic Programming*, pp. 17-23, San Francisco, California, (1987).

[2] R. Barbuti, M. Bellia, G. Levi and M. Martelli, LEAF: a language which integrates Logic, Equations and Functions, in: D. DeGroot and G. Lindstrom ed., *Logic Programming, Functions, Relations and Equations*, (Prentice-Hall, 1986) pp. 201-238.

[3] M. Bellia and G. Levi, The Relation between Logic and Functional Languages: A Survey, *J. Logic Programming*, **3** (1986), pp. 217-236.

[4] M. Bruynooghe, A Framework for the Abstract Interpretation of Logic Programs, Report, CW 62, Katholieke Universiteit, Leuven (1987).

[5] S. Cohen, The APPLOG Language, in: D. DeGroot and G. Lindstrom ed., *Logic Programming, Functions, Relations and Equations*, (Prentice-Hall 1986) pp. 239-276.

[6] D. DeGroot and G. Lindstrom ed., Logic Programming, Functions, Relations and Equations, (Prentice-Hall, Englewood Cliffs, NJ, 1986)

[7] P. Deransart and J. Małuszyński, Logic Programs and Attribute Grammars, *J. Logic Programming*, **2** (1985), pp. 119-155.

[8] J. Goguen and J. Meseguer, EQLOG: Equality, Types and Generic Modules for Logic Programming, in: D. DeGroot and G. Lindstrom ed., *Logic Programming, Functions, Relations and Equations*, (Prentice-Hall, 1986) pp. 295-363.

[9] J. Goguen and J. Meseguer, Models and Equality for Logical Programming, in: *Proc. TAPSOFT' 87*, Pisa, Italy, (1987).

[10] J-M. Hullot, Canonical Forms and Unification, in: *Proc. CADE-5*, pp. 318-334, (1980).

[11] J. Jaffar, J-L. Lassez and M-J. Maher, A Theory of Complete Logic Programs with Equality, *J. Logic Programming*, **3** (1984), pp. 211-223.

[12] J. Jaffar and S Michaylov, Methodology and Implementation of a CLP system, in: *Proc. 4:th Int. Conf. on Logic Programming*, Melbourne, Australia, (1987).

[13] N. Jones and H. Søndergaard, A Semantics-based Framework for the Abstract Interpretation of PROLOG, in: Abramsky and Hankin ed., *Abstract Interpretation of Declarative Languages*, (Ellis Horwood, 1987).

[14] J. Komorowski, QLOG - The Programming Environment for PROLOG in LISP, in: K. Clark and S-Å Tärnlund ed., *Logic Programming*, (Prentice-Hall, 1982).

[15] J. Leszczylowski, S. Bonnier and J. Małuszyński, Logic Programming with External Procedures: Introducing S-Unification, Report, R-88-01, Dep. of Comp. and Inf. Sc., Linköping University, Linköping, Sweden, a shortened version also in: *Information Processing Letters*, **27** (1988), pp. 159-165.

[16] J. Leszczylowski and J. Małuszyński, Logic Programming with External Procedures: Introducing S-Unification, Report, TR-86-21, Dep. of Comp Sc., Iowa State University, Ames (1986).

[17] C-S. Mellish, Abstract Interpretation of PROLOG Programs, in: Abramsky and Hankin ed., *Abstract Interpretation of Declarative Languages*, (Ellis Horwood, 1987).

[18] C-S. Mellish and S. Hardy, Integrating PROLOG in POPLOG Environment, in: J. Campbell ed., *Implementations of PROLOG*, (Ellis Horwood, 1984.)

[19] U. Nilsson, Inferring Restricted AND-Parallelism in Logic Programs using Abstract Interpretation, Report, R-88-02, Dep. of Comp. and Inf. Sc., Linköping University, Linköping, Sweden (1988).

[20] J-A. Robinson, A Machine-Oriented Logic Based on the Resolution Principle, *JACM*, *12* (1965), pp. 32-41.

[21] J. Robinson and E. Sibert, LOGLISP: Motivation, Design and Implementation, in: K. Clark and S-Å Tärnlund ed., *Logic Programming*, (Prentice-Hall, 1982).

[22] P. Subrahmanyam and J-H. You, FUNLOG: A Computational Model Integrating Logic Programming and Functional Programming, in: D. DeGroot and G. Lindstrom ed., *Logic Programming, Functions, Relations and Equations*, (Prentice-Hall, 1986) pp. 157-198.

AN APPLICATION OF ABSTRACT INTERPRETATION
IN SOURCE LEVEL PROGRAM TRANSFORMATION.

Daniel De Schreye, Maurice Bruynooghe
Department of Computer Science
Katholieke Universiteit Leuven
Celestijnenlaan 200A, B-3030 Heverlee, Belgium.

Abstract. We describe an application of abstract interpretation within the field of source-to-source program transformation for pure Horn clause logic programs. Using a very concrete setting, we aim to provide a comprehensible introduction to the technique of abstract interpretation, particularly suited for the novice in the field. Also, we argue that abstract interpretation is not only suited for applications in code optimization, but provides an excellent tool to support techniques in source level program transformation.

1. Introduction.

If one aims to prove general properties of programs, it is of crucial importance to have the ability of performing some kind of data abstraction. Although the runtime behavior observed during a concrete execution of a program may provide an example to support our expectations on the presence or absence of certain properties, a technique for interpreting the program using abstract data is needed to be able to prove these properties in general.

P.Cousot and R.Cousot in [10] were the first to thoroughly describe a general mechanism for the abstract interpretation of imperative programs. Very recently, several successful efforts were made to adapt their technique to logic programming. General reformulations have been presented by C.S.Mellish [22], N.D.Jones and H.Sondergaard [20],T.Kanamari and T.Kawamura [21] and M.Bruynooghe [6], applications in code optimization for logic programs have been described by S.K.Debray and D.S.Warren [12] and M.Bruynooghe et al. [5]. Also, a first description of the use of abstract interpretation in program transformation - more particularly in program specialization - is presented by J.Gallagher and M.Codish [16].

The increasing attention that abstract interpretation has obtained from researchers active in the field of logic programming can be explained by several reasons. First, there is the desire to obtain a better runtime efficiency for declarative programming languages such as Prolog. Through code optimizations obtained from mode inference, type inference and compile time garbage collection, there is high hope of eventually achieving runtime efficiencies of logic programs that are comparable to those of their imperative equivalents. Also, there is the ease with which abstract interpretation can be described and implemented within the setting of logic programming. This is partially due to the fact that a language such as Prolog contains its own meta-language, increasing the ability of writing various types of interpreters for the language. A second reason is that, because of its high declarativity and its data structuring facilities, the language is particularly well suited for symbol manipulation.

From the currently available literature on the abstract interpretation of programs, a general impression that one obtains, is that the theory is quite complex and hard to comprehend. Contributions to the field, such as [12], [5] and, most notably, [6], have improved the accesibility of the subject to some extend. However, most authors prefer to introduce the theory in a setting covering a wide range of potential applications. In doing so, they increase the level of abstraction of their presentation and end up giving the non-expert a hard time figuring out how this most powerful technique can be applied to solve his problem at hand.

This paper mainly addresses the novice in the field. It does not contribute any essential new features to the theory of [10], nor does it improve on the reformulation of abstract interpretation within the setting of logic programming by M.Bruynooghe [6]. It is merely an attempt to illustrate the type of considerations and the degree of creativity that are required to make abstract interpretation work for you.

In order to do so, we start with a concrete problem selected from the field of source-to-source transformation for logic programs. This application was thoroughly described in [3], [4] and [13] and deals with the compilation of ideal control rules into existing declarative Horn clause programs. It was selected for various reasons. First, it seemed appropriate not to focus on a problem within the field of code optimization, to illustrate that the applicability of the technique is not limited to this field of research. Secondly, several topics in program transformation, such as loop detection [2], [25], partial evaluation [16], fold/unfold [7], [19], [27], and the elimination of redundant computation [14], make use of techniques that are closely related to abstract interpretation, without explicitly refering to it. Finally, the selected problem involves a combination of mode-, structure- and aliasing inference and is composed of different layers where abstract interpretation is of use, so that even with one concrete application, we can illustrate most of the power of the technique.

We start off with some preliminaries on Horn clause logic and a first, high level introduction to the different steps that are encountered in building an application of abstract interpretation in section 2. Section 3, introduces the example application in program transformation and provides more details on the different steps that are encountered in a first layer solution for the application. In section 4, a more complete, second layer solution to the same problem is provided. Finally, we end with a discussion of the wide range of potential applications for the technique within the field of program transformation.

2. Preliminaries and high level approach.

The language for which both the transformation technique and the abstract interpretation are discussed is that of *pure* Horn clause logic with the SLD-resolution mechanism of Prolog. In this language, a program is a finite set of Horn clauses which are of the form:

$$A \leftarrow B_1, B_2, \cdots, B_n , \; n \geqslant 0,$$

and a goal clause or query

$$\leftarrow Q_1, Q_2, \cdots, Q_n , \; n \geqslant 1,$$

where A, B_1, B_2, $\cdots$, B_n and Q_1, Q_2, $\cdots$, Q_n are atomic formulae of the form

$$P(\, t_1, t_2, \cdots, t_m) \,, \; m \geqslant 0,$$

with an m-ary predicate symbol P and terms t_1, t_2, $\cdots$, t_m. Terms are either variables, constants or are constructed from functors whose arguments are again terms.

The query activates the program. The computation rule selects a subgoal Q_i from the query; the search rule selects a clause $A \leftarrow B_1, B_2, \cdots, B_n$ whose left hand side (head), A, has the same predicate symbol as Q_i. An attempt is made to find a most general unifier (mgu) θ such that $Q_i \, \theta = A \, \theta$ (for the clause a fresh set of variables is supplied). The query is replaced by the new goal

$$\leftarrow Q_1 \, \theta, \cdots, Q_{i-1} \, \theta, B_1 \, \theta, \cdots, B_n \, \theta, Q_{i+1} \, \theta, \cdots, Q_r \, \theta \,.$$

if unification succeeds. For some predicates (such as arithmetic operations) the predicate's definitions are built into the system. With a depth first strategy, the computation always proceeds with the most recently generated goal for which there are untried clauses matching the selected subgoal Q_i. The original query succeeds when the empty goal is derived and the composition of all mgu's applied on the variables of the original query yields the answer. All solutions are generated when all selected subgoals have exhausted their candidate clauses.

The order in which the subgoals in the query are selected for unification is determined by the computation rule. The standard computation rule of Prolog selects the subgoals in the query from left to right.

For a given query, we can represent the execution of a program under such a rule in a proof tree. The different goals obtained during the execution are the nodes in the tree. The proof tree contains an arc from one goal to another for every successful resolution step. The mgu is added as a label on the arc (for simplicity we will only specify the substitutions caused on the variables of the subgoal). The sequence of resolution steps performed by the theorem prover is found by tracing the tree depth-first, left-to-right.

Before giving an example to illustrate this, we sum up some conventions. Variable names start with a lower case character; constants, functors and predicate names with an upper case character. The infix notation x.y is used to denote a list with head x and tail y.

The example program is *Permutation_sort*, consisting of the following Horn clauses:

Sort(x, y) $\leftarrow$ Perm(x, y), Ord(y) .
Perm(Nil, Nil) $\leftarrow$.
Perm(x.y, u.v) $\leftarrow$ Del(u, x.y, w), Perm(w, v) .
Del(x, x.y, y) $\leftarrow$.
Del(x, y.u.t, y.v) $\leftarrow$ Del(x, u.t, v) .
Ord(Nil) $\leftarrow$.
Ord(x.Nil) $\leftarrow$.
Ord(x.y.z) $\leftarrow$ x $\leqslant$ y, Ord(y.z) .

This program sorts a list of numbers by first permuting it and next testing whether the permuted list is ordered. With an initial query $\leftarrow$ Sort(2.1.Nil, x), we get the proof tree of Fig.1 .

Along with the procedural interpretation of logic programs described above, there is a declarative one. Informally, in this second interpretation a Horn clause

$$A \leftarrow B_1, B_2, \cdots, B_n , n \geqslant 0,$$

expresses that for all possible assignments of values (taken from some predefined universe) to the variables occurring in A, B_1, B_2, $\cdots$ and B_n , the instantiated predicate A will hold if the conjunction of all the instantiated predicates B_1, B_2, $\cdots$, B_n holds. A query

$$\leftarrow Q_1, Q_2, \cdots, Q_n , n \geqslant 1,$$

states that no value assignment for the variables in Q_1, Q_2, $\cdots$ and Q_n can exist, such that the conjunction of instantiated predicates Q_1, Q_2, $\cdots$, Q_n holds. Augmenting the program with a query can be viewed as adding the hypothesis that no solutions for Q_1, Q_2, $\cdots$ and Q_n can be deduced from the given set of Horn clauses in the program. The computation uses unification and the *modus tolens* deduction rule from mathematical logic, to derive a new hypothesis

$$\leftarrow Q_1 \, \theta, \cdots, Q_{i-1} \, \theta, B_1 \, \theta, \cdots, B_n \, \theta, Q_{i+1} \, \theta, \cdots, Q_r \, \theta .$$

again expressing that no further substitutions for variables in these predicates can exist such that the conjunction holds. The ultimate goal is to obtain the empty query ($\leftarrow$.), which is a notation for contradiction. At this point, a proof by contradiction is completed for the initial conjunction of goals Q_1, Q_2, $\cdots$, Q_n, and the composition of all parameter substitutions yields a set of values such that the conjunction holds.

In this sense, a Prolog computation can be viewed as proving a theorem. For the Permutation_sort example above, the query $\leftarrow$ Sort(2.1.Nil, x) activates a proof for the fact that x/1.2.Nil is a substitution for which Sort(2.1.Nil, 1.2.Nil) is true. This is the main reason why Prolog is an excellent programming environment for performing abstract interpretation. The same theorem prover that is used to compute the results of programs, can - with some adaptation - be used to prove theorems concerning the program's behavior. As an easy example: if we redefine the builtin predicate $\leqslant$/2 to succeed for any two arguments, then by activating the program with a query $\leftarrow$ Sort(x.y.Nil, z) we prove that if the first argument of Sort/2 is a list of length 2 then the second argument of Sort/2 must also have this structure. Here, we made abstraction of the explicit content and type of the arguments x and y in the list. Therefore, the resolution mechanism had to be altered in such a way that any explicit reference to those values or types is omited. So, $\leqslant$/2 was redefined.

However, in this easy example, the abstractions x and y still constitute Prolog variables and the unification mechanism of Prolog can deal with them precisely in the way we expect it to. This is not always the case. If we would be interested in the mode behavior of our program for instance, then we could assign meaning to $\leftarrow$ Sort(Ground, Var) as being an abstract representation for the mode pattern we wish to investigate our program's behavior for. But without adaptation, the

Prolog unification algorithm, is unable to perform even one single resolution step starting from this query. Thus, along with the abstract representation we wish to use, the unification algorithm will be redefined.

In general, there are six different types of activities involved in building a concrete application using abstract interpretation:

1. Chosing the desired level of data-abstraction. What type of information do we wish to make abstraction of and what (other) information has to remain explicit during the interpretation. This step is highly dependent on the application at hand. It determines the class of abstract substitutions that are allowed for each predicate occurring in the program (the *abstract domain*).

2. Closely related to the choice of the abstraction level is the selection of a **representation** for the abstract substitutions.

3. The **unification mechanism** has to be redefined to be able to cope with resolution within the predefined abstract domain and its representation.

4. The behavior of **builtin predicates** has to be specified explicitly. More specifically, for each builtin predicate and each possible abstract pattern with which it may be invoked during the interpretation, the outcoming abstract substitution (and therefore the effect on the current set of pending goal statements) has to be made explicit.

5. A **special purpose interpreter** has to be written to support the abstract interpretation. This interpreter is not only intended to incorporate the new unification mechanism and builtin behavior, but should also serve the purpose of avoiding infinite loops, which will occur more frequently in an abstract interpretation than in a corresponding concrete execution due to the data abstraction.

6. Some applications require that the abstract interpretation behaves in a deterministic way. In particular, for code optimization problems, we are not interested in type- or mode inference within each branch in the search tree separately, but we want to deduce the strongest possible statement which holds for all possible solutions for the given procedure. This means that whenever nondeterminism occurs, a least generalization of all the computed abstract output substitutions has to be made.

Each of these six steps will be further explained and illustrated in the following sections.

3. A simple application : building abstract proof trees.

The problem discussed in [4] and [13] is as follows. Suppose that a highly declarative - but inefficient - Horn clause program is given, together with a special computation rule (different from the standard computation rule of Prolog, described above) for this program. From these two, synthesize a new Horn clause program that has the same computational behavior under the standard computation rule as the old program has under the special rule.

The solution for this problem, proposed in [4] and developed in more detail in [13], consists of two parts: first build a symbolic (abstract) proof tree for the execution of the original program under the new computation rule; then generate new Horn clauses that synthesize all the observed transitions in the obtained tree. Here, we focus on the first of these objectives. It gives rise to a first layer within the problem, where abstract interpretation is of use.

In this phase of the transformation method, an abstract query and an appropriate computation rule for the given program and query are specified. Then, the abstract proof is constructed. It traces the computation that will occur for any concrete query matching the abstract query pattern. Therefore - but also to distinguish it from a concrete proof tree -, we will refer to it as the trace tree in what follows.

3.1 Selecting the abstraction level.

The process of generating the trace tree must be guided by the computation rule. Therefore, it is essential to determine what kind of information the computation rule will need to perform this task. Several researchers have worked on the control of logic programs and have proposed mechanisms for expressing and enforcing new control rules. Some suggest the use of meta interpreters [17], [26] leading to languages with extremely rich control features. Others propose logic programming environments which include a separate control language to enforce the appropriate goal- or clause selection at run time [18], [8], [23], [30], [9]. A third group describe methods to compile control rules through source-to-source program transformation [19] , [27], [4], [24].

All the annotations, declarations or meta-predicates suggested in these papers aim at controlling the execution of programs on the basis of one of the following criteria:

- A goal is selected for expansion if it is sufficiently instantiated. This type of condition is quite simple to verify; it merely requires the ability to test whether some variable is either free (uninstantiated) or ground (fully instantiated). We call this type of control information 'static'.

- A goal is selected for expansion if certain of its variables will not become further instantiated due to this additional expansion. Here the condition is more complicated since a further resolution step has to be performed to detect whether a variable becomes instantiated. We call it control of the 'dynamic' type.

As in [4], [13] we use 'static' information to describe our computation rules, since the idea of selecting subgoals on the basis of their obtained instantiation pattern is quite natural and easy to understand and support. Since the computation rule will select a subgoal from the most recently obtained state (node) in the abstract trace tree, the abstraction level that we will use within the tree should contain information on whether a variable is free or ground. As an example, an appropriate abstract query pattern for the Permutation_sort program could be

$$\leftarrow \text{Sort}(x , y) \text{ , where x is ground and y is free.}$$

A second piece of information in our data of which we do not want to make abstraction are the functors appearing in the arguments of the goals. With the clauses for the predicate Ord/1 in the

Permutation_sort program, it seems quite appropriate to expand

        ← Ord(x) , where x is ground,

and

        ← Ord(x.y.z) , where x and y are ground and z is free

but inappropriate to expand goals of type

        ← Ord(x) , where x is free

and

        ← Ord(x.y) , where x is ground and y is free.

In the second of these four abstract queries, the two first members in the list are instantiated and therefore the test $x \leqslant y$ is ready to be performed. Obviously, this is not the case in query three and four.

Finally, we want to include in the abstraction level, all information concerning bindings between (free) variables. The reason why this is needed should be clear from the following example. Suppose that at some point during the computation we obtain a state of type

        ← A(x, y) , B(y, z) , C(z) , where x, y and z are free.

If the program contains a clause such as

        A(0, 0).

then selecting the goal A(x, y) for expansion will lead to a new state

        ← B(y, z) , C(z) , where y is ground and z is free.

However, without the information on the binding between the second parameter of A/2 and the first of B/2, this result could not be obtained and the information on instantiation in the trace tree would be incorrect. In fact, it is very unlikely that there exists an application of abstract interpretation which does not rely on binding or sharing between variables at all.

3.2 Representing the data-abstraction.

A general way to describe the abstract pattern which a predicate has obtained at some point during the computation uses abstract substitutions [6]. An abstract substitution is a high level description of the set of concrete substitutions for the arguments of the predicate. Through such sets of substitutions we can express abstract patterns. As an example, an abstract instantiation pattern for the predicate Ord/1

        Ord(x.y.y) , where x is ground and y is free

could be represented as the pair

(Ord(x),
$\quad$ { x ← y.z.t ,
$\quad$ y ← ground ,
$\quad$ z ← free ,
$\quad$ binding(t, z) }) .

Here, the second entry in the pair is a description of the set of all concrete substitutions for x which, during a concrete execution of the program, may still occur. In principle, there is no restriction on the syntax that is used to describe these abstract substitutions. The user is free to define them in any way he wants. Only, he must ensure that each syntactic expression occurring in the abstract substitutions is properly supported by his new definition of the unification algorithm and of the effect of calls to builtin predicates. As another example, the description

$\quad$ { x, y, possible_share(x, y), type(x, Int) }

is a typical abstract substitution of a type-inference application.

However, since the choice of syntax is free, we will use a more compact representation to describe the instantiation patterns of predicates in our application. The example pattern for Ord/1 given above, will be represented as

$\quad$ Ord($G.V_1.V_1$) ,

where G is a constant representing any ground term and V_i, i $\in$ IN is a constant representing a particular free variable. Bindings between variables are made explicit by using the same index i for all occurrences of the variable throughout the state.

Although this representation is elegant in the sense that it does not introduce complex new notations, it suffers from the inconvenience that different abstract patterns in this representation refer to the same state. Renumbering the indices i in the V_i's amounts to an equivalent representation and the replacement of a term including no V_i's by G results in a pattern which describes the state as well, e.g.

$\quad$ ← Perm($G.G.G, V_1$), Ord(V_1).

could also be represented as

$\quad$ ← Perm(G, V_2), Ord(V_2).

In order to overcome this, one must define a *canonical* abstract representation of a state. Here, it is introduced as a representation of the above type, in which the first occurrences of each V_i are numbered starting from 0 and ascending from the left hand to the right hand side in the state and where each term containing no V_i's is replaced by G.

3.3 Redefining the unification algorithm.

Obviously, some redefinition is needed since the unification for calls of type

$\leftarrow$ Ord(G).

or

$\leftarrow$ Ord(V_1).

with the clauses for Ord/1 using the Prolog unification mechanism will simply fail, which does not correspond to our intentions. This problem can easily be solved if the abstract interpretation is itself described as a Horn clause logic program. If this is the case, then the following steps can be taken:

1. Replace every occurrence of G in the abstract state by a fresh free variable and each different occurrence of a V_i as well (using the same variable for all occurrences of V_i with the same index i). At the same time, build a list containing all new variables associated to a G and a second list containing corresponding pairs of new variables and their associated V_i's (see the example below for a concrete illustration).

2. Perform a resolution step with the selected goal from the newly obtained state and a clause from the program, using the Prolog unification mechanism.

3. Now, because of the resolution step, the appropriate substitution has been applied to the free variables – not only in the state itself, but also in the two lists expressing the correspondences. What remains to be done is to reconvert the obtained state into the proper abstract form. It is for this purpose that the two correspondence lists are kept. They are used in three steps:

   • Replace all ground terms occurring in the first list by G and instantiate every free variable in it to G.

   • Replace all ground terms occurring in the first argument of a pair in the second list by G and unify each first argument of a pair which is still uninstantiated with the corresponding second argument.

   • Finally, instantiate all remaining free variables in the new goal list by V_j's, where the j's are fresh indices.

This leads to a program scheme of the form:

```
Expand_selected( selected_goal, other_goals, new_goals) ←

        Build_free_state( selected_goal.other_goals,
                        free_goal.free_others,
                        variables_for_Gs, pairs_of_variables_and_Vi),
        Clause( free_goal , goals_from_body),
        Append( goals_from_body, other_goals, new_goals),
        Instantiate_ground_list( variables_for_Gs),
        Instantiate_variables_list( pairs_of_variables_and_Vi),
        Instantiate_new_variables( goals_from_body).
```

and for an example query such as

$\leftarrow$ Expand_selected(Perm(G, V_1), Ord(V_1).Nil, new_goals).

and through unification with the second clause for Perm, this results in the following computation

- Build_free_state/4:
    free_goal.free_others $\leftarrow$ *Perm(x, y)*.Ord(y) ,
    variables_for_Gs $\leftarrow$ *x*.Nil ,
    pairs_of_variables_and_Vi $\leftarrow$ (V_1, y).Nil

- Clause/2:
    $x \leftarrow z.t$, $y \leftarrow v.w$
    goals_from_body $\leftarrow$ *Del(v, z.t, u)*.Perm(u, w).Nil

    Observe that these first two substitutions also cause the instantiations
    variables_for_Gs $\leftarrow$ *z.t*.Nil , and
    pairs_of_variables_and_Vi $\leftarrow$ (V_1, v.w).Nil

- Append/3:
    new_goals $\leftarrow$ *Del(v, z.t, u)*.Perm(u, w).Ord(v.w).Nil

- Instantiate_ground_list/1:
    $z \leftarrow G$, $t \leftarrow G$

- Instantiate_variables_list/1 performs no instantiations
  (pairs_of_variables_and_Vi = (V_1, v.w).Nil contains no ground terms nor free variables in a
  second argument of a pair)

- Instantiate_new_variables/1:
    $v \leftarrow V_2$, $w \leftarrow V_3$, $u \leftarrow V_4$

Thus, this results in the new abstract state:

$$\leftarrow \text{Del}(V_2, G.G, V_4), \text{Perm}(V_4, V_3), \text{Ord}(V_2.V_3)$$

3.4 Redefining the builtin predicates.

Again, the problem is that presenting abstract calls to builtin predicates causes failure (or runtime
errors) for most cases and results in an undesired behavior for others. Typical examples in our
setting are:

$\leftarrow V_1 = G$,   (fails, where it should instantiate V_1)

$\leftarrow V_1 = V_2$,   (fails, where it should cause a binding)

$\leftarrow V_1 \leqslant V_2$, (succeeds, where it should fail)

The only way it can be handled is by predefining the desired effect for calls to builtin predicates
for each possible call-pattern. This could, for instance, be done with a predicate
Abstract_builtin/2, for which we define - among many others - the following Horn clauses, in

order to deal with the examples above:

Abstract_builtin($V_1 = G$, $(V_1/G.Nil).Nil$).

Abstract_builtin($V_1 = V_2$, $(V_2/V_1.Nil).Nil$).

Abstract_builtin($V_1 \leqslant V_2$, Nil).

The first argument of Abstract_builtin/2 contains a *canonical* abstract call-pattern to a builtin predicate. The second is a list of lists, containing one sublist for each different abstract output substitution with which the given abstract call can succeed. These abstract substitutions are needed, since they must be applied to all goals occurring in the state where the abstract call to the builtin predicate was selected from.

In the clauses stated above, we express that the call-pattern $V_1 = G$ can only succeed with one possible output substitution, namely $V_1 \leftarrow G$. This is also the case for $V_1 = V_2$, with $V_2 \leftarrow V_1$. The third example deals with a failing call-pattern.

3.5 The interpreter for solving an abstract goal.

The techniques described in the previous subsections are sufficient to be able to develop an abstract trace tree for Permutation_sort with the abstract query pattern $\leftarrow$ Sort(G, V_1) and a computation rule that differs only from the standard computation rule in its eagerness to expand any call to Ord/1 with instantiation

Ord(G)   or   Ord(G.G.V1).

A finite part of the resulting trace tree is very similar to the one displayed in Fig.2, except that it contains additional branches originating from the expansion of the Del(V_i, G.G, V_j) goals.

The special way in which the expansion in the trace tree of Fig.2 deals with the Del(V_i, G.G, V_j) goals is due to the following pragmatic - but for large-size program transformations essential - observation. Often, a program consists of two types of procedures: those that need additional control directives - mostly coroutining - in order to become efficient, and those that already behave efficiently under the standard computation rule. In the example, calls to Del(V_i, G.G, V_j) do not play an active role in the coroutining process between Perm/2 and Ord/1 and are therefore of the second type. If we were to use the abstract interpretation to expand all goals, even when most of them do not need a transformation, then for real-life problems, the size of the resulting trace trees would become unacceptably large.

The way we will deal with goals for which transformation is unnecessary is very similar to the way we approach builtin predicates. The only information regarding them that should be made explicit in the trace tree consists of the abstract pattern of the goal before the call and the outcomming substitution obtained from completely solving it with the standard computation rule. This substitution must then be applied to the remaining goals in the state. In fact, we could make the approach completely similar to that of the builtin predicates by adding a fact of type Builtin_pattern/2 for each such call and abstract pattern. However, this would mean that new facts of this type would have to be produced by the user for each new transformation session. Instead, we will use the abstract interpretation itself to determine the abstract substitutions resulting from completely solving a given abstract goal. This is where some new and more interesting aspects regarding the design of the application turn up.

Solving an abstract goal is different from building (a finite part of) its abstract trace tree because recursive programs have infinite abstract trace trees. Thus, during the expansion we need criteria to determine whether or not additional output substitutions, different from the ones we already obtained, exist. In other words: abstractly solving a goal usually leads to an infinite number of success nodes, even if each corresponding concrete goal - each instance of the abstract pattern - results in a finite computation. The reason is that although certain calls occurring in a concrete execution contain different data, their abstractions may become identical and therefore the interpretation may infinitely loop.

The problem of infinite looping turns up when the recursive expansion of an abstract goal A_1 and the goals descending from it, eventually leads to the expansion of a descendent goal A'_1, such that A_1 and A'_1 have identical canonical patterns. A good way to formally describe and solve the problem is by representing the computation by means of an abstract AND-OR tree, since this type of tree is very explicit in representing the ancestor-descendent relation between the subgoals of the states.

An AND-OR tree is similar to the trace trees we have used so far, but instead of representing a conjunction of goal statements (what we called a *state*) as a node in the graph, we represent

- each subgoal individually (OR-node),

- for each clause which can be applied to the query in the OR-node, a descending node containing the conjuction of all the subgoals obtained from the body of the clause, after the unification of the query with the head has been performed (AND-node).

- for each AND-node, we represent all the subgoals in this node a second time, as the OR-nodes descending from it.

In Fig.3 we have drawn the - abstract - AND-OR-tree which describes the infinite loop situation in abstract interpretation.

To avoid entering infinite loops and still guarantee that all solutions be computed, the following technique is built into the abstract interpreter:

- We do not expand the descendent goal A'_1, but instead we freeze and record the entire computation (including the resulting substitutions) leading from the ancestor A_1 over all intermediate AND- and OR- nodes to A'_1.

- Then, the computation is continued as if the query $\leftarrow A'_1$ has failed. It backtracks to the latest OR-node in the tree for which there are untried clauses in the program.

- When eventually an output substitution for the goal A_1 has been computed, a proper renaming of the V_i's occurring in this output substitution yields an output substitution for the suspended OR-nodes A'_1 as well, because A_1 and A'_1 have identical canonical forms. Using the renaming as the output pattern that would result from solving A'_1, we can reactivate the suspended AND-OR-subtree and continue its computation in an attempt to derive additional output patterns for A_1.

- This process is continued until saturation occurs, i.e. until all output patterns obtained for A_1 have been used for A_1 and no further new patterns for A_1 can be derived in this way.

This method involves the following potential disadvantages:

1. If the computation for A_1 terminates without generating at least one output substitution for A_1, or if it does not terminate at all - due to an infinite subtree descending from some OR-node which is not of the loop type described above - then none of the suspended computations can ever be reactivated. Thus, we could possibly has lost some output patterns for A_1.

2. For some programs, infinitely many different output instantiation patterns exist, so that the point of saturation is never reached.

First, we discuss the reactivation of suspended goals. Assuming that the application has been built correctly - see [6] for criteria and proofs on correctness -, the AND-OR-tree for a concrete query with instantiation pattern $\leftarrow A_1$ is obtainable by taking a subtree from the abstract AND-OR-tree and replacing the abstract goals by their appropriate concrete instances. For the problem case with a terminating computation, this implies that the concrete AND-OR-tree will not produce a success node either. For a nonterminating computation the matter is more problematic. Here, it is possible that, although the abstract interpretation - using a depth-first search on the AND-OR-tree - can never continue its search for further solutions outside the infinite subtree, a corresponding concrete computation may fail at some point within the infinite branch and eventually lead to more solutions when backtracking.

Such infinite subtrees (different from the ones we suspend in the algorithm) can only occur in applications involving an infinite abstract domain. This is clear, since the OR-nodes in any descending path of a branch in the abstract AND-OR-tree must be either mutually distinct or suspended. This is why most applications of abstract interpretation make use of finite domains. This ensures termination of the interpretation and in most cases a finite domain is a necessary condition for completeness (see [6] for more details).

In our application, this is difficult to realize, because in principle recursive data structures can create functors with arbitrary complex instantiation patterns. The way that it is dealt with in [13], is by introducing an additional constant A to describe the abstract patterns. This constant takes its place among the abstract terms G and V_i and is used as an abstraction for any term, whatever its instantiation pattern. However, it is not allowed to occur within the actual abstract resolution, but only within some predefined declarations concerning certain positions within certain predicates. Its use is to express an upper bound beyond which the instantiation of a (recursively defined) term within a predicate becomes irrelevant to the computation.

For instance, a declaration of the form Ord(G.G.G.A) expresses that we are not interested in computations that provide instantiations of Ord(x) beyond the first three ground members of the list x.

Obviously, such declarations must be provided by the user, since they require knowledge regarding the semantics of the program. Their sole purpose is to interrupt possible infinite computations and to force the abstract interpretation to backtrack within the AND–OR-tree. In some sense, it can be regarded as an artificial way to reduce the abstract domain to a finite size.

Although the second problem, concerning the generation of infinitely many output patterns for a suspended query pattern has a quite different origine, the solution is identical. The declarations we have just described, will also cause the termination of these infinite processes.

3.6 Generalization.

Computing the output pattern obtained from solving an abstract goal is a non deterministic application of abstract interpretation. It generates a number of different solutions. Each different resulting pattern will give rise to a new branch in the abstract trace tree we originally set out to construct. For many applications however, it is more interesting to obtain only one abstract substitution that generalizes all those obtained in the different underlying branches. This is the case for all applications regarding code optimization. One implication is that the generalization of a set of abstract substitutions must be possible. To ensure this, the abstract domain of the application should be designed with the structure of a partially ordered set with a largest element. In order to obtain powerful results, a lattice is preferable. So, for each set of abstract substitutions (which are representations for sets of concrete substitutions themselves), there should be a least general abstract substitution, representing a set of concrete substitutions containing all concrete substitutions in the original abstract ones. A second implication is that the interpreter has to be developed with a breath-first approach instead of the depth-first approach we used in the previous subsection. The reason is that for every OR-node, all different solution should first be obtained, then generalized and finally the generalized solution should be passed to the ancestor nodes. With our previously described method, each individual solution to an OR-node is passed on to the ancestors.

We will not go into more detail on the matter of generalization, since it is our experience that in applications of program transformation there is very little need for it.

4. A second layer of abstract interpretation: completeness.

In the previous section we showed how the solutions of an infinite AND–OR-tree are computed by a special algorithm. However, if recursive clauses are expanded, the abstract tree for the original query is also infinite. After a finite number of steps, the expansion has to be stopped. The problem is to determine at which point sufficient information regarding the computation has been gathered in the tree, in order to be able to synthesize a new program from it, equivalent to the old one. Again, abstract interpretation is an adequate tool for performing this task.

The idea is as follows. The original program contains only a finite number of clauses. If we assume that the new computation rule is finitely expressable in terms of a finite number of different instantiation patterns which may occur during the computation (see [13] for a formal definition of *instantiation based computation rules*), then the number of essentially different transitions occurring in the trace tree is finite as well. With *essentially different* we mean that either

- a different instantiation atom was selected from the initial state, or

- a different clause from the program was used for the expansion, or

- the changes in the instantiation patterns of the remaining subgoals in the state caused by the expansion are different (i.e. the bindings between the selected subgoal and the other goals in the initial state are different).

The synthesis algorithm of [13] generates a new Horn clause for every equivalence class of mutually *similar* (not essentially different) transitions observed in the trace. The problem left to the abstract interpretation is to determine, at which point during the expansion of the tree, all the equivalence classes have been obtained.

In order to accomplish this, we introduce a further abstraction on nodes (states) in the abstract trace tree. This abstraction will be refered to as a *state description*. To introduce them on an informal basis, we recall some observations made in the manual completeness proof for the Sieve of Eratosthenos example in section 3 of [4].

The program is defined by the following set of Horn clauses:

Primes(n,p) ← Integers(2,i), Sift(i,p), Length(p,n).
Integers(n,Nil) ←.
Integers(n,n.i) ← m is n+1, Integers(m,i).
Sift(n.i,n.p) ← Filter(n,i,f), Sift(f,p).
Sift(Nil,Nil) ←.
Filter(n,m.i,f) ← Divides(n,m), Filter(n,i,f).
Filter(n,m.i,m.f) ← not Divides(n.m), Filter(n,i,f).
Filter(n,Nil,Nil) ←.
Length(Nil,0) ←.
Length(h.t,n) ← n > 0, m is n − 1, Length(t,n).

The completeness proof in [4] considers a number of *similar* states from a finite subtree of the abstract trace tree, e.g.

- Integers(G,V_1), Filter(G,G.V_1,V_2), Sift(V_2,V_3), Length(V_3,G)

- Integers(G,V_1), Filter(G,G.V_1,V_2), Filter(G,V_2,V_3), Sift(V_3,V_4), Length(V_4,G)

- Integers(G,V_1), Filter(G,V_1,V_2), Filter(G,G.V_2,V_3), Sift(V_3,V_4), Length(V_4,G)

- Integers(G,V_1), Filter(G,V_1,V_2), Filter(G,G.V_2,V_3), Filter(G,V_3,V_4), Sift(V_4,V_5), Length(V_5,G)

and associates to them a general description of instantiation patterns and bindings occurring in them:

Integers(G,V_1), Filter(G,V_1,V_2), $\cdots$, Filter(G,V_{i-1},V_i), Filter(G,G.V_i,V_{i+1}),
Filter(G,V_{i+1},V_{i+2}), $\cdots$, Filter(G,V_{n-1},V_n), Sift(V_n,V_{n+1}), Length(V_{n+1},G)

The pattern is that each example state contains precisely one goal of the types Integers(G,V_1), Filter(G,G.V_i,V_{i+1}), Sift(V_n,V_{n+1}) and Length(V_{n+1},G). Also, it contains 0 or more goals of type Filter(G,V_i,V_{i+1}). The binding pattern is a chain connecting the Integer/2 goal to 0 or more Filter(G,V_i,V_{i+1}) goals, then to the more instantiated Filter/3, which is again connected to 0 or more Filter(G,V_i,V_{i+1}) goals and finally to the pair Sift(V_n,V_{n+1}), Length(V_{n+1},G).

Different patterns of the above type are generated, so that eventually every state in the finite part of the trace tree is an instance of a state description. Then, it is proved that starting from any of these descriptions and performing a resolution step expanding the subgoal selected by the computation rule, an instance of another state description is obtained.

When for a given finite part of the abstract trace tree this result can be proved, it implies that all relevant transitions have been gathered from the trace and that the abstract expansion is in some particular sense (depending on the abstraction in the descriptions) *complete*.

4.1 A short review of the six steps.

We aim to perform resolution on the state descriptions. Therefore, these descriptions should at least contain the information retained for the previous application: the instantiation patterns of the goals within the state, functors within the arguments of those goals and bindings between their variables.

These leave little space for further abstraction. As shown in the example description for the Sieve of Eratosthenos program, what we make abstraction of is the *number* of goals that occur in chains of identically instantiated goals with identical bindings linking them together.

As an example, the state description in the Sieve of Eratosthenos program contains two such chains, both with base block

Filter(G, V_i, V_{i+1}),

which is linked to a previous block Filter(G, V_{i-1}, V_i) through its second argument and to the next Filter(G, V_{i+1}, V_{i+2}) through its third argument.

In order to deal with general states, a state description usually will contain chains, of which the base blocks reveal a much more complicated structure than the ones in the example. Often base blocks are sets of abstract goals (with connecting bindings) themselves. In some cases they even take the form of chains. We do not discuss these technical observations in more detail, but simply stress the fact that abstraction must be made of the frequency with which repeating structures occur within the state.

As for most applications, representing the abstraction can be performed in many different ways. The unification mechanism and the behavior for builtin predicates can be dealt with similarly as in the previous section. We do not discuss them in further detail.

In the interpreter, special care must be taken of the selection of subgoals and the generation of new descriptions. Both must be dealt with during each resolution step. A resolution step now consists of

- selecting a appropriate goal from the description - using the new computation rule -,

- expanding or solving the abstract goal using the mechanism of section 3,

- applying the resulting abstract substitution to the entire state description

- building a new description that represents the newly obtained state. This may include a case study, distinguishing between the presence of one or more base blocks in a chain. It also includes verifying whether or not newly created goals can be combined with existing goals to obtain new chains in the description.

After each resolution step, the obtained state description must be compared to all previously obtained descriptions (not just to the ancestors). If its canonical form is equal to that of a previous description, then no further resolution for that branch of the abstract trace tree is needed.

5. Discussion.

The main objective of this paper was to present an informal introduction to the topic of abstract interpretation with the aim of reducing the effort which is required from a novice in the field in order to be able to develop his application. Using an example from the field of source-to-source program transformation we illustrated the main activities involved in building such applications. The solution to the problem was split up into two different layers, with increasing difficulty, such that the combination of the two is both correct and complete. We deliberately did not provide rigorous proofs of the termination nor of the correctness of the method, since we are convinced that they would decrease the comprehensibility of the paper. For more details on these, within a general framework on abstract interpretation, we refer to [6]. In the more specific framework of program transformation, the topic is dealt with in [16].

We conclude by discussing the applicability of abstract interpretation as a basic tool for different kinds of program transformation. The motivation is simple: most program transformation methods start off with an analysis of the runtime behavior of the input program to detect which inefficiencies may occur. This is obviously the case for techniques for loop-detection and -avoidance (e.g. [2], [25]) as well as for those dealing with the detection and elimination of redundant computations [14]. Here, abstract interpretation will provide an automated way to detect these inefficiencies, together with sufficient information on the computational history to perform the transformation which is adequate.

Next, there are the methods based on the synthesis of programs from traces of example computations. Research in this field has been initiated by A. Biermann in [2]. Using abstract interpretation to construct the traces, significantly increases the power of these methods, because

1. more computational paths can be covered with a single (abstract) top level query,

2. completeness of the synthesized program can be ensured in an automated way.

Both these advantages where illustrated in our example application. [4] and [13] describe a technique of the above type aiming at the conversion of any generate and test program into a more efficient - but logically equivalent - one, involving a coroutining control regime. V.Turchin proposes a similar technique for functional languages in [28], majorly aiming at a further automation of the *Unfold/Fold* method.

A promising extension of the work presented in [4], again based on synthesizing example traces, is the conversion of generate and test algorithms into equivalent forward checking algorithms. Here, it will not be sufficient to abstractly interpret a given program following a new computation rule as a basis for synthesis, but minor transformations on the logical component of the program will be needed as well. P.Van Hentenryck in [29] has thoroughly studied the relationship between these two control mechanisms and in our further work we aim to develop a transformation scheme on the basis of his results.

The *Unfold/Fold* technique of Burstall and Darlington [7] offer another application of abstract interpretation. In [19] S.Gregory illustrates through his many examples that the mechanism of unfolding (abstract expansion) and folding (recognition of fixed points within an abstract execution trace) are strongly related to abstract interpretation. In a more recent paper [11], J.Darlington recasts the original ideas on *Unfold/Fold* within a setting based on symbolic execution.

Closely related to code optimization is the automatic generation of mode declarations using abstract interpretation. This source level transformation method has been successfully developed and implemented at our research centre as an auxiliary result of the interpretation described in the previous sections.

A final, but certainly not less important application domain is situated in the field of partial evaluation. Practical use of partial evaluation as an independent technique in program transformation has lost of its credibility in the last years, because no halting condition for the expansion of recursive clauses can be formulated. A possible solution to the problem is the use of automatically generated *wait*-declarations, as proposed by L.Naish in [23]. However, the range of applicability for this technique has not clearly been established. More convincing is the idea to derive partially evaluated programs for given top level query patterns, where abstract interpretation guides the evaluation of recursive clauses. This idea was elaborated by J.Gallagher and M.Codish in [16] for the case of program specialization. This paper recasts the theoretical framework of abstract interpretation within the field of program transformation in a rigorous manner and is therefore highly recommended as further reading. Possibly, the synthesis of the specialized program can be slightly improved using the flowchart analysis technique described in [3]. At this time, several other researchers in the field (e.g. H.Fujita [15]) are exploring the possibilities of combined partial evaluation and abstract interpretation. We are convinced that these efforts will lead to a further breakthrough of both.

6. Acknowledgement.

We are indebted to G.Janssens, A.Callebout, B.Demoen and A.Marien for communications on their early work in the field. Also thanks to B. Mignon for his implementation of a mode declaration generator. D.De Schreye is supported by the Belgian I.W.O.N.L.-I.R.S.I.A. under contract number 4856. M.Bruynooghe is supported as research associate by the Belgian National Fund for Scientific Research.

References.

[1] Biermann A., On the inference of Turing machines from sample computations, Artificial Intelligence, Vol. 3, 1972.

[2] Brough D.R., Walker A., Some practical properties of logic programming interpreters, in Proc. FGCS conference, 1984, pp. 149–156.

[3] Bruynooghe M., De Schreye D. and Krekels B., Compiling Control, Proc.Third International Symposium on Logic Programming, 1986, pp. 70–78.

[4] Bruynooghe M., De Schreye D. and Krekels B., Compiling Control, J.Logic Programming, to appear.

[5] Bruynooghe M., Janssens G., Callebout A., Demoen B., Abstract interpretation: towards the global optimisation of Prolog programs, Proc. Fourth International Symposium on Logic Programming, 1987.

[6] Bruynooghe M., A framework for the abstract interpretation of logic programs, report CW62, 1987, K.U.Leuven.

[7] Burstall R.M. and Darlington J., A transformation system for developing recursive programs, JACM, 24, 1977, pp. 44-67.

[8] Clark K.I., McCabe F.G., Gregory S., IC-Prolog language features, Logic programming, ed. Clark/Tarnlund, 1982, pp. 254-266.

[9] Colmerauer A., Prolog II, manuel de reference et modele theoretique, Marseille, 1982.

[10] Cousot P., Cousot R., Abstract interpretation: A unified lattice model for static analysis of programs by construction of approximation of fixpoints, in Proc. 4th ACM POPL symposium, 1977, pp. 238-252.

[11] Darlington J., Pull H., A program development methodology based on a unified approach to execution and transformation, in Proc.workshop on partial evaluation and mixed computation, 1987, Denmark.

[12] Debray S.K., Warren D.S., Automatic mode inferencing for Prolog programs, Proc.Third International Symposium on Logic Programming, 1986, pp. 78-88.

[13] De Schreye D., Bruynooghe M. On the transformation of logic programs with instantiation based computation rules, J.Symbolic Computation, to appear.

[14] Fronhofer B., Double work as a reason for inefficiency of programs, Technical report T.U.M. Munchen, 1987.

[15] Fujita H., Abstract interpretation and partial evaluation of prolog programs, ICOT technical report, 1986.

[16] Gallagher J., Codish M., Specialisation of Prolog and FCP programs using abstract interpretation, in Proceedings of the workshop on partial evaluation and mixed computation, 1987, Denmark.

[17] Gallaire H. and Laserre C., A control meta language for logic programming, in LogicProgramming, eds. Clark L. and Tarnlund S.A., Academic Press, 1982, pp. 173-185.

[18] Genesereth M.R. and Ginsberg M.L., Logic Programming, CACM 28(9), Sept. 1985, pp. 933-941.

[19] Gregory S., Towards the compilation of annotated logic programs, Res.Report DOC80/16, June 1980, Imperial College.

[20] Jones N.D., Sondergaard H., A semantics based framework for the abstract interpretation of Prolog, in Abstract interpretation of declarative languages, eds. Abramsky S. and Hankin C. , Ellis Horwood, in print.

[21] Kanamari T., Kawamura T., Analyzing succes patterns of Logic programs by abstract hybrid interpretation, ICOT technical report, TR 279, 1987.

[22] Mellish C.S., Abstract interpretation of prolog programs, in Proc. 3rd International Conference on Logic Programming, 1986, LNCS 225, Springer-Verlag, 1986, pp. 463–474.

[23] Naish L., Automating control for logic programs, J. Logic Programming 2, 1985, pp. 167–183.

[24] Narain S., A technique for doing lazy evaluation in Logic, J.Logic Programming 3 (3), 1986, pp. 259–276.

[25] Pelhat S., Analysis and control of recursivity in Prolog programs, Technical report CRIL, Universite de Paris-sud, 1987.

[26] Pereira L.M., Logic control with logic, in Implementations of Prolog, ed. Cambell, Ellis, Horwood, 1984, pp.177–193.

[27] Sato T., Tamaki H., Transformational logic program synthesis, FGCS '84, Tokyo, 1984.

[28] Turchin V.F., The concept of a supercompiler, ACM Transactions on Programming Languages and Systems 8 (3), 1986, pp. 292–325.

[29] Van Hentenryck P., Consistency techniques in logic programming, Ph.D. thesis FUNDF, Namur, Belgium, 1987.

[30] Warren D.H.D., Coroutining facilities for Prolog, implemented in Prolog, DAI working paper, Edinburgh, 1979.

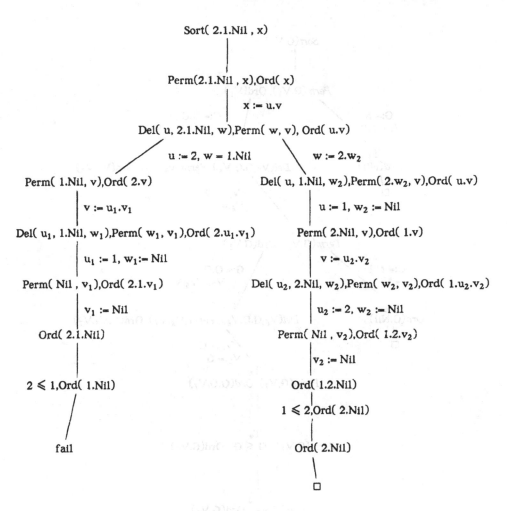

Fig. 1
Proof tree for ⟵ Sort(2.1.Nil) under the standard computation rule of Prolog.

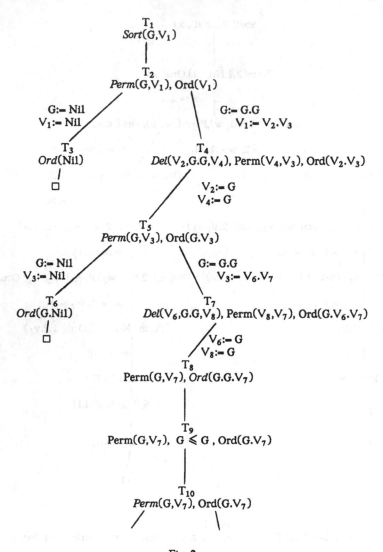

Fig. 2
Abstract trace tree of Slowsort
The selected subgoal is in Italic (e.g.$Perm(G,V_1)$).

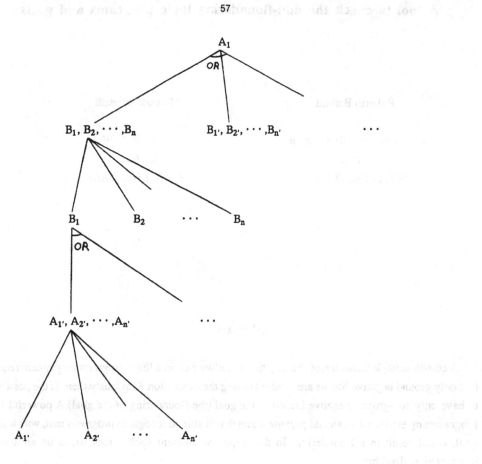

Fig.3 Abstract AND–OR-tree.

A tool to check the non-floundering logic programs and goals

Roberto Barbuti

Dipartimento di Informatica
Corso Italia 40,
56100 Pisa, ITALY

Maurizio Martelli

CNUCE-CNR
Via S. Maria 36,
56100 Pisa, ITALY

Abstract

A complete implementation of the negation as failure rule in a logic programming system requires that only ground negative literals are selected during the evaluation. Obviously there is the possibility to have only non-ground negative literals in the goal (the floundering of the goal).A powerful logic programming environment should provide a tool that is able to recognize programs that, with a given goal, could result in a floundering. In this paper we present such a tool based on an abstract interpretation algorithm.

1. Introduction

The completeness of SLDNF-Resolution has been widely investigated in many papers. Although there are completeness results for SLD-resolution and Negation as Failure separately [14, 11], when the two things are considered together (SLDNF–Resolution for general programs or goals) the proof procedure is not complete any longer. Recall that to obtain completeness, the proof procedure must be able to compute all correct answer substitutions relative to the completion of the program (comp(P)) [7].

There are two main different aspects responsible for the incompleteness of SLDNF-Resolution for logic programs. The first aspect is related to the fact that beside the incompleteness caused by the inconsistency of comp(P) [2], the SLDNF-resolution is unable to prove a formula F∨G if neither F nor G is a logical consequence of the theory. See [1, 12, 18] for discussions about this problem.

The second aspect is related to a specific peculiarity of the proof procedure, i.e. the need to restrict the evaluation of negative literals to the ground ones, thus avoiding the floundering. Let us consider the following program P:

p(x) ←.
q(a) ←.
r(b) ←.

and the goal

←p(x), ~q(x).

Resolving with the first clause, the goal becomes ←~q(x).

The tentative to prove the finite failure of ←q(x) does not succeed. The formula has not been proved, while ∃x. p(x), ~q(x) is a logical consequence of comp(P) since p(b), ~q(b) is a logical consequence.

This problem has been addressed in [15] with the introduction of a special class of programs and goals called *allowed* satisfying a syntactic condition. This condition is very strong, and in [4] we extended the concept of allowedness using concepts and techniques used in the abstract interpretations.

The idea is to have an algorithm that is able to check (sufficient condition) if a goal and a program will never flounder. Based on this algorithm a tool implemented in LPA Prolog is presented in the following.

2. Preliminary concepts

In this paper we assume the reader is familiar with the concepts of logic programming. For any terminology not explicitly defined see [14].

In the following we will refer to logic programs with negative literals in the clause bodies as *general programs* (and correspondingly to *general goals*).

Let us assume a proof procedure with a *safe* computation rule, i.e. one that will never select a non ground negative literal.

In [15] a class of non-floundering general programs and goals (*allowed*) is defined. This definition is based on a syntactic condition which roughly forbids non ground answers (for example programs containing non ground facts are not allowed). This condition seems to be too restrictive. In fact, in such systems, programs defining the usual relations *append* or *member* cannot be written.

The idea underlying our approach is that also predicates whose definition contains non ground facts can produce ground answers if suitably used (the use of a predicate in a goal is checked and not only its definition).

Let us give a simple example; consider the program P

$$r(x, x, z) \leftarrow$$
$$q(a) \leftarrow$$

and the goal G

$$\leftarrow r(a, y, z), \sim q(y)$$

$P \cup \{G\}$ is not allowed in the sense of [15] (the first clause of P is not allowed), but the evaluation of G does not flounder.

Using abstract interpretations techniques it is possible to give an algorithm able to infer that the variable y will be ground instantiated after the evaluation of r(a, y, z), and then that the goal G has to be considered allowed with respect to P.

Section 3. will illustrate the algorithm and Section 4. will present the tool implementation.

3. An algorithm to check the non-floundering of general programs and goals

Abstract interpretation is a general technique to check properties of programs which has been applied to the logic programming field in recent works [5, 8, 9, 16, 17]. The idea underlying the approach is to give the meaning of a program with respect to a suitable domain (generally finite) thus obtaining an approximation of the dynamic behaviour of the program itself. This technique has been mainly used to obtain information leading to the optimization of Prolog compilers.

The algorithm we propose is an extension of the algorithm for modes inference in [16]. In [4] the correctness and the termination of the algorithm is proved. Note that a similar analysis could be obtained using other techniques such as the ones in [10]. The algorithm performs an abstract evaluation of a goal on a domain composed by the two values **g** and **ng** (modes) corresponding to *ground* and *non ground* respectively. The abstract evaluation of positive literals results in an instantiation of modes for variables. The resulting modes are used to check the groundness of negative literals in the original goal and in those introduced during the evaluation. Obviously the algorithm gives only an approximation of the evaluation; it is possible that a goal does not flounder and that the algorithm is unable to give a positive answer. However, the correctness of the algorithm guarantees that no positively checked goal will flounder during its evaluation.

The algorithm operates by trying to apply the clauses of the program to positive literals in a (sub)goal. To each positive literal it is associated its input sequence of modes (the modes of the arguments of the literal before the abstract evaluation) and the algorithm results in an output sequence of modes (the modes of the arguments after the abstract evaluation). It is important to note that there are cases in which the output sequence for a literal cannot be computed; for example if no clause is applicable or a loop is detected. In this case the algorithm results in a special value **nc** corresponding to a SLDNF failure (either finite or infinite) of the literal.

The algorithm operates on abstract bodies corresponding to the concrete subgoals generated during the SLDNF evaluation

An element of the domain *AbstractBody* is a triplet in which the first element is a finite sequence of elements of the domain *AbstractAtom* (this part represents the positive literals in the body of a clause), the second one is a finite sequence of atoms (this part represents the negative literals in the body of a clause), and the third one is an element of the domain *Result*.

The domain *AbstractAtom* is defined as triplets in which the first element is an atom (in the following we will refer to it as concrete atom), the second is an element of the domain *Modes*, and the third is an element of the domain *Result* (this domain represents atoms with input and output annotations).

The domain *Result* is defined as pairs in which the first element is an element of the domain *Output* and the second one is a boolean (indicating non-floundering).

Output = *Modes*+ {**nc**} + {∅} (an element of *Modes*, or the sign of non-computable output **nc**, or the not yet computed output sign ∅)

Modes is the domain of all possible finite sequences of elements of {**g**, **ng**} (standing respectively for ground and non ground).

The clauses of a program W are numbered and denoted as $c_1,...,c_n$. Given a goal G, the clause c_0: goal $\leftarrow$ G is added to the program, thus obtaining the program W^+ which is checked for non-floundering.

The algorithm (NonFloundering) checks the non-floundering of the goal $\leftarrow$goal with respect to the program W^+. We will see that the algorithm always terminates. Pairs and triplets are denoted with (,) while sequences with ‹, ›. Atoms with any arity are denoted by P($\underline{t}$), where P is a predicate symbol and $\underline{t}$ is a tuple of terms.

NonFloundering (W^+)

1. Let (O,NFlou) = ProduceOut([], (goal,‹›))
2. NonFloundering (W^+) = NFlou

NonFloundering (W^+) is **true** if the original goal G does not flounder with respect to the program W, **false** if the original goal G could flounder.

Let us first describe some functions that will be used in the following.

---

norm (($e_1,...,e_m$)) =
Let {$e_1,...,e_m$} be a set of equations in which the right hand side is either g or ng.
Transform the set {$e_1,...,e_m$} using the following steps until a set {$e'_1,...,e'_k$} is reached such that none of the steps is applicable, then   norm (($e_1,...,e_m$)) = {$e'_1,...,e'_k$}.

1. Eliminate any equation with a constant in the left side.
2. For every equation e_i : f($t_1,...,t_n$) = s, eliminate e_i and add n equations t_i = s.
3. Eliminate any equation already in the set (leave a single copy).
4. For every pair of equations x = g and x = **ng**, eliminate x = **ng** (x is a variable).

Note that the result of norm is a set of equations with a variable as left hand side and either g or ng as right hand side. This can be considered a substitution which maps a set of variables into the set {g, ng}.

---

extract (a) =

Let a be an element of the domain *AbstractAtom*. The result is:

1. $\{t_s = i_s \mid 1 \leq s \leq n\}$ if $a = (P(t_1,..., t_n), \langle i_1,..., i_n \rangle, (\emptyset, \text{NFlou}))$, or

2. $\{t_s = o_s \mid 1 \leq s \leq n\}$ if $a = (P(t_1,..., t_n), \langle i_1,..., i_n \rangle, (\langle o_1,..., o_n \rangle, \text{NFlou}))$.

Given an abstract atom a, extract creates the set of equations in which the left parts are the arguments of the concrete atom in a and the right parts are the modes of the abstractly computed output or the modes of the input if the output of a has not yet been computed.

---

derive $(\langle t_1,..., t_n \rangle, a_1,..., a_m) =$

Let $t_1,..., t_n$ be terms and $a_1,..., a_m$ elements of the domain *AbstractAtom*. The result is:

$\langle s_1,..., s_n \rangle$ which is an element of *Modes*, such that

$s_i = \text{simplify}(\ t_i \theta)$ where θ is the substitution obtained by $\text{norm}(\bigcup_{k=1..m} \text{extract}(a_k))$ and

simplify (t) =	t	if t = g or t = ng, or		ng
		if t is a variable, or		
	g	if t is a constant, or		
	g	if $t = f(t_1,..., t_s)$ and for $1 \leq w \leq s$ simplify(t_w) = g, or		ng
	otherwise.			

The function derive is able to infer the modes of a set of terms using the informations contained in a set of abstract atoms.

---

compose $(out_1,..., out_n) =$

Let the out_i be $\langle s^i_1,..., s^i_m \rangle$ or nc, i.e. elements of *Output*.

The result is:

nc   if for $1 \leq w \leq n$ out_w = nc, or

$\langle r_1,..., r_m \rangle$ otherwise, where

         $r_j = g$ if for $1 \leq w \leq n$ $(out_w = nc \vee s^w_j = g)$, or

         $r_j = ng$ otherwise.

The function compose will be used to obtain the final output modes of an abstract atom starting from the outputs produced by each applicable clause.

ProduceOut(L,(P($\underline{t}$), I)) = (O, NF)

Let L be a list of pairs (n, I') where n is a clause number and I' an element of *Modes*.

1. Find all clauses applicable to P($\underline{t}$), that is the clauses whose heads contain the predicate symbol P and are unifiable with P($\underline{t}$).

2. For each applicable clause
   $$c_k = P(\underline{t}_{k0}) \leftarrow P_{k1}(\underline{t}_{k1}),\ldots, P_{km}(\underline{t}_{km}), \sim Q_{km+1}(\underline{t}_{km+1}),\ldots, \sim Q_{km+h}(\underline{t}_{km+h}),$$
   such that (k, I) does not belong to L (this condition prevents loops), perform:

   2.1. Let $N_k = (\langle a_1,\ldots,a_m \rangle, \langle na_{m+1},\ldots, na_{m+h} \rangle, (Out_k, NF_k))$ where
   each $a_i = (P_{ki}(\underline{t}_{ki}), derive(\underline{t}_{ki}, (P(\underline{t}_{k0}), I, (\varnothing, \_))), (\varnothing, NFlou_i))$, and
   each $na_j = Q_{kj}(\underline{t}_{kj})$.
   At this step the values of Out_k, NF_k, and $NFlou_i$ have not yet been determined.

   2.2 Select an element $a_z = (P_z(\underline{t}_z), I_z, (O_z, NFlou_z))$ in N_k, such that $O_z = \varnothing$ or $I'_z \neq I_z$,
   where.
   $I'_z = derive(\underline{t}_z, a_1,\ldots,a_m,(P(\underline{t}_{k0}), I, (\varnothing, \_)))$.
   Note that if $I'_z \neq I_z$ then I'_z contains more g's than I_z.

   a) If there is no such element a_z, let $Out_k = derive(\underline{t}_{k0}, a_1,\ldots,a_m ,(P(\underline{t}_{k0}), I, (\varnothing, \_)))$, and
   $$NF_k = \bigwedge_{i=m+1..m+h} checkNF(na_i, a_1,\ldots,a_m ,(P(\underline{t}_{k0}), I, (\varnothing, \_))) \wedge \bigwedge_{i=1..m} NFlou_i.$$
   Where:
   checkNF (Q($\underline{t}$), $a_1,\ldots, a_n$) = **true** iff $derive(\underline{t}, a_1,\ldots,a_n) = \langle g, g, \ldots, g \rangle$.

   b) Otherwise substitute a_z with $a'_z = (P_z(\underline{t}_z), I'_z, (O_z, NFlou_z))$, where
   $(O_z, NFlou_z) = ProduceOut ([(k, I) |L], (P_z(\underline{t}_z), I'_z))$
   If $O_z = nc$, then let $Out_k = nc$, $NF_k = $ **true** and terminate the step 2 for clause k.

3. Let $Out_1,\ldots, Out_v$ be the output computed by step 2 using all applicable clauses.
   O = nc if v=0;   otherwise O = compose($Out_1,\ldots, Out_v$).
   Let $NF_1,\ldots, NF_v$ be the non-floundering values computed by step 2.,
   then $NF = \bigwedge_{i=1...v} NF_i$.

This algorithm examines an abstract atom and it results in a pair. The first element of this pair is the computed output sequence of modes and the second one is a boolean value corresponding to the non-floundering of the part of computation regarding the abstract atom.

In step 1. all applicable clauses are selected and for each of them step 2. is performed. Step 2. examines each abstract atom in the abstract body of the selected clause.

The list L is used to check if an abstract atom has been previously computed with the same input sequence and the same clause, thus preventing infinite loops (step 2.). Recall that the number of possible abstract atoms and input sequences is finite.

In step 2.1 each abstract atom is initialized using the information in the input I.

Note that in step 2.2 an abstract atom can be selected to be computed more than once. This problem has been stressed in [5, 9] and is related to the aliasing of variables. Intuitively, the computation of an abstract atom can result in an output which can be used to further ground instantiate the input of a previously computed atom.

In step a), when all atoms are computed, the global result can be built. In step b) the algorithm is recursively applied to the selected abstract atom. Note that if the evaluation of an abstract atom results in nc then the whole computation of the abstract body can be considered to result in nc.

Finally, step 3. collects all results corresponding to all applicable clauses.

Remark 1 Note that if $c_k = P(t_{k0}) \leftarrow$ (a fact) step 2. produces
$N_k = (\diamond, \diamond, (\text{derive}(t_{k0}, (P(t_{k0}), I, (\emptyset, \_)), \textbf{true}))$. I.e. Out_k only depends from the input I and moreover if t_{k0} is ground $N_k = (\diamond, \diamond, (\langle g, g, ..., g \rangle, \textbf{true}))$.

In [4] the following theorems regarding the algorithm are presented.

Theorem 1 (Termination of ProduceOut)
Consider a program W^+. The evaluation of ProduceOut([], $(goal, \diamond)$) always terminates.

Theorem 2 (Correctness of non-floundering check)
Consider a program W^+. Let (O, NF) = ProduceOut ([], $(goal, \diamond)$).
If NF = **true** then the SLDNF-evaluation of the goal $\leftarrow goal$ never flounders.

4. Implementation

The algorithm has been implemented using the LPA-Prolog on Macintosh.

Because of the inefficiency of the algoritm in the presented form, the implementation is actually slightly different. In particular, two major changes have been made in order to cut the computation time:

- when an abstract output composed only by **g** values is computed, the corresponding abstract atom is nevermore selected for the recomputation. Its output cannot be furtherly instantiated.
- when an output is computed for an abstract atom, the result of the abstract computation is inserted in a data base (by means of the *assert* predicate). In this way the reinterpretation of the same abstract atom is avoided; the result is obtained directly from the data base.

The tool has been applied to a variety of logic programs. The interesting result of these computations is that the class of non-floundering programs contains most of the commonly used programs.

References

[1]   Apt K.R. Introduction to Logic Programming. To appear in: *Handbook of Theoretical Computer Science* (J. van Leeuwen Ed.), North Holland.

[2]   Apt K.R. Blair H.A. and Walker A. Towards a Theory of Declarative Knowledge. *Foundations of Deductive Databases and Logic Programming* (J. Minker Ed.), Morgan Kaufman, Los Altos, 1987.

[3]   Barbuti R. and Martelli M. Completeness of the SLDNF-resolution for a Class of Logic Programs. Third Int. Conf. on Logic Programming, London, 1986, 600-614.

[4]   Barbuti R. and Martelli M. A characterization of non-floundering logic programs and goals based on abstract interpretation techniques. Submitted for publication.

[5]   Bruynooghe M., Janssens G., Callebaut, A. and Demoen B. Abstract Interpretation: Towards the Global Optimization of Prolog Programs. 4th Int. Symp. on Logic Programming, San Francisco, 1987, 192-204.

[6]   Cavedon L. and Lloyd J.W. A Completeness Theorem for SLDNF-resolution. Report CS-87-06 University of Bristol, 1987.

[7]   Clark K.L. Negation as Failure. *Logic and Data Bases*. (H. Gallaire and J. Minker Eds.), Plenum Press, New York, 1978, 293-322.

[8]   Debray S.K. and Warren D.S. Automatic Mode Inference for Prolog Programs. Third Int. Symp. on Logic Programming, Salt Lake City, 1986, 78-88.

[9]   Debray S.K. Efficient Dataflow Analysis of Logic Programs. Fifteenth ACM Symp. on Principles of Programming Languages, San Diego, 1988, 260-273.

[10]   Deransart P. and Maluszynski J. Modelling Data Dependencies in Logic Programming by Attribute Schemata. INRIA Internal Report, 1984.

[11]   Jaffar J. Lassez J-L. and Lloyd J.W. Completeness of the Negation as Failure Rule. IJCAI 83, Karlsruhe, 1983, 500-506.

[12]   Kunen K. Negation in Logic Programming. *J. Logic Programming 4*, 4 (1987), 289-308.

[13]   Kunen K. Signed Data Dependencies in Logic Programs. University of Wisconsin. To appear.

[14]   Lloyd J.W. *Foundations of Logic Programming*. Second Edition, Springer-Verlag, Symbolic Computation Series, 1987.

[15]   Lloyd J.W. and Topor R.W. A Basis for Deductive Database Systems II. *J. Logic Programming 3*, 1 (1986), 55-67.

[16]   Mannila H. and Ukkonen E. Flow Analysis of Prolog Programs. 4th Int. Symp. on Logic Programming, San Francisco, 1987, 205-214.

[17]   Mellish C.S. Abstract Interpretation of Prolog Programs. Third Int. Conf. on Logic Programming, London, 1986, 463-474.

[18]   Shepherdson J.C. Negation in Logic Programming. *Foundations of Deductive Databases and Logic Programming* (J. Minker Ed.), Morgan Kaufman, Los Altos, 1987.

Towards a Framework for the Abstract Interpretation of Logic Programs

Ulf Nilsson

Department of Computer and Information Science

Linköping University

S–581 83 Linköping, Sweden

Abstract: *A new framework for abstract interpretation of logic programs is presented. The idea is to take as the basis a simplified semantics that approximates the standard operational semantics of logic programs but still makes it possible to derive non-trivial abstract interpretations. The relative simplicity of the basic semantics facilitates systematic derivation of abstract interpretations and static analyses of logic programs. Sufficient conditions for termination and correctness of the derived interpreters are provided. The approach is illustrated by inferring groundness information for an example program.*

1   Introduction

A logic program and a set of goal-clauses together describe a set of computations in a universe of substitutions. If we restrict our attention to *definite* programs and goals and adopt SLD-resolution as our operational semantics, they denote a set of SLD-derivations. A naïve approach to determine whether the program exhibits some run-time property would be to construct the set of all possible derivations and to explicitly test whether the property holds. Needless to say, the method would not, in general, terminate in finite time.

Abstract interpretation (e.g. [AH87], [Bru87], [CC77], [DW88], [MS88]) is a general method which allows us to effectively approximate the semantics of a program. In abstract interpretation the domain(s) of the concrete interpretation is replaced by some abstract domain(s) and the operations on the concrete domain(s) are replaced by abstract operations on the abstract domain(s).

The aim of the paper is to provide a general and simple framework for abstract interpretation of logic programs, facilitating construction of different abstract interpretations in a simple and systematic way. We intend to exploit the ideas and results as the basis for efficient implementation of abstract interpretation in different abstract domains.

The approaches presented in the literature takes as a starting point some precise semantics of concrete interpretation — e.g. the *static* semantics of [CC77] and the *collecting* semantics of [JS87]. Such a semantics may become quite complicated. Therefore development of correctness proof for an abstract interpretation may be difficult. In this paper we suggest a concrete semantics which is in itself an approximation of the precise static/collecting semantics. Our semantics (which is called a static$^+$ semantics) uses the same domain as the static semantics but is a superset of it. We then demonstrate how further abstractions may be achieved by replacing the concrete domain by an abstract domain and by giving abstract interpretations to the operations of the static$^+$ interpretation. Because of the relative simplicity of the static$^+$ semantics such abstractions can be obtained in a systematic way. We also formulate some simple sufficient conditions which guarantee the termination and correctness of abstract interpretations.

The rest of the paper is organized as follows — section 2 provides the necessary definitions and notation. Section 3 informally introduces the concept of abstract interpretation, assertions and contexts. Section 4 develops a static$^+$ semantics based on the set of possible SLD-derivations. Section 5 presents some properties and requirements necessary to guarantee correctness and termination of abstract domains and operations. Section 6 gives an abstract domain and operations to infer groundness information for an example program. Section 7, finally, contains conclusions and comparisons with related work.

2 Preliminaries

If nothing else is said we adopt the notation and terminology of e.g. [Llo87] and [Apt87]. Below some of the most important concepts are outlined.

Without lack of generality we assume that the standard (leftmost) computation rule of Prolog is employed. Moreover, to avoid having to refer to "the i:th subgoal in the j:th clause" we assume, for notational convenience, that all literals in a program are unique.

The substitutions we consider in this paper are all idempotent. The *composition* $\theta' \circ \theta''$ of substitutions θ' and θ'' will be defined in the standard way (see [Llo87]).

Definition 2.1 Let $\theta = \{X_1/t_1, \ldots, X_n/t_n\}$ be a substitution and denote by $Var(x)$ the set of variables in a term/formula, x. Then $Dom(\theta) = \{X_1, \ldots, X_n\}$ is called the *domain* of θ and $Range(\theta) = Var(t_1) \cup \ldots \cup Var(t_n)$ is called the *range* of θ. ∎

Definition 2.2 The *restriction* $\theta|_V$ of a substitution θ to a set of variables V is the substitution $\{X/t \mid X/t \in \theta \land X \in V\}$. ∎

The notation $\theta' \bullet \theta''$ denotes the substitution $(\theta' \circ \theta'')|_{Dom(\theta')}$. Throughout the paper we assume that $\circ$ binds stronger than $\bullet$, i.e. $\theta \bullet \theta_1 \circ \ldots \circ \theta_n$ is identical to $\theta \bullet (\theta_1 \circ \ldots \circ \theta_n)$ ($\circ$ is associative). Usually $\circ$ is omitted altogether.

Definition 2.3 A *renaming* (substitution) of a term/formula, x, is a substitution $\sigma = \{X_1/Y_1, \ldots, X_n/Y_n\}$ such that $X_1, \ldots, X_n, Y_1, \ldots, Y_n$ are distinct variables and $Dom(\sigma) = Var(x)$. ∎

Definition 2.4 Let P be a definite program and G_0 a definite goal. An *SLD-derivation* of G_0 is a sequence $\langle G_0, C_0\sigma_0 \rangle, \ldots, \langle G_{n-1}, C_{n-1}\sigma_{n-1} \rangle, G_n$ where:

- σ_i is a renaming of $C_i \in P$ such that $C_i\sigma_i$ and $G_0, \ldots, G_i$ contain no common variables, and

- if $C_i = (x \leftarrow x_1, \ldots, x_m)$, $G_i = (\leftarrow y_1, y_2, \ldots)$ and $\theta_{i+1} = mgu(x\sigma_i, y_1)$ then $G_{i+1} = (\leftarrow x_1\sigma_i, \ldots, x_m\sigma_i, y_2, \ldots)\theta_{i+1}$.

The *computed substitution* of the derivation above is the composition $\theta_1 \ldots \theta_n$ of all mgu's in the derivation. ∎

Definition 2.5 The (initial) *connection graph*[1] of a program P (including one or more goal clauses) is the set

$$\{x \rightarrow y \mid (\ldots \leftarrow \ldots, x, \ldots) \in P \wedge (y \leftarrow \ldots) \in P \wedge \exists\theta(x\theta = y\sigma\theta)\}$$

where σ is a renaming of y such that $Var(x) \cap Var(y\sigma) = \emptyset$ ∎

Example 2.1 The connection graph of the *reverse*/2-program below is depicted in Figure 1.

$\leftarrow reverse(X, Y).$
$reverse([], []).$
$reverse([X|Xs], Ys) \leftarrow reverse(Xs, Zs), append(Zs, [X], Ys).$
$append([], Xs, Xs).$
$append([X|Xs], Ys, [X|Zs]) \leftarrow append(Xs, Ys, Zs).$

∎

We conclude the section with the following result due to [Tar55] and [Kle52].

Theorem 2.1 Let $\mathcal{D}$ be a complete lattice with bottom element $\bot$, f be a mapping $f : \mathcal{D} \rightarrow \mathcal{D}$ and denote by:

$$f \uparrow 0 = \bot$$
$$f \uparrow (n+1) = f(f \uparrow n)$$
$$f \uparrow \omega = \bigcup_{i=0}^{\infty} f \uparrow i$$

If f is continuous then $f \uparrow \omega$ is the least fixed point of f. ∎

---

[1]The definition given here diverges slightly from the one in e.g. [Kow79]

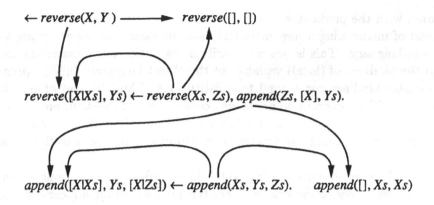

Figure 1: Connection-graph of *reverse*/2-program

3 Abstract Interpretation

Operationally the body of a (definite) clause may be viewed as a sequence of
procedure-calls. For each call there are two distinguished program points — the
point immediately to the left of a call x will be referred to as the *calling point* of x,
and the point to the right will be called the *success point* of x. The leftmost and
rightmost points in a clause will be called the *entry-* and *exit points* respectively
of the clause.

Let p be the calling point of some literal x. We say that the program point p
is *current* (in a derivation d) when (an instance of) x is the selected subgoal in d.
For instance, the calling point of B_1 is current in the last goal of the derivation in
Figure 2. By analogy the success point of x is current whenever x is immediately
solved. Similarly entry- and exit-points may be current. Notice that several points
may be current simultaneously — in the last step of Figure 3 the success point of
A_i, the calling point of A_{i+1} and the exit point of $(B \leftarrow \ldots)$ are current (among
others).

With every program point we want to associate some invariant assertion —
i.e. an expression which is always true whenever the program point is current.
Roughly speaking, the objective of abstract interpretation is to produce correct
assertions for the program points of a program.

This idea is similar to [DM87] except that abstract interpretation generates
assertions whereas [DM87] verify assertions. In contrast to [DM87] we are not
going to introduce any specific meta-language for assertions. Another difference is
that our assertions are associated with the program points — in [DM87] they are

associated with the predicates.

Instead of introducing a new meta-language for assertions we are going to use the object-language. This is not necessarily a restriction since assertions usually refer to the bindings of (local) variables of the object language. In logic programming variable bindings correspond to substitutions. Thus, instead of associating an assertion with a program point we may collect a set of substitutions — namely all substitutions, θ, such that there exists a derivation where the program point is current and the computed substitution is θ. However, this leads to three complications.

First of all we are usually not interested in the whole substitutions — only in bindings for variables in the clause where the program point appears. Secondly, assertions refer to the variables in a clause of the program whereas, in derivations, *renamed* clauses are used. Consequently the substitutions contain bindings not for the program clause but for a renamed clause. Finally there are infinitely many ways to rename the variables in the clauses of a derivation. These problems will be handled as follows;

Consider a derivation $\ldots, \langle G_i, C\sigma \rangle, \ldots, G_j$ and assume that one of the program points in C is current in G_j. Then $\sigma \bullet \theta_1 \ldots \theta_j$ should be contained in the set of substitutions associated with the program point. This solves the first two problems — it gives us a substitution whose domain is exactly the variables in the program clause C. Such a substitution will be called an *environment*.

The third problem will not be dealt with — we shall simply not consider assertions which refer to the actual names of variables in the range of an environment. This is not a great restriction since no standard treatment is available how to rename the variables of a clause in a derivation.

Now, with every program point of a program we want to associate the set of all possible environments when the point is current. This set will be called a *context*.

If no restrictions are imposed on the use of a program practically any context may appear at each program point of the program and no useful assertions will be deduced. To limit the set of possible derivations we shall assume that the user provides information about the set of possible goals given to the program. Such a set will be called a *call-pattern*. To simplify the notation we assume that it is given on the form $\leftarrow p(X_1, \ldots, X_n), \{\theta_1, \ldots, \theta_m\}$ where $X_1, \ldots, X_n$ are distinct variables, θ_i is a substitution and $Dom(\theta_i) = \{X_1, \ldots, X_n\}$ for $1 \leq i \leq n$. I.e. as a definite goal with distinct variables as arguments together with a context for the goal. For instance, $\leftarrow reverse(X, Y), \{\{X/[a, b, c], Y/Y_1\}, \{X/[], Y/Y_1\}\}$ may be a possible call pattern of Example 2.1.

Let $\mathcal{C}_i$ be the set of all contexts which may be associated with point i of a program P. Then clearly $\langle \mathcal{C}_i, \subseteq, \cup, \cap \rangle$ is a complete lattice with $\cup$ and $\cap$ as least upper- and greatest lower bound respectively.

Let P be a program with n program points. The set $\mathcal{C}_0 \times \ldots \times \mathcal{C}_n$ of *context*

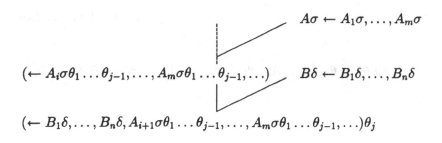

Figure 2: Entry-point of B is current

vectors will be denoted $\mathcal{CV}$. It is easy to see that $\langle \mathcal{CV}, \widetilde{\subseteq}, \widetilde{\cup}, \widetilde{\cap} \rangle$ where

$$\langle x_1, \ldots, x_n \rangle \widetilde{\subseteq} \langle y_1, \ldots, y_n \rangle \ \Leftrightarrow\ x_1 \subseteq y_1 \wedge \ldots \wedge x_n \subseteq y_n$$
$$\langle x_1, \ldots, x_n \rangle \widetilde{\cup} \langle y_1, \ldots, y_n \rangle \ =\ \langle x_1 \cup y_1, \ldots, x_n \cup y_n \rangle$$
$$\langle x_1, \ldots, x_n \rangle \widetilde{\cap} \langle y_1, \ldots, y_n \rangle \ =\ \langle x_1 \cap y_1, \ldots, x_n \cap y_n \rangle$$

is also a complete lattice. We will use the symbol Θ to denote context vectors and refer to its components by subscripts. E.g. $\Theta_{call(x)}$ refers to the value of the calling point of x in the context vector Θ. Sometimes we use integers as indices.

4   A Static$^+$ Semantics

In this section we develop a semantics which associates with every program point of a program (at least) the set of all possible contexts which may occur in a derivation whenever the point is current.

Consider the entry-point of a clause $B \leftarrow B_1, \ldots, B_n$. Clearly, in order for this point to become current there has to be a derivation like that depicted in Figure 2. For each such derivation the context $\delta \bullet \theta_1 \ldots \theta_j$ must be contained in $\Theta_{entry(B)}$.

It is straightforward to see that:

$$\delta \bullet \theta_1 \ldots \theta_j = \delta \bullet \theta_j = \delta \bullet mgu(A_i \sigma \theta_1 \ldots \theta_{j-1}, B\delta)$$

and since $A_i \sigma \theta_1 \ldots \theta_{j-1} = A_i \sigma \bullet \theta_1 \ldots \theta_{j-1}$ we get the following equation for each clause, $x \leftarrow x_1, \ldots, x_n$, of the program:

$$\Theta_{entry(x)} = \bigcup_{y \rightarrow x} \{ \delta \bullet mgu(y\theta, x\delta) \mid \theta \in \Theta_{call(y)} \wedge \delta = Ren(x, y\theta) \}$$

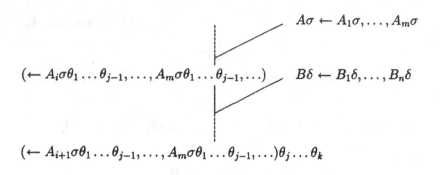

Figure 3: Success-point of A_i is current

where $Ren(x, y)$ returns a renaming substitution of $x \leftarrow x_1, \ldots, x_n$ whose range is disjoint from the variables in y. For the sake of brevity we shall use $f(\Theta, y \rightarrow x)$ to the denote the set former.

Next we consider the success-point of a body literal, x. To reach this point there has to be a derivation which first "passes" the calling point of x with some computed substitution θ. Then $x\theta$ must be unified with a clause head and all subgoals in the body of that clause must be satisfied (i.e. we have to reach the exit-point of the clause). In other words there has to be a derivation like the one depicted in Figure 3. For each such derivation $\sigma \bullet \theta_1 \ldots \theta_k$ must be contained in $\Theta_{succ(x)}$.

Theorem 4.1 For the derivation in Figure 3 it holds that:

$$\sigma \bullet \theta_1 \ldots \theta_k = (\sigma \bullet \theta_1 \ldots \theta_{j-1}) \circ mgu(B\delta \bullet \theta_1 \ldots \theta_k, A_i\sigma \bullet \theta_1 \ldots \theta_{j-1})$$

∎

Proof: Initially we observe that:

$$B\delta\theta_1 \ldots \theta_k = B\delta\theta_j \ldots \theta_k = A_i\sigma\theta_1 \ldots \theta_k$$

Now let

$$B' = B\delta\theta_j \ldots \theta_k = B\delta \bullet \theta_j \ldots \theta_k$$
$$A_i' = A_i\sigma\theta_1 \ldots \theta_{j-1} = A_i\sigma \bullet \theta_1 \ldots \theta_{j-1}$$

Clearly B' is an instance of A_i' and thus:

$$B' = A_i'\alpha \text{ where } \alpha = mgu(A_i', B')$$

Consequently
$$Dom(\alpha) \subseteq Var(A_i') \subseteq Range(\sigma \bullet \theta_1 \ldots \theta_{j-1})$$
and
$$A_i'\alpha = A_i'\theta_j \ldots \theta_k$$

Thus, $\alpha \mid_{Var(A_i')} = (\theta_j \ldots \theta_k) \mid_{Var(A_i')} = \alpha$.

Now $\theta_j \ldots \theta_k$ is obtained by satisfying the goal $\leftarrow A_i'$. Consequently the domain of $\theta_j \ldots \theta_k$ will contain only variables in $Var(A_i')$ and some new variables which do not appear in $Range(\sigma \bullet \theta_1 \ldots \theta_{j-1})$. Thus:

$$Dom(\theta_j \ldots \theta_k) \cap Range(\sigma \bullet \theta_1 \ldots \theta_{j-1}) \subseteq Var(A_i')$$

and finally

$$
\begin{aligned}
\sigma \bullet \theta_1 \ldots \theta_k &= (\sigma \bullet \theta_1 \ldots \theta_{j-1}) \circ (\theta_j \ldots \theta_k) \mid_{Range(\sigma \bullet \theta_1 \ldots \theta_{j-1})} \\
&= (\sigma \bullet \theta_1 \ldots \theta_{j-1}) \circ (\theta_j \ldots \theta_k) \mid_{Var(A_i')} \\
&= (\sigma \bullet \theta_1 \ldots \theta_{j-1}) \circ \alpha
\end{aligned}
$$

∎

It is worth noticing that if there is a derivation like the one in Figure 3 then $B\delta \bullet \theta_1 \ldots \theta_k$ has to be an instance of $A_i\sigma \bullet \theta_1 \ldots \theta_{j-1}$. Thus for each body literal, x, we get the equation:

$$\Theta_{succ(x)} = \bigcup_{x \to y} \{\theta \circ mgu(y\delta, x\theta) \mid \theta \in \Theta_{call(x)} \wedge \delta \in \Theta_{exit(y)} \wedge \exists \omega(y\delta = x\theta\omega)\}$$

The set former will be abbreviated $g(\Theta, x \to y)$.

Since all points in a program are either entry- or success-points we may formulate an equation for every point of the program. However, the entry point of the goal given in the call pattern needs special treatment since its context is already provided in the call pattern.

Example 4.1 Denote by A the literal $reverse(X, Y)$ in Example 2.1, by B the literal $reverse([], [])$ etc. We then get the following set of equations:

$$
\begin{aligned}
\Theta_{call(A)} &= \{\{X/[a, b, c], Y/Y_1\}, \{X/[], Y/Y_1\}\} \\
\Theta_{succ(A)} &= g(\Theta, A \to B) \cup g(\Theta, A \to C) \\
\Theta_{entry(B)} &= f(\Theta, A \to B) \cup f(\Theta, D \to B) \\
\Theta_{entry(C)} &= f(\Theta, A \to C) \cup f(\Theta, D \to C) \\
\Theta_{succ(D)} &= g(\Theta, D \to B) \cup g(\Theta, D \to C) \\
\Theta_{succ(E)} &= g(\Theta, E \to F) \cup g(\Theta, E \to G) \\
\Theta_{entry(F)} &= f(\Theta, E \to F) \cup f(\Theta, H \to F) \\
\Theta_{entry(G)} &= f(\Theta, E \to G) \cup f(\Theta, H \to G) \\
\Theta_{succ(H)} &= g(\Theta, H \to F) \cup g(\Theta, H \to G)
\end{aligned}
$$

∎

For the general case, we want to find a Θ such that

$$\{\Theta_1 = \Delta_1(\Theta), \ldots, \Theta_n = \Delta_n(\Theta)\}$$

This is equivalent to finding a fixed point of the function $cv : \mathcal{CV} \to \mathcal{CV}$

$$cv(x) = \langle \Delta_1(x), \ldots, \Delta_n(x) \rangle$$

Obviously cv may have several fixed points (corresponding to several solutions to the set of equations). All solutions contain the set of all possible contexts at each point. Clearly we want to find the the most accurate of the solutions, i.e. the *least* fixed point of cv (assuming the existence of a least fixed point).

It can be shown that cv is continuous and since we know that $\mathcal{CV}$ is a complete lattice we conclude that $cv \uparrow \omega$ is the least fixed point of cv. The fixed point $cv \uparrow \omega$ will be called the static[+] semantics of the program. The static[+] semantics is similar to the static semantics of [CC77]. However, the latter gives precise information about the set of possible environments whereas the static[+] semantics may be seen as an approximation (i.e. a superset) of the static semantics.

5 Abstract Domains

Unfortunately it is usually not possible to compute the static[+] semantics of a program in finite time. The natural way to avoid this problem is to find some *abstract domain* $\mathcal{CV}'$ which is isomorphic to a suitable subset of $\mathcal{CV}$. In this section some general guidelines are outlined how to find such an abstract domain.

Let $C_1 \times \ldots \times C_n$ be the set $\mathcal{CV}$ of context vectors of some program. The set of *abstract* context vectors $\mathcal{CV}'$ is the set $C_1' \times \ldots \times C_n'$ where each C_i' is isomorphic to a subset of C_i.

The first requirement is that $\mathcal{CV}'$ is a complete lattice. For this to hold, $\langle C_i', \sqsubseteq_i, \sqcup_i, \sqcap_i \rangle$ should be a complete lattice and there should be a monotonic injection

$$\gamma_i : C_i' \to C_i$$

which will be called the *concretization mapping* (of C_i').

Clearly $\langle \mathcal{CV}', \widetilde{\sqsubseteq}, \widetilde{\sqcup}, \widetilde{\sqcap} \rangle$ is a complete lattice if

$$
\begin{aligned}
x \mathbin{\widetilde{\sqsubseteq}} y &\Leftrightarrow x_1 \sqsubseteq_1 y_1 \wedge \ldots \wedge x_n \sqsubseteq_n y_n \\
x \mathbin{\widetilde{\sqcup}} y &= \langle x_1 \sqcup_1 y_1, \ldots, x_n \sqcup_n y_n \rangle \\
x \mathbin{\widetilde{\sqcap}} y &= \langle x_1 \sqcap_1 y_1, \ldots, x_n \sqcap_n y_n \rangle
\end{aligned}
$$

Furthermore, there is an injection

$$\gamma : \mathcal{CV}' \to \mathcal{CV}$$

based on the concretization of the components. It is easy to see that γ is monotonic, i.e.

$$x \stackrel{\sim}{\sqsubseteq} y \Rightarrow \gamma(x) \stackrel{\sim}{\sqsubseteq} \gamma(y)$$

Definition 5.1 Let there be two lattices $\langle \mathcal{A}, \preceq \rangle$, $\langle \mathcal{B}, \sqsubseteq \rangle$ and a monotonic injection $\gamma : \mathcal{B} \to \mathcal{A}$ (i.e. $x \sqsubseteq y \Rightarrow \gamma(x) \preceq \gamma(y)$). We say that $f' : \mathcal{B}^n \to \mathcal{B}$ is a *safe γ-approximation* of $f : \mathcal{A}^n \to \mathcal{A}$ iff

$$\forall x_1, \ldots, x_n \in \mathcal{B}^n \ (f(\gamma(x_1), \ldots, \gamma(x_n)) \preceq \gamma(f'(x_1, \ldots, x_n)))$$

∎

Informally this definition states that $f'(x_1, \ldots, x_n)$ contains at least as much information as f applied to the objects denoted by $x_1, \ldots, x_n$.

For instance, it is easy to show that $\tilde{\sqcup} : \mathcal{CV}' \times \mathcal{CV}' \to \mathcal{CV}'$ above is a safe γ-approximation of $\tilde{\sqcup} : \mathcal{CV} \times \mathcal{CV} \to \mathcal{CV}$ — because of the monotonicity of γ we have that $\gamma(x) \stackrel{\sim}{\sqsubseteq} \gamma(x \tilde{\sqcup} y)$ and $\gamma(y) \stackrel{\sim}{\sqsubseteq} \gamma(x \tilde{\sqcup} y)$. Hence, $\gamma(x) \tilde{\sqcup} \gamma(y) \stackrel{\sim}{\sqsubseteq} \gamma(x \tilde{\sqcup} y)$.

It is now possible to prove the following

Theorem 5.1 If the monotonic operation cv' is a safe (γ-) approximation of cv and $\mathcal{CV}'$ is a *finite height* lattice then

- There exists an $n \geq 0$ such that $cv' \uparrow (n+1) = cv' \uparrow n$, and

- for that n, $cv \uparrow \omega \stackrel{\sim}{\sqsubseteq} \gamma(cv' \uparrow n)$

∎

Proof: The first proposition is proved using the monotonicity of cv' and the finite height of the domain. The second proposition follows from the more general result that $cv \uparrow \alpha \stackrel{\sim}{\sqsubseteq} \gamma(cv' \uparrow \alpha)$ for *any* ordinal α. The latter is shown via transfinite induction. ∎

It is easy to see that $cv'(x) = \langle \Delta_1'(x), \ldots, \Delta_n'(x) \rangle$ is a safe approximation of $cv(x) = \langle \Delta_1(x), \ldots, \Delta_n(x) \rangle$ if Δ_i' is a safe approximation of Δ_i for $1 \leq i \leq n$. Notice that $\Delta_i : \mathcal{CV} \to \mathcal{C}_i$ and by "safe approximation" we mean that

$$\forall x \in \mathcal{CV} \ (\Delta_i(\gamma(x)) \subseteq \gamma_i(\Delta_i'(x)))$$

A sufficient condition for safeness of Δ_i' (wrt. Δ_i) follows

- $\Delta_i' \in \mathcal{C}_i'$ is a safe approximation of $\Delta_i \in \mathcal{C}_i$ if $\Delta_i \subseteq \gamma_i(\Delta_i')$.

- $\Delta_i' = f'(x,1) \sqcup_i \ldots \sqcup_i f'(x,m)$ is a safe approximation of $\Delta_i = f(x,1) \cup \ldots \cup f(x,m)$ if $f'(x,y)$ is a safe approximation of $f(x,y)$ for each edge y of the connection graph.

- $\Delta_i' = g'(x,1) \sqcup_i \ldots \sqcup_i g'(x,m)$ is a safe approximation of $\Delta_i = g(x,1) \cup \ldots \cup g(x,m)$ if $g'(x,y)$ is a safe approximation of $g(x,y)$ for each edge y of the connection graph.

The last two points are easy to prove using the fact that $\sqcup_i : \mathcal{C}_i' \times \mathcal{C}_i' \to \mathcal{C}_i'$ is a safe γ_i-approximation of $\cup : \mathcal{C}_i \times \mathcal{C}_i \to \mathcal{C}_i$.

6 Groundness Analysis (Example)

In this section we use the results above to derive groundness information for the $reverse/2$-programs. I.e. to determine whether some predicate is always called with some specific argument being ground, or succeeds with some argument always being ground.

Let $\mathcal{V}_i$ denote the set of variables in the clause containing the program point i. Then C'_i shall be the set $\wp(\mathcal{V}_i)$ and γ_i is defined thus

$$\gamma_i(x) = \{\theta \in C_i \mid X \in x \Rightarrow ground(X\theta)\}$$

Now, obviously $\langle \wp(\mathcal{V}_i), \supseteq, \cap, \cup \rangle$ is a complete lattice of finite height (with $\mathcal{V}_i$ and $\emptyset$ as bottom and top elements respectively). If $CV' = C'_1 \times \ldots \times C'_n$ then $\langle CV', \tilde{\supseteq}, \tilde{\cap}, \tilde{\cup} \rangle$ is a complete lattice when the operations are applied component-wise.

Next, consider the abstract operations f' and g'. The core of both operations are the unification of the literals in the second argument. Let x and y be two literals with mgu θ (we assume that x and y contain no common variables). What can we say about the mgu of $x\sigma$ and $y\sigma$ if our only knowledge about σ is that for some $X/t \in \sigma$, t is ground? Let $v = \{X \mid X/t \in \sigma \wedge ground(t)\}$. There are two cases to consider — if $X/t \in \theta$ and $X \in v$ then all variables in t will be ground. Secondly, if $X/t \in \theta$ and t is ground or contains only variables in v or in those which are ground from case 1, then X will be ground. Using this we may define the abstract operations f' and g' as follows

$$f'(\Theta, x \to y) = close(mgu(x\sigma, y), \Theta_{call(x)}\sigma, y)$$
$$g'(\Theta, x \to y) = \Theta_{call(x)} \cup close(mgu(x, y\delta), \Theta_{call(x)} \cup \Theta_{exit(y)}\delta, x)$$
$$close(\theta, x, y) = Var(y) \cap (case1(\theta, x) \cup case2(\theta, case1(\theta, x) \cup x))$$
$$case1(\theta, x) = \{X \mid Y/t \in \theta \wedge Y \in x \wedge X \in Var(t)\}$$
$$case2(\theta, x) = \{X \mid X/t \in \theta \wedge Var(t) \subseteq x\}$$

where σ (δ) is a renaming of x (y) such that $x\sigma$ $(y\delta)$ and y (x) contain no common variables. Furthermore $\{X_1, \ldots, X_n\}\sigma = \{X_1\sigma, \ldots, X_n\sigma\}$.

In addition to taking the union of the two cases, $close$ also restricts the resulting set of ground variables to those which appear in the third argument. The definition of f' simply is a call to $close$ whereas g' is the intersection of $close$ and the variables which are know to be ground before the call (clearly variables which become bound remain bound while executing the subgoals to the right of the point where they become bound).

The mapping cv' is now defined as $cv'(x) = \langle \Delta'_1(x), \ldots, \Delta'_9(x) \rangle$ where (cf. Examples 2.1 and 4.1)

$$\Delta'_1(x) = \{X\}$$
$$\Delta'_2(x) = g'(x, A \to B) \cap g'(x, A \to C)$$

$$\vdots$$

$$\Delta_9'(x) \;=\; g'(x, H \to F) \cap g'(x, H \to G)$$

Here the first equation says that the program is always called with the first argument being ground. It does not say anything about the second argument — it may be any term.

Clearly, the bottom element in $\mathcal{CV}'$ is

$$cv' \uparrow 0 \;=\; \langle \{X, Y\}, \{X, Y\}, \emptyset, \{X, Xs, Ys, Zs\}, \{X, Xs, Ys, Zs\},$$
$$\{X, Xs, Ys, Zs\}, \{Xs\}, \{X, Xs, Ys, Zs\}, \{X, Xs, Ys, Zs\} \rangle$$

and the fixed point of cv' is reached after four iterations (where " ..." denotes components which do not change)

$$cv' \uparrow 1 \;=\; \langle \{X\}, \ldots, \ldots, \{X, Xs, Ys\}, \ldots, \ldots, \ldots, \ldots \rangle$$
$$cv' \uparrow 2 \;=\; \langle \ldots, \ldots, \ldots, \{X, Xs\}, \ldots, \ldots, \ldots, \ldots \rangle$$
$$cv' \uparrow 3 \;=\; \langle \ldots, \ldots, \ldots, \ldots, \{X, Xs, Zs\}, \ldots, \ldots, \ldots, \ldots \rangle$$
$$cv' \uparrow 4 \;=\; \langle \ldots, \ldots, \ldots, \ldots, \ldots, \ldots, \{X, Xs, Ys\}, \ldots \rangle$$
$$cv' \uparrow 5 \;=\; cv' \uparrow 4$$

As a result of the analysis we may conclude e.g. the following "assertions":

- if *reverse*/2 is called with the first argument being ground, then the second argument is ground on success (second component of $cv' \uparrow 5$).

- whenever *reverse*/2 is called the first argument is ground (components 1 and 4).

- all calls to *append*/3 are made with the first two arguments being ground (components 5 and 8).

7 Conclusions

A theoretical framework for the abstract interpretation of logic programs was presented. We developed a static$^+$ semantics for definite programs to provide a basis for further abstractions. The static$^+$ semantics plays the rôle of the static semantics in [CC77] and the collecting semantics in [JS87]. However, the static$^+$ semantics is an approximation (a superset) of these two.

From the static$^+$ semantics further abstractions are possible. This is achieved by constructing abstract domains and by giving alternative, abstract interpretations to the operations used to define the static$^+$ semantics. The first step towards an abstract interpretation would be to construct an abstract domain. By selecting a complete lattice of finite height as domain, termination can be ensured. Secondly if there exists a monotonic injection, γ, from the abstract domain to the concrete one and if there is a monotonic mapping, cv', which safely approximates cv wrt. γ, then for some finite n, $\gamma(cv' \uparrow n)$ approximates (contains) $cv \uparrow \omega$ — i.e. the static$^+$ semantics (and of course as a consequence also the static semantics). We also showed how safeness of cv' wrt. cv can be broken down to safeness of more primitive operations (like f' and g' in our case).

Roughly speaking, the consequence of having only a static$^+$ semantics is that we do not keep full track of "where information originates from". More precisely, two different calls to a clause may give different contexts at the exit point of that clause, however, when we compute the success point of a call we take into account *all* contexts at the exit point — not just the ones which were due to the call. This leads to three consequences

- The result of abstract interpretation may become worse. That is, the approximation *may* be less accurate;

- The efficiency (speed) of the analysis is usually improved;

- The formulation of the concrete semantics becomes less complicated.

To some extent accuracy can be traded against efficiency in our approach by performing "unfolding" in the connection graph. Clauses which are called from several body literals may be copied. Thus, avoiding some imprecision at the expense of extra analysis time.

Some previous attempts to provide general frameworks for abstract interpretation are available (e.g. [Bru87], [JS87], [Mel87], [DW88]). Like [Bru87] we have based our framework on the standard operational semantics (SLD-resolution) of definite programs. This is by no means the only possibility — in [JS87] denotational semantics is used and in [MS88] a bottom-up fixed point semantics.

In one respect [Mel87] and [DW88] distinguish themselves from the other three. Neither of them records the set of contexts associated with (what we call) program points. Instead they record the set of all calls and successes of each predicate. For some important run-time properties this information is not sufficient. It is e.g. not possible to deduce whether two subgoals in the body of a clause are always independent (contain a common variable) during run-time. However, both [Mel87] and [DW88] are primarily interested in, so called, mode analysis of logic programs.

In [JS87] contexts are recorded only at the entry point of each clause.

The aim of this paper was to provide a theoretical framework for efficient implementation of abstract interpretation in different abstract domains. Some preliminary tests indicate that cv' can be implemented efficiently in a language with constant access time to arrays (to represent the context vector). This follows from the observation that $cv' \uparrow (n + 1)$ and $cv' \uparrow n$ usually only differ in some of their components. Therefore it is not necessary to compute a completely new context vector in each iteration — some (most) components will remain the same.

This paper covers only static analysis of *definite program*. However, it would not be very hard to include also some of the *extralogical features* of most Prolog implementations. For instance, taking the operational semantics of most Prolog systems into account we know that for a subgoal $t_1 < t_2$ all of the variables in t_1 and t_2 are ground on success. However, some built-in predicates cause additional problems — in particular those which modify the database (*assert*/1 and *retract*/1) and those which are implemented in terms of *call*/1 (*setof*/2, *not*/1 etc).

Acknowledgements

The author is grateful to Jan Małuszyński for his continuous support and advice. S.Bonnier, M.Bruynooghe, W.Drabent and H.Søndergaard provided many useful and constructive comments on previous versions of the paper. Fundings were supplied by the Swedish National Board for Technical Development (STU).

References

[AH87]   S. Abramsky and C. Hankin, editors. *Abstract Interpretation of Declarative Languages*. Ellis Horwood, 1987.

[Apt87]   K. Apt. *Introduction to Logic Programming*. Report TR-87-35, Dept. of Computer Science, The University of Texas at Austin, 1987. Revised and Extended Version in 1988.

[Bru87]   M. Bruynooghe. *A Framework for the Abstract Interpretation of Logic Programs*. Report CW62, Katholieke Universiteit, Leuven, 1987.

[CC77]   P. Cousot and R. Cousot. Abstract interpretation: a unified lattice model for static analysis of programs by construction or approximation of fixpoints. In *Proc. of POPL*, Los Angeles, 1977.

[DM87]   W. Drabent and J. Małuszyński. Proving runtime properties of logic programs. In *Proc. of TAPSOFT'87*, Pisa, LNCS 250, Springer-Verlag, 1987.

[DW88]   S. Debray and D.S. Warren. Automatic mode inference for logic programs. *J. Logic Programming*, 5(3), 1988.

[JS87]   N.D. Jones and H. Søndergaard. A semantics-based framework for the abstract interpretation of prolog. In S. Abramsky and C. Hankin, editors, *Abstract Interpretation of Declarative Languages*, Ellis Horwood, 1987.

[Kle52] S.C. Kleene. *Introduction to Metamathematics*. North-Holland Publ. Co, Amsterdam-New York, 1952.

[Kow79] R. Kowalski. *Logic For Problem Solving*. Elsevier, North-Holland, New York, 1979.

[Llo87] J.W. Lloyd. *Foundations of Logic Programming*. Springer-Verlag, second edition, 1987.

[Mel87] C. Mellish. Abstract interpretation of prolog programs. In S. Abramsky and C. Hankin, editors, *Abstract Interpretation of Declarative Languages*, Ellis Horwood, 1987.

[MS88] K. Marriott and H. Søndergaard. Bottom-up abstract interpretation of logic programs. In *Proc. of 5th International Conf/Symp. on Logic Programming*, Seattle, MIT Press, 1988.

[Tar55] A. Tarski. A lattice theoretical fixpoint theorem and its applications. *Pacific J. Math*, 5, 1955.

An implementation of retargetable code generators in Prolog

Annie DESPLAND* Monique MAZAUD** Raymond RAKOTOZAFY*

* L.I.F.O. Université d'Orléans BP 6759, 45067 Orléans CEDEX2, France and I.N.R.I.A.
* * I.N.R.I.A. Domaine de Voluceau, BP 105, 78153 Le Chesnay CEDEX, France.

Abstract

A major problem in deriving a compiler from a formal definition is the production of correct and efficient object code. In this context, we propose a solution to the problem of code generator generation.

Our approach is based on a target machine description where the basic concepts used (storage classes, access modes, access classes and instructions) are hierarchically described by tree-patterns. These tree-patterns are written in an abstract tree language which is also used to write the program intermediate representation (input to the code generator). The code generation process is based on access mode template-driven rewritings in which the program intermediate representation is progressively transformed. The result is that each program instruction is reduced to a sequence of elementary machine instructions, each of them representing an instance of an instruction template. A data base of clauses is derived automatically from the target machine description. It is used by the kernel of the rewriting system implemented in Prolog.

First, this paper presents a way of structuring formal specifications of target machines in order to decrease the size of the description. We propose to get complete specification components by instances of parameterized specifications. As a consequence, legibility which is an important requirement of large specifications is improved.

Second a theoretical support of the intermediate rewritings based on abstract data types is given.

Third the code generation algorithm is presented and illustrated.

Finally an implementation in Prolog of a code generator based on our appoach is developped.

Introduction

Considerable research effort has been put into making the compiler construction as modular and automatic as possible.

Numerous works have developped techniques and tools for the implementation of retargetable code generators. Such tools should combine portability features and ease of writing for the compiler writer. Moreover they must make it possible :

- to clearly separate the description of a general technique from its application to a particular machine.
- to describe and achieve various code generation subtasks without imposing any particular ordering on them.
- to accept as input a description easy to deduce from the handbook of the machine.

The use of formal description of a target machine within a compiler writing system has given rise to several techniques such as the works of Cattell [Cat 77], Graham-Glanvillle [GG 78][GH 84], Ganapathi-Fischer [GF 82], Ganzinger-Giegerich [Gan Gie 82][Gie 85].

As the properties of the source and the target languages are quite different, it is necessary to introduce an **intermediate representation (I.R)**. The main drawback of the systems above is that the input I.R can not be parameterized by the features of both the source language and the target machine. The solution proposed here overcomes this. It produces, as in the Perluette system [GDM 84] [Des 82], a compiler from a specification in three parts : a source language definition, a target language definition and the description of the implementation choices (see fig 1). As the source and target language definitions are **algebraic data types**, the I.R may be parameterized.

The target machine description is hierarchically structured in three levels [DMR 87] :
- storage description (sets of available locations i.e registers, memory locations, stacks ...) as storage classes ;
- addressing modes description (various ways to access locations) as access modes;
- instruction set description.

As an operand of an instruction may accept several **access modes**, the access modes are assembled in **access classes.** So the access classes are instruction parameters. The semantics of access modes and instructions is given as terms of the target data type. Once the correct **I.R** term is produced, the code generation will proceed in four steps (omitting optimization tasks) :
- **access modes templates** and **instructions templates pattern-matching**. The bottom up matching process of the **I.R** is carried out until the **I.R** is identified to instructions templates. In order to identify an instruction template, operand subterms are matched with access mode templates. When it succeeds the subterm is remplaced by a representative tree of the access mode recognized. This representative is called in the sequel "canonical form". When it fails, an inner subterm matching an access mode template is replaced by a temporary variable. This requires the insertion of elementary universal store trees of temporary results in temporary storages.
- **binding.** Each temporary occurrence is bound with the list of the allowed access modes. Considering a preference order on the allowed access modes, this step binds a physical storage to each temporary with the corresponding access mode.
- **register assignment**. A name is chosen for each temporary depending on the available storage locations
- **code production**. Now, the **I.R** is a tree built up with intances of instruction templates rooted by the sequence operator. As each instruction template is decorated with the corresponding assembly instruction mnemonic, the code emission can be simply achieved by a left-right sequential tree traversal of these instances.

This solution allows a modular multi-pass code generation process with the different optimization tasks inserted as rewritings according to the compiler writer's wishes. Such an approach confers modularity and independence to our system while preserving the descriptive features approaches. Our solution to automatic production of code generators is complete in the sense that it tackles correctly both the code selection and the storage allocation problems.

This paper is divided into four sections.

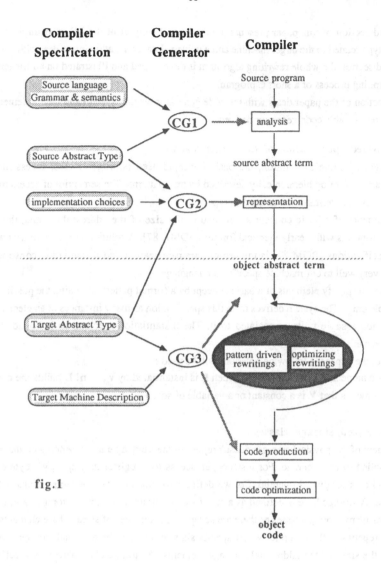

The first one presents the formal specification of the target machine required as input to the code generator generator. Our initial goal was to propose a machine description technique which was homogeneous, exhaustive and correct. Our experience concerning the description of general purpose registers machines such as **PDP-11** [MRS 86] and **VAX** was encouraging. Nevertheless we observed the proliferation of nearly identical formulas which leads to a large size of the formal specification. Thus there was also a risk to lose the reader in such a description.

Since the specification becomes larger and larger when multiplying the storage classes, we propose now to get complete specification components by instances of parameterized specifications. In this paper, a component of the description (storage class, access mode or instruction) may be described as a pattern of the component followed by its instances. Concepts developed here are illustrated by **MC68000** examples throughout the paper.

The second section of this paper presents the theoretical support of the **LR** rewritings. It needs an abstract data type related to the target machine and a universal data type allowing to deal with temporaries.

In the third section the whole rewriting algorithm is developped and illustrated on an **LR** term issued from the compiling process of a short C program.

The last section of the paper deals with the code generator writing system and the implementation in Prolog of the retargetable code generator derived.

1. Parameterized specification of the target machine

In our target machine description, the basic concepts used (storage classes, access modes and instructions) are bottom-up hierarchically described by tree-patterns. The semantics of access modes and instructions is given in terms of the target data type.

As the elements of a basic concept are related to the size of the addressable units, this leads to repetitive descriptions with nearly identical formulas [DMR 87]. A solution proposed to deal with large algebraic specifications [BGM 87] is the use of parameterization and instantiation constructs. Such constructs fit very well to our machine specification language.

We propose to specify elements of a basic concept by a formal pattern including the possible sizes of the addressable units. The system derives from this specification as many instances of an element as there are sizes of addressable units asssociated to it. The instantiation mechanism is bound to a name generation mechanism.

Throughout the paper the following notations will be used :

. If n is a name and **L** is a variable,   when **L** is instantiated by **v** ,   n! **L** builds the name n_v

. <S V> means that **V** is a constant or a variable of sort S.

1.1 Parameterized storage classes

A component of the physical storages doesn't represent the same operand depending on the type of the operation applied to this operand. For instance, an access to a register may specify a byte operand, a word operand or a longword operand. So, we define two fundamental concepts : **storage base** and **storage class**. A storage base is defined as a set of storage units. For a given storage base, the system must derive as many storage classes as there are acceptable sequences of storage base elements. In order to avoid the repetition, the compiler writer specifies a storage class by a formal storage class pattern followed by the sizes of the addressable storage elements. A storage class pattern is specified by its denotation, its storage base, an access operation to the contents of an element of the storage class(dereference operation) and the symbolic names of the elements of this class in the assembly language. In the instances the sizes of the addressable units are defined. As the **MC68000** has two kinds of registers, the compiler writer defines two storage bases for registers : *data register* and *address register* bases and the corresponding storage classes.

Storage_base DREG   - - Data registers
        Set **is** { DREG [k] **where** k in 0 .. 31 }

End

Storage_class
    Denotation   <dregister!size reg>

    Attributes
        $Base = DREG

    Dereference_operation
        cont_of_dreg!size (<dregister!size Dk>)

    Symbolic_notation
        D_k is DREG[4*k .. 4*k + length - 1] **where** k in 0 .. 7

    Instances
        size **in** {B, W, L}
        case size **is**
            B : length **is** 1
            W :   length **is** 2
            L : length **is** 4
        End case

    End

The specification of the address register class is similar to that of the data register class. The only difference is that the byte access to an address register is not available.

1.2 Parameterized access modes

For a given addressing mode of the machine, the system derives as many access modes as there are associated storage classes from the formal access mode specification.

A formal access mode pattern is specified by :

- *a canonical form representative of the access mode including its name and its parameters. These parameters are formal storage or value classes.*
- *its related attributes length, format and cost.*
- *templates that describe the access path to the corresponding operand when it is respectively in destination position and in source position.*

Let us consider the *data register* addressing mode of the **MC68000**. Its associated storage classes are byte data register, word data register, longword data register. Thus the compiler writer defines a formal access mode pattern "dreg_am!size" parameterized by the formal data register "dregister!size" defined in the **§1.1.** Its instances are the effective *data register* access modes with their appropriate storage class.

```
Access_mode                                    - - Data register access modes
   Canonical_form
      dreg_am!size ( <dregister!size reg> )

   Attributes
      $length = size                           - - length of the addressable unit
      $fmt    = ~reg~                          - - Assembly language format
      $cost   = 0

   Templates
      dst    = <dregister!size reg>            - - access path on destination position
      src    = cont_of_dreg!size (dst)         - - access path on source position

   Instances
      size in {B, W, L}

End
```

When an access mode template in source position is defined by the dereference operation (here "cont_of_dreg!size") applied to the term which defines the access mode template in destination position, the compiler writer uses the abbreviation **dst** to denote the access mode template in destination position. Using the preceding definition, the system deduces the definition of the "dreg_am_B" access mode.

```
Access_mode
   Canonical_form
      dreg_am_B ( <dregister_B reg> )

   Attributes
      $length (dreg_am_B (<dregister_B reg> ))  = B
      $fmt (dreg_am_B(<dregister_B reg> ))      = ~reg~
      $cost (dreg_am_B(<dregister_B reg> ))     = 0

   Templates
      dst (dreg_am_B(<dregister_B reg> ))       = <dregister_B reg>
      src (dreg_am_B(<dregister_B reg> ))       = cont_of_dreg_B (<dregister_B reg> )

End
```

The indirect with displacement access mode has instances which depend on the contents of the location in source position.

Access_mode   - - Indirect with displacement access modes
   Canonical_form
      disp_am!size (<aregister_L reg> , <value_W val>)

   Attributes
      $length = size   - - length of the addressable unit
      $fmt   = ~val(reg)~   - - Assembly language format
      $cost   = 1

   Templates
      dst   = index   - - access path in destination position
                  (cont_of_areg_L(<aregister_L reg>)
                  ,<value_W val>)
      src   = cont_of_laddress!size (dst)   - - access path in source position

   Instances
      size **in** {B, W, L}

End

1.3 Parameterized instructions

An instruction may be viewed differently depending on its particular use. It may be characterized by the following properties:

- *the access classes on which the instructions applies*
- *its related attributes : the length and the format, i.e the syntax in the assembly language*
- *the template describing what is performed by the instruction (term of the abstract data type)*

Nearly every instruction of the target machine may be applied to the different lengths of operand. In order to avoid the repetition of such descriptions, the compiler writer specifies a pattern of an instruction and its instances.

Let us consider the *move* instruction. The size of the operation may be specified to be a byte, a word or a longword. We get the following specification :

Instruction
      move!size (<All_access!size AM1>, <Altdata_access!size AM2>)

   Attributes
      $length = size
      $fmt   = ~MOVE!size $fmt (<All_access!size AM1>)
                     , $fmt (<Altdata_access!size AM2>)~

   Template
      assign!size   (src (<All_access!size AM1>)
                  , dst (<Altdata_access!size AM2>))

   Instances
      size **in** {B, W, L}

End

The most general comparison instruction template may be specified as following.

Instruction
cmp!size (<All_access!size AM1>, <Dregister_access!size AM2>)

Attributes
$length = size
$fmt   = ~CMP!size $fmt (<All_access!size AM1>)
                       , $fmt (<Dregister_access!size AM2>)~

Template
compare!size (src (<All_access!size AM1>)
                    , src (<Dregister_access!size AM2>))

Instances
size **in** {B, W, L}

End

The operands of an instruction are access classes which are defined as sets of access modes. An access class is also specified by a pattern including the instantiation of its elements. There are as many instances of instructions as there are possible sizes of operand.

Access_class
<All_access!size AM>
     = dreg_am!size (<dregister!size reg>)   **where** size **in** {B, W, L }
     = areg_am!size (<aregister!size reg>)   **where** size **in** {W, L }
     = ...
End

2. Theoretical support of the intermediate representation rewritings

2.1 Introduction

Let us summarize the specification mechanism of the code generator for a given target machine. The machine is specified by the description of available locations, access modes and instructions. As the locations are defined, names of sorts are associated to them. The access modes and instructions are specified by operators on locations. Thus, a set of operations with the corresponding domains and co-domains can be defined. Therefore the specification of the code generator includes two parts :
- the target machine description
- the target abstract data type related to the target machine.

In the framework of a translator writing system which works in three steps (see fig 1), the intermediate form input of the code generator is the target abstract term. It is the representation of the source abstract term which is the semantic value associated to the source program. The source term corresponding to the semantic value of a statement is a **modification** as defined in [GDM 84]. The representation of a modification of the source abstract data type is a modification of the target abstract data type.

The translation of the semantic value of the source program into the semantic value of the object program is specified and proved [GDM 84] to be the representation of one abstract data type into another. The basic **I.R** for the code generation process is the tree corresponding to the abstract target term. During attribute evaluation passes, this tree is decorated and transformed.

2.2 Abstract data type related to the target machine

In order to emit the code related to an instruction, it is necessary to recognize an instance of an instruction template. As in the syntactic analysis process, an automaton is derived automatically. It is used by a target machine independant kernel which consists of an analyser and modules of tree construction and rewritings. The object term, input to the code generation process belongs to the target abstract data type. The specification of the target abstract data type includes:
- a set of names of sorts
- a signature, i.e a set of names of operations with their corresponding domains and co-domains
- a set of axioms.

Sorts are defined from the machine description elements such as storage classes and value classes.

2.3 Universal operations and temporaries

Since to recognize an instruction template, the system have to recognize the access classes of its children, first all access modes must be recognized. The largest possible subtree corresponding to an access mode will allow to produce better code ("maximal munch" method). If the father of this tree is not the root of an instruction template, it will be necessary to store this identified access mode in a temporary location. This operation needs :
- the use of a universal temporary storage location, associated with its access mode, known by the code generator writing system ; we shall denote them "temporary" and "temporary_am" respectively.
- the use of a store operator known by the code generator writing system and which can apply to each kind of temporary. The universal store "Univ_assign" is used for this purpose, its rightmost operand is the destination.

In order to ensure compatibility with the I.R, the system needs to know how to make the correspondence between "Univ_assign" and the specific machine stores, when the corresponding instruction is emitted.

Trees are generated for temporary stores and they must be rooted in the sequence. A sequence operator must be available for the code generator writing system, by convention, we denote it by "Univ_seq".

Thus, the compiler writer must specify equivalence declarations between the machine operators and the universal operators. This is done in an interface between the machine specification and the code generator writing system. The temporary access mode is bound to all access modes selected for the management of temporary locations specified in a preference order. For the MC68000, the equivalence declarations will be specified :

```
Univ_seq                          : seq
Univ_assign                       : assign!size                       where size in {B, W, L}
temporary_am(<temporary temp>) : areg_am!size (<aregister!size temp>)  where size in {W, L }
                                  I dreg_am!size (<dregister!size temp>) where size in {B, W, L }
                                  I relative_am!size (<code_label!size temp>) where size in {B, W }
```

Here, the universal sequence operator "Univ_seq" is bound to the "seq" operator (sequence operator) of the target data type. The universal store operator "Univ_assign" is bound to different assign operators of the target data type (assignment on byte, word and longword operands). The access mode on temporaries is bound to access modes allowing direct access to an *address register* , to a *data register* or relative access to the memory. They are given in the preference order according to their cost.

3. The code generation process
3.1 Introduction

The code generation process involves matching the I.R with instruction templates because an instruction template corresponds exactly to one assembly instruction. The code generator works in four steps :
- first the bottom-up matching process of the each modification is carried out until the I.R is identified to an instruction template. For each such a modification, the pattern matching process tries to identify an access mode. If the rewritten modification does not represent an instance of an instruction template, the location designated by the access mode is stored in a temporary and the modification is rewritten. The process goes on in order to make the modification closer to an instruction template.The temporary storage allocation is done as needed.

   At the end of the rewriting process, we get a sequence of instructions instances including references to temporary locations.
- The goal of the second step is to connect a temporary to a concrete storage location. We shall call this step "binding" in the following.

   In fact, the system selects a set of possible access modes for a temporary access mode. This leads to bind the temporary to a set of sorts of storage classes. This is done using the rewriting rules of the interface, taking into account the two following points :
   - the access classes of the instruction ; the temporary access mode must be rewritten by an access mode belonging to the right access class,
   - on the context constraints of the other trees of the sequence.

   As a consequence the universal operators are bound with effective assignment ones (assign_L, assign_W...).

   The rewriting process has created as many names of temporaries as needed. All temporaries could not be hold into registers and a great amount of space will have to be allocated. In order to decrease the number of temporaries, those that are not live simultaneously can be packed into the same name.
- The "register assignment" step can now take place. According to the available storages, first the system picks for each temporary the storage class related to the cheapest access mode of the preceding set. Second the system chooses the name of an actual available location of this storage class for the temporary.
- Finally the code is emitted during a left-right sequential tree traversal.

3.2 Algorithm

The algorithm belongs to the target machine independent kernel of the code generator. At present, the rewriting algorithm applies to an I.R corresponding to a sequence of modifications.

For each **I.R** term the rewriting algorithm needs to know the frontier where the access mode pattern matching can stop and where the instruction pattern matching can begin. For this purpose, we define a partition of instruction templates into instruction classes that have the same frontier.

The leaves of instruction templates are denotation of access classes (they can be considered as typed variables) or access modes. Two templates of an instruction class can only differ on the type of the variables. We are interested in the "canonical representative" of such a class, i.e., a tree in which all the sons of src and dst are replaced by variables. Each variable has a single occurrence. If we consider all the substract instruction templates, the canonical representative of the instruction class is :

$$\text{assign!size (sub(src(X), src(Y)), dst(Z))}$$

- - general substract
assign!size
    (sub
        (src (<Dregister_access!size AM2>)
        , src (<All_access!size AM1>))
        , dst (<Dregister_access!size AM2>))

- - substract quick
assign!size
    (sub
        (src (<Alterable_access!size AM2>)
        , src (<Quick_access!size AM1>))
        , dst (<Alterable_access!size AM2>))

- - substract immediate
assign!size
    (sub
        (src (<Altdata_access!size AM2>)
        , src (<Immediate_access!size AM1>))
        , dst (<Altdata_access!size AM2>))

- - negate
assign!size
    (sub
        (src (val_immediate_am(<value!size 0>))
        , src (<Altdata_access!size AM>))
        , dst (<Altdata_access!size AM>))

Steps of the algorithm are :
1. **For each tree T** of a sequence
        rewrite_modification(T)
2. Binding step.
3. Register assignment.
4. Code emission.

rewrite_modification(T)

- done = false
- nomore_class = false

Repeat

- choose an instruction class CI which matches T with respect to the class ordering
- **If** there is no more instruction class to examine, **then** nomore_class = **true** ; **exit**
  else the subtrees S_j ($1 \leq j \leq n$) of T matching the CI n variables are decorated with the corresponding position attribute (src or dst)
- **For each** son S_j
      may_blocking[S_j] = false ;
      canonicalize(S_j, position)

  EndFor
- **If** match_template(T).

      then done = true

      else - deal_with_nested_arithmetic_operators(T)

          - **If** (**not** blocking[CI])

              then

                 - choose I_i a template of CI under the better partial match with T criterion
                         match_access_modes_with_access_classes(T, I_i)

                if match_template(T)

                   then done = true

                   else partial_instruction_match(T, I_i)

    until (done or nomore_class)

end   rewrite_modification

3.3 Example

Let us consider a short program written in the C language :

```
proc (c1, c2, e1, e2)
int c1, c2 ;
int *e1, *e2 ;
{      int t ;
       if (c1 > c2)
          t = *e1 ;
       else
          *e2 = 0 ;
}
```

A tree which designates a variable in a call can be written by indexing the offset of the variable to the base content of the procedure to which this variable is local. We assume that :

- the *address register* a_6 points to the beginning of the activation record of the current call
- 8 and 12 are respectively the offsets of c1 and c2 from the base of the procedure
- 16 and 20 are respectively the offsets of e1 and e2 from the base of the procedure
- - 4 is the offset of t from the base of the procedure.

The I.R term corresponding to the conditionnal statement is :

```
seq
- - if (c1 > c2)
    ( compare_L
      ( cont_of_laddress_L
          ( index  ( cont_of_areg_L (<aregister_L a6>)
                   , <value_W 12 > ))                         T1
        , cont_of_laddress_L
            ( index  ( cont_of_areg_L (<aregister_L a6>)
                     , <value_W 8 > )))


      , branch_if_le (<code_label ELSE>)                      T2


- - t = *e1


      , assign_L
        ( cont_of_laddress_L
          ( cont_of_laddress_L
              ( index( cont_of_areg_L (<aregister_L a6>)      T3
              , <value_W 16 > ))
          , index  ( cont_of_areg_L (<aregister_L a6>)
              , <value_W -4 > )))


        , bra (<code_label ENDIF>)                            T4

- - else *e2 = 0 ;
      ......
```

For legibility reasons, we shall apply the full code generation process to each modification successively. Let us consider the first modification T_1 of the sequence, i.e., the term of root "compare_L". The instruction class which matches T_1 with respect to the class ordering is the set of instructions tempates such that :

$$\text{compare\_L (src(X), src(Y))}$$

Step 1 : The rewriting step

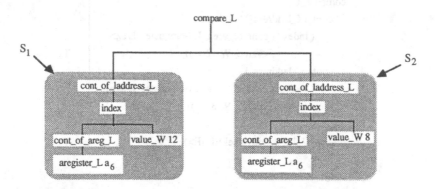

The *disp_am _L* access mode in source position is recognized for S_1, as its father is the son of an instruction template, we replace by the canonical form in the tree T_1. The same rewriting is applied to S_2.

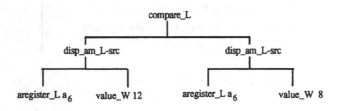

The instruction template which matches the best the tree T_1 is :

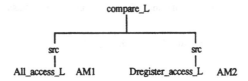

As the right son of T_1 does not match the Dregister_access_L access class, we apply the partial instruction match rewriting.

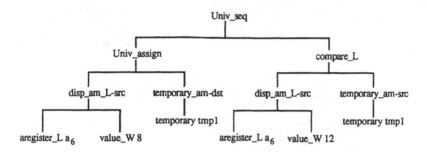

Step 2 : the binding step

The binding of tmp1 must be done considering the "compare_L" tree. As its second son must belong to the "Dregister_access_L" access class, the only rewriting of the temporary access mode using the interface is "dreg_am_L". It is only necessary to do the overloading of the universal operators "Univ_seq" is overloaded by "seq" and "Univ_assign" is overloaded by "assign_L" according to the size of the operands.

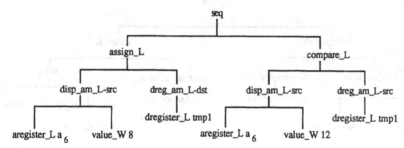

Step 3 : The register assignment step

If d_0 is chosen for tmp1, we get the following sequence :

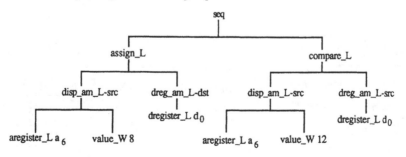

Step 4 : Code emission

$$\text{MOVE.L} \qquad 8(a_6), \quad d_0$$
$$\text{CMP.L} \qquad 12(a_6), \quad d_0$$

Now let us consider the third modification T_3 of the sequence :

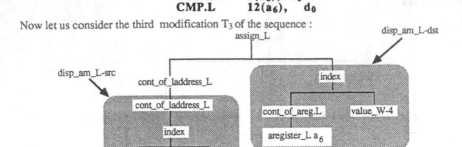

Let us denote S_1 and S_2 the two sons of the root assign_L

Step 1 : The rewriting step

The *disp_am_L* access mode in source position is recognized inside S_1. As its father is not the son of an instruction template a universal store is generated.

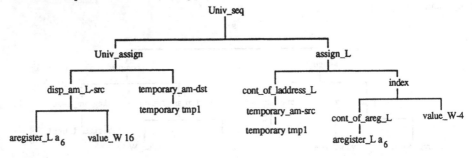

The temporary access mode is bound to the address register access mode via the interface.

As src(areg_am_L (<aregister_L tmp1>)) is the canonical form of cont_of_areg_L (<aregister_L tmp1>), temporary_am-src (<temporary tmp1>) is rewritten in cont_of_areg_L (<aregister_L tmp1>). Thus the address register indirect *areg_ind_am_L* access mode is recognized for the left son of assign_L.

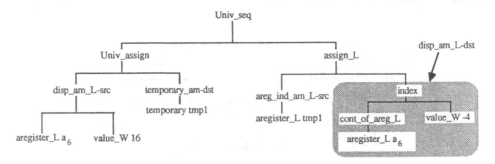

The *disp_am* access mode in destination position is recognized for S_2,

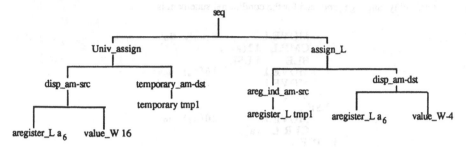

Step 2 : The binding step

The temporary tmp1 is bound to a long address register (because of the left son of the second tree) for each occurrence of tmp1 in the sequence. Then the overloading of the universal operators takes place according to the size of the left child. And at last the temporary access mode in the first assign tree is overloaded by the "areg_am_L" access mode.

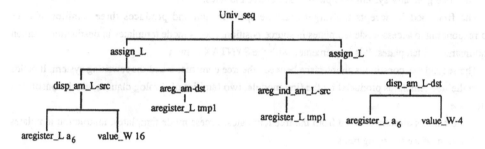

Step 3 : The register assignment step : if the name a_0 is chosen for tmp1, we get the following sequence :

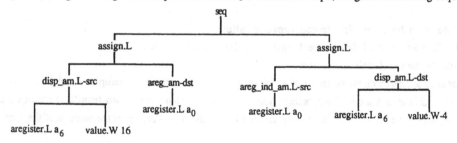

Step 4 : Code emission

$$\begin{array}{l} \textbf{MOVE.L 16(a}_6\textbf{), a}_0 \\ \textbf{MOVE.L (a}_0\textbf{), -4(a}_6\textbf{)} \end{array}$$

As the code emitted for the branch term branch_if_le(<code_label ELSE>) is "BLE ELSE", the full sequence of assembly language produced for the conditional statement is :

```
        MOVE.L          8(a₆), d₀
        CMP.L   12(a₆),   d₀
        BLE     ELSE
        MOVE.L          16(a₆), a₀
        MOVE.L          (a₀), -4(a₆)
        BRA     ENDIF
ELSE :
        MOVE.L          20(a₆), a₀
        CLR.L   (a₀)
ENDIF :
```

4 System implementation

The kernel of the code generator generator is a tree transformation system. That is the reason why Prolog was chosen to implement the experimental system.

4.1. Introduction

The code generator system is implemented in three modules.

The first module accepts the target machine specification and produces three families of trees corresponding to access mode templates in source position, access mode templates in destination position and instruction templates. It is implemented with the SYNTAX system.

The second one constitutes an interface between the tree constructor and the rewriting system. It builds from the tree templates produced by the first module, two families of Prolog clauses which constitute a data base:

- the clauses directly derived from the tree templates: access mode templates, instruction templates and interface rewriting rules.
- the clauses describing the properties of the instruction templates for the rewriting algorithm.

The third one corresponds to the rewriting step : the clauses translating the rewriting algorithm make up the kernel of the code generator generator.

4.2 The data base and its Prolog representation

4.2.1 Clauses derived from the target machine specification

a) Access modes implementation

For each access mode the system derives Prolog clauses that represent the templates and the attributes related to this access mode. Two "access_mode" clauses implement the two templates (source and destination) of an access mode. Their last parameter is a predicate that describes the position of the access path.

The long data register access mode is described by the following clauses :
access_mode (denotation (dregister_L, REG),

dst (dreg_am_L (denotation (dregister_L, REG))), is_dest)
access_mode (cont_of_dreg_L (denotation (dregister_L, REG)),

src (dreg_am_L (denotation (dregister_L, REG))), is_source).

Among the access mode attributes, the assembly format must be described by an "access_format" clause.
access_format (dreg_am_L (denotation (dregister_L, REG)), [REG]).

The long indirect with displacement access mode is described by the following clauses :
access_mode (index (cont_of_areg_L (denotation (aregister_L, REG)), denotation (value_W, VAL))

, dst (disp_am_L (denotation (aregister_L, REG), denotation (value_W, VAL))

, is_dest).
access_mode (cont_of_laddress_L (index (cont_of_areg_L (denotation (aregister_L, REG)),

denotation (value_W,VAL)))

, src (disp_am_L (denotation (aregister_L, REG), denotation (value_W, VAL)))

, is_source).
access_format (disp_am_L (denotation (aregister, REG), denotation (value_W, VAL)),

[VAL, '(', REG, ')']).

The rewriting algorithm searches for the largest subtree corresponding to an access mode This can be achieved using the reading strategy of the Prolog clauses. Thus it is necessary to sort the clauses according to a decreasing order criterion on tree templates. Such a sort is performed by the tree constructor.

b) Access classes implementation

An access class is a set of access modes. The access classes clauses declare the following fact : an access mode is a member of an access class.

All_access_L (dreg_am_L).

All_access_L (areg_am_L).

c) Instructions implementation

There are as many clauses for an instruction as there are attributes and templates. All the clauses related to an instruction take their meaning only in the context of this instruction. As Prolog gathers the clauses which have the same name and reads them sequentially), the context in which these clauses are defined is completely lost. In order to fix the context of the clauses bound to an instruction, a unique name is associated to each instruction. This name is the first parameter of the head of the corresponding clauses. This allows us to consider that each instruction defines parallel module to that of others instructions.

The *move* and the *clear* instruction template are implemented as follows :
instruction (move_l, assign_L (src(AM1), dst (AM2))) :
- All_access_L (AM1) , Altdata_access_L (AM2).
instruction (clear_l, assign_L (src(immediate_am(denotation(value, 0))), dst(AM))):
- Altdata_access_L (AM).

Among the attributes related to an instruction, let us describe the format of the move instruction. It requires first the access mode formats of its operand and the code list including the assembly mnemonic
ins_format (move_l, assign_L (src(AM1), dst (AM2))) :
- access_format (AM1, L1) , access_format (AM2, L2)
, CODE = ['MOVE.L', L1, ', ', L2].

d) Interface rewriting rules

There are as many clauses as there are equivalence rules between the temporary access mode and an effective access mode of the target machine. For the **MC68000**, we get the following clauses :
interface_assoc (temporary_am (denotation (temporary, X)), areg_am_L(<aregister_L, X)).
interface_assoc (temporary_am (denotation (temporary, X)), dreg_am_L(<dregister_L, X)).
interface_assoc (temporary_am (denotation (temporary, X)), relative_am_W(<code_label_W, X)).
...

4.2.2 Clauses describing properties of instruction templates

As we have defined a partition of instruction templates into equivalence classes, it is necessary to build the clauses that reflect the notion of instruction class.

For each instruction class, a clause declares the instruction class name and its "canonical representative". For instance the instruction class including the *move* and the *clear* instructions is defined as follows :
ins_ class (assign_l, assign_L (src (AM1), dst (AM2))).
The fact that an instruction template belongs to a given class is described by :
belong_ins_class(Instruction_class_name, Instruction_name).
Thus we have for the *move* instruction :
belong_ins_class(assign_l, move_l).
Similarly, we get for the *clear* instruction :
belong_ins_class(assign_l, clear_l).
In order to identify an instruction template of a given instruction class, the rewriting algorithm tests whether a given access mode belongs to the right access class. For instance the first son in source position of a *move* instruction must belong to the *All_access_L* access_class :
belong_access_class (move_l, src(X), 1) :- All_access_L(X).

4.3 Prolog implementation of the rewriting algorithm

The rewriting algorithm may be translated directly into Prolog clauses.

rewrite_modification (T, SEQ)
   If T is an abstract target term
      then SEQ is the sequence of trees obtained at the end of the rewritings

rewrite_modification (T, SEQ) : -   choose_inst_class (IC, T)
                                   , canonicalize (IC, T, New_T, S)
                                   , match_template (IC, New_T, S, SEQ).

choose_inst_class(T, IC)
   If T is a tree
   then IC is a canonical representative of an instruction class such that T is an instance of that class

canonicalize(IC, T, New_T, S)
   If IC is a canonical representative of an instruction class
      and T is a tree which is an instance of IC
   then IC gives the context for access mode research in the tree T.
      New_T is the tree T in which access modes are replaced by their canonical form.
      S is a sequence of universal stores , resulting from the processing of the nested access modes.

match_template(IC, T, S, SEQ)
   If IC is a canonical representative of an instruction class
      and T is a tree which is an instance of IC
      and S a sequence of universal stores, resulting from the processing of the nested access modes
   then SEQ is the sequence of S followed by the result of matching the tree T with an instruction of the IC instruction class.

4.4 Comments on the choice of Prolog

Prolog allows us to make quickly an experimental system to achieve the production of code generators from target machine specifications based on tree templates. The code produced is locally optimal.

The most serious problem we had to face is that the rewriting algorithm is based on the filtering mechanism whereas Prolog uses the unification mechanism.

Another problem encountered is the clause ordering. The access modes, the instructions and the instructions classes may be partially ordered. The clause writing order fits for a total ordering but not for a partial ordering. Furthermore, in the rewriting algorithm, we choose an instruction template of an instruction class under the better match criterion. This induces a new ordering of the instructions belonging to the instruction class.

Finally one can ask if some of the problems encountered are not due to the choice of the Prolog representation of our tree templates. In this case, the choice of the data structure is as crucial as in other programming languages.

Conclusion

We have provided ways to specify target machines in the framework of an abstract data type writing system. The correctness proof of the code generator can be done by means of axioms on universal operators of the target abstract data type, thus it is machine independant.

The code generators built by the prototype produce locally optimal code.

Currently, we are working in two directions : to make an operational system and to deal with global optimization subtasks viewed as attributed tree rewritings.

Bibliography

[BGM 87]   Bidoit M., Gaudel M. C., Mauboussin A. : "How to make algebraic specifications more understandable ? an experiment with the PLUSS specification language", Rapport LRI N° 343, Université d'Orsay, France 1987.

[Cat 77]   Cattell R. G. G. : "A Survey and Critique of some Models of Code Generation", Carnegie-Mellon University, Computer Sciences Department, Technical Report, CMU-CS-115, 1977.

[Cat 80]   Cattell R. G. G. : "Automatic Derivation of Code Generators from Machine Description", ACM Transactions on Programming Languages and Systems, Vol. 2, N°.2 p173-199, April 1980.

[DMR 87]   Despland A., Mazaud M., Rakotozafy R. : "Code generator generation based on template-driven target term rewriting", LNCS n° 256 p 105-120, Proceedings of Rewriting Techniques and Applications, Bordeaux, France, May 1987.

[Des 82]   Deschamp Ph. : "PERLUETTE : a compiler producing system using abstract data types", Proceedings of International Symposium on Programming, Turin, April 1982.

[Gan Gie 82] Ganzinger H, Giegerich R. : "A truly Generative Semantics-Directed Compiler Generator", Proceedings of the SIGPLAN 82 Symposium on Compiler Construction, ACM SIGPLAN n° 17, 6, June 1982.

[GDM 84]   Gaudel M. C., Deschamp Ph., Mazaud M. : "Compiler Construction From High Level Specification", Automatic Program Construction Techniques, Macmillan Inc, 1984.

[GF 82]   Ganapathi M., Fischer C. N. : "Description-Driven Code Generation Using attributed Grammars", Conference of the Nineth Annual ACM Symposium on Programming Languages, Albuquerque New-Mexico, p 108-109, January 25-27, 1982.

[GG 78]   Graham S. L, Glanville R. S. : "A New Method for Compiler Code Generation", Conference Record of the Fifth Annual ACM Symposium on Principles of Programming Languages, p 231-240, January 1978.

[GH 84]   Graham S. L., Henry R. R. & Al. : "Experiment with a Graham-Glanville Style Code generator", Proceedings of the SIGPLAN 84, Symposium on Compiler Construction, ACM Not. 19, 6, June 1984.

[Gie 85]   Giegerich R. : "Logic specification of Code Generation Techniques", LNCS n° 217, p 96-111, Programs as data objects, Copenhague October 17-19 , 1985.

[Mad 83]   Madelaine E. : "Système d'aide à la preuve de compilateurs", Thèse de 3ème cycle, Université de Paris VII, Septembre 1983.

[MRS 86]   Mazaud M., Rakotozafy R., Szumachowski-Despland A. : "Code generator generation based on template-driven target term rewriting", Rapport de recherche INRIA RR-582, 1986.

Towards a "Middle Road" Methodology
For Writing Code Generators

Feliks Kluźniak
Mirosława Miłkowska

Institute of Informatics
Warsaw University

Abstract

We describe a simple experiment in using Prolog for the code selection part of a code generator. The results suggest a new methodological approach that could be generally useful in compiler writing/retargeting undertakings.

1. Introduction

In [Colm75] Alain Colmerauer showed how to use Prolog for writing a simple and elegant compiler for a toy programming language. Since these techniques were made more generally known by [Warr80] it has become more or less widely accepted that Prolog is a very convenient tool for writing compiler front ends (at least on an experimental scale). As far as we know, however, to date there had been no attempts to investigate whether Prolog is equally convenient as a tool for constructing non-trivial back ends. We have recently begun experimenting to satisfy our curiosity in this respect.

This paper describes one such experiment, in which we tried to develop a fairly sophisticated code selector in very limited time. Our results are encouraging and indicate that cheap and efficient code generators might be constructed using what seems to be a novel methodology.

In Section 2 we describe our experiment. Section 3 is devoted to more general considerations.

2. An experiment in code selection

2.1. Initial assumptions

In our experiments with code generation we decided to start with the problem of code selection: we find it fascinating, and it is very inadequately treated in most of the standard texts on compiler construction. At this stage we avoided dealing with details of register allocation, generation of spill code etc. by assuming that we will never run out of registers. Registers are assigned in a stack-like manner.

Our target machine was a slightly idealised PDP-11 (we glossed over the fact that multiplication and division involve pairs of registers). This is the standard machine model in [AhU176] and [ASU86]. The instruction set is elegant and convenient, yet code selection is non-trivial: there are usually many different ways to achieve the same result.

For the sake of completeness we will now present those aspects of the target code that appear in the examples in this paper.

There are two types of instructions: those that have two operands
        operation   source, target
and those that have only one
        operation   operand

Instructions with two operands are
        mov   (data transfer)
        add   (addition)
        sub   (subtraction)
        mul   (multiplication)
        div   (division)

Instructions with one operand are

    inc   (increment)

    neg   (negate, i.e. subtract from zero)

    asl   (arithmetic shift left, by one position)

Any operand can be in one of the following forms

    rn   (general register *n*)

    *rn   (memory cell indicated by general register *n*)

    i   (memory cell at address *i*)

    #i   (the literal *i*, in source position only)

    i(rn)   (memory cell whose address is the sum of *i* and the
               contents of general register *n*)

Whenever an instruction has an operand in one of the last three
forms, the value of *i* is given in the word directly following the
instruction. An instruction with two operands can occupy one, two
or three words depending on its operands. The length of the code is
a convenient overall measure of its cost.

In assembler code integer operands can appear in symbolic form, to
be resolved at load time.

Example 1

    The assignment   x := -(x - 7)

    could be translated to

            mov   #x,r0   ;; address of x to register 0
            mov   *r0,r1   ;; value of x to register 1
            sub   #7,r1   ;; subtract 7 from register 1
            neg   r1   ;; negate register 1
            mov   r1,*r0   ;; store result in x

    (cost 7, two registers used).

    The same effect could be achieved by

            neg   x   ;; x:= -x
            add   #7,x   ;; x:= x + 7

    (cost 5, no registers used).

End of example 1

108

In our experiments we generated code for single Pascal-like assignments in the domain of integers. We assumed that the address of variable *v* can be represented by the symbol *v* (static allocation, real addresses assigned at load time).

Since Prolog can be thought of as a "tree-oriented" language, we immediately decided to adopt TCOL-like trees (see [Lev80]) as our intermediate language. This notation is best described by an example.

Example 2

PDP-11 is byte addressable, and an integer occupies two bytes. The operator @ is used to distinguish between the address of a memory cell and its contents (@ *address*).

The assignment

    a[x + i] := a[x] + i

is therefore converted by the front end to

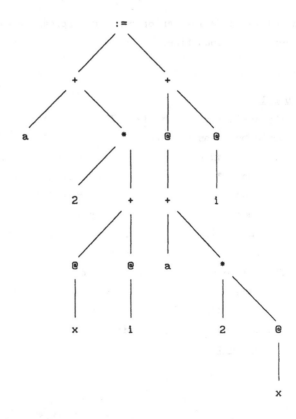

This is represented by the term

$$:=(+(a,*(2,+(@(x),@(i)))), +(@(+(a,*(2,@(x)))),@(i)))$$

or, given appropriate "operator" declarations in Prolog,

$$a + 2 * (@ x + @ i) := @ (a + 2 * @ x) + @ i$$

End of example 2

2.2. The initial version

We began by writing the simplest code generator we could think of. There is a clause for each type of tree node:

```
% gen_code( + (sub)tree, + number of target register )
gen_code( Dest := Exp, I ) :- !,
                    gen_code( Dest, I ), J is I + 1,
                    gen_code( Exp, J ), emit( mov rJ,*rI ).
gen_code( L - R, I ) :- !,
                    gen_code( L, I ), J is I + 1,
                    gen_code( R, J ), emit( sub rJ,rI ).
gen_code( @ AdrExp, I ) :- !,
                    gen_code( AdrExp, I ), emit( mov *rI,rI ).
gen_code( Lit, I ) :- is_literal( I ), !,
                    emit( mov #Lit,rI ).
gen_code( T, _ ) :- eRROR( bad_tree( T ) ).
```

(To save space we omit clauses for arithmetic operators other than subtraction. For clarity, we omit the details of making arguments to the code-producing procedure *emit* palatable to Prolog's parser.)

Of course, this produces horrible code. For the assignment of Example 2 we obtained

```
    mov #a,r0          ;;  a
    mov #2,r1          ;;  2
    mov #x,r2          ;;  x
    mov *r2,r2         ;;  @x
    mov #i,r3          ;;  i
    mov *r3,r3         ;;  @i
```

```
add r3,r2              ;;   @x+@i
mul r2,r1              ;;   2*(@x+@i)
add r1,r0              ;;   a+2*(@x+@i)
mov #a,r1              ;;   a
mov #2,r2              ;;   2
mov #x,r3              ;;   x
mov *r3,r3             ;;   @x
mul r3,r2              ;;   2*@x
add r2,r1              ;;   a+2*@x
mov *r1,r1             ;;   @(a+2*@x)
mov #i,r2              ;;   i
mov *r2,r2             ;;   @i
add r2,r1              ;;   @(a+2*@x)+@i
mov r1,*r0            ;;   a+2*(@x+@i):= @(a+2*@x)+@i
```
(cost 28, 4 registers used)

However, this code generator is rather obviously correct.
Moreover, the effort needed to write it was negligible: it took
one person one day to write and have running both the generator
and the front end for our mini language. (The program was somewhat
more complicated than shown here, as it included automatic
generation of comments and instrumentation to gather information
about length of code and the number of registers used.)

2.3. Improving the code

This code generator is very easy to improve. To give the simplest
example, if one wants to utilise the increment instruction one
need only write

```
    gen_code( E + 1, I ) :- !,  gen_code( E, I ),
                    emit( inc rI ).
    gen_code( 1 + E, I ) :- !,  gen_code( E, I ),
                    emit( inc rI ).
```

These two clauses must be inserted in front of the general clause
for addition, which always remains as a "catch-all" general case.
If a new clause does not of itself generate incorrect code, the
whole generator remains correct.

Notice that the patterns in clause heads play the role of "templates" used to "tile" the tree according to a top-down, "maximal munch" strategy (see [Catt78]). This rather advanced method of code generation turns out to be the natural first choice when one programs in Prolog.

Strictly speaking, the generator uses maximal munch only if we are careful to put clauses with "larger" templates in front of those with "smaller" templates for the same root node. This is usually the best strategy to follow, as witnessed by the following example, which also illustrates the power of the method.

Example 3

    To avoid recomputing the index in code for statements such as

        a[x + i] := a[x + i] + k * l

we simply add the clause

        gen_code(E1 := @ E1 + E2, I) :- !,
                        gen_code(E1, I),   J is I + 1,
                        gen_code(E2, J),   emit(add rJ,*rI).

However, if this were preceded rather than followed by

        gen_code(E1 := E2 + 1, I) :- !,
                        gen_code(E1, I),   J is I + 1,
                        gen_code(E2, J),
                        emit(inc rJ),   emit(mov rJ,*rI).

then the code for   a[x]:= a[x]+1   would be significantly worse than for   a[x]:= a[x]+2.

The correct ordering is not quite satisfactory, as the code for   a[x]:= a[x]+1   will use general addition instead of the increment instruction. This can be remedied by inserting yet a third clause, in front of the other two:

        gen_code(E := @ E + 1, I) :- !,
                        gen_code(E, I),   emit(inc *rI).

End of example 3

As shown in the example, the difficulty of finding a proper ordering can often be solved by adding new special cases. A less obvious problem is that a slight improvement may sometimes worsen the situation: a new large template may cover the root nodes of subtrees for which particularly efficient code was already being produced. It might therefore be a good idea to have a benchmark of "average" constructs that could be used to check the effects of introducing such uncertain improvements.

It is a good heuristic to think carefully about general cases before writing clauses for many special cases. For example, if we decided to evaluate the right-hand side of an assignment before evaluating the destination address (such code could use less registers in certain cases), we would have to modify most of the special rules involving the assignment operator.

The improvements come so easily that one may be tempted to introduce too many new rules (eg. to cover a[E1]:= E2+a[E1], a[E]:= a[E] + a[E] etc., also for the other arithmetic operators). One must remember that a clever code generator should not attempt to replace an optimiser of intermediate code, and that an optimising pass is necessary if we want to obtain really good code. It would be very useful to prepare the tree by:
- folding constant expressions
- taking advantage of arithmetic identities (eg. a*(b+c) is easier to compile than a*b+a*c)
- ordering operands of commutative operators (so that it is always 1+E, never E+1, allowing us to make do with only one clause for increment)
- eliminating redundant subexpressions etc.

Of course, writing such a "tree simplifier" in Prolog is a relatively straightforward task.

2.4 Results

Once we had the initial, inefficient but correct version of the code generator, the two of us spent a single afternoon running it on small examples and repeatedly adding improvements. This activity was rather enjoyable, and the results were quite encouraging.

For the assignment of Example 2 we obtained

```
    mov x,r0              ;;   @x
    add i,r0              ;;   @x+@i
    asl r0               ;;   2*(@x+@i)
    mov x,r1             ;;   @x
    asl r1              ;;   2*@x
    mov a(r1),r1        ;;   @(a+2*@x)
    add i,r1            ;;   @(a+2*@x)+@i
    mov r1,a(r0)        ;;   a+2*(@x+@i):= @(a+2*@x)+@i
```
(cost 14, two registers used)

For   a[x + i] := a[x + i] + 1   the code was

```
    mov x,r0
    add i,r0
    asl r0
    inc a(r0)
```
(cost 7, one register used)

To gain some perspective on the achievements of that afternoon, we ran our examples through three commercial compilers available on a PDP-11 running RSX 11-M. The compilers were:
- OMSI Pascal-1 v1.1G
- DECUS C Language System
- Fortran IV-PLUS v3.0

The results are shown in the following table. The column marked with asterisks refers to our experimental code generator. The first number indicates the length of generated code, the second - the number of registers used. Results marked with   *) do not include the cost of passing arguments and calling a multiplication procedure.

(These tests are somewhat unfair to the Fortran compiler, which was the only one that maintained information about machine state between successive statements. We had to compile one statement at a time to make the results comparable. On the other hand, the comparison is advantageous for C. We used special forms such as a[x+i]++, a[x]+=i*5 etc.: the code for straightforward assignments was much worse. Note that in Pascal and C all variables are addressed with respect to an activation record accessed by a register. However, using static allocation in C had no effect on the cost.)

Statement	Pascal	C	Fortran	***
a[x+i]:= a[x] + i	16 + 2	16 + 2	14 + 2	14 + 2
a[x+i]:= a[x+i] + 1	17 + 2	8 + 1	7 + 1	7 + 1
a[b[x]]:= a[b[x]]+1	21 + 2	10 + 1	8 + 1	8 + 1
a[b[x]]:= a[b[x]+1]	20 + 2	20 + 2	9 + 1	17 + 2
a[x+1]:= a[x] + 1	14 + 2	14 + 2	8 + 2	12 + 2
y := 0 * x	2 + 0	8 + 1 *)	2 + 0	2 + 0
y := 0 - x	5 + 1	5 + 1	5 + 1	5 + 1
y := 1 * x	3 + 0	3 + 0	3 + 0	4 + 1
y := 2 * x	5 + 1	5 + 1	5 + 1	5 + 1
z := (x-y) * (w-v)	10 + 2 *)	13 + 1 *)	11 + 2	11 + 2
x := 123	3 + 0	3 + 0	3 + 0	3 + 0
x := 0	2 + 0	2 + 0	2 + 0	2 + 0
x := y	3 + 0	3 + 0	3 + 0	3 + 0
x := x + 1	2 + 0	2 + 0	2 + 0	2 + 0
x := x - 1	2 + 0	2 + 0	2 + 0	2 + 0
x := 1 + x	2 + 0	2 + 0	2 + 0	2 + 0
a[x] := a[x] + i*5	13 + 2 *)	12 + 2	9 + 2	9 + 2
a[7] := a[7] + 2	3 + 0	3 + 0	3 + 0	5 + 1

It should be noted that in all cases where our generator is inferior, it could be improved with two or three additional rules: these would undoubtedly have been added if we had not limited ourselves to a single afternoon's work before making this comparison.

3. What have we learned ?

There are, in general, two approaches to the problem of constructing a new code generator.

The traditional, "low road" approach is to get together a small group of programmers conversant with the target machine and/or compiler writing techniques. Given enough time, they will come up with a program that is not too unreasonable. Given more time, they will attempt to make the code more efficient by taking advantage of special cases.

The disadvantages of this approach are many. It is time-consuming and it requires expert labour. The product is not retargetable. It is also seldom demonstrably correct: as the number of clever optimisations grows, so does the time needed to "debug" the generator; in the final count, to say that it produces correct code is to demonstrate faith in the skills of its authors.

The "high road" approach is based on methodological considerations: what goes on when good code is being produced? on what grounds do we prefer one instruction sequence to another? how can we usefully classify different instructions, operand types, registers for a wide class of machines?

This general approach resulted in a number of methods that attempt to make the process of constructing code generators more or less mechanical (the bibliography is too large to include here: we refer the reader to [ASU86] as a good entry point). Some of these methods are useful in writing code generators "by hand", many require special tools. A few of them, notably PQCC ([Lev80]), come within sight of the ultimate goal: completely automatic production of good code generators from formal descriptions of the target machines.

Those who choose to travel the high road do so in the hope that an initial large investment in research and construction of special tools will pay for itself by enabling them to quickly produce good compilers over a long period of time, for many target machines and with a relatively small additional investment for each new machine. Consequently, both the tools and detailed information about the techniques used are not always generally available. It is known, however, that access to such tools does not always solve all the problems. Insufficiently expert preparation of input (such as a machine description) may cause the resultant generator to block or loop for certain constructs. The tools themselves sometimes require heavy computational resources, and the constructed compilers are not always sufficiently small and fast to make them acceptable in certain production environments (eg. on popular microcomputers). For reasons such as these, the low road is not likely to fall into disuse anytime soon.

However, there may be other alternatives. Our experiment in code generation was very limited: in particular we did not yet address the problem of adequate register assignment, not to mention the subtle interplay between code selection and register allocation. But once we assume that our method can be extended (if only by using a prepackaged set of standard techniques), it seems to constitute a third, "middle road" approach towards constructing code generators.

The approach consists in constructing a trivial, inefficient but obviously correct code generator, and then incrementally augmenting it with a set of rules formulated by an expert. The expert is any competent assembly programmer who knows the target machine, and the demands on his time and attention are quite modest (since he works in "small pieces", he can even apply himself to the problem intermittently, taking advantage of slack time in other projects). There is no attempt to extract any general rules about the expert's behaviour: we are interested only in the results of such behaviour. The code generator consists of an (almost) unstructured set of rules, but it is not an "expert system": all this is hard-core computer science.

There is no way to ensure that the generated code will always be optimal, but we can expect it to be sufficiently sophisticated. Optimality is nowhere near as important as correctness, and the correctness of a code generator produced with this method can be verified quite easily (albeit not automatically): we need only check that each individual rule produces correct code for the case that it covers, and the "knowledge" embodied in such a rule is simple and virtually explicit.

Finally, the only tool that is needed is a decent implementation of Prolog, and these are now available even on personal computers. Efficiency is likely to be better than in more conventional compilers based on template matching. A good Prolog compiles away most of the matching overhead. In any event, the structure of the code generator is so simple that - once it is found to generate satisfactory code - it is relatively easy to rewrite it into a more conventional language.

The middle road approach is quite informal, but in many situations it may enable us to strike the right balance between the cost of implementation, the efficiency of code generation and the quality of the generated code. Above all, there are no compromises where correctness is concerned.

References

[AhUl76] Aho, A.V.; Ullman,J.D.: Principles of Compiler Design.
Addison-Wesley, Reading, MA 1976

[ASU86] Aho, A.V.; Sethi, R.; Ullman, J.D.:
Compilers: Principles, Techniques and Tools.
Addison-Wesley, Reading, MA 1986

[Catt78] Cattell, R.G.G.: Formalization and Automatic Derivation
of Code Generators. Ph.D. Thesis, Dept. of Computer
Science, Carnegie-Mellon University, April 1978

[Colm75] Colmerauer, A.: Les grammaires de métamorphose.
Groupe d'Intelligence Artificielle, Université
d'Aix-Marseille, 1975
(English version: Metamorphosis Grammars.
In L.Bolc (ed.): Natural Language Communication with
Computer. Springer-Verlag, Berlin and Heidelberg 1978)

[Lev80] Leverett, B.W.; Cattell, R.G.G.; Hobbs, S.O.; Newcomer,
J.M.; Reiner, A.H.; Schatz, B.R.; Wulf, W.A.:
An Overview of the Production-Quality Compiler Compiler
Project. *Computer* **13**:8, 38-49

[Warr80] Warren, D.H.D.: Logic Programming and Compiler Writing.
Software Practice and Experience **10** (2), 97-125

A compiler written in Prolog: the Véda experience

Jean-François Monin

CNET LAA-SLC-EVP
BP 40
F–22301 Lannion

Tel : (33) 96 05 26 79

abstract : *We present our experience in developing a system called Véda in which Prolog was used for writing a real-size compiler. We give the main techniques used for increasing the performances of the compiler up to a usable level, and for keeping some flexibility to Véda. Finally we give a few hints about performances.*

I. Introduction

We present here a tool development that began in the end of 1983 and which is known under the name of *Véda*, in which Prolog was used for writing a compiler that will be soon be commercially distributed. Véda is mainly a simulator, specially tailored for protocol validation [Jard 85b]. The way of using Véda can roughly be sketched as follows :

1. describe protocol *P* in a *specification language* (which in this case is close to a programming language);

2. analyse statically this protocol with a parser; in particular check consistency of interfaces and structuration;

3. describe properties that should belong to the protocol *P* in the form of an *observer O* ;

4. generate a code that simulates *P* observed by *O* ;

5. run the simulation, and interpret the results.

Of course, steps 2 and 4 are done in the same compilation step. Let us indicate that the latter does not directly produce machine code, but a Pascal program.

Details of the implementation of Véda can be found in [Jard 85a], [Jard 88] and [Monin 88]; this paper is essentially devoted to the features of Véda bound to the choice of Prolog as a language for writing compilers.

Why Prolog? Partly because of the choice of a new language called *Estelle* [ISO 86, Courtiat 87] as the protocol specification language used for Véda. Reasons for choosing Estelle are given in [Jard 88]. One of them is that Estelle is an ISO standard for protocol specification.

In 1983 no Estelle compiler was yet available. And our group was much more interested in getting quickly a compiler rather than getting a quick compiler. Moreover the definition of

Estelle was evolving with the process of standardisation, so the handiness of the compiler description was of prime necessity. These reasons among others made us choose Prolog.

This paper is organized as follows. First we have a short overview of the Estelle language, then the meaning of compiling in Véda, and the main techniques for increasing the performances of the compiler up to a usable level, and for keeping some flexibility to the compiler. In concluding remarks we analyse some of the results and give a few hints about performances.

II. Overview of Estelle

From a compiler writer point of vue, Estelle is firstly a superset of Pascal ; more precisely all the Pascal grammar – excepted the axiom – is contained in the Estelle grammar.

Furthermore Estelle includes structuring notions such as *module type*, *module body*, *module instance*, *channel*, *interaction point*, for describing a distributed system by stepwise refinement, with strongly typed interfaces between the entities of same level. The behavior of an elementary component (called *process*) is described under the form of an "extended" automaton, where each transition has a *guard* and an *action*.

The guard is a conjunction of firing conditions about the *main state*, internal Pascal variables of the process, end of a delay, or presence of a message on an interaction point. The action is a Pascal statement that modify the state of the process (including its internal variables), and in which messages could be sent.

All in all, the Estelle grammar is twice the size of Pascal grammar. This shows that Estelle is not a toy language.

III. Extent of compilation in Véda

Although the target language is Pascal, an Estelle description must be entirely analysed ; even the Pascal parts cannot be simply copied. There are at least two reasons for this :

— The Pascal non-terminal "statement" is extended in Estelle to communication statements, connection statements, etc...

— all identifiers have to be renamed in target code.
A third reason is that errors should be detected in the source program (even spelling errors) rather than in the generated Pascal program.

In the parser, Prolog is used in the extended attributes grammars style's – see [Simonet 81] for a comparison. Moreover the part of the compiler concerning Pascal is taken from [Watt 79].

Separate compilation.

Véda gives the possibility of managing applications that are divided into several compilation units. This involves two advantages :

— the user can logically split her/his protocol description ;

— memory space limitations cannot allow compilation of very big units : the source code cannot exceed 500 to 2000 lines of source code, depending on the host operating system ; however Véda allowed dealing with real protocols involving several thousands lines of Estelle [Dinsenmeyer 87], thanks to separate compilation.

Notice that this is not only the question of independant compilation : type checking would be the same if all the protocol was described in just one compilation unit.

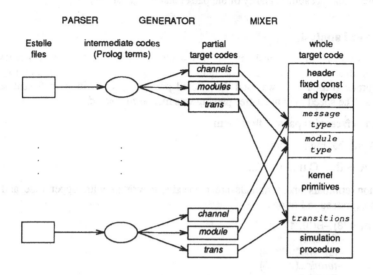

Figure 1. target code generation

Target code.

The target code is a mixture of *fixed parts* (the *kernel*) and *variable parts* (protocol dependant). Fixed parts include on the one hand declarations of basic data structures, primitive procedures for handling the event queue, process contexts, communications, and on the other hand the general simulation procedure. Variable parts include data structures for interactions, module interfaces, process contexts and two procedures for each transition (one for the guard, one for the action). The different steps for generating the target code are presented in figure 1.

Vocabulary

Compiling in Véda uses two steps. The first includes lexical analysis, parsing and semantic analysis, and generates an *intermediate code* representing an Estelle description under a termal form. The second step generates the *target code* (a Pascal program) from the intermediate code. In Véda we call *parser* the program implementing the first step, and *generator* the one implementing the second step. Files generated by the latter are split and pasted in a appropriate manner by the *mixer*, and the output is a complete Pascal program. The functionality achieved by the mixer is similar to the link phase in traditional compiling.

IV. The main techniques

We present here some techniques used in Véda. Their purpose is to speed up compilation, or to increase manageability, clarity of the parser and the generator.

IV.1 Lexical analysis

In a very first time, lexical analysis was written in Prolog, but it was very quickly dropped. The Prolog dialect used (Prolog/P) was quite well integrated with the programming language of the interpreter (Pascal), so we used the offered possibility of writing in Pascal some built-in predicates. The speed of context-free parsing was increased *tenfold*.

IV.1.1 Interface with parser, first form

A rule having the form :

A -> B ... C u ... v D ....

where non-terminals and terminals are respectively written with upper case and lower case letters, is expressed in Prolog :

```
A(*0,*8) −B(*0,*1) ...
         −C(*2,*3)
         −terminal(u,*3,*4) ...
         −terminal(v,*5,*6)
         −D(*6,*7) ...
```

In this syntax [Barberye 83], litterals of the body of a clause are preceded by "−", and variables begin with a star. The two arguments added to each symbol are similar to the ones presented in [Colmerauer 75], but here their type is different. Instead of representing a difference list, they represent an interval in the sequence of implicitly numbered terminals : each couple of variables is a couple of integers. The built-in predicate $terminal(t, *x, *y)$ calls for the $*x^{th}$ terminal (this variable is then instantiated to an integer); lexical analysis of the asked symbol is processed when necessary; at the same time, $*y$ is instantiated to $*x + 1$.

An advantage of this approach on the usual method (in Prolog) is that lexical analysis and parsing are done during the same pass. As a consequence, error reporting is made easier.

IV.1.2 Interface with parser, second form

In a last evolution, the built-in predicate *terminal* became backtrackable, so the two added arguments were no longer useful. So the parser became easier to handle, easier to read, and space for substitutions was spared at running time. Let us notice that the latter step involves a global Pascal variable, and few Prolog have this kind of feature. For example Quintus Prolog cannot handle global variables.

The previous grammar rule would be now expressed :

```
A −B ...
  −C
  −terminal(u) ...
  −terminal(v)
  −D ...
```

For a detailed presentation of the implementation see [Barrielle 87].

IV.2 Handling environments

Another key point in a compiler is access to the symbol table (called "dictionnary" in [Warren 80]). Recall that the problem consist in representing a (partial) function mapping identifiers I onto context dependant informations such as value, type, coded under the form of terms T_I.

IV.2.1 Traditional approaches

[Colmerauer 75] and [Warren 80] proposition is to represent this function as a couple *(E,access)*, where E is the *environment term*, which is an argument of the non-terminals, and *access* is a search predicate for these environment terms. Practically, E is a binary search tree, having couples $<I,T_I>$ as nodes.

In the proposition of [Garetta 86], the function is directly coded with clauses $I(T_I)$.

The advantage of the latter method on the former is the speed, because it implicitly uses the internal hashing function used by Prolog for accessing clauses. But the trouble is the use of the built-in predicate "assert", which is not consistent with the declarative features of Prolog. Even from an operating point of vue, problems happend in the following situations :

— T_I is progressively known, and it would be nice to built this term by growing instantiations ;

— a couple $<I,T_I>$ must be deleted due to backtracking.

Such questions are not relevant with the first method, because it uses only right first order logic where the resolution principle correctly works.

IV.2.2 Approach used in Véda

In Véda, we try to represent the environment function in such a way that advantages of twice methods above are preserved. As in the former, effective information is represented by an argument E of each non-terminal. On the other hand, the information T_I associated to I is no longer accessed by a recursive predicate, but using a single unification step, with a predicate call such as :

$$-I(E, T_I).$$

As a matter of fact a relations base of the form

$I (<environment\ term\ skeleton> , <place>).$

is built and updated each time a *new* identifier occurs. For example, if the data structure of E was a list, its "skeleton" would be :

*1.*2.*3.*4.*5...

Let us suppose that the three first identifiers of a source program are Ariane, Venus and Cleopâtre, then the base of relations would be :

```
Diane      (*1.*r,       *1).
Venus      (*1.*2.*r,    *2).
Cleopâtre (*1.*2.*3.*r , *3).
```

Practically of course, E is structured as a balanced binary tree and *<environment skeleton>* is reduced to the path between the root and *<place>*.

So the parser keeps a clean declarative semantics. The important fact is that asserted clauses really contain *no* information. From an abstract point of vue we could imagine without drawback that the compiler contains a predefined base of relations for all identifiers.

Remarks

1. For two different identifiers the relations between *<environment skeleton>* and *<place>* are different by construction.

2. In case of backtracking the clause $I(,)$ remains, but I shall not be considered new any longer.

Implementation and justifications are detailed in [Monin 84].

IV.3 Parasits

IV.3.1 Need for non local information

The parser was built in an incremental manner, so that tests may become easier. Initially only context-free parsing was done (non-terminal were without parameters). Then we successively introduced arguments (or *attributes*) for contextual analysis, such as the environment parameter E, and then those for building intermediate code. In general these are synthetized attributes, except E. But in some typical situations inherited attributes are necessary.

— When parsing expressions: $a - b - c$ implicitly means $(a - b) - c$; but for processing the corresponding intermediate code with only synthetized attributes, a left recursive grammar is necessary; such a grammar is not compatible with the *LL* type parsing method used.

— When processing the type of a variable reference: for example the type of $A.B.C$ is processed in function of the type of $A.B$ which is again a function of the type of A.

In such situations, the addition of an inherited attribute remains quite local, only some non-terminals must be modified. On the other hand, a computation done in a non-terminal sometimes depends on information produced far away in the derivation tree (*proof tree* in the terminology of [Deransart 85]).

For example Estelle includes a notion of "pure function" (i.e. without side effect); expressions occuring in the guard of a transition cannot use a function considered as impure. This constraint is especially annoying to control, because the non-terminal *expression* occurs in many right members. Quite a natural solution would consist in adding an inherited attribute to the non-terminal *expression*, that would indicate the origin of the call. Unfortunately this additional parameter propagates on all the numerous descendants of *expression*, in particular *var_reference*, and on all occurences of them in right members.

So a good part of the parser is turned upside down, all sorts of risks arise, evolution of the compiler becomes difficult. Another solution using a modified copy of *expression* cannot be retained for quite analogous reasons.

Let us point out that with an algorithmical programming language, this problem would have quite simply be resolved, by the use of a global variable. Then how could a similar fonctionality be available in Prolog, without abandoning, if possible, the frame of pure logic?

IV.3.2 A solution without "global variable"

In the parser of Véda, we use for passing such contextual information the environment parameter E, which has the advantage of being already available in almost all non-terminals. The identifier I of couples $<I,T_I>$ of E is simply replaced by a composed form *parasite(P)*, in order to avoid potential conflicts with identifiers of the parsed source text. Accessing information associated to a parasit follows the same way than for normal identifiers. We saw that in the case of Véda, this mechanism is quite efficient : it roughly requires one unification step.

For example in the case of "pure functions", parasit *pure-expr* is by default associated to the constant *false*, but in the non-terminal *provided-construct* (contributing to describe the guard of a transition), this pseudo-declaration is hidden by another that maps *pure-expr* onto *true*. The value associated to this parasit is consulted only in one place, the non-terminal that describes the call of a function. So modifications remain circumscribed where they are relevant, they don't anarchically propagate in the compiler. Different parasits were introduced as and when required, but the compiler remained relatively manageable.

IV.4 Code generation

The aim is now to produce a Pascal program from a Prolog term representing a source text. The problematics is quite simple, it is about walking through this term in order to build a partial Pascal program. A single pass is sufficient, i.e. the Pascal text can sequentially be built. So an intermediate step building an abstract form of the target code from the abstract form of the source code can be avoided, and we prefer this for efficiency reasons.

On the other hand the target code is composed of a fixed part, the *kernel*, and of a variable part which only depends on the source protocol. This distinction is especially due to the implementation of separate compilation. So generating code requires in Véda three different texts : the *generator*, the kernel and the *mixer* (see figure 1).

IV.4.1 First Version

In a first time, these three texts were written by hand (the generator and the mixer were Prolog programs). So we quickly got an operative version of Véda. Nevertheless this approach is a quite low level one.

— Dispersal in three strongly coupled parts is a big handicap for managing the product.

— The Prolog generator is composed of a sequence of more or less structured "write" statements ; what are we doing with the good old declarative semantics of Prolog, since only side effects are interesting, and not a substitution answer?

— In order to save memory space, many clauses that logically should have been expressed :

$A - B - C \ldots - D$.

are split in pieces when no information is passed between them :

$A - B - IMPASSE$.
$A - C - IMPASSE$.
$\ldots$
$A - D$.

So target code generation becomes quite acrobatic in first version.

IV.4.2 Spécode

Fortunately it came to light that these unpleasant things could be automatically handled. Target code is now specified in a language called *Spécode*; the mixer is henceforth target code independant, and the two other texts (generator and kernel) are generated from the target code specification by ... Prolog programs. Spécode was especially tailored for Véda's needs. It consists essentially in a formalism of rewriting rules parametrized by Prolog terms. Here are some favourable arguments to this choice.

— It easily deals with structuration, and has undeniable qualities of clarity.

— Its nature is mainly descriptive; in particular a semantics other than operational can be attached to it. As a matter of fact it is quite identical to metamorphosis grammars ([Colmerauer 75]), but used in a frame where attributes are in general purely inherited.

— These attributes are coded as Prolog terms, so intermediate code can directly be used.

— We can easily imagine a (however simplistic) translation of such rewriting rules into Prolog clauses: each non-terminal corresponds to a predicate, each rule to a clause, and each terminal to the call of a built-in predicate that writes this terminal.

— Thanks to recursivity, rewriting rules give a versatility which is necessary in some circumstances.

— It is possible to design a syntax of Spécode suitable to specific requirements of Véda. See the following paragraphs.

The form of Spécode (its syntax) was chosen on the basis of a practical consideration: the rules specifying the target code contain long strings of consecutive terminals (this is not the case for the grammars of programming languages). In order to make the specification of such strings easier, we adopt an entirely mark-free designation of terminals. On the other hand, the other symbols occuring in a right member (non-terminals, end-of-rule delimiter for example) are indicated by the presence of an escape character: the "#". Predicates are prefixed with a slash "/".

Example:

```
enum_interact(*CI) ->
    typeinteraction = ( sivide0
                            #noms_de_messages(*CI)
                        ) ;
#.
noms_de_messages(*CI) ->
            #X #/mesg(*CI,*im)
            , #*im
#.
```

Figure 2. Some Spécode rules

The ouput of these rules would be of the form:

```
typeinteraction = ( sivide0
                  , id_msg₁

                  , id_msgₙ
                  ) ;
```

The purpose of this example is to built the type declaration *typeinteraction* containing the enumeration of all interaction identifiers. *CI* is a variable instantiated to a term representing the whole intermediate code. It is an argument of every non-terminal and predicate. Here we write it explicitly, but actually it is an implicit argument. *#*im* indicates the target representation of a source identifier. *#X* is the *repetition operator*. It is similar to the *star* operator of Kleene, and it applies on the rest of the right member. It has a predicate *(mesg(*CI,*im))* as a parameter, synthetizing one of its arguments (*im*); its semantics is on this example: let *lim* be the list of answers to: *−/*mesg(*CI,*im); then *noms-de-messages* has the equivalent definition showed in figure 3.

```
noms_de_messages(*CI) ->
              #/liste_des_mesg(*CI,*lim)
              #noms_de_messages_bis(*lim)
#.
noms_de_messages_bis(nil).
noms_de_messages_bis(*im.*lim) ->
              , #*im
              #noms_de_messages_bis(*lim)
#.
```

Figure 3. Equivalent rules

The general definition of *#X* is left to the reader.

IV.4.3 Implementation principles

Now we roughly explain how Spécode is implemented. Specification of the target code is parsed: each rule is put under the form of a list of terms. Then the generator and the kernel are generated. The first step to do that is to distinguish terminal occurrences which belong to the kernel from those which belong to the variable part.

This computation is based on the existence, in the derivation tree starting from the axiom of the target code specification, of a demarcation line crossing over each *minimal* predicate which depends on intermediate code (*MPIC*). The partial order $<*$ used for *minimal* is defined between nodes of the derivation tree, as the reflexive-transitive closure of the relation $<$, itself defined by: $N_1 < N_2$ iff N_2 is a right brother or a son of N_1, where N_i are nodes of the derivation tree. For example, *mesg(*CI,*im)* is a MPIC. Let S be the string of terminals of the derivation tree (in left to right order). The variable part is the substring of S restricted to terminals T "under" the demarcation line, i.e. such that there exist a MPIC P such that $P <* T$. The kernel is the complementary substring in S. These notions are informally illustrated in figure 4.

A top-down walk of the grammatical specification is used to determine if a terminal belongs to the kernel or to the variable part. It allows building two derived programs from this grammar: in one case all kernel terminals are erased, and in the other all variable part terminals are erased. The former *is* the generator. whereas running the latter *generates* the kernel. Marks are inserted at the level of the demarcation line in both programs, for the final mixing step.

128

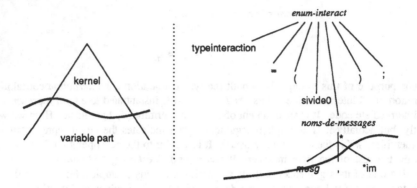

Figure 4. the demarcation line

Unlike the prototype of generator written by hand, it is basically the same derivation of the same grammar that produces in two different steps the kernel and variables parts. This two phases derivation scheme could be formalized with grammar transformations.

To take memory space constraints into account, we saw that a clause corresponding to a Spécode rule has to be split, whenever possible. This splitting is computed from a static dataflow analysis in the target code specification. This analysis is highly simplified and sped up by two constraints and hypothesis on the mode of arguments :

— arguments in the same position of several occurences of the same non-terminal (or predicate) must have the same mode ;

— after a predicate (or non-terminal) call, all variables occuring in its arguments are ground terms.

The second hypothesis could seem severely restrictive, but :

— it is practically usable in such a context, at least for Véda ;

— it is in fact considerably weakened : Spécode actually includes a kind of functional syntax for terms (more precisely : relations between terms) that allows partly circumventing the constraint ; but it is beyond the scope of the paper ; here we only indicate that it generalizes in some sense the difference lists ;

— this constraint could entirely be deleted by introducing in Spécode a possibility of explicitly specifying the mode of non-terminals and predicates arguments.

These remarks show the interest, for the developper of Véda, of mastering the definition of Spécode.

IV.4.4 Using Spécode

Spécode was first used to improve the target code generated for simulation ; many peculiarities were discovered and corrected on this occasion. Then we built (with Spécode) a new version of Véda wherein the input language was the last ISO standard proposal – it involved a deep reorganisation of the target code structure. It seems quite a good estimation that using Spécode reduces code generation development time within a factor of three to five. Spécode will soon be used for another performance evaluation oriented version of Véda. The fact that Spécode are compiled rather than directly interpreted is certainly harmful during the development step, But as a compensation many static checking are done during the translation in Prolog, for example about compatibility between non-terminal calls and their definition. Notice that these checks are sometimes very specific and would be too restrictive in the general frame of first order logic.

Details about Spécode will be found in [Monin 88].

V. Conclusion

Véda has certainly a place among significant applications written in Prolog; at least it is a well known tool in Estelle's community. We hope that some ideas in this paper are reusable in other contexts, in particular:

— "parasits" technique, more precisely the use of an environment parameter where global variables would be used in an imperative programmation language; in Véda, this technique was reused in the Spécode translator;

— usage of other levels of language. Prolog is certainly not the perfect language usable, just as it is, in every situation. However Prolog has indisputable good features for handling tree structures, which contribute to make Prolog a good tool for processing languages. Then one hesitates less to design an ad-hoc language whenever necessary. One gets a multi-level programmation, and then is faced with new and interesting problems: designing at the same time a language, its translator and text using this language. However the experience of Véda shows that sometimes "le jeu en vaut la chandelle". Moreover this approach is close to the one defined as *metaprogramming* by [Levy 86].

We end with some indications about performances. When we began (in the end of 1983), no realistic compiler written in Prolog seemed to exist. A failure was even described in [Hayter 83]. Véda's performances are certainly quite far from those of more classical compilers. However this experience can be considered as a success on the following points.

— Véda has gained a large number of users within our PTT research center (CNET), but also outside its place of design, in french universities and public research laboratories [Jard 88].

— A software company (Vérilog) is currently industrializing Véda *in its Prolog form.*

— Significant applications were processed using Véda, notably in the switching field [Dinsenmeyer 87]. Compilation units having more than 2000 lines passed in Véda. An application of 5000 lines of code and 30-odd compiling units was achieved with Véda.

— Compilation speed is low but tolerable: roughly ten lines per second on a workstation such as Apollo DN3000.

So the well known slowness of Prolog should not be a crippling argument: even in the compilation field, Prolog can be useful.

Acknowledgements

I thank Pierre Bérubé and Roland Groz for their help in translating the french version of this paper.

References

[Barberye 83] G. Barberye, T. Joubert, M. Martin: "Manuel d'utilisation du Prolog-CNET". *Note technique* NT/PAA/CLC /LSC /1058, CNET, France, Sept. 1983.

[Barrielle 87] E. Barrielle, JF. Monin: "Est-ce que Prolog sait lire?" Actes du seminaire *programmation en logique* de Trégastel, 19–21 mai 1987, pp 131–140

[Bekkers 86] Y. Bekkers, B. Canet, O. Ridoux, L. Ungaro: "A Memory Management Machine for Prolog Interpreters". *Proc. of the 3rd Symposium on Logic Programming*, IEEE, sept 1986, Salt-Lake City, USA.

[Colmerauer 75] A. Colmerauer: "Les grammaires of métamorphoses". *Rapport de recherche*, GIA, Univ. Marseille-Luminy, France, Nov. 1975.

[Courtiat 87] JP. Courtiat, P. Dembinski, R. Groz, C. Jard: "Estelle, un langage ISO pour les algorithmes distribués et les protocoles". *TSI*, March 1987.

[Deransart 85] P.Deransart, J. Maluszynski: "Relating Logic Programs and Attribute Grammars". *J. of Logic Programming*, 1985, 2 pp 119–155. INRIA, RR 323,Avril 1985.

[Dinsenmeyer 87] I.Dinsenmeyer, O.Louvet, R. Groz: "Utilisation de techniques of description formelle (TDF) pour la spécification de logiciels de commutation". *Annales des télécommunications*, tome 42,num. 7–8, pp 448–460, juillet 1987.

[Garetta 86] Garetta: "Un compilateur de Modula-2 écrit en Prolog" (?) *thèse de troisième cycle*, Université de Marseille, 1986 (?)

[Hayter 83] R.Hayter: "Edison in Prolog'. *Logic Programming Newsletter*, winter 83–84, p 11.

[ISO 86a] ISO/TC97/SC21/WG16-1 DP9074: "Estelle: a Formal Description Technique based on an Extended State Transition Model". Sept. 1986.

[Jard 85a] C. Jard, JF. Monin, R. Groz: "Experience in implementing X250 in Véda". *V IFIP WG6.1 workshop*, Moissac, June 1985, France, North-Holland, M. Diaz ed.

[Jard 85b] C. Jard, R. Groz, JF. Monin: "Véda: a Software Simulator for the Validation of Protocol Specifications". COMNET'85, Budapest, Oct. 1985, published by North-Holland in *Computer network usage : recent experiences*, L. Csaba, K. Tarnay, T. Szentivanyi ed.

[Jard 88] C. Jard, JF. Monin, R. Groz: "Development of Véda, a Prototyping Tool for Distributed Algorithms". *Special Issue of IEEE trans. on Software Engineering on Computer communication Systems*, Vol 13, March 1988.

[Levy 86] LS. Levy: "A Meta-programming Method and its Economic Justification". *IEEE trans. on Software Engineering*, Vol 12, Nu 2, Feb. 1986, pp 272–277.

[Monin 84] JF. Monin: "Ecriture d'un compiler réel en Prolog". *Journées sur la programmation en logique*, Plestin, France, Avril 1984, Cnet ed.

[Monin 88] JF. Monin: "Véda" *Thèse de doctorat of l'université de Rennes I*, 1988.

[Simonet 81] M.Simonet: "W Grammaires et logique du premier ordre pour la définition and l'implantation des langages". *thèse d'état*, Grenoble, 1981.

[Warren 80] D.H.D. Warren: "Logic Programming and Compiler Writing". *Software, Practice and Experience*, Vol 10, pp 97–125, 1980.

[Watt 79] D.A. Watt: "An Extended Attribute Grammar for Pascal". *SIGPLAN Notice*, Vol 14, Nu 2, pp 60–74.

Coupled context-free grammar
as
a programming paradigm

Yoshiyuki YAMASHITA and Ikuo NAKATA,

Institute of Information Sciences and Electronics, University of Tsukuba,
Tsukuba-shi, Ibaraki-ken, 305, Japan.

Abstract

The formal grammar: Coupled Context-Free Grammar (CCFG) is interpreted as a programming system, in which context-free grammars (CFGs) represent input/output data structures and a CCFG, called a CCFG program, represents the relation between the input/output data structures. The mathematical properties of logic programs and CCFG programs are dual with each other. An arbitrary logic program can be automatically transformed into the equivalent CCFG program and vice versa. Because a data structure of the CCFG program is expressed as the CFG, the execution mechanisms of CCFG programs are the extensions of the parsing techniques for the CFGs.

1 Introduction

In the field of programming languages, the theory of formal grammars, especially the context-free grammars (CFGs), has mainly contributed to language specifications and compiler constructions. In this paper we introduce another contribution of CFGs to a programming paradigm, in which CFGs are viewed as the representations of input/output data structures and a couple of the CFGs is considered as the program representing the relation between the input/output data structures. We call such a couple as a **Coupled Context-Free Grammar** (CCFG).

The main purpose of our study of CCFGs is to develop a programming language based on a data-directed programming paradigm. Any programs can be specified by the relations between the input and the output data. If these data have some kind of structures and their relations depend, heavily or somewhat, on their structures, the structures of the programs can be derived from their data structures. We call such a method of program design, i.e. designing programs based on their input and output data structures, the *data-directed* (or *data structure-directed*) *programming paradigm* [NaSa][YaNa 1]. One such programming paradigm is the well-known Jackson method [Ja].

Our CCFG can also be regarded as an extension of the syntax-directed translation schemes [AhUl] or the attribute grammars. Although these schemes have provided excellent tools in the field of program translations, their expressive powers are too small to be used as general purpose programming systems. For example, they have only one input grammar, i.e. only one to specify the input data. We have succeeded to broaden the expressive power of CCFG by allowing to interpret several grammars as input grammars and by introducing a metasymbol ≈ which means equality.

One of the main purposes of this paper is to show the duality between logic programs and CCFG programs. Therefore, we introduce here our CCFG programs comparing the equivalent logic programs.

It is well known that logic programs can express any CFGs. For example, we see that the set of the following context-free rules

$$X \rightarrow \varepsilon,$$
$$X \rightarrow aX,$$
$$X \rightarrow bX,$$

where X is the start symbol and ε is an empty string, has the same meaning as the following logic program (the set of definite Horn clauses),

$$p([]),$$
$$p([a|X]):-p(X),$$
$$p([b|X]):-p(X),$$

if we identify the string "abb" with the linear list [a, b, b]. The terminal string x can be derived from X if and only if the goal $p(x)$ can be proved by the logic program, where x is the linear list corresponding to x. In the same sense, the grammar

$$Y \rightarrow \varepsilon,$$
$$Y \rightarrow cY,$$
$$Y \rightarrow dY,$$

and the logic program

$$q([]),$$
$$q([c|Y]):-q(Y),$$
$$q([d|Y]):-q(Y),$$

have the same meaning.

Coupling the above logic programs, we can obtain the program such as

$$pq([], []),$$
$$pq([a|X], [c|Y]):-pq(X, Y),$$
$$pq([b|X], [d|Y]):-pq(X, Y).$$

This expresses the binary relation. Each definite clause pq(..):-... is obtained by combining the two corresponding definite clauses p(...):-... and q(...):-... Similarly, we can introduce the combinations of the production rules X→... and Y→... such as the following sets,

$$\{X \rightarrow \varepsilon, \quad Y \rightarrow \varepsilon\},$$
$$\{X \rightarrow aX, \quad Y \rightarrow cY\},$$
$$\{X \rightarrow bX, \quad Y \rightarrow dY\},$$

where all the production rules in a set must be simultaneously applied. The couple (X, Y) of start symbols can derive couples of terminal strings. One of such derivation sequences is given as follows,

$$(X, Y) \Rightarrow (aX, cY) \Rightarrow (abX, cdY) \Rightarrow (abbX, cddY) \Rightarrow (abb, cdd).$$

We see that the couple (x, y) of the terminal strings can be derived form (X, Y) if and only if the goal $p(x, y)$ can be proved by the logic program, where x and y are the linear lists corresponding to x and y, respectively. We call these sets as a CCFG or a CCFG program, and we say that the logic program and the CCFG have the same meaning.

In this way, we can introduce the formal grammars: CCFGs whose mathematical structure is equivalent to that of logic programs (this is shown in section three), though the syntax of CCFGs looks quite different from that of logic programs. The difference between both syntaxes may give us new insights into logic programs. The first is the data-directed programming methodology just like the Jackson method, in which a programmer first defines the input/output data structures by the Jackson diagrams just like regular right-part grammars or CFGs. The study of CCFGs is expected to formalize the Jackson method. The second is the efficient execution methods. We can apply the efficient parsing techniques such as LL(k) or LR(k) for subsets of CFGs to the CCFG program execution methods. We expect, further more, that new methods of program transformations may be derived for CCFG programs from the study of CCFG programs. In this paper, we mainly discuss the execution methods.

In section two, we first define CCFGs and CCFG programs precisely. These can treat only the string type data. Then we extend them to the term-based CCFG programs in which the right-hand sides of production rules are terms. Because the values of the terms are defined by their normal forms derived by a term-rewriting system, the extended programs can treat various data types.

In section three, we introduce the program transformation rule from an arbitrary logic program into the equivalent CCFG program. This rule is so simple that we can automatically carry out the transformation. In addition, we can clearly understand the simple relationship between logic programs and CCFG programs.

In section four, we briefly explain our ideas of the efficient execution methods of CCFG programs. Lookahead is the major technique in the well-known efficient parsers for CFGs. This technique can also be used in the CCFG program execution. Some kind of CCFG programs can be regarded as the scheme of the syntax-directed translation. In this case these programs can be executed in the forms of the corresponding syntax-directed translators. Because the term-based CCFG programs can treat data not only of the string type but also of the integer type, all these execution methods should be extended to deal with all these types.

In section five, the relations between CCFG programs and some other grammar systems, such as the attribute grammar, the attribute coupled grammar and the two-level grammar, are discussed. In addition to the relation between CCFG programs and logic programs described in section three, these relations will clarify the characteristics of CCFG programs.

2 CCFG programming

Here we define CCFGs and the interpretation of them as programs. The details have been given in [YaNa 1].

2.1 Definitions of CCFG programs

Definition(CCFG) A Coupled Context-Free Grammar (CCFG) is defined as the quadruple (N, T, Ω_S, R), where N is a finite set of nonterminal symbols, T a finite set of terminal symbols, Ω_S an n-tuple ($n \geq 1$) of start symbols ($\in N$), and R a finite set of **rule-sets**. A rule-set is a finite set of production rules, which are context-free rules or **left-hand-omitted rules**. The right-hand side of a rule is composed of nonterminal symbols, terminal symbols and metasymbols $\approx$.

Example(a program to calculate the Fibonacci sequence) The following quadruple is a CCFG,

Fib = ({Fin, Fout, Fin', Fout'}, {@}, (Fin, Fout), R_{Fib}),

R_{Fib} = {	{Fin→ε,	Fout→@},	...(Fib.1)
	{Fin→@,	Fout→@},	...(Fib.2)
	{Fin→@Fin≈@@Fin',	Fout→FoutFout'},	...(Fib.3)
	{Fin'→Fin,	Fout'→Fout} }.	...(Fib.4)

We will fully explain later that the above grammar **Fib** can be interpreted as a program to calculate the Fibonacci sequence. Roughly speaking, the intuitive meaning of the rule-set (Fib.1) is the same as the functional relation $fib(0) = 1$, when we consider a string of n "@"s as an integer n. The meaning of (Fib.2) is $fib(1) = 1$, and that of (Fib.3) is $fib(n) = fib(n_1)+fib(n_2)$ where $n=n_1+1=n_2+2$. The rule-set (Fib.4) expresses that the relation between Fin' and Fout' is the same as the relation between Fin and Fout. ✦

Before we define the derivation rule in CCFG, consider the following derivation sequence,

$$(Fin, Fout) \Rightarrow (@Fin≈@@Fin', FoutFout') \quad\quad \text{by (Fib.3)}$$
$$\Rightarrow (@Fin≈@@Fin, FoutFout). \quad\quad \text{by (Fib.4)}$$

The two couples (Fin, Fout) and (Fin', Fout') can be extracted from (@Fin≈@@Fin', FoutFout') in the first line. But these couplings can not be *uniquely* extracted from the second line, because we can not understand which of the two Fin and which of the two Fout correspond to each other as input/output of a Fibonacci number. In order to avoid such confusions, the history of derivations is added to every nonterminal symbol in a derivation sequence as follows.

Definition(numbered nonterminal symbols) For a nonterminal symbol X and an integer k ($k≥0$), the **nonterminal symbol X numbered with k** is expressed as X[k]. For a string α, $\alpha[k]$ expresses the same string as α except that all the nonterminal symbols are numbered with k, and is called α numbered with k. For a tuple $\Omega = (\alpha_1, ..., \alpha_n)$ of strings, $\Omega[k]$ expresses $(\alpha_1[k], ..., \alpha_n[k])$. For a set N of nonterminal symbols, N[k] expresses the set $\{X[k] \mid X \in N\}$. ✦

Definition(tuples of sentential forms) Given a CCFG: $G = (N, T, \Omega_S, R)$, a **tuple** Ω_k ($k≥0$) **of sentential forms** is defined as follows.

(1) The tuple $\Omega_S[0]$ numbered with zero is the initial tuple Ω_0 of sentential forms.
(2) The tuple Ω_{k+1} is a tuple of sentential forms if Ω_k is a tuple of sentential forms and satisfies the relation $\Omega_k \Rightarrow \Omega_{k+1}$.

Here the relation $\Rightarrow$ is described in the next definition. ✦

Definition(derivation rule) Given a CCFG: $G = (N, T, \Omega_S, R)$ and a tuple of sentential forms $\Omega_k = (\omega_1, ..., \omega_n)$ ($k≥0$), let $N_{\Omega k}$ be the set of all the numbered nonterminal symbols which appear in Ω_k and $Left_r$ be the set $\{X_1, ..., X_p\}$ of all the nonterminal symbols which appear in the left-hand sides of a rule-set

$$r = \{X_1 \to \alpha_1, ..., X_p \to \alpha_p, \beta_1, ..., \beta_q\} \in R, (p≥1, q≥0),$$

where $\beta_1, ..., \beta_q$ are left-hand-omitted rules. If it holds that for a certain integer m≥0,

$$Left_r[m] \subseteq N_{\Omega k},$$

then the relation $\Omega_k \Rightarrow \Omega_{k+1}$ by r is defined as follows,

$$\Omega_{k+1} = \Omega_k\{X_1[m]/\alpha_1[k+1], ..., X_p[m]/\alpha_p[k+1]\}:(\beta_1[k+1], ..., \beta_q[k+1]).$$

where $\{X_1[m]/\alpha_1[k+1], ..., X_p[m]/\alpha_p[k+1]\}$ is a multiple substitution of $\alpha_i[k+1]$ into $X_i[m]$ (p≥i≥1), and ":" is a concatenation operator for tuples. We say that Ω_k derives Ω_{k+1} by applying the rule-set r. ◄

Here the precise definition of the substitutions are omitted (see [YaNa 1]). Roughly speaking, the distributive law $\alpha(\beta \approx \gamma)\delta = \alpha\beta\delta \approx \alpha\gamma\delta$ for the metasymbol $\approx$ holds. Therefore the result of applying the substitution $\{X[i]/b \approx Z[k+1]\}$ to the string $aX[i]c \approx Y[j]$ is

$$aX[i]c \approx Y[j]\{X[i]/b \approx Z[k+1]\} = a(b \approx Z[k+1])c \approx Y[j] = abc \approx aZ[k+1]c \approx Y[j].$$

The reflexive and transitive closure of $\Rightarrow$ is expressed as $\Rightarrow^*$.

Next we define the language generated by a CCFG. Since more than one start symbol can be defined in a CCFG, the language is not a set of terminal strings but a relation over several sets of terminal strings derived from these start symbols.

Definition(CCFL) Given a CCFG: $G = (N, T, \Omega_S, R)$, where Ω_S is a n-tuple, the **Coupled Context Free Language** (**CCFL**): L(G) is a set of n-tuples of terminal strings defined as follows,

$$L(G) = \{(x_1, ..., x_n) \mid \Omega_0 \Rightarrow^* (\omega_1, ..., \omega_n, ..., \omega_m),$$
$$\omega_i = x_i^{(1)} \approx x_i^{(2)} \approx ... \approx x_i^{(ki)}, x_i^{(j)} = x_i \in T^* \text{ for all } m \geq i \geq 1, ki \geq 1, ki \geq j \geq 1\}.$$
◄

This definition means that if any ω_i which is derived from a start symbol (n≥i≥1) or a left-hand-omitted rule (m≥i≥n+1) has at least one metasymbol $\approx$, all the sides of $\approx$s in ω_i have the same terminal string as x_i. The tuple $(x_1, ..., x_n)$ is an element of the language, called a solution. If one derivation derives a solution, it is called a **successful** derivation. Otherwise a **failed** derivation.

Example(continued) Consider the derivations by the CCFG: **Fib**. First the initial couple Ω_0 of sentential forms is $\Omega_S[0] = (Fin[0], Fout[0])$. The set $N_{\Omega 0}$ of all the numbered nonterminal symbols in Ω_0 is $\{Fin[0], Fout[0]\}$. The sets of all the nonterminal symbols which appear in the left-hand sides of the rule-sets (Fib.1), (Fib.2), (Fib.3) and (Fib.4) are

$$Left_{(Fib.1)} = Left_{(Fib.2)} = Left_{(Fib.3)} = \{Fin, Fout\} \text{ and } Left_{(Fib.4)} = \{Fin', Fout'\}.$$

Because the following two conditions hold that

$$Left_{(Fib.1)}[0] = Left_{(Fib.2)}[0] = Left_{(Fib.3)}[0] \subseteq N_{\Omega 0},$$

and that for any n≥0

$$Left_{(Fib.4)}[n] \not\subset N_{\Omega 0},$$

one of the rule-sets (Fib.1), (Fib.2) and (Fib.3) can be applied to Ω_0, and the rule-set (Fib.4) can not be applied. For example, when the rule-set (Fib.3) is applied, Ω_1 is obtained as follows,

$$\Omega_1 = (@Fin[1] \approx @@Fin'[1], \qquad\qquad Fout[1]Fout'[1]).$$

When the rule-set (Fib.4) is further applied to Ω_1, then

When the rule-set (Fib.4) is further applied to Ω_1, then
$$\Omega_2 = (@\text{Fin}[1]{\approx}@@\text{Fin}[2], \qquad\qquad \text{Fout}[1]\text{Fout}[2]),$$
and the derivation may go on as follows,
$$\Omega_3 = (@@\text{Fin}[3]{\approx}@@@\text{Fin}'[3]{\approx}@@\text{Fin}[2], \ \text{Fout}[3]\text{Fout}'[3]\text{Fout}[2]),$$
$$\Omega_4 = (@@\text{Fin}[3]{\approx}@@@\text{Fin}[4]{\approx}@@\text{Fin}[2], \ \ \text{Fout}[3]\text{Fout}[4]\text{Fout}[2]),$$
$$\Omega_5 = (@@@{\approx}@@@\text{Fin}[4]{\approx}@@\text{Fin}[2], \qquad @\text{Fout}[4]\text{Fout}[2]),$$
$$\Omega_6 = (@@@{\approx}@@@{\approx}@@\text{Fin}[2], \qquad\qquad @@\text{Fout}[2]),$$
$$\Omega_7 = (@@@{\approx}@@@{\approx}@@@, \qquad\qquad\qquad @@@).$$
Because all the sides of "$@@@{\approx}@@@{\approx}@@@$" in Ω_7 are the same, the above derivation is successful and the resolvent is $(@@@, @@@)$. If the length of a terminal string is interpreted as the value of an integer, this resolvent indicates that the third number of the Fibonacci sequence is three.

In this way, the language generated by this grammar is obtained as follows,
$$\text{L(Fib)} = \{(\varepsilon, @), (@, @), (@@, @@), (@@@, @@@), (@@@@, @@@@@), ...\},$$
and for a couple (x, y) of terminal strings in L(Fib) the $|x|$-th value of the Fibonacci sequence is $|y|$, where $|x|$ means the length of x. ◧

Definition(CCFG program) A CCFG is a **CCFG program**. Its semantics is defined by the language generated by the CCFG. ◧

A CCFG program represents the relation, which is a subset of n-tuples of terminal strings derived from the program.

2.2 An extension of CFG and CCFG

In order to make CCFG programming practical, it is necessary to be able to treat various kinds of data types such as integers, lists, structures. Although a string of the length n can be used for an integer n as described above, it is not effective for the practical uses. Therefore we extend the string-based CCFG programs to the programs which can treat such data types naturally.

For example, a production rule of the form A→bB means that one of the values of A is the result of the concatenation operation between the constant value b and one of the values of B. In the same manner, we think that A→3+B means that one of the values of A is the sum of 3 and one of the values of B.

Definition(term) Let N be a finite set of nonterminal symbols and F be a finite set of functors. A **term** is defined as follows,
  (1)   A functor $c \in F$ of the arity zero is a term called a constant.
  (2)   A nonterminal symbol $X \in N$ is a term.
  (3)   If $t_1, ..., t_n$ $(n \geq 1)$ are terms and $f \in F$ is an n-ary functor, then $f(t_1, ..., t_n)$ is a term.
A term which contains no nonterminal symbols is called a ground term. ◧

Definition(t-CFG) A **term-based Context-Free Grammar** (t-CFG) is a quadruple: G = (N, F, S, P), where N is a finite set of nonterminal symbols, F a finite set of functors, S a start symbol ($\in N$) and P a finite set of context-free production rules whose right-hand side is a term. The derivation rule for the t-CFG is defined in the same manner as the string-based one. The language L(G) generated by G is the set of all the values of the ground terms derived from the start symbol S. Namely

$$L(G) = \{t\downarrow \mid S \Rightarrow^* t, t \text{ is a ground term}\},$$

where $t\downarrow$ expresses the value of the term t.　　　　　　　　　　　　　　　　　　　　🍎

More precisely speaking, $t\downarrow$ expresses the normal form of t defined in a relevant term rewriting system. For example, if we discuss the integer data type, we assume the existence of the term rewriting system which define the addition, subtraction, multiplication and division. In such a case we write **Integer** as the finite set of functors of a t-CFG. In this paper we do not discuss the relation between CFGs and term rewriting systems.

　　Definition(t-CCFG and t-CCFL) A **term-based Coupled Context-Free Grammar (t-CCFG)** and a **term-based Coupled Context-Free Language (t-CCFL)** are defined in the same way as a t-CFG and a t-CFL. A t-CCFG is also regarded as a t-CCFG **program.** 🍎

　　In the following, we call t-CCFG as CCFG if no confusions occur.

　　Example(factorial) In the following program **Fac**, the nonterminal symbol F means factorial(N) for the integer (nonterminal symbol) N.

　　Fac = ({N, F}, Integer, (N, F), R_{Fac}),

$$R_{Fac} = \{ \quad \{N\rightarrow 0, \qquad F\rightarrow 1\},$$
$$\{N\rightarrow N+1, \qquad F\rightarrow (N+1)*F\} \quad \}.$$　🍎

　　Example(car operation for lists) Supposing that a list is composed of nil, a constant c and the constructor cons, the following is the program to obtain the car-part of such a list, where the car-part of InputList is CarList, and List and List' are arbitrary lists.

　　Car = ({InputList, CarList, List, List'}, {nil, c, cons}, (InputList, CarList), R_{car}),

$$R_{car} = \{ \quad \{\text{InputList}\rightarrow\text{nil}, \qquad\qquad \text{CarList}\rightarrow\text{nil}\},$$
$$\{\text{InputList}\rightarrow\text{c}, \qquad\qquad \text{CarList}\rightarrow\text{nil}\},$$
$$\{\text{InputList}\rightarrow\text{cons(List, List')}, \quad \text{CarList}\rightarrow\text{List}\},$$
$$\{\text{List}\rightarrow\text{nil}\},$$
$$\{\text{List}\rightarrow\text{c}\},$$
$$\{\text{List}\rightarrow\text{cons(List, List')}\},$$
$$\{\text{List'}\rightarrow\text{List}\} \qquad\qquad\qquad\qquad \}. \quad 🍎$$

　　Example(Fib rewritten in t-CCFG) The program **Fib** to calculate the Fibonacci sequence is the string-based one. Here we rewrite it as the following term-based one.

　　Fib' = ({Fin, Fout, Fin', Fout'}, Integer, (Fin, Fout), R_{Fib}),

$$R_{Fib} = \{ \quad \{\text{Fin}\rightarrow 0, \qquad\qquad \text{Fout}\rightarrow 1\}, \qquad\qquad ...(\text{Fib'}.1)$$
$$\{\text{Fin}\rightarrow 1, \qquad\qquad \text{Fout}\rightarrow 1\}, \qquad\qquad ...(\text{Fib'}.2)$$

$$\{Fin \rightarrow 1+Fin \approx 2+Fin', \quad Fout \rightarrow Fout+Fout'\}, \qquad \qquad ...(Fib'.3)$$
$$\{Fin' \rightarrow Fin, \quad \quad \quad Fout' \rightarrow Fout\} \qquad \qquad \}. \quad ...(Fib'.4) \quad \clubsuit$$

3 On the relation between logic programs and CCFG programs

We find that logic programs and CCFG programs have similar characteristics. The first is that a logic program [Ll][ClMe] represents an n-ary relation between data objects by using an n-ary predicate symbol whereas a CCFG program represents the same relation by using an n-tuple of nonterminal symbols. Therefore both declarative semantics are similar to each other. The second is that a definite Horn clause in a logic program is regarded as a rewriting rule to replace a goal which is unifiable with the head of the clause by the body, and a rule-set in a CCFG program is, of course, a rewriting rule.

Such similarities are clearly understood by using the following transformation rule.

Definition(transformation rule) Transform every definite Horn clause in a (given) logic program of the form

$$p(s_1, ..., s_i):-q(t_1, ..., t_j), ..., r(u_1, ..., u_k),$$

into the rule-set of the form

$$\{P_1 \rightarrow s_1, ..., P_i \rightarrow s_i, Q_1 \approx t_1, ..., Q_j \approx t_j, ..., R_1 \approx u_1, ..., R_k \approx u_k\},$$

where $P_1, ..., P_i$ are the nonterminal symbols corresponding to the i-ary predicate symbol p, and $Q_1, ..., Q_j$ and $R_1, ..., R_k$ correspond to q and r, respectively. If two or more goals of the same predicate name q appear in the body of the clause, attach the second suffix n to every nonterminal symbol Q_m of the n-th such goal, as $Q_{m,n}$ (n=2, 3, ...).

The set of all the transformed rule-sets defines a CCFG program. $\clubsuit$

If a logic program L is transformed into a CCFG program G by the above rule, we can prove that the semantics of L for an n-ary predicate symbol p is the same as that of G with start symbols $P_1, ...P_n$ [YaNa 3].

Example The following is the logic program to calculate the Fibonacci sequence,

fib = {	fib(0,1).	...(fib.1)
	fib(1,1).	...(fib.2)
	fib(2+X, Y+Z):-fib(1+X,Y),fib(X,Z). } .	...(fib.3)

Each clause in the above logic program is transformed as follows,

$$\{Fib_1 \rightarrow 0, \quad Fib_2 \rightarrow 1\},$$
$$\{Fib_1 \rightarrow 1, \quad Fib_2 \rightarrow 1\},$$
$$\{Fib_1 \rightarrow 2+X, \quad Fib_2 \rightarrow Y+Z, \quad Fib_1 \approx 1+X, \quad Fib_2 \approx Y, \quad Fib_{1,2} \approx X, \quad Fib_{2,2} \approx Z\}.$$

We find that the first and second rule-sets are equal to the rule-sets (Fib'.1) and (Fib'.2) in the previous example if Fib_1 and Fib_2 are identified with Fin and Fout, respectively. Considering the variables X, Y and Z as expressing *arbitrary* values, the third rule-set can be further transformed into the following equivalent rule-set.

$$\{Fib_1 \rightarrow 1+Fib_1 \approx 2+Fib_{1,2}, \quad Fib_2 \rightarrow Fib_2+Fib_{2,2}\}.$$

This is equal to the rule-set (Fib'.3) if $Fib_{1,2}$ and $Fib_{2,2}$ are identified with Fin' and Fout', respectively. Because the relation between $Fib_{1,2}$ and $Fib_{2,2}$ is the same as the relation between Fib_1 and Fib_2, we can add the following rule-set as an auxiliary one,

$\{Fib_{1,2} \rightarrow Fib_1, \quad Fib_{2,2} \rightarrow Fib_2\}$.

This is equal to the rule-set (Fib'.4). In this way, we understand that the above logic program is automatically transformed into the equivalent CCFG program.

The inverse transformation from a CCFG program to the equivalent logic program has also been given in [YaNa 3]. The correctness of these transformations have been proved in [YaNa 3] by using the least fixpoint semantics.

4 Execution methods of CCFG programs

Here we briefly describe our ideas of the efficient execution methods of CCFG programs.

A CCFG program consist of several CFGs. Therefore roughly speaking, we can regard the analysis of input data as the parsing for the input CFG, and the output data can be obtained by the generator which synchronizes with the parser. Consequently the fruitful results for parsing and compiling techniques that have long been studied are expected to be applicable to the CCFG program execution.

In general, a CCFG program needs to run nondeterministically. However, in a simple case, a CCFG program can be transformed into a procedural program which runs deterministically. This can be accomplished by applying deterministic parsing methods in which the lookahead techniques play an important role. These techniques can be applied to more general cases, i.e. nondeterministic program executions. Here, we show these ideas informally by examples.

The following is the CCFG program.

$\mathbf{Exp} = (N_{Exp}, T_{Exp}, (Ei, Ep), R_{Exp})$,

$N_{Exp} = \{Ei, Ti, Fi, Ep, Tp, Fp, Id\}$,

$T_{Exp} = \{i, +, *, (,)\}$,

$R_{Exp} = \{$

$\{Ei \rightarrow Ei+Ti,$	$Ep \rightarrow +EpTp\}$,	...(Exp.1)
$\{Ei \rightarrow Ti,$	$Ep \rightarrow Tp\}$,	...(Exp.2)
$\{Ti \rightarrow Ti*Fi,$	$Tp \rightarrow *TpFp\}$,	...(Exp.3)
$\{Ti \rightarrow Fi,$	$Tp \rightarrow Fp\}$,	...(Exp.4)
$\{Fi \rightarrow Id,$	$Fp \rightarrow Id\}$,	...(Exp.5)
$\{Fi \rightarrow (Ei),$	$Fp \rightarrow Ep\}$,	...(Exp.6)
$\{Id \rightarrow i\}$	$\}$.	...(Exp.7)

This program expresses the relation between the infix and prefix notations of an arithmetic expression. For example, the first rule-set means that the expression Ei of the infix notation is composed of the expression Ei, the symbol "+" and the term Ti of the infix notation if and only if the corresponding expression Ep of the prefix notation is composed of the symbol "+", the corresponding expression Ep and the corresponding term Tp of the prefix notation. The other rules are also understood in the same way.

Here let us solve the problem to obtain the expression in the prefix notation which corresponds to the expression, such as i*i+i, in the infix notation. In this case, the start symbol Ei is in the input mode and the corresponding Ep is in the output mode, and the above CCFG program can be identified with a scheme of the syntax-directed translation [AhUl]. The translator from infix forms of expressions to prefix forms of equivalent expressions is easily implemented in a form of procedural program and this translator can produce the solution +*iii. Because the input grammar is a LR(k) grammar, the action of the translator can be deterministic.

The above example is easily understood because it can be identified with the scheme of syntax-directed translation. If there is only one input start symbol, it can be implemented as such a translator.

This method can be extended to CCFG programs which treat integers such as **Fac** or **Fib'**.

A simple program such as **Fac** can be translated to a recursive procedure by an extended recursive descent parser generator and to an iterative one by an extended LR parser generator.

We suppose that for the CCFG program **Fib'** the start symbols Fin and Fout are in the input and output modes, respectively. The input grammar is not a CFG because the right-hand side of the rule (Fib'.3) contains the metasymbol $\approx$. However in this case, considering the semantics of the metasymbol, we know that **Fib'** can be transformed into the following equivalent procedural program.

> **function** fib(Fin : integer) : integer;
> > **begin if** Fin = 0 **then** fib := 1
> > > **else if** Fin = 1 **then** fib := 1
> > > > **else** fib := fib(Fin-1)+fib(Fin-2)
> > **end**

The original CCFG program has three rule-sets. The rule-set (Fib'.1) is transformed into the part "**if** Fin = 0 **then** fib := 1", because (Fib'.1) can be applied if the nonterminal symbol Fin can be rewritten as 0. The rule-set (Fib'.2) is transformed in the same way. The rule-set (Fib'.3) is transformed into the recursive-call statement "fib := fib(Fin-1)+fib(Fin-2)", because (Fib'.3) is the recursive definition. The rule Fin→1+Fin≈2+Fin' in (Fib'.3) is translated into the equivalent two rules Fin-1→Fin and Fin-2→Fin', and these left-hand sides Fin-1 and Fin-2 are substituted into the two argument positions of the function-calls in the statement, respectively. The rule-set (Fib'.4) is implicitly applied in the second function call. We see that the above procedural program is equivalent to the original CCFG program. This is obtained by applying a top-down parsing method, the recursive descent one. However, expressions (e.g. 1+Fin) in the right-hand sides of production rules are directly applicable only in bottom-up parsing. Hence, we need, in this case, the inverted expressions (e.g. Fin-1). This may sometimes cause the implementation of this kind of transformation difficult. We are also investigating another type of transformations by extending the LR-parsing methods.

As well as logic programs, CCFG programs can express the problems which need bidirectional computations. For example, given two equivalent incomplete expressions "i*??+i)" in the infix notation and "*??i?" in the prefix notation, where each ? expresses an unknown terminal symbol, the problem is to substitute the appropriate symbol into each ? and obtain the complete equivalent expressions. This problem can be expressed as the following CCFG program,

$$\mathbf{Exp'} = (N_{Exp} \cup \{Si, Sp, V, W, X, Y, Z\}, T_{Exp}, (Si, Sp), R_{Exp} \cup R_{Exp'}),$$
$$R_{Exp'} = \{ \quad \{Si \rightarrow i*VW+i) \approx Ei, \; Sp \rightarrow *XYiZ \approx Ep\}$$

$$\{V\rightarrow i\}, \{V\rightarrow *\}, \{V\rightarrow +\}, \{V\rightarrow (\}, \{V\rightarrow)\},$$
$$\{W\rightarrow i\}, \{W\rightarrow *\}, \{W\rightarrow +\}, \{W\rightarrow (\}, \{W\rightarrow)\},$$
$$\{X\rightarrow i\}, \{X\rightarrow *\}, \{X\rightarrow +\},$$
$$\{Y\rightarrow i\}, \{Y\rightarrow *\}, \{Y\rightarrow +\},$$
$$\{Z\rightarrow i\}, \{Z\rightarrow *\}, \{Z\rightarrow +\} \qquad\qquad \},$$

where N_{Exp}, T_{Exp}, and R_{Exp} have been defined in the program **Exp**. If (Si, Sp) successfully derives the couple $(x{\approx}x, y{\approx}y)$ of terminal strings, (x, y) gives the solution. Here we show one efficient method to obtain them which uses the lookahead technique.

Before to begin the execution we first compute the two kinds of lookahead sets, directors

$$DIRECTOR_L(X\rightarrow\alpha,k) = \{x \mid S\Rightarrow^*\beta X\gamma\Rightarrow\beta\alpha\gamma\Rightarrow^*\beta x..., |x| = k, x\in T^*\},$$

and

$$DIRECTOR_R(X\rightarrow\alpha,k) = \{x \mid S\Rightarrow^*\beta X\gamma\Rightarrow\beta\alpha\gamma\Rightarrow^*...x\gamma, |x| = k, x\in T^*\},$$

for every production rule $X\rightarrow\alpha$ in the CCFG program and a certain k. Let k=2 in the following example. Some of the directors are

$$DIRECTOR_L(Ep\rightarrow+EpTp, 2) = \{+i, ++, +*\},$$
$$DIRECTOR_L(Ep\rightarrow Tp, \quad 2) = \{i, +i, ++, +*, *i, *+, **\},$$
$$...$$

The first derivation of the derivation sequence from the couple of start symbols is given as follows,

(Si[0], Sp[0]) $\Rightarrow$ (i*V[1]W[1]+i)$\approx$Ei[1], *X[1]Y[1]iZ[1]$\approx$Ep[1]).

Next we can rewrite (Ei[1], Ep[1]), V[1], W[1], X[1], Y[1] or Z[1]. However, the actual rewriting should be the application of (Exp.2) as follows,

$\Rightarrow$ (i*V[1]W[1]+i)$\approx$Ti[2], *X[1]Y[1]iZ[1]$\approx$Tp[2]), $\qquad\qquad$ by (Exp.2)

because *...$\approx$Ep[1] and we see that *...$\in$ DIRECTOR$_L$(Ep$\rightarrow$Tp,2) but *...$\notin$ DIRECTOR$_L$(Ep$\rightarrow$+EpTp,2). This derivation is deterministic. The next derivation is

$\Rightarrow$ (i*V[1]W[1]+i)$\approx$Ti[3]*Fi[3], *X[1]Y[1]iZ[1]$\approx$*Tp[3]Fp[3]), by (Exp.3)

because i*...$\approx$Ti[2] and i*$\in$ DIRECTOR$_L$(Ti$\rightarrow$Ti*Fi,2) but i*$\notin$ DIRECTOR$_L$(Ti$\rightarrow$Fi,2). This derivation is also deterministic. The next is

$\Rightarrow$ (i*V[1]W[1]+i)$\approx$Ti[3]*(Ei[4]), *Tp[3]Ep[4]$\approx$*X[1]Y[1]iZ[1]), by (Exp.6)

because ...)$\approx$...Fi[3], and ...)$\in$ DIRECTOR$_R$(Fi$\rightarrow$(Ei),2) but ...)$\notin$ DIRECTOR$_R$(Fi$\rightarrow$Id,2)....

In this way, the couple of sentential forms can be rewritten as (i*(i+i)$\approx$i*(i+i), *i+ii$\approx$*i+ii). This is the solution. In the above derivation sequence, the number of the deterministic derivations is 16 and that of the nondeterministic is zero. In the case that k=1, the numbers of the deterministic and of the nondeterministic are 21 and 3, respectively. These facts mean that the longer the lookahead strings are, the more deterministic the execution is.

5 Relations between CCFG programs and some other grammar systems

There are many formal systems based on Chomsky's formal grammars. CCFG programs are, of course, one of them, and so are attribute grammars, attribute coupled grammars, two-level grammars and so on. In this section, we discuss the relation between CCFG programs and each of them.

An attribute grammar (AG) [Kn][Pa] defines the syntax of input data by using its underlying

CFG and the semantics by attribute evaluation rules. It can be automatically transformed into the equivalent CCFG program. The underlying grammar is transformed into an input CFG in the transformed CCFG program. The semantic rules which compute the values of synthesized attributes are transformed into output CFGs in the CCFG program, and the semantic rules which compute the values of inherited attributes are transformed into auxiliary CFGs. For example, the following AG computes the value of an input binary number string.

$$
\begin{aligned}
F \rightarrow L \quad \{ \quad & F.val = L.val \\
& L.pos = 0 \quad \} \\
L \rightarrow B \quad \{ \quad & L.val = B.val \\
& B.pos = L.pos \quad \} \\
L_1 \rightarrow L_2 \, B \quad \{ \quad & L_1.val = L_2.val + B.val \\
& L_2.pos = L_1.pos + 1 \\
& B.pos = L_1.pos \quad \} \\
B \rightarrow 0 \quad \{ \quad & B.val = 0 \quad \} \\
B \rightarrow 1 \quad \{ \quad & B.val = 2^{B.pos} \quad \}
\end{aligned}
$$

Here "$... \rightarrow ...$" is a production rule, "$\{ \, ...=... \, \}$" is a set of the corresponding semantic rules and F is the start symbol. If the input is "101", its value 5 is computed as the attribute F.val. This AG is transformed into the following CCFG program,

$$Ag = (\{F, Fval, L, Lval, Lpos, B, Bval, Bpos\}, \{0, 1\} \cup Integer, (F, Fval), R_{Ag}),$$

$$
\begin{aligned}
R_{Ag} = \{ \quad & \{F \rightarrow L, Fval \rightarrow Lval, Lpos \approx 0\}, \\
& \{L \rightarrow B, Lval \rightarrow Bval, Lpos \rightarrow Bpos\}, \\
& \{L \rightarrow LB, Lval \rightarrow Lval + Bval, Lpos \rightarrow Bpos, Lpos \approx Bpos + 1\}, \\
& \{B \rightarrow 0, Bval \rightarrow 0, Bpos \rightarrow Any\}, \\
& \{B \rightarrow 1, Bval \rightarrow 2^{Any}, Bpos \rightarrow Any\} \quad \}.
\end{aligned}
$$

Here Any is the special symbol which means an arbitrary value. We see that

$$(F, Fval) \Rightarrow^* (101, 5, ...).$$

In this way, it might be easy to understand that every AG can be automatically transformed into the equivalent CCFG program, though we omit the precise discussion.

An attribute coupled grammar (ACG) [GaGi][Gi] is a kind of AG which has only one synthesized attribute with its start symbol. One grammar describes one part of compiler specifications and a set of grammars, chained by connecting the output of one grammar with the input of another grammar, describe the whole compiler. Such a connection is useful to support modularity of compiler specifications. We can see the relation between CCFG programs and ACGs in the same way as the above discussion. Namely, arbitrary ACGs and their connections can be automatically transformed into the equivalent CCFG program. For example, suppose that two ACGs are transformed into the two equivalent CCFG programs, whose tuples of start symbols are (X, Xval) and (Y, Yval), respectively. Then the connection between Xval and Y is implemented as the following rule-set,

$$\{Z \rightarrow X, Xval \approx Y, Zval \rightarrow Yval\}.$$

Considering n ACGs whose tuples of start symbols are $(X_1, X_1val) ... (X_n, X_nval)$ $(n \geq 2)$, their connections are implemented as follows,

$$\{Z \rightarrow X_1, X_1val \approx X_2, X_2val \approx X_3, ..., Zval \rightarrow X_nval\}.$$

In [GaGi][Gi], there is the algorithm to transform several ACGs into one ACG. It will be possible to develop this kind of transformation algorithm for CCFG programs by using unfold/fold program transformation methods described in [YaNa 4].

We have just shown the similarities of CCFG programs to AGs and ACGs. An AG (or ACG) is a special class of CCFG programs in the sense that the AG (or ACG) has only one input grammar, which is sufficient because the main purposes of such an AG and ACG are to express translators or compilers, and it is certain that AGs and ACGs can express them easier than CCFG programs. On the other hand, CCFG programs is to express general purpose programs rather than translators or compilers. For this purpose CCFG programs have several facilities such as multiple input and output grammars, bidirectional nondeterministic computations, arbitrary constraints expressed by $\approx$ and various kinds of data types.

Two-level grammars or W-grammars [Wi][Pa] increase their expressive power by introducing higher order concept into CFGs. On the other hand, CCFG programs are based on a first order theory and increase their expressive power by combining several CFGs horizontally, i.e., by putting rules side by side, and introducing the metasymbol $\approx$. In this sense, the central concepts of two-level grammars, in which grammars are connected vertically, and CCFG programs are quite different and, adding to say, orthogonal to each other. Hence it is possible to define *two-level CCFG* by mixing them. Since the concept of two-level grammars is considered to give the polymorphism of data types, it will become our advanced subject for extending CCFG programs.

There is a new approach to understand two-level grammars and logic programs [DeMa]. In [DeMa], logic programs are recognized as a special class of two-level grammars mainly from the view point of operational semantics. The SLD-resolution can be simulated by the derivation procedure of the equivalent two-level grammar, and vice versa. This is different from our approach described in section three, because CCFG programs and logic programs are the first-order and the relation between them is considered from the view point of declarative semantics, especially of the least fixpoint semantics [YaNa 3], and it is emphasized that CCFG programs express *relations* between data objects. The two approaches in [DeMa] and ours to understand the relationship between logic and grammar are quite different.

6 Concluding remarks

In this paper, we have introduced CCFG and its interpretation as a programming language, and described the relationship between CCFG programs and logic programs. We can say that both programs have the *dual* structures with each other. The major syntactic difference between CCFG programs and logic programs is that CFGs are embedded in CCFG programs. Therefore, it is expected that lookahead techniques in the parsing methods may be effectively used for the methods of program executions. Some examples of the executions have been shown.

The study of CCFG programming has just started. Other interesting topics which we are studying but have not mentioned here are:

(1) to define the least fixpoint semantics of CCFG programs [YaNa 2].

(2) to unify CCFG programs with logic and functional programs.

(3) to obtain the program transformation rules, including unfolding and folding, for

CCFG programs [NaYa][YaNa 4].

(4)   to design a practical programming language based on CCFG.

(5)   to implement the processor (interpreter and compiler) for such a language [YaNa 5].

References

[AhUl]   Aho, A. V. and Ullman, J. D. : *The Theory of Parsing, Translation, and Compiling*, Volume I: Parsing, Prentice-Hall (1972).

[DeMa]   Deransart, P. and Maluszynski, J. : A Grammatical View of Logic Programming, in this volume.

[GaGi]   Ganzinger, H. and Giegerich, R. : Attribute Coupled Grammars, Proc. ACM SIGPLAN '84 Symposium on Compiler Construction, *SIGPLAN Notices*, Vol.19, NO.6 (1984).

[Gi]   Giegerich, R. : Composition and Evaluation of Attribute Coupled Grammars, *Acta Informatica*, Vol.25, pp.355-423 (1988).

[ClMe]   Clocksin, W. F. and Mellish, C. S. : *Programming in Prolog*, Springer-Verlag (1981).

[Ja]   Jackson, M. A. : *Principles of Program Design*, Academic Press (1975).

[Kn]   Knuth, D. E. : Semantics of Context-Free Languages, *Math. Syst. Th.* Vol.2, NO.2 (1968), correct ibid. Vol.5, No.1 (1971).

[Ll]   Lloyd, J. W. : *Foundation of Logic Programming*, Springer-Verlag (1984).

[NaSa]   Nakata, I. and Sassa, M. : Regular Expressions with semantics and their Application to Data Structure Directed Programs, *Computer Software*, Vol.3, No.1, pp.47-56 (1986).(*In Japanese*)

[NaYa]   Nakata, I. and Yamashita, Y. : Program transformations in Coupled Context-Free Grammar, *Computer Software*, Vol.5, NO.2 (1988). (*In Japanese*)

[Pa]   Pagan, F. G. : *Formal Specification of Programming Languages*, Prentice-Hall (1981).

[Wi]   van Wijnggaarden, A. : *Revised Report on the Algorithmic Language ALGOL 68*, Springer-Verlag (1976).

[YaNa 1]   Yamashita, Y. and Nakata, I. : Programming in Coupled Context-Free Grammars, Technical Report ISE-TR-88-70, University of Tsukuba (1988).

[YaNa 2]   Yamashita, Y. and Nakata, I. : The Least Fixpoint Semantics of CCFG Programs, an internal document (1987).

[YaNa 3]   Yamashita, Y. and Nakata, I. : On the Relation between CCFG Programs and Logic Programs, Technical Report ISE-TR-88-71, University of Tsukuba (1988).

[YaNa 4]   Yamashita, Y. and Nakata, I. : The Unfold/Fold Program Transformation in CCFG Programs, Technical Report ISE-TR-88-72, University of Tsukuba (1988).

[YaNa 5]   Yamashita, Y. and Nakata, I. : The Execution Methods in the Programming Language Based Coupled Context-Free Grammar, *Proc. 28-th Programming Simposium*, Japan Information Processing Society (1987). (*In Japanese*).

A bottom-up adaptation of Earley's parsing algorithm

Frédéric Voisin

Laboratoire de Recherche en Informatique, U.A. 410 du CNRS
Bât 490, Université Paris-Sud, 91405 Orsay CEDEX (France)

Introduction: in a compiler for a standard programming language, parsing is surely the step which is, by now, the best handled. Although the design of an efficient error recovery scheme, for example, is a still difficult problem, most of the work may be automated using parser generators or, more generally, compiler-compilers [4]. Although parsing may no longer be a problem for programming languages, there are still areas where this automatic generation of parsers is not possible, due to the limited class of grammars which can be handled this way. This happens, for example, for the processing of natural languages, whose underlying grammars are ambiguous, or for the interactive environments built for the "new generation of programming languages" (specification languages, functional or logic programming languages) which offer, often, a too restricted user-interface. These new programming languages, with a very high degree of abstraction, should include syntactical facilities to ease, as most as possible, the work for the user: presence of a flexible syntax, overloading of operators, user-defined coercions to introduce sub-types...

The work described in this paper is related to such an environment: the **Asspegique** system is an integrated algebraic specification environment, which allows to write, test and use algebraic specifications in various ways (assisted program construction, automatic generation of data tests from specifications...) [2,5,7]. We recall that algebraic specifications are composed of declarations of domain names (sorts), operator names over these sorts (the signature) and logical formulæ describing the relationships between the operators (the axioms). These formulæ must be checked for syntactical correctness (are they valid combinations of operators?) and the need for a parsing system is clear. In addition to the semantic aspects, the legibility and correctness of these specifications are also related to the ease, for the designer, of expressing the axioms: it should be possible to use classical notations when they exist (mathematical operators), as well as less usual, more textual, notations when they are preferable (arbitrary combination of operands and symbols) [3]. A complete description of the consequences of such syntactical problems is presented in [11]. The main characteristic is that the designer of the parser no longer has the choice of the grammar for the language to be parsed, and this grammar can therefore have undesirable features (left recursivity, ambiguities due to the user-defined syntax or to overloaded operators and coercions) which make deterministic parsing methods not applicable.

In such a case, one has to use a general parsing method, which does not require any property of the grammar to be considered [1,8,10]. Among these methods, the best known is due to J. Earley [6]: it computes "in parallel" the set of all partial derivations which are compatible with a prefix of the input. By sharing the steps which are common to several partial derivations, it allows for a time complexity which is acceptable (cubic), at least in contexts where the inputs are not too long. In [11], we presented another parsing method, based on tries, well-adapted to our context of parsing in an environment for algebraic specifications. Our method works by privileging a particular parse tree in the case of ambiguous expressions, using heuristics to select the next move when several moves are possible. These heuristics allow to predict which parse tree will be returned in the case of an ambiguous expression (and therefore decrease the need for disambiguating indications), but can lead to the rejection of correct inputs.

```
algorithm Earley(w₁ ... wₙ)
I₀ ← Closure({ [S→.α, 0] / (S→α) ∈ G })
for i := 1 to n do
    if Iᵢ₋₁ = ∅ then return (failure)
    else Iᵢ ← Closure({ [X→αwᵢ.β, j] / [X→α.wᵢ β, j] ∈ Iᵢ₋₁}) fi
end
if {(S→α) ∈ G / [S→α., 0] ∈ Iₙ} ≠ ∅ then return (success) else return (failure) fi
end algorithm


function Closure(I)
while it is possible to add new items to I do
    if [Y→α.Xβ, j] ∈ I then  for every (X→γ) ∈ G do add [X→.γ, i] to I end  fi
    if [X→γ., j] ∈ I then  for every [Y→α.Xβ, k] ∈ Iⱼ do  add [Y→αX.β, k] to I end  fi
end
end function
```

Figure 1: A high-level description of Earley's algorithm

The method we present here is derived from Earley's parsing method and from our previous work. It can be viewed as a bottom-up adaptation of Earley's algorithm, guided by a representation of the grammar by tries. It leads to improved performances, although it does not change the main order term of the complexity, and a better error diagnostic. This last point is a classical benefit of bottom-up algorithms over top-down ones. We shall first review Earley's algorithm and then present our method, in an implementation-oriented way. A more abstract description, along with the proof of its correctness and complexity, is presented in [12].

Notations: we do not recall here the classical notions of languages, grammars or derivations [1]. We note $G = (V_N, V_t, S, P)$ the grammar used, where V_N and V_t are the disjoint sets of non-terminal and terminal symbols. One of the characteristics of our overall context is that the axiom S derives directly into any non-terminal symbol, or conversely any non-terminal can be taken for axiom. Non-terminals symbols will be represented by upper-case letters, terminal symbols by lower-case letters and undistinguished combinations of symbols by greek letters, with ε standing for the empty word. We note $w = w_1 \ldots w_n$ the input to be parsed, n being its length.

1. Earley's Algorithm: the algorithm aims at computing a collection of sets, noted $I_0 \ldots I_n$, of all items of the general form $[A\to\alpha.\beta, j]$, where $(A \to \alpha\beta)$ is a production in G, for which the following property holds:

$$([A \to \alpha.\beta, j] \in I_i) \Leftrightarrow (\exists\, \gamma, \delta \in (V_N \cup V_t)^* : S\to^*\gamma A\delta \wedge \gamma \to^* w_1 \ldots w_j) \wedge \alpha\to^* w_{j+1} \ldots w_i.$$

An item symbolizes the progression in a production $(A \to \alpha\beta)$, with α deriving $w_{j+1} \ldots w_i$, which can be used to extend a partial derivation of the prefix $w_1 \ldots w_j$. Once these sets are computed, we have the following characterization: $w \in L(G) \Leftrightarrow \exists\, (S \to \alpha) \in P : [S \to \alpha., 0] \in I_n$.

A high-level description of an algorithm to compute this collection of items is given in Figure 1 and the sets of items computed for a short example are presented in Figure 2.

Here, we want to emphasize the following property, an easy consequence of the definition of items:

$$([A \to \alpha.\beta, j] \in I_i) \Leftrightarrow \alpha \to^* w_{j+1} \ldots w_i \wedge (\exists [Y \to \gamma.X\delta, k] \in I_j : A \in Init(X)).$$

It is valid except for the initialization of I_0, where $Init$ is the classical function defined over V_N by: $Init(X) = \{A \in V_N\ /\ \exists\, \eta \in (V_t \cup V_N)^* : X\to^* A\eta\}$.

$$GEA : \begin{cases} E \rightarrow E + T \mid T \\ T \rightarrow T \times F \mid F \\ F \rightarrow a \end{cases}$$

I_0	I_1	I_2	I_3	I_4	I_5
$[E \rightarrow .E + T, 0]$	$[F \rightarrow a., 0]$	$[E \rightarrow E + .T, 0]$	$[F \rightarrow a., 2]$	$[T \rightarrow T \times .F, 2]$	$[F \rightarrow a., 4]$
$[E \rightarrow .T, 0]$	$[T \rightarrow F., 0]$	$[T \rightarrow .T \times F, 2]$	$[T \rightarrow F., 2]$	$[F \rightarrow .a, 4]$	$[T \rightarrow T \times F., 2]$
$[T \rightarrow .T \times F, 0]$	$[T \rightarrow T. \times F, 0]$	$[T \rightarrow .F, 2]$	$[T \rightarrow T. \times F, 2]$		$\mathbf{[E \rightarrow E + T., 0]}$
$[T \rightarrow .F, 0]$	$[E \rightarrow T., 0]$	$[F \rightarrow .a, 2]$	$[E \rightarrow E + T., 0]$		$[T \rightarrow T. \times F, 2]$
$[F \rightarrow .a, 0]$	$[E \rightarrow E. + T, 0]$		$[E \rightarrow E. + T, 0]$		$[E \rightarrow E. + T, 0]$

For grammar GEA, with axiom E, and input $w = a + a \times a$ the algorithm computes the sets of items above and accepts w as correct, because of the presence of the item in Boldface in I_5.

Figure 2: the sets of items computed for grammar GEA and input $w = a + a \times a$

This property makes explicit when an item $[A \rightarrow \alpha.\beta, j]$ should appear in a set I_i: in addition to the derivation of the corresponding substring $w_{j+1} \ldots w_i$, its left-hand side A must be in the $Init$ set for at least one symbol X of V_N such that there is an item in I_j with the dot in front of X. This last condition is satisfied by the selection, by the first rule of function $Closure$, of relevant left-hand sides. This is the so-called "prediction" step. Our algorithm will avoid this step and use a more direct computation of relevant items.

Complexity: we recall that this parsing algorithm can handle any context-free grammar and works with a time complexity which is cubic and a space complexity which is quadratic wrt. the length of input. The algorithm works with a lower complexity when used with an appropriate grammar: time complexity becomes quadratic for a non-ambiguous grammar and even linear if the grammar has a LR-like property. A less favorable point is that the coefficients of the main order terms of the complexities are quite high: they are related to the size of the grammar, that is to the sum of the length of the right-hand sides of the productions in G.

Although it computes the set of all the contexts (i.e. partial derivations) in which the parser can be at a given point, Earley's algorithm can be viewed as a top-down algorithm: parsing starts from the axiom and, for a given non-terminal, uses for the remaining input only derivations starting from this non-terminal. It thus avoids all the productions which are useless in a given context and detects an error on the first character for which this is possible in a left to right parsing of the input. In fact, this benefit may sometimes be inadequate for error explanation: in the case of an input which is incorrect only because of a "type mismatch", the parser will stop at the beginning of the wrong operand, with the simple but unsatisfactory explanation that parsing is blocked at that point.

2. Algebraic specifications and context-free grammars: we recall that the actual use of our algorithm is an algebraic specification environment. The user defines his/her own operators by providing their syntax and profile. The syntax is any combination of symbols and of occurrences of the reserved symbol "_" which stands for the position of an operand in a call to this operator (distfix syntax [9]). The only restrictions are that the number of sorts in the domain must be equal to the number of "_" and the coercions (operators whose syntax is made by a unique "_") must define an acyclic relation over sorts. No other restriction exists, either on a single operator or on the global set of operators. We give in Figure 3 two specifications to illustrate these points.

The data structure: A specification defines a context-free grammar with the sorts standing for non-terminal symbols. By "reversing the arrow" in its declaration, each operator is viewed as a production of the grammar, its left-hand side being the range and its right-hand side the syntax, with every occurrence of "_" replaced by the corresponding sort of the domain. For example the

```
SPEC : NATURAL WITH : BOOLEAN          SPEC : POLYNOMIAL WITH : NATURAL
SORT: Nat                              SORTS: Mono Poly
OPERATIONS :                           OPERATIONS:
  zero  :            → Nat               _ + _  : Poly Mono → Poly
  s _   : Nat     → Nat                  _      : Mono      → Poly
  _ + _: Nat Nat → Nat                   _ X** _ : Nat Nat   → Mono
  _ × _: Nat Nat → Nat                   _      : Nat       → Mono
  _ ≤ _: Nat Nat → Bool                  _ < _ > : Poly Nat  → Nat
VARIABLES : x, y : Nat                 VARIABLES: coef, exp, val : Nat;
AXIOMS :                                          M : Mono; P : Poly
  plus-a  : zero + y    = y            AXIOMS :
  plus-b  : (s x) + y   = s (x + y)      eval-cst : coef < val >          = coef
  times-a : zero × y    = zero          eval-0  : coef X** 0 < val >     = coef
  times-b : (s x) × y   = y + (x × y)    eval-s  : coef X** s exp <val> =
  inf-a   : zero ≤ y    = true                        val × (coef X** exp <val>)
  inf-b   : (s x) ≤ zero = false        eval-+  : (P + M) < val >     =
  inf-c   : (s x) ≤ (s y) = x ≤ y                   (parse-as Nat (P < val >) + (M < val >))
END                                    END
```

Figure 3: two pieces of specification

production $Nat \rightarrow Nat + Nat$ is associated with the operator $\_ + \_ : Nat \; Nat \rightarrow Nat$ and $Polynomial \rightarrow Monomial$ with $\_ : Monomial \rightarrow Polynomial$.

Following [11], we associate a trie with every set of operators: a grammar is stored as a trie built with the right-hand sides of the productions, each arc being labelled by a symbol of $V_N \cup V_t$. Each leaf stores the left-hand side(s) of the production(s) associated with the path leading to that leaf. It contains several non-terminals if there are several productions with the same right-hand side. The coercions from a sort X to a sort Y, which correspond, from a parsing standpoint, to a *chain derivation* $Y \rightarrow^* X$, deserve a special handling, since coercions usually introduce, in algebraic specifications, the notion of subsorts. The coercions are not included in the trie and their use will be represented in this paper by the relation over sorts $X \subseteq Y$, recalling the relation which holds between the languages generated by X and Y. As ε-productions have no meaning in algebraic specifications, they are not used and will not be considered. Our algorithm can nevertheless be readily extended to handle ε-productions. Finally, the grammar is defined incrementally and can be very ambiguous, especially because of coercions and overloaded operators.

Note: except for coercions, every prefix of a right-hand side of a production in G corresponds to the sequence of labels on the path from the root to exactly one vertex in the trie, thanks to the trie structure. This gives a convenient and unambiguous way to name the corresponding vertex, similar to the usual notion of *occurrence* in a tree, except that we use sequences of symbols rather sequences of ranks in lists of successors. We shall therefore name each vertex by its corresponding occurrence. The root is referenced by ε, as usual.

We add new arcs to the trie representing a grammar, to embed part of the computation done in the *Closure* function of Earley's algorithm. These new arcs make our algorithm closer to a classical tree traversal (with the use of a stack to recognize a context-free language !):

- first, for each occurrence αY, with $\alpha \neq \varepsilon$, we add an arc between this occurrence and the root of the trie (cf. Figure 4a). Such an arc, implicitly labelled by ε, is therefore added for every instance of a non-terminal which is not the first symbol of a production. Intuitively, if one is expecting a non-terminal, one is expecting everything it can derive ! The new arcs bypass every sequence of derivations corresponding to the replacement of leading non-terminals, by directly pointing to the productions with a leading terminal symbol. All these productions are represented by a unique

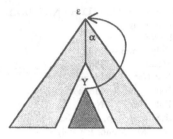

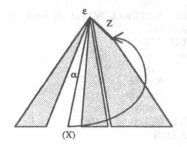

Figure 4.a

Figure 4.b

vertex: the root. $O(|P|)$ different first parts of items may be represented by a unique pointer and this can occur for every second part of items. This happens, for example, for I_0 which will include a unique element instead of the $|P|$ items required with the standard algorithm: since every non-terminal can be derived from the axiom, every production would be included in I_0. Nevertheless, the target of the arc being the root of the whole trie, one is ready to accept not only what can be derived from a given non-terminal but, more generally, any terminal symbol directly derived from a non-terminal. This leads to useless moves if no left-hand side of the production about to be started is included in the *Init* set for the expected non-terminal.

- other arcs, noted *first-op*, connect each leaf α to some of the occurrences Z at height 1: there is an arc $\alpha \longmapsto Z$ for each production $(X \to \alpha)$ in G such that $X \subseteq Z$ (cf. Figure 4.b). This kind of arc will be used to simulate the derivations by leading non-terminals which have been suppressed, according to the preceding point. Again, this leads to useless moves each time the target of the new arc corresponds to productions whose left-hand sides are not included in the *Init* set for an expected non-terminal.

The possibility to perform useless moves implies that an error would not be detected as soon as possible, since we can consider productions which are useless in the current context of parsing. We shall explain in Section 3 how this problem can be dealt with.

Note: The reader may have noticed similarities between our data structure and the one used in the Knuth-Morris-Pratt's (KMP) algorithm for fast string matching. When described in terms of a finite automaton, KMP represents the set of patterns to be matched by a trie (special case of finite automaton) enriched by additional transitions: an arc connects every prefix of a pattern to its longest suffix, which is also a prefix of (another) pattern. In case of failure of a partial match, these arcs give the smallest backtracking on the input needed to find another partial match of a pattern, without having to test again the letters stored between the root of the trie and the target of the arc. Similarly, our arcs explicitly show how to combine productions ! Of course parsing is not as easy as string matching: arcs are labelled not only by terminal symbols but also by non-terminals, corresponding to whole substrings. Finally, there must be no overlapping, nor holes, in the parts of the input derived by non-terminals: incorrect parts of input are not discarded !

3. An informal description of the algorithm: the input is scanned from left to right and, for each letter of input, we compute the set of all the occurrences in the trie which can derive the corresponding prefix of input. With every such occurrence α we shall dynamically associate a pair $<\beta, j>$, called the context of occurrence α. Here, j is an index in the input and β an occurrence which can be extended by at least one non-terminal symbol X. The meaning of the association between α, and $<\beta, j>$ is the following: the path leading to the occurrence α has been initiated by the arrival at step j on occurrence β; β was then suspended, waiting for a derivation of X, and α is expected to be part of such a derivation.

As other parsing methods, our algorithm aims at pasting partial derivations: if $(A \rightarrow \alpha)$ and $(B \rightarrow \beta C \gamma)$ are two productions such that $\beta \rightarrow^* w'$ and $\alpha \rightarrow^* w''$, could the tree rooted by A be grafted in C ? In such a case, one should have $A \subseteq C$ and w' and w'' should be adjacent. This last constraint is represented by the index in the context: it is the index in the input at which w'' must have started. The first part of the context shows where the grafting will occur: here, after β. In Earley's algorithm our context corresponds to the set of all the items which have a non-terminal at the right of the dot, in the set of items referenced by the index.

Our algorithm computes, for each step, the list of the "active" occurrences with their context. It also computes the list of the occurrences and contexts, suspended at that step. Given an active occurrence α, three kinds of moves compute the list of occurrences that will be used at the next step. They correspond to the different ways to extend a partial derivation:

a) α is the source of an arc labelled by the current input symbol: the target vertex is added to the new list of occurrences and is associated with the context of α. The input character is shifted.

b) α is the source of some arcs labelled by non-terminals: α is then suspended with its context, until a derivation of one of the expected non-terminals is found. To initiate such a derivation, the root of the trie is added to the new list of occurrences, with a context formed by the suspended occurrence α and the current index in the input.

c) α is a leaf: it is time to consider its context, of the form $<\beta, j>$, where β is an occurrence suspended at step j. Two kinds of moves are performed:

- if there are any, the arcs between the leaf α and the occurrences at height 1 are considered and their targets added to the list of occurrences with the same context than α.

- one tries to reactivate the suspended occurrence β: suppose that βY is a prefix of production and let $(X \rightarrow \alpha)$ be a production associated with leaf α. If $X \subseteq Y$, then βY is added to the new list of occurrences, with the context that β had at the time it was suspended. We just find an instance of the expected non-terminal Y and may go further down the path.

In addition to the list of active occurrences and their contexts, one only needs to keep the lists of occurrences and contexts suspended during the previous steps. It is worth noticing that an occurrence can be reactivated several times, even at different steps, should the input be ambiguous.

The algorithm is started with an initial list of occurrences restricted to the root of the trie, ε, with $<\varepsilon, 0>$ as context ! It simplifies the handling of the prefixes of the input included in the language, via the moves computed for a leaf. Once the end of the input is reached, the algorithm succeeds if and only if the current list of occurrences includes a leaf whose context is the starting context $<\varepsilon, 0>$.

The new algorithm: at the moment, the algorithm described in Figure 5 is only a recognizer: it does not built any parse tree but computes the set of all non-terminals which can derive into the input. The algorithm returns "success" if this set is not empty and "failure" otherwise.

Notations: - *is-a-leaf* : a predicate which characterizes the leaves
- $X \subseteq Y : Y \rightarrow^* X$ by a chain derivation
- *Suspended*$[j]$, $0 \leq j \leq n$: the list of occurrences and contexts suspended at step j
- *first-op* : $Z \in$ *first-op*$(\alpha) \Leftrightarrow \exists(X \rightarrow \alpha) \in G : X \subseteq Z$

Remarks :
- the inner loop of the algorithm applies the three kinds of moves described above to all the occurrences computed, until nothing new can be obtained. The passage from one letter to the next one only occurs at the end of this loop: it would allow a correct handling of possible ε-productions, via the call of function *Reduction* for the leaves representing ε-productions.

algorithm Upley($w_1 \ldots w_n$)
var *actives* $\leftarrow$ {$<\varepsilon, <\varepsilon, 0>>$}; *new, computed, aux* $\leftarrow \emptyset$
for $i \leftarrow 0$ **to** n **do**
  if *actives* $= \emptyset$ **then return** (failure) **fi** ;
  new $\leftarrow$ *actives*; *computed* $\leftarrow$ *actives*; *actives* $\leftarrow \emptyset$
  while *new* $\neq \emptyset$ **do**
    for every $<\alpha, <\beta, j>> \in$ *new* **do**
      new $\leftarrow$ *new* $\setminus$ {$<\alpha, <\beta, j>>$};
      if $\exists x \in V_t : \alpha x$ is an occurrence **then** add $<\alpha, <\beta, j>>$ to *actives* **fi** ;
      if there is an arc $\alpha \longmapsto \varepsilon$ **then**
        add $<\varepsilon, <\alpha, i>>$ to *actives*; add $<\beta, j>$ to *Suspended*[i] **fi** ;
      if *is-a-leaf*(α) **then**
        aux $\leftarrow$ *Reduction*($<\alpha, <\beta, j>>$) $\setminus$ *computed*;
        add *aux* to *new* ; add *aux* to *computed* **fi**
    end
  end
  if $i \neq n$ **then** *actives* $\leftarrow$ { $<\alpha w_{i+1}, <\beta, j>> / <\alpha, <\beta, j>> \in$ *actives*} **fi**
end
if { $T \in V_N / \exists (X \rightarrow \alpha) \in G : <\alpha, <\varepsilon, 0>> \in$ *computed* $\wedge X \subseteq T$} $\neq \emptyset$
  then return (success) **else return** (failure) **fi**
end algorithm ;

function *Reduction*($<\alpha, <\beta, j>>$)
var *res* $\leftarrow$ {$<Z, <\beta, j>> / Z \in$ *first-op*(α)};
for every $(X \rightarrow \alpha) \in G$, βY an occurrence : $X \subseteq Y$ **do**
  for every $<\gamma, k> \in$ *Suspended*[j] **do** add $<\beta Y, <\gamma, k>>$ to *res* **end**
end ;
return (res)
end function

Figure 5: the new algorithm

- the context could be reduced to the index in the input where the search for an operand to match a non-terminal started, as in Earley's algorithm. By including the suspended occurrence in the context, we save an equivalent search for it when the operand is completed.

Figure 6 presents the complete trie for the grammar *GEA* of Figure 2 (remember that coercions $F \subseteq T \subseteq E$ are not included in the trie) and the list of occurrences computed for the parsing of $w = a + a \times a$. The leaf in Boldface included in the last line shows that w is correct. The reader may have noticed that the pairs $<E, <E+, 2>>$ computed at step 3, $<E, <T\times, 4>>$ and $<E, <E+, 2>>$ computed at step 5 are useless, since they cannot occur in any derivation. Similarly, $<T, <T\times, 4>>$ is useless in step 5. They illustrate the problem of useless moves, evoked earlier in this section.

More insights into the algorithm: when we described Earley's algorithm, we emphasized the role of the *Init* relation for the computation of items. How is the relation used in our algorithm?

- it should be clear that all items [$X \rightarrow .a\delta$, j] are implicitly represented by the arcs between the non-terminals and the root of the trie, since ε is the common prefix of all the productions with a leading terminal symbol. The passage from one step to the next one by a shift of the current input symbol in Earley's algorithm is obtained here by using the arcs labelled by this input symbol (if there are any such arcs...)

- it may be more difficult to see how the items [$Y \rightarrow .X\delta$, j] are handled, since they have no equivalent in our algorithm. Let us consider an item [$Y \rightarrow \alpha.X\beta$, k] in $A(j)$, with $\alpha \neq \varepsilon$. A sequence of insertion in $A(j)$ of items [$X \rightarrow .X_1\delta_1$, j], [$X_1 \rightarrow .X_2\delta_2$, j] $\ldots$ [$X_{n-1} \rightarrow .X_n\delta_n$, j], finally

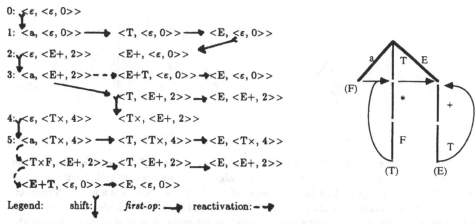

0: $<\varepsilon, <\varepsilon, 0>>$

1: $<a, <\varepsilon, 0>> \longrightarrow <T, <\varepsilon, 0>> \longrightarrow <E, <\varepsilon, 0>>$

2: $<\varepsilon, <E+, 2>>$ $<E+, <\varepsilon, 0>>$

3: $<a, <E+, 2>> - - \blacktriangleright <E+T, <\varepsilon, 0>> \rightarrow\!\!\bullet <E, <\varepsilon, 0>>$

   $<T, <E+, 2>> \rightarrow\!\!\bullet <E, <E+, 2>>$

4: $<\varepsilon, <T\times, 4>>$ $<T\times, <E+, 2>>$

5: $<a, <T\times, 4>> \longrightarrow <T, <T\times, 4>> \rightarrow\!\!\bullet <E, <T\times, 4>>$

   $<T\times F, <E+, 2>> \rightarrow <T, <E+, 2>> \rightarrow <E, <E+, 2>>$

   $<E+T, <\varepsilon, 0>> \rightarrow\!\!\bullet <E, <\varepsilon, 0>>$

Legend: shift: first-op: $\longrightarrow$ reactivation: $- \blacktriangleright$

Figure 6: the list of occurrences computed for grammar *GEA* and input $w = a + a \times a$

ending with $[X_n \rightarrow .a\gamma, j]$, leads to $[A \rightarrow \alpha X.\beta, j]$ in a subsequent set $A(i)$ only if all the productions $(X_n \rightarrow a\gamma)$, $(X_{n-1} \rightarrow X_n \delta_n)$, ..., $(X_1 \rightarrow X_2 \delta_2)$ and $(X \rightarrow X_1 \delta_1)$ are found in order during the parsing of $w_{j+1} \ldots w_i$. This is what the first rule performed when a leaf is reached computes: once a right-hand side of a production is completed, it includes all the productions whose first symbol is (one of) its left-hand side. Therefore, when $(X_n \rightarrow a\gamma)$ succeeds, it starts $(X_{n-1} \rightarrow X_n \alpha_n)$, and again when this production succeeds, it starts $(X_{n-2} \rightarrow X_{n-1} \alpha_{n-1})$, etc..., and we finally get the same result than Earley's algorithm. But, if one of these derivations ever fails, then nothing useless had been computed in advance: the order of insertion of the items respects the order of completion of the productions corresponding to these items. One may notice that our algorithm works in a bottom-up way...

Due to a lack of space we do not prove our algorithm here (cf. [12]) but only state the result: let L be the set of inputs for which the algorithm returns "success", then $L = L(G)$.

4. How to compute only valid occurrences?

Using the LR terminology, an occurrence with its context is said to be "valid" if it derives a prefix of a word which can be completed into a word of the language. Therefore, when this occurrence is computed, it is not yet possible to say if it will be used in the derivation of the input, and it must not be discarded. As mentioned in Section 2, at the moment our algorithm may compute invalid pairs of occurrences and contexts, since it may consider occurrences independently of the context in which they are to be used. This fact may be illustrated by the two main situations:

- use of a production with a leading terminal symbol (cf. figure 7a): the result is useless if for every production $(X \rightarrow a\gamma)$, X is not included in $Init(Y)$, where Y is an expected non-terminal. This is an easy situation to handle with a lookahead character, but the general case is more complicated (it generalizes to any shift of symbol): there could exist two productions $(X_1 \rightarrow a\delta_1)$ and $(X_2 \rightarrow a\delta_2)$ such that X_1 is in $Init(Y)$ but X_2 is not ! Then, a should be shifted but $(X_2 \rightarrow a\delta_2)$ should not be used, even if $(X_1 \rightarrow a\delta_1)$ fails.

- Similarly, the use of the arcs *first-op* may add invalid items (cf. figure 7b): here, let us consider a leaf α, associated with a production $(X \rightarrow \alpha)$, and a context, for a given index, made of an occurrence β, source of an arc labelled by Y. A useless move occurs for each production $(T \rightarrow Z\delta)$ with X in $Init(Y)$, $X \subseteq Z$ but Z not in $Init(Y)$. The use of production $(T \rightarrow Z\delta)$ is worthless in a context limited to Y.

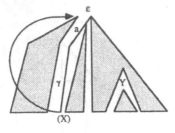

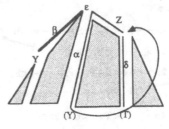

Figure 7.a   Figure 7.b

If an early detection of errors is preferred to what may be a better explanation of errors, one can deal with this problem without much changes in the algorithm: we store at each occurrence α of the trie the list, noted $LHS(\alpha)$, of all left-hand sides of productions whose α is a prefix. Moreover, we associate with each occurrence source of some arcs labelled by non-terminals, the union of the sets $Init$ for these non-terminals. During parsing, this last information is dynamically added to the context of any new path started to get an operand for the expected non-terminals.

For the example of grammar GEA, the trie will be completed with the following relations:

- $LHS(T) = LHS(T\times) = LHS(T \times F) = \{ T \}$
- $LHS(E) = LHS(T+) = LHS(E + T) = \{ E \}$
- $LHS(a) = \{ F \};\ LHS(\varepsilon) = \{ E, T, F \}$
- $Init(E) = \{ E, T, F \};\ Init(T) = \{ T, F \};\ Init(F) = \{ F \}$

At each step of the algorithm (use of an arc labeled by a terminal or non-terminal symbol, use of the *first-op* arcs...), the target of the arc is added to the new list of occurrences only if its set LHS is not disjoint with the sets $Init$ stored in its context. If the test succeeds, the occurrence is added with the same set of initial symbols. In the special case where an occurrence is suspended while one looks for an operand, a new path is started only if, after shifting by at least one of the expected non-terminals, one gets an occurrence valid in the current context. A new path is then started, with a list of initial symbols restricted to the union of $Init$ sets for the relevant non-terminals. An occurrence is discarded as soon as the intersection between the LHS relation and the list of non-terminals included in its context becomes empty: the corresponding productions can no longer be part of any derivation rooted by the expected non-terminals.

This test introduces a relationship between any current occurrence (more precisely, between the left-hand sides of the derivations which have this occurrence as prefix) and the suspended productions, which is quite similar to the one we emphasized in the description of Earley's algorithm.

5. Complexity of the new algorithm: first of all, one should notice that all the relations we use can be precomputed and stored in the trie and will thus have a constant cost during the parsing on an input: this is the case for all the arcs added between the occurrences in the trie, which are fixed as long as the grammar is constant: this is the case for the *first-op* arcs and for the arcs between the occurrences having some arcs labelled by non-terminals and the root of the trie. This is also the case for the relations $Init$ and LHS...

In the same way, the coercion relation $\subseteq$ can be precomputed and stored in an array. More generally the "type checking" can also be precomputed: for every non-terminal X stored in a leaf, and for every occurrence β, one can compute whether $X \subseteq Y$, for each Y such that βY is an occurrence. This information is stored with β. The check for the validity of an occurrence with respect to a given context can also be partly precomputed.

The **while** loop is implicitly guarded by the detection of already computed occurrences: for each pair one must check if it has already been considered during the current step. This check, which is equivalent to the one needed in Earley's algorithm, can be achieved in constant time.

Finally, in most of the moves of the algorithm, the indexes stored in the context are not used: they are only important in the function *Reduction*. We can thus use a factorized representation of pairs by grouping pairs with common occurrences, all the indexes included in the contexts associated with these occurrences being stored in a linked list. This representation allows us to ignore the indexes when they are not needed, by simply copying a pointer to this list. A variable number of pairs can thus be dealt with in a constant time. The counterpart of this facility is that all the computed pairs must be refactorized before being inserted in *Suspended* or in the list of active occurrences. As the number of distinct occurrences is fixed, this can be achieved by a "radix sort" in time proportional to the number of pairs to be sorted.

In the worst case, our algorithm works with the same complexity as Earley's algorithm [6] :

- the 0th step is trivial: only $<\varepsilon, <\varepsilon, 0>>$ is needed (if there is no ε-production !).

- the outer loop is trivially bounded by the length of the input. With the test for the detection of already computed occurrences, the number of traversals of the inner loop is bounded by the number of distinct pairs that may exist at the current step, i.e. the number of occurrences in the trie, times the number of distinct contexts; this is linear in the number of letters shifted. At the ith step, the number of different pairs is thus linear in i. The cost of going from a step to the next one by shifting the current letter is linear in the number of pairs to be tested, i.e. linear in i. In fact, with our factorization, it can be achieved in constant time, since we do not need to scan the list of indexes.

- cost of handling a pair in the inner loop at the ith step: the only step which does not have a straightforward cost is the computation needed for the leaves: let $<\alpha, <\beta, j>>$ be such a pair, where α is a leaf, β a suspended occurrence and j an index. The use of *first-op* arcs is bounded by the number of occurrences at height 1: $min(| V_N |, | P |)$. For the reactivation of the suspended occurrence β, we mentioned that the time requested by the time-checking is constant. The cost for this part of the algorithm is thus proportional to the number of pairs that will be considered at that point (since these new pairs are included in the total number of pairs, the cost of their handling needs not to be considered here). This number is equal to the cardinal of $Suspended[\gamma, j]$: it is proportional to the index j. One must consider each occurrence, at least for the detection of a pair already considered and for the check of its validity.

Finally, as with the standard algorithm, we find that at the ith step, the number of pairs to consider is linear in i, each pair having a cost of computation also proportional to i. The cost for the ith step is then proportional to i^2 and the cost for an input of length n is proportional to n^3. Space complexity is related to the total number of pairs that may be stored at a given point, and is given by the size of the current list of occurrences plus the number of all occurrences kept in *Suspended*, the total being proportional to n^2. One may notice that both complexities are strongly related to the number of pairs to be computed. A last point is that the complexity of our algorithm is also improved, like for Earley's algorithm, when it is applied to well-formed grammars ...

Comparison with the standard algorithm: although both algorithms have the same order of complexity in the worst case, could they be compared in a more precise way ? One should first notice that the constants of the main order terms of the complexity are different :

- on one hand we replace a constant (the size of the grammar) by a term which is always less than or equal to it: the number of vertices in the trie built over the right-hand sides of productions. In the case where the trie is degenerated, our algorithm behaves like Earley's algorithm: an example of such a situation is given by grammar GRE in Annex where the main gain of our algorithm is due to the factorization of two productions into a unique occurrence. The gain may be higher for other kinds of grammars, especially for operators grammars, with productions of the form $E \rightarrow E\,x\,E$, where x is an operator in V_t.

- on the other hand, for every suspended occurrence, we replace several items by a unique occurrence (this is the case for I_0). As explained in Section 3 we save the prediction step ! This happens for grammar PCG in Annex: whenever a symbol F is expected, we replace 15 items by a unique occurrence, giving a total saving of two-thirds of the total number of items, for the examples presented ! This is valuable.

With our data structure and the precomputation of most of the relations, our algorithm requires a minimal information on the context of parsing... yielding to a decrease in the number of elements to be computed at each step. To illustrate this property let us consider a grammar with four productions $(A \rightarrow \alpha B\beta)$, $(B \rightarrow \delta)$, $(B \rightarrow C\gamma)$ and $(C \rightarrow \eta)$ and suppose that α had been derived and that we are looking for a derivation of B: either the next moves will correspond to the production $(B \rightarrow \delta)$ and then $(B \rightarrow C\gamma)$ and $(C \rightarrow \eta)$ are useless, or they will correspond to $(C \rightarrow \eta)$, and $(B \rightarrow \delta)$ is useless as well as $(B \rightarrow C\gamma)$ until $(C \rightarrow \eta)$ is completed, or both moves are possible and, again, $(B \rightarrow C\gamma)$ is not to be considered before the completion of $(C \rightarrow \eta)$ ... In the three cases our algorithm uses the same information: the right-hand sides of productions η and δ are about to be started and their common prefix, ε, has been derived...

Although our algorithm has the same main order term for its time complexity, the benefit may be interesting when the inputs involved are not very long, as is the case in our environment, the constant of the main order term being sometimes more significant. Remember that the complexity of the algorithm is strongly related to the number of elements computed. The annex shows that the difference may be valuable... For longer inputs, the gain is weaker, but one can argue that neither algorithm is really well adapted.

- our algorithm seems easier to understand and to implement than the standard (optimized) algorithm [1,8] because more relations can be precomputed: the use of coercions, the type-checking, how to combine productions... All these relations are represented in a natural and straightforward way in the trie and they make the algorithm look like a tree traversal, with a detection of repeated elements and the suspension of paths...

- error explanation : we mentioned how our algorithm can be modified to compute only valid pairs and therefore share with other parsing algorithms the property of early detection of errors. For programming languages this property is crucial, because it helps a better error detection and, above all, a better error recovery. This is not always true in our environment where "sort errors" may be more frequent than other kinds of errors. Moreover, the grammar not being known in advance, it is difficult to expect a very precise error diagnostic, not to speak of a possible error recovery ! In opposite, it may be more interesting to consider a different strategy, implemented by our original algorithm, which tries to parse the input as far as possible, by partioning it in substrings which may be derived by some prefixes of productions. It is then more easy to detect "sort errors", characterized by the presence of a prefix αA of a right-hand side of production, with α deriving $w_1 \ldots w_j$, and a derivation $B \rightarrow^* w_{j+1} \ldots w_i$ but with B not in $Init(A)$. Our algorithm is not blocked at the jth step but may work until the ith step and thus explicits the incorrect operand. A similar situation occurs when prefix α of αA derives $w_1 \ldots w_j$, production $(A \rightarrow \beta B\gamma)$ is available and $B \rightarrow^* w_{j+1} \ldots w_i$. Here, with the derivation of β missing, the detection of an operand rooted by B is a helpful information to explain the error.

Of course, in both cases the source of the error may be different ! This is only a heuristic... The detection of a correct operand, of a wrong type or at the wrong place, may be an helpful information and the two examples above correspond to situations where an operand is expected. If the parsing does not end with a complete operand, it is still possible to go back to the first location of an error and to emit the first diagnostic. The use of this strategy does not change the main order term of the complexity for parsing correct sentences although the practical efficiency may decrease... The algorithm being quite the same with these two error explanation strategies (use, or not, of the *LHS* and *Init* relations), one may imagine a system where the final balance is left to the user, between a faster algorithm or an algorithm with better error explanation facilities.

6. Building parse trees   Having an algorithm which works as a recognizer is not enough, since one usually needs to access the parse tree(s) corresponding to the input. One may be interested in counting the different trees, in enumerating either all these trees or only one of them, or in choosing a specific tree, which can be specified in one way or another. The data structure built during parsing should ease all these operations.

Earley's data structure: the sets of items computed for testing the correctness of the input contain enough information to build the parse trees: the first part of each item gives the production used and the second part gives its history, i.e. a way back to its father and older brothers. Going backwards from the final item, it is possible to recompute any parse tree for the input. Alternatively, during the recognition step, one can also build a "graph of items", including a link between an item and every items whose computation yield to its insertion. At the end of parsing, this graph is used to get the parse trees [1]. Nevertheless, one must be careful when using this graph, since a given item may correspond to very different situations with respect to the part of the input derived from it. This problem may be illustrated by the following example, introduced in [10]: let us consider the grammar $S \to S\,S \mid 1$ and the input 1 1 1: the graph of items is given below (it contains two different parse trees) and one may notice that the two derivations from item (*) are not compatible:

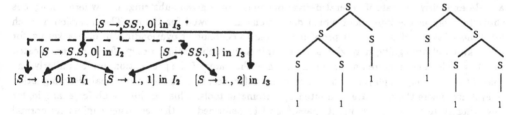

Our data structure: parse trees will be represented by a graph whose nodes are triplets of the general form $<X, j, i>$ where X is a non-terminal and $j \le i$ are two indexes in the input, with the following meaning: $<X, j, i>$ is a node in the graph if $X \to^* w_{j+1} \ldots w_i$.

With each node we associate a list of tuples of the general form $(op\ g_1 \ldots g_m)$, where op is a production in G and the g_i's are nodes such that one gets the substring $w_{j+1} \ldots w_i$ by replacing each non-terminal in the right-hand side of op by the substring derived from the corresponding node. Each tuple differs from the others either by the production used or by the nodes referenced (for ambiguous inputs). In our tuples, any derivation from a node g_k is compatible with any derivation of another node $g_{k'}$ of the same tuple, avoiding the problem of Earley's data structure.

Our data structure aims at building, during the parsing of the input, a representation for parse trees which can later be used in a straightforward way, while keeping an acceptable complexity by a maximal sharing of the derivations which are common to several parse trees. The complexity remains sub-exponential, even for grammars with an exponential number of parse trees for a given input. Nevertheless, the total complexity for parsing and building the graph is no longer always cubic and may be an arbitrary polynomial, depending on the ambiguity of the grammar.

The construction of the graph takes place during the computation of the leaves of the trie. For that, we must add to the context of an occurrence the list of all the nodes associated with the non-terminals stored on the current path . Once a leaf is reached, we create, if it does not already exist, a node $<X, j, i>$ for every left-hand side X of a production associated with this leaf, j being the step at which the path was initiated and i being the current step. Moreover, a tuple made with the name of the production and the list of nodes created along the path is associated with the newly created node. There can be more than one list of nodes in the context of an occurrence, and we must keep the list of all the possibilities. This list is updated:

- after using an arc *first-op* between a leaf and an occurrence at height 1, in which case a new list is started, since we know that the new node is the first operand of a production.

- after each computation of a leaf which reactivates a suspended occurrence: the node corresponding to the non-terminal derived is appended to every sublist.

In both cases, we must create the nodes corresponding to the possible use of coercions !

Display at request: the graph we build gives a shared structure for all the parse trees which correspond to an input. A classical graph traversal, started from the root $<S, 0, n>$, which selects a tuple for every node, gives in an easy way one of the possible parse trees for the input. Nevertheless, most of the trees are usually worthless for the user: in fact, (s)he minds a particular parse tree but does not care to add enough indications in the input to fully disambiguate it. To accommodate to this behavior, we have designed a *display-and-select* system in which it is possible to reject in a single step a whole class of unwanted parse trees by selecting in order the root production of a subtree. This graph traversal for the selection of the desired parse tree may be used to compute at the same time a minimal disambiguation of the input, i.e. a word which corresponds to the selected parse tree but which is unambiguous and differs from the original input by the least amount of indications. This can easily be achieved from our parsing graph since the tuples associated with a node explicitly indicate if several derivations exist for a given substring, i.e. where ambiguous substrings lay in the input and which derivations are allowed for them. The insertion at such locations of type indications, for problems related to coercion or overloading, or of bracketing, for other kinds of ambiguity, may give such a minimal disambiguation, except for very complicated inputs which would require an explicit mention of the name of the production used. Similarly, the role of the user may be played by a tree used as a reference, to offer such a minimal disambiguation in systems where the trees are computed by automatic tools. This can be useful, for example, for rewriting systems: a term is input, parsed and transformed by the rewriting engine; its normal form is then flattened and parsed to obtain its parsing graph. By comparison between the parsing graph and the original tree, the normal form can then be pretty-printed to the user in the most legible, but still unambiguous, form.

Conclusion: in this paper we have described a new, bottom-up, parsing algorithm, derived from the standard Earley's algorithm. It is easier to understand and more efficient, thanks to the precomputation of some closure relations and to the minimization of the number of items that it computes, and yields an improved practical efficiency and a better error explanation capability which make it well adapted to be the parsing system of many experimental environments.

Acknowledgments: special thanks to M.C. Gaudel for her support and to J.C. Raoult for many fruitful discussions. This work is partially supported by PRC-Programmation and the Esprit contract Meteor.

References

[1] A. Aho & J. Ullman: *The theory of Parsing, Translation and Compiling*, Vol. 1 : Parsing, Prentice-Hall, Englewoods Cliffs, N.J.

[2] M. Bidoit, F. Capy, C. Choppy, N.Choquet, C. Gresse, S. Kaplan, F. Schlienger & F. Voisin: *ASSPRO: an Interactive and Integrated Programming Environment*, Technology and Science of Informatics (John Wiley and Sons), Vol. 6, N. 4, 1987, pp. 259-278.

[3] M. Bidoit, M.C. Gaudel & A. Mauboussin: *How to make algebraic specifications more understandable? An experiment with the PLUSS specification Language*, L.R.I. Research Report 343, April 1987.

[4] P. Boullier: *Contribution à la construction automatique d'analyseurs lexicographiques et syntaxiques*, Thèse d'Etat, Université d'Orléans, Jan. 1984.

[5] F. Capy: *ASSPEGIQUE: un environnement d'exceptions. Une sémantique opérationnelle des E,R-algèbres, formalisme prenant en compte les exceptions.*, Thèse de 3ème cycle, Université de Paris-Sud, Orsay, Déc. 87.

[6] J. Earley: *An Efficient Context-Free Parsing Algorithm*, C.A.C.M., Vol. 13, N. 2, Feb. 1970, pp. 94-102.

[7] M.C. Gaudel: *Towards Structured Algebraic Specifications*, ESPRIT Technical Week, Bruxelles 1985, ESPRIT'85 Status Report, North-Holland, pp. 493-510.

[8] S. Graham, M. Harrison & W. Ruzzo: *An Improved Context-Free Recognizer*, A.C.M.-T.O.P.L.A.S., Vol. 2, N. 3, Jul. 1980, pp. 415-462.

[9] S.L. Peyton-Jones: *Parsing Distfix Operators*, Computing Practices, Vol. 29. N. 2, 1986, pp. 118-122.

[10] M. Tomita: *An Efficient Context-Free Parsing Algorithm for Natural Languages*, Proc. 9th I.J.C.A.I., Los Angeles, Aug. 1985, pp. 756-764.

[11] F. Voisin: *CIGALE: a Tool for Interactive Grammar Construction and Expression Parsing*, Science of Computer Programming, Vol. 7, N. 1, 1986, pp. 61-86.

[12] F. Voisin: *Une version ascendante de l'algorithme d'Earley*, L.R.I. Research Report, to appear, 1988.

- ANNEX -

In Table 1 below, we give a practical comparison of both parsing algorithms. The criterion we use is the total number of items, including doubles, computed for a given input. This abstract criterion is characteristic of the inherent complexity of parsing the input and is not biased by the quality of the implementations. Grammars *PCG* and *GRE* are taken from [6], where they were used to compare Earley's algorithm to other parsing methods. The first one is unambiguous (actually Lalr) and the second one is ambiguous due to an associativity problem in the last production. Inputs used in the comparison are also from the original paper. The two last grammars *GEXP* and *GEA* are more representative of actual inputs than *GRE*. Both generate the same language, but only the first one is ambiguous. They generalize to any number of operators, given by increasing precedence for *GEA*. In Table 1, the first columns give the results for Earley's algorithm. The numbers are slightly less than the original ones because we delete any item related to the axiom, since this notion does not exists in our algorithm (this saves two items plus as many items as there are prefixes of the input included in the language). The second columns give our results, counted as indicated in Section 5.

PCG	GRE	GEXP	GEA
F → C | S | P | U	X → a | Xb | Ya	E → E+E	E → E+T | T
C → U ⇒ U	Y → e | YdY	E → E×E	T → T×F | F
U → (F) | ¬ U | L		E → a	F → a
L → L' | p | q | r			
S → U ∨ U | U ∨ S			
P → U ∧ U | U ∧ P			

PCG			GRE				GEA		GEXP	
p	22	4	ededea	30	21	$(a+)^4 a$	46	28	80	55
$(p \wedge q)$	65	17	$ededeab^4$	38	29	$(a*)^4 a$	38	28	80	55
$(p' \wedge q) \vee r \vee p'$	143	39	$ededeab^{10}$	50	41	$(a+)^8 a$	82	52	282	198
$p \Rightarrow ((q \Rightarrow \neg(r' \vee (p \wedge q)))$	273	79	$ededeab^{200}$	430	421	$(a*)^8 a$	66	52	282	198
$\Rightarrow (q' \vee r))$			$(ed)^4 eabb$	74	61	$(a+ax)^2 a$	42	30	96	64
$\neg(\neg p' \wedge (q \vee r) \wedge p')$	138	54	$(ed)^7 eabb$	189	155	$(a \times a+)^2 a$	42	29	96	64
$((p \wedge q) \vee (q \wedge r) \vee (r \wedge p'))$	395	123	$(ed)^8 eabb$	246	204	$(a+ax)^4 a$	74	56	394	288
$\Rightarrow \neg((p' \vee q') \wedge (r' \vee p))$			$(ed)^{10} eabb$	394	333	$(a \times a+)^4 a$	74	55	394	288

Table 1: Comparison between Earley's and the new algorithm

For grammar PCG, our algorithm computes only one-third of the items required by Earley's algorithm. This impressive gain is mainly due to the saving of the items computed by the prediction phase: for example, each time a F term is expected we save 15 items... Even with unambiguous grammars, efficiency may be improved ! In the second example, the saving is low and partly due to the trie structure (items $Y \rightarrow .YdY$ and $Y \rightarrow .e$ share a unique occurrence, as do items $Y \rightarrow Y.dY$ and $X \rightarrow Y.a$) and partly to the fact that indexes are not always tested. For input $w = (ed)^n e$ the saving is $O(n^2)$, for a total number of elements which is $O(n^3)$. Time complexity, for both algorithms, is therefore cubic.

For the two grammars GEA and $GEXP$, the saving for most of the examples is about one-third of the total number of items, although the grammars are very small ones. For $GEXP$, one may notice an interesting property: the total number of elements computed by our algorithm for a given input depends on the actual number of operators used in the input (the number of parse trees does not depend on the number of distinct operators, but more elements are needed to represent them) but not on the total number of operators in the grammar. This is not true for the original algorithm, where each unused operator increases the complexity by a $O(n^2)$ term. This straightforward consequence of the trie structure makes our method more stable. This property is not exactly true for GEA, since we must deal with the "coercions" used to reflect the precedence levels: for every prefix of the input included in the language, we must add coercions even if the corresponding operators are not used. Nevertheless, our algorithm is still more stable than Earley's algorithm, because of the saving of the prediction phase, as illustrated by the results for inputs with only one operator, like $(a+)^n a$ or $(a\times)^n a$...

USING AN ATTRIBUTE GRAMMAR AS A LOGIC PROGRAM

Günter Riedewald , Uwe Lämmel
Wilhelm-Pieck-Universität Rostock
Sektion Informatik
Albert-Einstein-Str. 21
DDR-2500 Rostock

0. Introduction

In [DM84] Deransart and Maluszynski showed the way to transform logic programs into semantically equivalent attribute grammars, and vice versa. Furthermore, in [DM88] was additionally shown that Definite Clause Programs (DCP) can be looked upon as a special kind of Relational Attribute Grammars (RAG).
A concept related to RAG´s is the Grammar of Syntactical Functions (GSF) [RDM83]. This special kind of attribute grammars was developed during 1970-1972 from two-level grammars for parsing ALGOL-68 programs [R72]. In 1976 an experimental compiler transforming ASPLE [CU73] into FORTRAN-63 [R76], and in 1985 a generator for dialogue systems RUEGEN-KS [L84], both based on GSF, were developed.
Now GSF´s are exploited for software engineering and logic programming. A GSF which is L-attributed and has an underlying LL(k)-grammar can be directly used as a PROLOG program. That means that the same rules can be considered a GSF as well as a PROLOG program. Contrary to the DCG [PW80] there is no need for a GSF to be transformed into a PROLOG program. This kind of GSF´s is suited for a program development system combined with rapid prototyping by a PROLOG system.
GSF´s are introduced in section 1. Some relations between GSF´s and PROLOG programs are treated in section 2. Finally, section 3 presents a proposal for a program development system.

1. Grammars of Syntactical Functions

The basic idea of the GSF originates from interpreting hypernotions of two-level grammars as functions supplying nonterminal or terminal symbols. For instance, the hypernotion "MODE source", or in a more

functional notation "source(MODE)", represents a set of nonterminal
symbols such as "source(real)" or "source(boolean)", obtained after
substituting values for the metanotion MODE. Therefore, "source(MODE)"
is a function, mapping the domain of MODE into the set of nonterminal
symbols consisting of "source" followed by a value of MODE closed in
brackets. Such syntactical functions are the basic elements of the GSF.
In order to specify the computation of the arguments of syntactical
functions we use semantic functions. Auxiliary syntactical functions
define constraints which must be satisfied by the parameters.
We will define a GSF by two steps: first we will introduce a GSF scheme
defining the main structure of a GSF by relations between functions. A
GSF is derived from a GSF scheme by an interpretation which associates
the scheme with particular semantic functions and constraints.

Definition 1 :

A GSF scheme is a tuple

$$S = \langle\ B,\ A,\ SF,\ V,\ C,\ F,\ AR,\ R\ \rangle,$$

where

B = < N, T, R′, ST > (N - set of nonterminal symbols,

                          T - set of terminal symbols,

                          R′- set of production rules,

                          ST N - start symbol)

is a context-free grammar (the basic grammar of the GSF);
A, SF, V, and C are finite sets of names of auxiliary syntactical
functions, names of semantic functions, variables and constants resp.;
V∪C is the set of parameters;
F is the forbidden symbol;
R is a finite set of production rule patterns, each of the form

$$f(P_{f,1}\ ,\ldots,P_{f,nf})\ :\quad f1(P_{f1,1},\ldots,P_{f1,nf1}),\ldots,\ fr(P_{fr,1},\ldots,P_{fr,nfr}),$$
$$h1(P_{h1,1},\ldots,P_{h1,nh1}),\ldots,\ hs(P_{hs,1},\ldots,P_{hs,nhs}).$$

$$(*)$$

where h1,...,hs ∈ A∪SF, $P_{f,1}$,...,$P_{hs,nhs}$ ∈ V∪C and f:f1,...,fr ∈ R′.
N, T, A, SF, and {F} are pairwise disjoint. V and C are disjoint, too.
We say that (*) is related to f:f1,...,fr.
AR the arity of a function name maps each element of N T A SF into
the set of integers.
The elements of N are called names of syntactical functions and the
elements of T names of basic syntactical functions.
g(P1,...,Pn) is a syntactical_function, a basic_syntactical function, a
semantic function, or an auxiliary syntactical function if g∈N, g∈T,

$g \in SF$, $g \in A$ resp. . Each syntactical function ST(P1,...,Pn) occuring on
a left-hand side of a production rule pattern is a __start element__ of the
GSF.
#

__Remark__:
Basic syntactical functions represent classes of terminal symbols. E.g.
"identifier(X)" represents the class of possible identifiers.
A particular terminal symbol can be derived from a basic syntactical
function by substituting values for each variable.

__Example 1__:
We illustrate the definition 1 by a GSF scheme describing simple programs together with their symbol table.

```
B  = <{program, block, declaration_list, dec_list, statement_list,
          stat_list,identifier_declaration,type, statement,expression},
        {begin,end,var, ;, :, :=,bool,int,identifier}, R´,program >,
A  = { NIN, INID },
SF = { IDDECL, ENTRY, INIT },
V  = { S, S0, SN, IT, B, I, T },
C  = { bool, int },
R :
/1/ program(S) : ´begin´,block(S),´end´.
/2/ block(S) : declaration_list(S),statement_list(S).
/3/ declaration_list(SN) : ´var´,identifier_declaration(IT),´;´,
                           dec_list(S,SN), INIT(S,IT).
/4/ dec_list(S,SN) : identifier_declaration(IT),´;´, dec_list(S0,SN),
                     NIN(S,IT),ENTRY(S0,S,IT).
/5/ dec_list(S,S): .
/6/ statement_list(S) : statement(S),stat_list(S).
/7/ stat_list(S) : ´;´,statement(S),stat_list(S).
/8/ stat_list(S) : .
/9/ identifier_declaration(IT) : type(T),´:´,identifier(I),
                                 IDDECL(IT,I,T).
/10/ type(bool) : ´bool´.
/11/ type(int)  : ´int´ .
/12/ statement(S) : identifier(I),´:=´,expression(S), INID(S,I).
/13/ expression(S) : identifer(I), INID(S,I).
```

The set of production rules R´ of the basic grammar B can be easily obtained from the set of production rule patterns R by omitting auxiliary syntactical functions, semantic functions, and parameter lists.

For better understanding of GSF schemes we will informally define the semantic functions and auxiliary syntactical functions as follows:

- INIT(S,IT) initializes the symbol table S with the first entry IT
- ENTRY(SO,S,IT) makes an entry IT into the symbol table S. The resulting symbol table is SO.
- IDDECL(IT,I,T) forms an entry IT from an identifier I and its type T.
- NIN(S,IT) checks whether the identifier of a new formed entry IT has been declared yet and consequently is contained in the symbol table S or not.
- INID(S,I) checks whether an identifier I has been declared. That means whether the symbol table S contains an entry for the identifier I or not.

The meaning of parameters of all·functions can be seen by these definitions.

#

Definition 2:

Suppose S = < B, A, SF, V, C, F, AR, R> is a GSF scheme as introduced in definition 1. A GSF G is a pair <S,IP>, where IP is an interpretation. An interpretation IP = <M,D,I> consists of a family of domains D, a function I associating with each element f A SF an n-ary relation on the domains from D(n=AR(f)) and a function M assigning with the i-th parameter position of a syntactical function, auxialiary syntactical function and semantic function f a particular domain M(f,i) from D. Moreover, the following conditions must be satisfied:

- A variable occuring on the i-th parameter position of a function f stands for a value from the domain M(f,i). It represents the same value whenever it occurs in a given production rule pattern.
- A constant occuring on the i-th parameter position of a function f is an element from the domain M(f,i).
- Suppose $f \in A \cup SF$, AR(f)=n, and $a_i \in M(f,i)$, i=1,...,n.
  Then

$$f(a_1,\ldots,a_n) = \begin{cases} \text{empty string, iff } (a_1,\ldots,a_n) \in I(f) \\ \\ F \quad \text{else} \end{cases}$$

#

Remark: Using this condition it is possible to associate each production rule pattern

$$f(P_{f,1}, \ldots, P_{f,nf}) : f1(P_{f1,1}, \ldots, P_{f1,nf1}), \ldots, fr(P_{fr,1}, \ldots, P_{fr,nfr}),$$

$$h1(P_{h1,1}, \ldots, P_{h1,nh1}), \ldots, hs(P_{hs,1}, \ldots, P_{hs,nhs}).$$

with a relation consisting of tuples $(v_1, \ldots, v_m)$ with $m=nf+f1+\ldots+nfr$ and v_l from some domain of D. A tuple $(v_1, \ldots, v_m)$ is constructed as follows:

- In the above production rule pattern a value from the domain corresponding to the parameter position is substituted for each variable in such a way that the value of each auxiliary syntactical function is the empty string.
- The parameter lists of the syntactical functions and basic syntactical functions (which now contain only values from the domain of D) are pasted together from left to right.

By this construction the relationship between RAG's and GSF's can be seen. In the case of GSF's auxiliary syntactical functions and semantic functions are as important as logic formulae in the case of RAG's, whereas logic formulae tell us how to construct the elements of the relations auxiliary syntactical functions and semantic functions say what are the elements.

The distinction betweeen the sets A and SF is not necessary from the theoretical point of view, in practical applications it is more comfortable however.

Example 2:

For the GSF scheme in example 1 we specify an interpretation for each program that allows to construct a symbol table from the declaration part of the program. Then, this symbol table is submitted to the statement sequence to check, whether each identifier has been declared before being used. Here, symbol tables are simply lists of entries (<identifier>,<type>). Each identifier may be declared only once. The domains associated with the parameter positions together with the corresponding parameter positions identified uniquely by a variable are shown in the following table :

domain	variable
identifiers	I
{bool,int}	T
entries into a symbol table	IT
symbol tables	S,S0,SN

The relations associated with the names of the auxiliary syntactical functions and semantic functions are as follows:

I(INIT)   = {([e],e)¦ e is an entry} initializes the symbol table
I(IDDECL) = {((i,t),i,t)¦i-identifier, t-type} forms an entry
I(ENTRY) = {([o,e],[o],e)¦[o]-old symbol table, e-new entry}
            makes an entry into the symbol table
I(INID)   = {(s,i)¦ identifier i is contained in symbol table s}
I(NIN)   = {(s,i)¦ identifier i is not contained in symbol table s}

Now, e.g. with the 4th production rule pattern we can assign a relation the elements of which are
  (v1,v2,v3,v4,v5) with v2=v5, (v4,v1,v3) ∈ I(ENTRY), (v1,v3) ∈ I(NIN)
#

By substituting values from the domains of D for each variable in a syntactical function, a basic syntactical function, an auxiliary syntactical function or a semantic function resp. we get a new value, which is a nonterminal symbol in the first case, a terminal symbol of the GSF in the second case, and the empty string or the forbidden symbol F in the other two cases .
Thus, using a suitable substitution for each variable in a given production rule pattern of the GSF it is possible to generate a context-free production rule of the GSF iff the value of each semantic function and auxiliary syntactical function is the empty string.
We can say: By substituting values from the corresponding domains of the parameter positions for the variables in a production rule pattern we get special parameter lists of the syntactical and basic syntactical functions . If the tuple pasted together from these parameter lists is an element of the relation associated with the production rule pattern we get a context-free production rule. By it each production rule pattern acts as a generator for a set of context-free production rules. Since each production rule pattern r is related to a context-free production rule r´ of the basic grammar of the GSF the set of production rules p derived from r can be considered as a refinement of r´.

Example 3:
We can get the production rule from the 4th production rule pattern of example 1 by substituting values for IT, SO, and SN and taking into account the interpretation from example 2 :

```
  dec_list([(y,int)],[(y,int),(x,int)]) :
                   identifier_declaration((x,int)),';',
                   dec_list([(y,int),(x,int)],[(y,int),(x,int)]).
because NIN([(y,int)],(x,int)) = empty string, and
        ENTRY([(y,int),(x,int)],[(y,int)],(x,int)) = empty string.
Nonterminal symbols are dec_list([(y,int)],[(y,int),(x,int)]),
identifier_declaration((x,int)), and
dec_list([(y,int),(x,int)],[(y,int),(x,int)]).
( [(y,int)],
  [(y,int),(x,int)],
  (x,int),
  [(y,int),(x,int)],[(y,int),(x,int)]
)
```

is an element of the relation associated with the 4th production rule
pattern of example 2.
#

The generation of context-free production rules from production rule
patterns enables the definition of a language generated by a GSF
through the derived production rules.

Definition 3:
Let G be a GSF with the set R of production rule patterns. A string w
consisting of terminal symbols of G is a word generated by G iff there
is a value ST(v1,...,vn) of some start symbol of the GSF and a set of
production rules of the GSF derived from R such that ST(v1,...,vn)$\overset{+}{=}$=>w.
The language L(G) generated by the GSF G is the set of words generated
by G.
#

Remark:
L(G) is a sublanguage of the language generated by the basic grammar.
The language generated by a GSF associates relations with names of
syntactical function.

Definition 4:
Let G be a GSF and f a given name of a syntactical function. R(f) is a
n-ary relation (n=AR(f)) and ER(f) a (n+1)-ary relation associated with
f, where
     (v1,...,vn) R(f) and (w,v1,...,vn) ER(f)
     iff f(v1,...,vn) $\overset{+}{=}$=> w, uwv ∈ L(G).
#

The structure of a word generated by a sequence of production rules of a GSF can be represented by a decorated derivation tree pasted together from elementary decorated trees corresponding to the production rules. The nodes of a tree are labeled by syntactical or basic syntactical functions. Omitting the parameter lists from the functions we get a derivation tree of the given word according to the underlying basic grammar of the GSF. Obviously, a decorated derivation tree will be constructed beginning with this tree.

Because a GSF is a special kind of attribute grammars the evaluation of parameters (attributes) can be done by some well known method. It's also possible to exploit systems of equations, which have a uniquely determined solution iff the GSF is a well-defined attribute grammar. That means, it is consistent and not circular.

The construction of such a system of equations is based on the following facts:

Suppose w is a word generated by a GSF G and therefore by the underlying basic grammar B of G and $r1',r2',\ldots,rn'$ are the only production rules of B generating w. If ri is a production rule pattern related to ri', $i=1,\ldots,n$, then w is also generated by the context-free production rules $r1'',r2'',\ldots,rn''$ of the GSF, where ri'' is derived from ri by suitable substitutions for each variable in ri, $i=1,\ldots,n$. These substitutions are not independent of each other.

Suppose m is an inner node of the derivation tree of w which is labeled by the nonterminal symbol $f(v1,\ldots,vn)$ with vj from corresponding domains of D. Then this nonterminal must occur on the right hand side of some derived production rule rk'' and on the left hand side of some derived production rule rl'' (connection condition). Therefore, the substitutions for the variables in rk and rl must be done in such a way that the connection condition will be satisfied. We will formulate this fact by equations. Another kind of equations originates from the last condition of definition 2.

Example 4:

To illustrate this we will construct the decorated derivation tree of the word

    begin var int:x; int:y; x:=y end   (*)

generated by the GSF with the GSF scheme from example 1 and with the interpretation from example 2. The word (*) is generated by the production rules:

    $1',2',3',9',11',4',9',11',5',6',12',13',8'$.

Decorating the corresponding derivation tree means to derive context-

free production rules from the production rule patterns :
    1,2,3,9,11,4,9,11,5,6,12,13,8
from example 1. These production rules generate (*).
Before substituting a value from the corresponding domainf or each
variable in the production rule patterns we will rename the variables
to avoid collisions. Therefore, our starting-sequence of production
rule patterns will be :
/ 1"/ program(S8) : ´begin´,block(S8),´end´.
/ 2"/ block(S) : declaration-list(S),statement_list(S).
/ 3"/ declaration_list(SN) : ´var´,identifier_declaration(IT),´;´,
                              dec_list(S1,SN), INIT(S1,IT).
/ 9"/ identifier_declaration(IT1) : type(T),´:´,identifier(I),
                                      IDDECL(IT1,I,T).
/11"/ type(int):´int´.
/ 4"/ dec_list(S2,SN1) : identifier_declaration(IT2),´;´,
                        dec_list(S0,SN1),
                        NIN(S2,IT2),ENTRY(S0,S2,IT2).
/ 9"/ identifier_declaration(IT3) : type(T1),´:´,identifier(I1),
                                      IDDECL(IT3,I1,T1).
/11"/ type(int) : ´int´.
/ 5"/ dec_list(S3,S3): .
/ 6"/ statement_list(S4) : statement(S4),stat_list(S4).
/12"/ statement(S5) : identifier(I2),´:=´,expression(S5),
                        INID(S5,I2).
/13"/ expression(S6) : identifier(I3), INID(S6,I3).
/ 8"/ stat_list(S7) : .
From the connection conditions we get the following equations:
    S8=S , S=SN , IT=IT1 , T=int , I=x , S1=S2 , SN=SN1 , IT2=IT3 ,
    T1=int , I1=y , S0=S3 , SN1=S3 , S=S4 , S4=S5 , I2=x , S5=S6 ,
    I3=y , S4=S7   .
From the last condition of definition 2 we get:
    INIT(S1,IT)= IDDECL(IT1,I,T)= NIN(S2,IT2)= ENTRY(S0,S2,IT2)=
    IDDECL(IT3,I1,T1)= INID(S5,I2)= INID(S6,I3)= empty string .
According to these equations the variables in the above production rule
patterns must be replaced as follows:
    - S0,S,S3,S4,S5,S6,S7,S8,SN,SN1 by [(x,int),(y,int)]
    - S1,S2   by [(x,int)]
    - IT,IT1   by (x,int)
    - IT2,IT3   by (y,int)
    - T,T1   by int
    - I,I2   by x
    - I1,I3   by y .

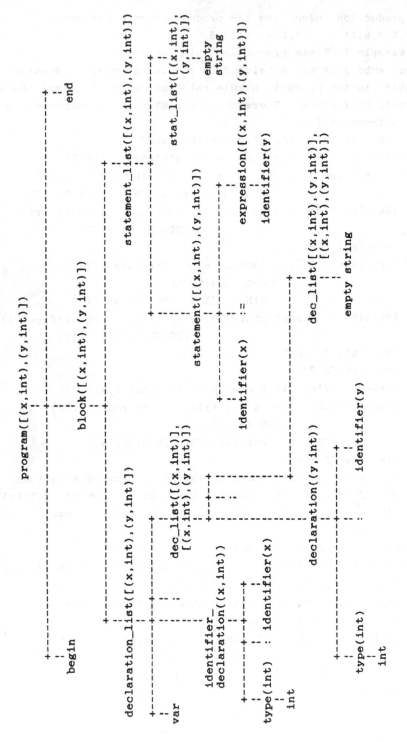

Fig. 1.

The decorated derivation tree is shown in fig. 1 .
#
In practical applications (RUEGEN-KS,compiler ASPLE-FORTRAN63) we used a more restricted version of the GSF than that from definition 2. Because it is related to the Functional Attribute Grammars (FAG) [DM85] we will call it Functional Grammar of Syntactical Functions - FGSF (up to now there hasn't been a special name). For these grammars semantic functions are interpreted as implicit functions rather than relations and obviously, implemented by external procedures. Their first parameter is the only output parameter which is computed in dependence on the other parameters from the parameter list of a semantic function. This enables the computation of the value of parameters in a deterministic way.

Example 5:
The GSF with a GSF scheme from example 1 and with the interpretation from example 2 can be interpreted as a FGSF. For this purpose we redefine the semantic functions:
- INIT(S,IT)   : S = INIT(IT), where S=[e], if IT=e ,
- IDDECL(IT,I,T) : IT=IDDECL(I,T), where IT=(i,t),if I=i and T=t .
- ENTRY(S0,S,IT) : S0=ENTRY(S,IT), where S0=[0,e], if S=[o], IT=e.
Now, the system of equations from example 4 can be rewritten:

S8 =S   , S =SN   ,S1=INIT(IT)   ,IT=IT1   ,
IT1=IDDECL(I,T) ,   T =int   ,I =x   ,S1=S2   ,
SN =SN1,   NIN(S2,IT2)=empty string ,S0=ENTRY(S2,IT2),IT2=IT3   ,
IT3=IDDECL(I1,T1), T1=int   ,I1=y   ,S0=S3   ,
SN1=S3   , S =S4   ,S4=S5,   INID(S5,I2)=empty string,
I2=x ,   INID(S6,I3)=empty string ,S5=S6   ,I3=y   ,
S4=S7
#
FGSF's give rise to compute the values of parameters in form of terms. Now, a system of equations is interpreted as follows:
- V=W, where V and W are variables, means both variables represent the same term.
- V=t, where V is a variable and t is a term, but not a variable, assigns the term t to the variable V.
- t= empty string, where t is a term, but not a variable, defines a constraint for the values of the variables occuring in t.

Example 6:

With the above interpretation of equations the values of the variables
computed by the system of equations from example 5 are :
- S0=S=S3=S4=S5=S6=S7=S8=SN=SN1=
                    ENTRY(INIT(IDDECL(x,int)),(IDDECL(y,int)),
- S1=S2= INIT(IDDECL(x,int)),
- IT=IT1= IDDECL(x,int),
- IT2=IT3= IDDECL(y,int),
- T=T1=int,
- I=I2=x,
- I1=I3=y,
where NIN(INIT(IDDECL(x,int)),IDDECL(y,int))=
      INID(ENTRY(INIT(IDDECL(x,int)),IDDECL(y,int)),x)=
      INID(ENTRY(INIT(IDDECL(x,int)),IDDECL(y,int)),y)=empty string
#

Parameter values in form of terms are not very legible. Nevertheless,
they are useful in practical applications. Such a term gives an information about the dependence between semantic functions computing a
value of a parameter and between auxiliary syntactical functions
defining   constraints   on   these   values.   Therefore,   the   term
interpretation of a system of equations may be applied to test FGSF´s
without a particular interpretation of the semantic functions. It is
used e.g. in the system RUEGEN-KS, where it is possible to test
dialogue systems generated by RUEGEN-KS without particular application
procedures implementing semantic functions.
In the case of termal interpretation of FGSF´s the construction of
systems of equations corresponds to the unification within PROLOG
programs (cf. remarks after theorem 1).

2. Using a GSF as a logic program

By the definition of a GSF scheme and the relations associated to it
the similarity with logic programs can be seen. The following question
arises: Is it possible to exploit a GSF as a logic program, especially
as a PROLOG program ? Before answering the question we will carry out
some "cosmetic" changes of the GSF notation:
- The notation of variables, constants and names of functions must
  correspond to the notational convention of PROLOG programs.
- ":" will be replaced by ":-", ": ." by "." , "´X´" by " @ X",

f(p1,...,pn) with f T by @ f(p1,...,p3) .
- h(p1,...,pn), where h A SF, will be preceded by # , & resp.
- Auxiliary syntactical functions and semantic functions may occur
  everywhere on the right hand side of a production rule pattern.

Example 7:
We transform the production rule pattern from example 1:
```
/* 1*/ program(S) :- @ begin,block(S),@ end.
/* 2*/ block(S) :- declaration_list(S),statement_list(S).
/* 3*/ declaration_list(SN):- @ var,identifier_declaration(IT),@ ;,
                            & init(S,IT), dec_list(S,SN).
/* 4*/ dec_list(S,SN) :- identifier_declaration(IT),@ ; ,
                      # nin(S,IT), & entry(S0,S,IT),dec_list(S0,SN).
/* 5*/ dec_list(S,S).
/* 6*/ statement_list(S) :- statement(S),stat_list(S).
/* 7*/ stat_list(S) :- @ ; ,statement(S),stat_list(S).
/* 8*/ stat_list(S).
/* 9*/ identifier_declaration(IT):- type(T),@ : ,@ identifier(I),
                                  & iddecl(IT,I,T).
/*10*/ type(bool) :- @ bool.
/*11*/ type(int)  :- @ int.
/*12*/ statement(S) :- @ identifier(I),@ := ,expression(S),
                     # inid(S,I).
/*13*/ expression(S) :- @ identifer(I), # inid(S,I).
#
```
To use the above modified production rule patterns as clauses of a
PROLOG program we must define the new symbols @, & , and # as operators
[L87]. The operator @ causes a lexical scan of terminal symbols. & and
cause the computation of semantic and auxiliary syntactical
functions. In our example the operator @ could be defined by the
following clauses:
```
  @ identifier(Id) :- !,next(id,Id).
  @ integer(N) :- !,next(int,N).
  @ X :- next(term,X).
  next(Type,X) :- (clause(t(Z));getnext(Z),assert(t(Z))),!,
                    test(Type,Z),!,Z=X,kill.
  test(term,_).
  test(int,X) :- integer(X).
  test(id,X) :- atom(X),not key(X) .
  kill :- retract(t(_)).
  kill.
  getnext(X) :- read(X).
```

The use of the built-in predicate "read" would be the simplest variant
having an important disadvantage: every input of a terminal symbol must
end with a full stop "." . Instead of "read" a self-made lexical
analyzer brings much more convenience. Moreover, the database must
contain the reserved words in the form "key(X)" . @ X, where
X=f(P1,...,Pn) and f T, means that a terminal symbol of the class X is
expected from the input. E.g. "@ integer(X)" expects an integer. If X
is a reserved symbol then this symbol is expected. the expected symbol
is locked for the database of the program. Usually, it is not contained
there and the next symbol is read from the input stream and added into
the database. Its type (identifier, integer, reserved symbol) is
checked. Now, if the entered and expected symbols are equal, the symbol
is removed from the database. In this way, the database contains only
the next expected symbol. Clearly, the definition of the operator @
depends on the particular PROLOG system its built-in predicates and
operators.

In dependence on the aim of the PROLOG program several variants exists
to define the operators & and #, for instance:

- The auxiliary syntactical functions and semantic functions are not
  yet implemented and we are only interested to know the connections
  between them rather than the computational result:

      & X :- write(X),nl. # X :- write(X),nl.

Example 8:

We consider the GSF from example 7 as a PROLOG program.

Asking ?- program(S).   ,

and giving the input: begin var int :x; int:y ; x := y end

the system will answer :

      iddecl(_22,x,int)
      init(_23,_22)
      iddecl(_24,y,int)
      nin(_23,_24)
      entry(_25,_23,_24)
      inid(_25,x)
      inid(_25,y)
      S=_25
      yes

where _22, _23,... are representations for variables. The same
number stands for the same value whenever it occurs. From this
output the dependence between the functions can be seen.

      #

- We would like to implement a symbolic computation of the parameters
  (termal interpretation):

```
& X :- X=..[Func,Out|Args], Out=..[Func|Args].
# X :- write(X),nl.
```

<u>Example 9</u>:
For the GSF from example 7 and for the same input as in the example
before the PROLOG system gives the following answer to the question
?-program(S).   :

```
nin(init(iddecl(x,int)),iddecl(y,int))
inid(entry(init(iddecl(x,int)),iddecl(y,int)),x)
inid(entry(init(iddecl(x,int)),iddecl(y,int)),y)
S=entry(init(iddecl(x,int)),iddecl(y,int))
yes
```
It corresponds to the result from example 6.
```
#
```
- The auxiliary syntactical functions and semantic functions are
implemented in PROLOG and they will be executed :
```
& X :- call(X).    # X :- call(X).
```

A mixed case with termal interpretation and computed terms is possible,
too. The mentioned variants are very profitable to different phases of
program development. Now the following theorem can be proved.

<u>Theorem 1</u>:
Suppose G is a GSF with underlying LL(k)-grammar and G is L-attributed
in the sense of attributed grammars. Then a PROLOG program G´ derived
from G by the above modifications exists, which is semantically
equivalent to G. That means,   G´ as well as G define equal relations.
If G is consistent,   unification for G´ means only renaming variables
and assigning terms to variables.
#
The atomic formulae (or simple atoms in the sense of predicate
calculus) in clauses of a PROLOG program G´ are arranged in three
groups. The first group contains atoms, which are identical with the
syntactical functions of the production rule patterns of G. The second
group contains atoms derived from auxiliary syntactical (auxiliary
syntactical functions preceded by #) and the atoms of the third group
are derived from semantic functions (preceded by &). The assumptions -
the basic grammar of G is LL(k) and G is L-attributed - guarantee an
evaluation of the parameters of G from left to right during top-down
parse, which corresponds to the strategy of PROLOG systems to satisfy
goals and therefore enables the computation of G´ by a PROLOG system.

This strategy may be only disturbed by atoms from the second or third group. But the modifications of a FGSF to get a PROLOG program allow a reordering of these atoms.

An atom l of the third group must be placed after all atoms with input parameters from l and before atoms with the only output parameter of l. An atom l of the second group must be placed after all atoms containing variables from l. Such ordering is always possible because of the assumptions that G is a functional GSF and L-attributed.

For example, by modifying the fourth production rule pattern from example 1 we get the fourth clause of the PROLOG program from example 7 with the atom & entry(S0,S,IT) occuring immediately before the atom dec_list(S0,SN). Because S0 is the output parameter of the semantic function entry(S0,S,IT), it's computed in dependence on S and IT and then submitted to dec_list(S0,SN).

From the consistence of G follows that the value of a parameter will be determined by only one term. Therefore, matching two corresponding parameter of two given atoms from G´, the case that terms both not being variables are unified is excluded.

There is no need for carrying out the occur-check, because G is acyclic (cf. [DM84]).

Remarks:

- A PROLOG program G´ derived from a GSF G can be considered a notational variant of the GSF G, e.g. the operator @ can be interpreted as follows:
  - If the rules for G´ are used in a PROLOG system, @ X means a lexical scan of a given input. @ X is a subgoal in the sense of PROLOG.
  - If the rules of G´ are considered production rule patterns, @ X means X is a terminal symbol or a class of terminal symbols.
- Generally it's not possible to replace the assumption for the GSF G to be L-attributed by the more general assumption to be one-sweep, because the syntactical functions in a production rule pattern can´t be reordered (Reordering of these functions implies also reordering of the terminal symbols in the processed input stream). In this case the standard strategy of PROLOG systems can´t be used.

Example 10:

The rules from example 4 extended by the definitions of operators @, & and # represent a PROLOG program semantically equivalent to the GSF from example 2. The basic grammar is a LL(1)-grammar according to the used definition of the operator @ .

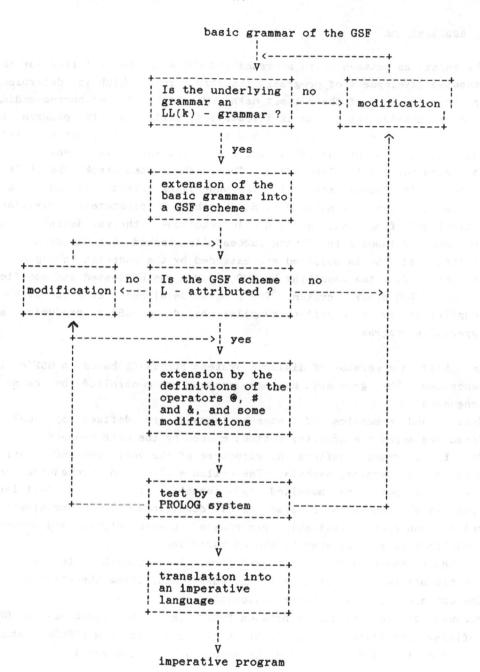

basic grammar of the GSF

Is the underlying grammar an LL(k) - grammar ? — no → modification

yes

extension of the basic grammar into a GSF scheme

modification ← no — Is the GSF scheme L - attributed ? — no →

yes

extension by the definitions of the operators @, # and &, and some modifications

test by a PROLOG system

translation into an imperative language

imperative program

Fig. 2

3. Applications

The relations between logic programs and GSF´s can be exploited for the stepwise development of programs the structure of which is determined by the structure of their input data. The basic idea of corresponding program development system is illustrated in fig. 2. The program is step by step developed as a GSF and tested as a PROLOG program. First the basic grammar of the GSF is defined by the author in dependence on the structure of the input data. Then, the system checks the LL(k)-property (obviously k=1). If the underlying grammar is an LL(k)-grammar, it can be completed to a GSF scheme by parameters, auxiliary syntactical functions, and semantic functions, thereby defining the treatment of input data. Having succesfully checked that the grammar is L-attributed it is modified and extended by the cosmetic changes of section 2. Now, the resulting PROLOG program can be tested and modified by a PROLOG program system. The program development ends up with a compilation by a compiler compiler based on GSF´s producing an imperative program.

In [L84] a generator of dialogue systems RUEGEN-KS based on GSF´s is described. The generated dialogue systems are controlled by command languages.
Syntax and semantics of a command language are defined by FGSF´s. Semantics means the computer actions caused by the user commands.
The basic grammar defines the structure of the user commands, which consist of terminal symbols. The called application procedures and system outputs are modelled by semantic functions. Auxiliary syntactical functions realize context conditions. The communication between commands, application procedures, system outputs, and context conditions is accomplished by shared variables.
If the commands have some standard form, it is possible to generate the production rule patterns of the FGSF, describing the structure of the commands, from a signature automatically.
Because of the relations between FGSF´s and PROLOG programs a GSF defining particular dialogue systems can be tested by a PROLOG system, if the mentioned GSF satisfies the assumptions of theorem 1.

References

[CU73]   Cleaveland,J.C.,Uzgalis,R.C. :
          What every programmer should know about grammar.
          Preliminary version, Univ. of California,
          Los Angeles,1973.
[DM84]   Deransart,P.,Maluszinski,J.:
          Relating Logic Programs and Attribute Grammars
          LiTH-IDA-R-84-07, Computer and Information Science
          Department, Linkoeping Univ.,Sweden.
[DM88]   Deransart,P.,Maluszinski,J.:
          A grammatical view of logic programming.
          Proceedings of PLILP'88,Orleans,France,
          May 16-18,1988.
[L84]   Lämmel,U.:
          Spezifikation und Implementation von Kommandosprachen
          fuer Dialogsysteme mit Hilfe einer attributierten
          Grammatik.
          Dissertation, Sektion Informatik, W.-Pieck-Univ.
          Rostock,DDR,1984.
[L87]   Lämmel,U.:
          Realisierung von Grammatiken syntaktischer Funktionen
          in PROLOG.
          Vortraege des Problemseminars "Programmiersprachen
          und Sprachimplementation" Helmsdorf 9.-13.11.87, DDR
          to be published in: Schriftenreihe des Weiterbildungs-
          zentrum fuer Mathematische Kybernetik und Rechen-
          technik/Informationsverarbeitung der Technischen
          Univ. Dreseden, DDR.
[PW80]   Pereira,F.,Warren,D.:
          Definite Clause Grammars for Language Analysis -
          A survey of the formalism and a Comparison with
          Augmented Transition Networks.
          Artificial Intelligence 13(1980),231-278.
[R72]   Riedewald,G.:
          Syntaktische Analyse von ALGOL68-Programmen
          Dissertation,Sektion Mathematik, W.-Pieck-Univ.
          Rostock,DDR,1972.
[R76]   Riedewald,G.:
          Compilermodell auf der Grundlage einer Grammatik
          syntaktischer Funktionen
          Interner Bericht,Sektion Mathematik, W.-Pieck-Univ.
          Rostock,DDR,1976.
[RDM83]   Riedewald,G.,Maluszinski,j.,Dembinski,P.:
          Formale Beschreibung von Programmiersprachen
          Akademie-Verlag Berlin,1983.
          also: R.Oldenburg Verlag Muenchen Wien,1983.

Structure sharing in attribute grammars

Henning Christiansen

Roskilde University Centre
P.O. Box 260, DK-4000 Roskilde, Denmark

Structure sharing is commonplace in Prolog implementations in order to achieve a compact representation of data values and to provide the ability to update sets of interrelated values simultaneously. This paper describes a representation of attributed syntax trees — as they appear in syntax-oriented editors — based on structure sharing.

Although the two formalisms, attribute grammars and Prolog programs, do have much in common we can only hope for a partial application of structure sharing: The attributes in a typical attribute grammar concern structural objects as well as other values defined by arbitrary functions. In the present approach, the attribute defining expressions are filtered and classified in order to recognize the potential applications of structure sharing. The propagation of changes when updating the shared attribute representation is measured by an abstract interpretation, the so-called flow algebra.

The results in this paper provide a basis for the study of efficient updating algorithms for attributed syntax trees — and existing algorithms may be improved.

1 Introduction

This paper concerns the use of structure sharing in the representation of attributed syntax trees with special reference to incremental editors.

An incremental editor based on attribute grammars keeps a user's program text in the shape of a consistently attributed syntax tree. The attributes may, for example, be symbol tables used in order to check context-sensitive syntax or a persistently compiled version of the program. Whenever the user alters the program text, the editor state, i.e., the representation of the syntax tree and its attributes, must be updated in order to reflect the change. And the editor should re-use as much of the previous state as possible: A small change in the program should only imply a similarly small amount of work for maintaining the attributes.

It is well-known in the context of automatic theorem provers, (Boyer, Moore, 1972), including Prolog systems, (Warren, 1977), that structure sharing provides for a space-efficient representation which allows for simultaneous update of interrelated data structures. The inherent structure sharing in (most implementations of) LISP is also appreciated by experienced programmers (and feared by the unexperienced ones) for its far-reaching side-effects.

Deransart and Maluszynski, (1985), have demonstrated the close relationship between pure Prolog programs and attribute grammars whose attributes are terms over free algebras: The proof trees of the former are isomorphic to the syntax trees of the latter. One might, then, expect that the structure sharing method used in Prolog systems applies for the representation of attributed syntax trees as well. However, there are some fundamental differences in the needs of a Prolog interpreter and of an incremental editor based on attribute grammars: First of all, the techniques applied in the Prolog system are not intended to be incremental, in fact, it is a virtue to avoid building the proof tree and to store as few parameters as possible. Secondly, the attributes in a syntax tree are, as opposed to the parameters of a proof tree, defined by expressions which may contain arbitrary functions. A typical attribute grammar uses a mixture of term or tuple constructors and other functions. This implies that structure sharing only makes sense for a part of all attributes.

In the approach described here, the attribute defining expressions are filtered in order to recognize which attributes and parts thereof should be stored in a global heap, as opposed to reside directly in the syntax tree, and hence referenced by a pointer. Sharing of structure may appear whenever these pointers (via an alternative interpretation of the attribute expressions) are made part of attributes recognized as freely constructed data structures.

Whenever the editor user alters the tree structure, some new attribute values appear which in turns may affect other attributes in the tree. For measuring the flow and the degree of these changes, I use a three-valued, abstract interpretation (cf. Mycroft, 1981) of the attribute expressions. An attribute value may be totally unaffected, it may be physically changed, to a new pointer or integer constant, for example, or it may be in an intermediate state called 'Indirectly-changed': Its physically represented value is same before and after the event, but the 'true', abstracted value may be another due to a change in the content of some storage cell maybe far, far away. A special treatment is given to the class of attributes characterized as pure structures which are (potential) pointer structures guaranteed not to be dereferenced in order to determine other attribute values. The explicit propagation of changes in these attributes is suppressed, they are treated as if they were unaffected, even when they are actually indirectly changed: Exactly as in a Prolog system, the applied structure sharing implies an instant execution of all related changes.

Most formal results in this paper are formulated with respect to noncircular attribute grammars in order to obtain a simple presentation. However, the results can be generalized to go for a class of circular grammars based on reflexive domains as well. Informal remarks concerning this generalization will appear now and then.

Related work

This paper describes a model for the use of structure sharing in incremental editors and its impact on the propagation of changes. The concepts of structure sharing used here and in Reps' work, (Reps, 1984), are radically different: Reps uses comparison of pointers in order to achieve efficient equality test for large structures and hence the opportunity for simultaneous updating is lost; even a minor change in the bottom of a large structure may cause the entire structure to be re-built in order to preserve the pointer-to-value correspondence. (Section 7 provides for an enhancement of Reps' algorithm based on my use of structure sharing; the abstract flow interpretation eliminates the need for explicit equally tests).

In order to extend the scope of Reps' original work, Hoover, (1986), and Reps, Marceau, and Teitelbaum, (1986), suggest in slightly different settings for a special treatment of chains of attributes recognized as copies of each other: Not every instance in the chain needs actually to receive a new value — only those that are used directly to determine other attribute values. Such chains represent a special case of structure sharing, each attribute value in the chain can be represented by a pointer to a common storage cell and efficient updating is gained for free.

The paper by Reps, Marceau, and Teitelbaum, (1986), describes, furthermore, an algorithm in which a change in a component of a structured object (of a certain kind) implies re-evaluation of only those other attributes that depend on exactly that component. This sort of fine-grained change flow measurement is not covered by the abstract flow interpretation as it is presented here; a possible generalization will be discussed in the final section. It should be noted, however, that my work, in contrary to the references above, is concerned mainly with the underlying data representation and its properties.

In systems based on parsing, e.g., traditional compilers and compiler writing systems, the construction and maintenance of syntax trees are avoided in order to save space. Various techniques with a flavour of structure sharing have been used to reduce the number of stored attributes and the amount of attribute calculations. Räihä, (1979), Ganzinger, (1979), and others have improved storage allocation by using the same global variable for different instances of the same attribute when certain conditions are satisfied. Furthermore, Räihä uses pointers to represent attributes whose values are known to be copies of each other. These ideas has been elaborated by, among others, Kastens, Hutt, Zimmermann, (1982), for their GAG system, and Sonnenschein, (1985). Actually, an algorithm described in the present paper indicates that my approach to structure sharing applies to parsing-based systems as well.

The NEATS system, (Jespersen, Madsen, Riis, 1978; Madsen, 1980), constructs an expression graph describing the synthesized attributes for the root node of the syntax tree while parsing and evaluates it afterwards. This graph contains, of course, also expressions for all other attributes needed in order to determine these final, synthesized attributes. Whenever an attribute, via an attribute variable, is used in order to determine another attribute, no copying takes place, a pointer to its defining expression graph is used instead. In the case of freely constructed data structures (which denote themselves), this yields a shared representation similar to what is described in this paper. NEATS can also handle circular attribute grammars, the expression graph may then contain circularities — in the same way that the heap storage representation proposed in the present paper may contain meaningful circularities.

Deransart, Jourdan, and Lorho, (1985, 1986a, 1986b), provide for an overview of results on attribute grammars and a recent bibliography.

Finally, an attribute grammar can be considered as a Prolog program — extended in the sense that arbitrary functions may be used and restricted in that one out of the two parties in a 'unification' is guaranteed to be a variable. It may, then, be reasonable to believe that some of the results in this paper may apply to logic programs involving functions as well. However, this possibility has not been investigated.

Outline

Section 2 gives the definitions for attribute grammars and the potential interpretations of their attribute expressions: Representations which preserve the attribute values and abstract interpretations that may be used for classification of attributes. The filtering of attributes expressions into various pieces is described in section 3.

The shared representation of the attributes, in which certain attributes and parts thereof are referred to a heap storage, is described in section 4. The flow algebra is introduced in section 5, whereas section 6 is concerned with the relation between the shared representation and the flow algebra: This leads to lemma which captures the use of the flow algebra as a controlling device in updating algorithms and that can be used for proving such algorithms correct.

Section 7 provides for two sample updating algorithms: First of all, an illustrative algorithm that visits every attribute in the syntax tree is described. This algorithm covers, as a special case, a strategy for using structure sharing in systems based on top-down parsing. Secondly, it is illustrated how structure sharing (in my sense) gives rise to an immediate enhancement of an algorithm described by (Reps, 1984).

The final section is a discussion which gives some more detailed comments on recent, related work. Furthermore, I consider possible generalizations of the results and techniques presented in this paper.

2 Attribute grammars and interpretations

The notation for attribute grammars used here is taken over from the so-called extended attribute grammars of Watt and Madsen, (1979). However, I will ignore their general pattern matching which allows for implicitly specified constraints and inverse functions. This notation has two advantages over the notation used originally by Knuth, (1968), which for some reason still is the most commonly used:

- It has a compact expression and a concise reading.

- It accentuates the algebraic properties of a grammatical definition: An attribute is not viewed as a value produced by some unaccessible 'semantic' function, rather, it is the value of an explicit term whose structure can be analyzed and transformed.

In fact, my whole method is based on a detailed analysis of the expressions that define the attribute values — they will be chopped into pieces and interpreted in various, different ways.

Definition 1. An *attribute grammar* is a set of *rules* of the form

$$\langle N_0 \dagger exp_{0,1} \dagger \ldots \dagger exp_{0,no} \rangle ::=$$
$$\alpha_0 \langle N_1 \dagger exp_{1,1} \dagger \ldots \dagger exp_{1,n1} \rangle \alpha_1$$
$$\ldots$$
$$\alpha_{n-1} \langle N_n \dagger exp_{n,1} \dagger \ldots \dagger exp_{n,nn} \rangle \alpha_n.$$

where

- $N_0, \ldots, N_n$ are *nonterminal symbols*,

- $\alpha_1, \ldots, \alpha_n$ sequences of *terminal symbols*,

- $\dagger$ stands for either $\uparrow$, preceding an inherited attribute (position), or $\downarrow$, preceding a synthesized attribute (position),

- $exp_{0,1}, \ldots, exp_{n,nn}$ are *attribute expressions* which are terms built out of typed function symbols, constants, and variables.

It is required that any inherited attribute expression of N_0 and synthesized attribute expression of $N_1, \ldots, N_n$ consists of a single, distinct variable; these attribute positions are called *defining* positions. Any variable used in a rule should appear in exactly one defining position.

Furthermore, the number, the types, and classifications as either inherited or synthesized of the attribute expressions associated with a given nonterminal symbol should be consistent throughout every rule in the grammar. One distinct nonterminal symbol is recognized as the *start symbol*; it should not have any associated, inherited attribute positions.
□

The attribute expressions will be made subject of various transformations in the sequel so a basic, algebraic terminology is necessary. Readers unfamiliar with universal, many-sorted algebra and abstract interpretations are referred to, e.g., (Goguen, Thatcher, Wagner, 1979), and to Mycroft, (1981).

A fixed signature of sorts, operator symbols with given arity (or rank),

$$f: s_1 \ldots s_n \rightarrow s, \text{ where } s_1, \ldots, s_n, \text{ and } s \text{ are sorts,}$$

and constant symbols is assumed. As usual, an *interpretation* is an algebra, i.e., an assignment of (maybe partial) functions to function symbols and constants to constant symbols. An *environment* is a mapping from a set of variables to appropriate values; we may hence refer to the *value* of term with respect to a given interpretation in given environment.

The *canonical* interpretation describes the 'obvious' or 'true' meaning of terms; we may expect, for example, that the canonical value of the symbol '7' is the natural number seven and that '+' denotes addition. The *term algebra* associates terms with themselves.

By a *representation* is understood an interpretation, Repr, such that there exists an *abstraction function* which maps the values of terms wrt. Repr to their canonical values. Hence a representation associates distinct values to terms that describe distinct, canonical values. An *abstract interpretation* is an interpretation which is not (necessarily) a representation. An abstract interpretation may clash canonically distinct terms and may thus serve as a device for classification of terms.

Example 1. The following attribute grammar describes a simple language of integer expressions which will be referred to throughout this paper. The string

let a = 2 **in** a + a **end**

is a sample program. Each expression is decorated with three attributes:

- A symbol table describing the currently available named constant; an inherited attribute.

- The value of the expression which is an integer number; a synthesized attribute.

- The translation of the expression into the language of an abstract stack machine; a synthesized attribute. This machine applies two stacks, an evaluation stack and a stack of bindings of constant names to their values.

The two synthesized attributes, the value and the translation, will be used in the sequel to exemplify two different classes of attributes. It should be noted, though, that either one could be removed from the grammar without affecting the other. The grammar has three nonterminal symbols, 'exp' for expressions with the attributes described above, 'int' for integer constants and 'id' for identifiers, each having one obvious, synthesized attribute, and 'program', the start symbol, equipped with two synthesized attributes, the value of and the stack machine code for the program.

The constant and function symbols used in the grammar are intended to be self-explanatory; variables can be distinguished from other symbols due to their appearances in defining positions. As an aid to the reader, variables and only variables are italized.

$\langle$program$\uparrow val \uparrow code \rangle ::= \langle$exp$\downarrow$empty$\uparrow val \uparrow code \rangle$

$\langle$exp$\downarrow table \uparrow val_1 + val_2 \uparrow code_1; code_2;$ ADD$\rangle ::=$
    $\langle$exp$\downarrow table \uparrow val_1 \uparrow code_1 \rangle + \langle$exp$\downarrow table \uparrow val_2 \uparrow code_2 \rangle$

$\langle$exp$\downarrow table \uparrow val \uparrow$PUSH-BIND$(id, n); code;$ POP-BIND$\rangle ::=$
    let $\langle$id$\uparrow id \rangle = \langle$int$\uparrow n \rangle$ **in** $\langle$exp$\downarrow$extend$(table, id, n) \uparrow val \uparrow code \rangle$ **end**

$\langle$exp$\downarrow table \uparrow$find$(table, id) \uparrow$FETCH$(id) \rangle ::= \langle$id$\uparrow id \rangle$

$\langle$exp$\downarrow table \uparrow n \uparrow$LOAD$(n) \rangle ::= \langle$int$\uparrow n \rangle$

$\langle$int$\uparrow 1 \rangle ::= 1, \ldots$

$\langle$id$\uparrow a \rangle ::= a, \ldots$

$\square$

Definition 2. An *instance* of an attribute grammar rule (wrt. to some interpretation) is the structure that results from a substitution of its attribute expressions by their respective values in a common environment. Hence, a rule instance takes the form

$$A_0 ::= \alpha_0 A_1 \ldots A_n \alpha_n$$

where $\{A_i\}$ are *attributed nonterminal symbols*,

$$A_i = \langle N_i \uparrow a_{i,1} \uparrow \ldots \uparrow a_{i,ni} \rangle.$$

The values, $\{a_{i,j}\}$, are called *attributes*.

The class of *attributed syntax trees* for an attribute grammar (wrt. some interpretation) is defined as follows.

• Whenever

$$A_0 ::= \alpha_0 A_1 \ldots A_n \alpha_n$$

is a rule instance and $T_1, \ldots, T_n$ are attributed syntax trees whose root nodes are $A_1, \ldots, A_n$, resp., then

$$\alpha_1 T_1 \ldots T_n \alpha_n$$

is an attributed syntax tree.

• Nothing else is an attributed syntax tree.

$\square$

Lemma 1. The abstraction function for a representation naturally extends to a function mapping the syntax trees wrt. that representation to similarly shaped, canonically attributed syntax trees.
$\square$

In this paper, the focus is on the attributes and their representation, the actual syntax tree structure is of minor interest. The following definition represents an abstraction in which only the attributes and their mutual dependencies remain.

Definition 3. An *attribute descriptor*, D, is an environment mapping a set of variables to terms, observing their respective sorts, and which satisfies the following condition:

Whenever v_1 and v_2 are variables such that v_2 occurs in $D(v_1)$, there exists a term, t, such that $D(v_2) = t$.

An *attribute record* for a given attribute descriptor, D, wrt. a given interpretation, is the smallest environment, R, such that:

If $D(v) = t$, then $R(v)$ is the value of t wrt. the given interpretation in the environment R.

□

Two comments to definition 3 are needed. First of all, a given attributed syntax tree gives rise to an attribute descriptor: Each attribute is represented by a descriptor variable which is bound to its defining expressions (with an appropriate substitution of variables). This attribute descriptor captures all essential properties concerning the attributes, namely their definition and interrelation. The corresponding attribute record contains the set of all the attributes in the tree. Therefore it is reasonable to apply the designations of attributes, attribute expressions, and attribute variables for the components of attribute descriptors and records.

Example 2. The following figure displays an attributed syntax tree (wrt. the canonical interpretation) for the grammar in example 2 and its corresponding attribute descriptor. The subscripts (not actually part of the syntax tree) indicate the correspondence between the attributes and their matching attribute variables in the descriptor.

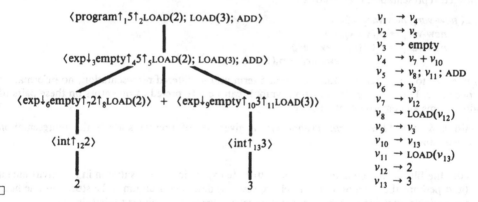

□

The second comment on definition 3 concerns the well-definedness of attribute records. If the descriptor does not contain circularities, i.e., no variable is defined in terms of itself, directly or indirectly, the descriptor constitutes a set of equations which can be solved uniquely in a finite number of elimination steps. Circular descriptors may or may not give rise to attribute records; however, there are some meaningful and useful cases. Consider, for example, the recursively defined environments (symbol tables) used in denotational semantics, cf. (Milne, Strachey, 1976). Particular elements of such reflexive domains are naturally specified by circular attribute descriptors. In order actually to handle this, the definition of attribute records should properly be formulated by means of a least fixed-point construction. Finally, the question as to whether an attribute grammar may give rise to circular attribute descriptors is simply a rephrasing of the familiar notion of circularity of an attribute grammar, cf. (Knuth, 1968).

3 Filtering the attribute expressions

In the shared representation, a given attribute value may reside either directly in the syntax tree or in a global heap store; in the latter case, the syntax tree holds a pointer to the appropriate storage cell. The actual choice of what to do about a certain attribute sort is a trade-off between an efficient implementation of operations on the one hand and storage economy and efficient change propagation on the other. I will not put any restrictions on this choice, instead an arbitrary set of *pointer sorts* is assumed: Values of attribute expressions and subexpressions of pointer sort, and only those, will be referred to the heap.

The shared representation of attribute values is described in two steps: First of all, the attribute expressions are filtered in order to factor out those subexpressions whose values should go to the heap. Secondly, the values of the remaining expressions are defined by a (partial) representation which is described in section 4.

The result of filtering a term is a new term and a, maybe empty, environment. The new term is similar to the original one, except that each subterm (exclusive of the term itself!) of pointer sort is replaced by an entirely new variable which in turns is bound in the environment to the (recursively filtered representation of that) subterm. However, variables in the original term, irrespective of their sorts, are not affected. It is important to stress that a term is not considered to be a subterm of itself, otherwise the filtering of a term of pointer sort would result in an infinite chain of mutually embedded environments.

Consider the following example term in which p_1, p_2, and p_3 are function symbols of pointer sort whereas a and b are of non-pointer sort; '12' and '25' are constants of non-pointer sorts, x_1, x_2, x_3, x_4 arbitrary variables.

$$a(\ p_1(x_1, x_2, x_3),\ p_2(\ b(x_4),\ p_3(12)),\ 25)$$

Its filtered representation is as follows.

$$a(\ \textit{new-var}_1,\ \textit{new-var}_2,\ 25)$$
$$\textit{new-var}_1 \rightarrow p_1(x_1, x_2, x_3)$$
$$\textit{new-var}_2 \rightarrow p_2(\ b(x_4),\ \textit{new-var}_3)$$
$$\textit{new-var}_3 \rightarrow p_3(12)$$

It is possible to map back and forth between a term and its filtered representation, no information has been lost. Furthermore, the function symbols can be interpreted as operators on these pairs of residual terms and environments. Hence:

Definition 4. The *filtered term algebra* wrt. a given set of pointer sorts is the representation described above.
□

Consider the filtered representation of some attribute expression. Each subterm in the environment part (and perhaps the remaining 'top-level' expression) describes a datum to be stored in one heap cell, the variable referring to it mirrors the (future) existence of a pointer to that datum.

The term filtering is generalized to filtering of attribute descriptors as follows.

Definition 5. Let D be an attribute descriptor. The corresponding *filtered attribute descriptor* is the smallest attribute descriptor, FD, that satisfies the following condition:

Whenever v is a variable such that $D(v) = t$ and t's filtered representation is $\langle t', env \rangle$, then

$$FD(v) = t'$$

and for any binding, $v_i \rightarrow \langle t_i, env_i \rangle$, in env or any of its embedded environments,

$$FD(v_i) = t_i.$$

The terms $\{t_i\}$ are called *local attribute expressions* and their values in any attribute record are called *local attributes*. The terms in FD of pointer sort distinct from singleton variables are called *proper pointer expressions*.
□

The notion of local attributes is justified by the fact that they are associated with a given node in a syntax tree and they only appear (qua some variable) in the defining expressions for other attributes associated with that node. The proper pointer expressions are those that give rise to allocation of new heap cells.

The filtering of an attribute descriptor does not affect its semantic properties, rather, it provides for a more detailed specification:

Lemma 2. Let D be an attribute descriptor and FD its filtered version and let R and FR be their respective attribute records wrt. some interpretation, then

$$R \subset FR$$

□

4 The shared representation

The precise notions of heaps and pointers are given by the following definition.

Definition 6. For any set, S, assume the following.

- Two sets,
    S-Pointers, and
    S-Heaps.

- Three functions with the indicated properties,
    new: S-Heaps $\rightarrow$ S-Pointers $\times$ S-Heaps
        - allocates a new and unused heap cell,
          yielding a pointer to it and a modified heap,
    put: S $\times$ S-Pointers $\times$ S-Heaps $\rightarrow$ S-heaps
        - stores a value in the heap cell referred to by
          the given pointer, destroying any previous content and
          yielding a modified heap,
    get: S-Pointers $\times$ S-Heaps $\rightarrow$ S
        - fetch the most recent value in the heap cell referred
          to by the given pointer.

Whenever F is a family of sets,

$$F\text{-Heaps} = \Pi_{S \in F} S\text{-Heaps}$$

and the functions new, put, and get are generalized accordingly.
□

In order to represent selected attributes in the heap and to use these as components of data structures, an alternative to the canonical interpretation is needed. What is meant by a data structure is captured by the following definition.

Definition 7. The set of *structural sorts* (in the fixed, basic signature) is the set of all sorts, s, such that each function symbol,

$$f: s_1 \ldots s_n \rightarrow s,$$

is a free operator with respect to the canonical interpretation, i.e., it constructs tuples or thereby isomorphic objects.
□

Example 3. The grammar of example 1 uses four attribute sorts, namely integers, identifiers, symbol tables, and stack machine code. Integers are not structures due to the plus operation. Identifiers, on the other hand, are vacuously structures, no function symbol creates identifiers — each potential identifier is named by an individual constant symbol.

The stack machine language represents a structural sort, a stack machine program is viewed as a tree. (No semantics is associated with this language and hence no 'equations' such as associativity of the sequencing operator, ';', are recognized). Similarly, symbol tables are viewed as structures, i.e., lists of bindings constructed from the constant symbol, 'empty', and the function symbol, 'extend(− , − , −)'.

In the examples to follow, symbol tables and stack machine code will, furthermore, be considered as pointer sorts.

□

Now, the reason for paying attention to structural sorts is the possibility to replace a value of pointer sort in a structure by a matching pointer. This is made precise in the following definition and lemma.

Definition 8. The *pointer interpretation* (wrt. to a given set of pointer sorts) is defined as follows.

- Any pointer sort, ps, is associated with the union of the actual representation of ps (which is defined by one of the cases below) and the associated pointer set. {The former are the values of sort ps to be stored in the heap, the latter are the values given to operators whose arguments are expected to belong to ps.}

- Any structural sort, ss, is represented by a set of tuples, such that the interpretation of any operator,
     f: $s_1 \ldots s_n \rightarrow$ ss,
  creates tuples of its arguments. However, these tupling operations are defined only when their arguments of pointer sorts actually are pointers.

- Any non-structural sort, ns, is represented by its canonical value set, and hence an operator
     f: $s_1 \ldots s_n \rightarrow$ ns
  must dereference its arguments (if necessary) in order to produce a reasonable value.

□

Lemma 3. Given a heap, h, the pointer interpretation above serves as a representation for the class of terms that can appear in filtered attribute records. The required abstraction function, i.e., the re-construction of canonical values, is as follows.

- Values that are not pointers or structures containing pointers are already in their canonical form.

- For any other value, all pointers are replaced by their recursively dereferenced value.

□

It should be noted that the verb 'dereference' in definition 8 properly refers to the abstraction function in lemma 3. In the case of circularities in the heap, the abstraction may or may not be defined. Circular heaps may be used for representation of elements of reflexive domains, cf. the discussion of circular attribute descriptors above. This allows for the representation of syntax trees for a useful class of circular attribute grammars. Actually, the parsing-based NEATS systems, (Madsen, 1980), employs circular structures in a similar way.

The following definition generalizes the pointer representation to go for filtered attribute descriptors.

Definition 9. Consider a filtered attribute descriptor, FD. A *shared representation state* for FD (or *state*, for short) is a pair

   ⟨P, h⟩

where h is a heap and P is the smallest environment such that the following conditions hold.

- Whenever FD(v) = t and t is of non-pointer sort, then
    P(v) = val
  where val is the value of t wrt. the pointer representation in the environment P and heap h.

- Whenever FD(v) = t and t is of pointer sort, then
    P(v) = p
  where p is a pointer such that
    get(p, h) = val
  where val is the value of t wrt. the pointer representation in the environment P and given the heap h.

- Whenever v_1 and v_2 are distinct variables of pointer sort such that their defining expressions, FD(v_1) and FD(v_2), are proper pointer expressions, then
    P(v_1) ≠ P(v_2).

□

The first two requirements state that each represented attribute value (i.e., value stored in P) is, in fact, the value of its defining expression; the second one, furthermore, implies structure sharing. The third requirement excludes 'casual' structure sharing: Two attributes share the same heap cell if and only if they can be traced back, via chains of singleton variables in FD, to a common, proper pointer expression.

Lemma 4. The attributed syntax trees for a class of attribute grammars which include all noncircular grammars can be represented by a generalization of shared representation states. There exists an abstraction function which maps such represented trees to similarly shaped, canonically attributed attributed syntax trees.
□

Example 4. The following figure displays an attributed syntax tree for the sample grammar represented by means of a shared representation state. Heap cells are presented as boxes scattered around the syntax tree; a pointer is shown as an arrow pointing to its matching heap cell.

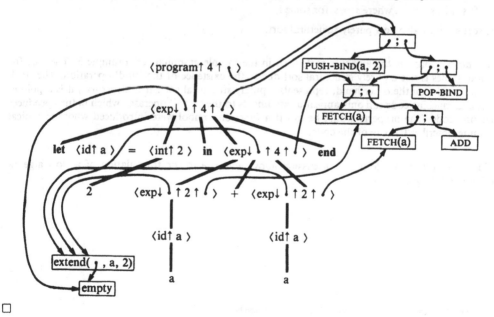

□

5 The flow algebra, a measurement of change

Each attribute in a syntax tree is defined by means of an expression whose variables stand for other attributes in the tree. Whenever the tree structure is altered, some new attributes values occur and the attributes defined in terms of these values must be updated and the attributes depending on these in turns must also be updated, etc.

Whether or not a given attribute really needs to be evaluated from scratch is determined by the state of the attributes referred to in its defining expression. The use of structure sharing provides for a distinction between whether the actual, physical representation of an attribute has been changed or only the 'abstracted' or dereferenced value it stands for — due to a modification of a heap cell maybe far, far away. A structural value needs only be re-evaluated when some attribute on which it directly depends has changed its represented value. Any other attribute must be re-evaluated whenever a change in one of the attributes on which it depends is reported — irrespective of the degree of that change.

When an attribute has been re-evaluated, the advent of a potentially new value must be reported and the report should explain the degree of that change. Assume that an attribute is represented by a pointer to a heap cell whose contents has achieved a new value. Seen from the rest of the world, the physical value, i.e., the pointer, is the same as before: The inserted pointer link diminishes the degree of the change. However, the change in the abstract value should be reported — even if no actual re-evaluation has taken place — such that other attributes that really depend on the abstracted or dereferenced value 'know' when to re-evaluate.

A special treatment is given for the class of pure structures (defined below) which are pointer structures guaranteed not to be dereferenced in order to determine the values of other attributes. For such structures only hard, physical changes need to be announced, the applied structure sharing implies an instant execution of all other necessary updates.

Definition 10. The set of *purely structural* sorts (in the fixed, basic signature) is the maximal[1] set of sorts which are structural and pointer sorts that satisfy the following condition: For any purely structural sort, s, and function symbol,

$f: s_1 \ldots s_n \to s'$, where $s = s_i$ for some i,

the sort s' must also be a purely structural sort.

$\square$

Example 5. Consider the attribute sorts used in the sample grammar, cf. example 3. The sort for symbol tables is not a purely structural sort due to the existence of the 'find' operation. The stack machine code, on the other hand, represents a purely structural sort: It is structural, it is a pointer sort, and machine code can only appear as arguments to the ' − ; − ' operator which in turn produces machine code. The property would be lost if a function symbol were introduced whose canonical meaning describes the size of the code.

$\square$

The observations made in the discussion above give rise to the formulation of a flow algebra defined as follows.

---

1. The fact that there exists one and only one such maximal set can be seen as follows.
   - There exist such sets, $\emptyset$, for example.
   - The property is closed wrt. set union.
   - The union of all such sets can be shown to be *the* maximal set.

Definition 11. The *flow algebra* wrt. a given set of pointer sorts is defined as follows. The algebra comprises three values ordered as follows.

Unaffected $<$ Indirectly-changed $<$ Changed

The flow function associated with each function symbol is defined as follows.

- The flow function associated with a function symbol,
  $$f: s_1 \ldots s_n \to s,$$
  where s is a purely structural sort always yields 'Unaffected'.

- The flow function associated with a function symbol,
  $$f: s_1 \ldots s_n \to s,$$
  where s is any non-pure, structural sort, returns the maximal flow value of its arguments; however, if, furthermore, the sort s is a pointer sort, a value of 'Changed' is reduced to 'Indirectly-changed'.

- The flow function associated with a function symbol,
  $$f: s_1 \ldots s_n \to s,$$
  where s is a non-structural sort returns 'Changed' if any of its arguments differ from 'Unaffected', 'Unaffected' otherwise; however, if, furthermore, the sort s is a pointer sort, a value of 'Changed' is reduced to 'Indirectly-changed'.

□

The use of flow values to determine whether or not a given attribute needs to be re-evaluated is described more precisely in definition 14 and lemma 6 below.

6 Properties of the flow algebra

Here I will examine the properties of the flow algebra that relate to its intended use as an instrument for tracing the flow of changes in updating processes. The flow value for a given attribute tells something about whether or not the attribute has changed its value in the transition from one state to another. Whether or not an attribute really needs to be re-evaluated depends on the flow values of the attributes referenced in its defining expression. In other words, the flow algebra concerns the period of time between two well-defined states, i.e., shared representation states.

Definition 12. Let $\Sigma = \langle P, h \rangle$ and $\Sigma' = \langle P', h' \rangle$ be two shared representation states. A flow environment, F, which is a mapping from a set of variables to flow values, is said to *report the transition* from Σ to Σ', written

$$F: \Sigma \Rightarrow \Sigma',$$

whenever the following properties hold.

- F binds the same variables as P'.

- If, for some variable, v,
  $$P(v) \neq P'(v), \text{ or }$$
  $$P(v) \text{ is undefined, whereas } P'(v) \text{ is defined}$$
  then $F(v) = $ Changed,

- If, for some variable, v, for which
  $$P(v) = P'(v),$$
  but the abstracted values of v are different in the respective Σ and Σ', then
  $$F(v) = \text{Indirectly-changed}.$$

□

An editing session is a sequence of events, each specifying a modification of the structure of a tree (or generally, a set of trees) represented in the editor's execution state. Following such an event, an algorithm for restoring the consistency of the attribute values is set to work and the set of affected attributes are re-evaluated in an appropriate sequence.

Described in terms of shared representation states, an updating process may be viewed as follows. Given an old state, Σ_{old}, a new state is reached via a series of intermediate states, $\Sigma_0, \Sigma_1, \ldots, \Sigma_n = \Sigma_{new}$, which include more and more attributes.

Definition 13. A (shared representation) state, $\Sigma_{n+1} = \langle P_{n+1}, h_{n+1} \rangle$ is a *successor* of a state $\Sigma_n = \langle P_n, h_n \rangle$ wrt. a previous state $\Sigma_{old} = \langle P_{old}, h_{old} \rangle$ whenever

$$\Sigma_n \{v := t\} \Sigma_{n+1}$$

where this notation is defined as follows; the variable, v, should be unbound in Σ_n whereas any variable that occurs in t should be defined in Σ_n.

Let val be the value of t in Σ_n wrt. the pointer representation.
If t is not a proper pointer expression,

$$P_{n+1} = P_n \cup \{v \to val\},$$
$$h_{n+1} = h_n.$$

If t is a proper pointer expression,

$$P_{n+1} = P_n \cup \{v \to p\}$$

where p is a pointer defined as follows.
If v is bound in P_{old}, then

$$p = P_{old}(v) \text{ and}$$
$$h_{n+1} = put(val, p, h_n),$$

otherwise, (i.e., t is a completely new, proper pointer expression),

$$\langle p, h_{n+\frac{1}{2}} \rangle = new(h_n) \text{ and}$$
$$h_{n+1} = put(val, p, h_{n+\frac{1}{2}}).$$

$\square$

The following monotonicity lemma and its corollary describe in a constructive way a sequence of increasing flow environments corresponding to a given sequence of successive states. The lemma may serve as an induction hypothesis in correctness proofs for attribute update algorithms.

Lemma 5, monotonicity. Let Σ_{old}, Σ_n, and Σ_{n+1} be states such that

$$\Sigma_n \{v_n := t_n\} \Sigma_{n+1}$$

wrt. Σ_{old} and assume F_n is a flow environment such that

$$F_n: \Sigma_{old} \Rightarrow \Sigma_n.$$

Now, let

$$F_{n+1} = F_n \cup \{v_n \to fv_n\}$$

where, if v_n is bound in Σ_{old}, fv_n is the flow value of t_n in F_n; otherwise, fv_n is by convention set to Changed. Then

$$F_{n+1}: \Sigma_{old} \Rightarrow \Sigma_{n+1}.$$

$\square$

Corollary. Let $\Sigma_0, \ldots, \Sigma_n$ be a sequence of states such that

$$\Sigma_i \{v_i := t_i\} \Sigma_{i+1}, \quad i = 0, \ldots, n-1$$

wrt. a state $\Sigma_{old} = \langle P_{old}, h_{old} \rangle$ and that

$$\Sigma_0 = \langle \varnothing, h_{old} \rangle \text{ and}$$
$$\Sigma_n = \Sigma_{new}.$$

Now, let $F_0 = \varnothing$ be the empty flow environment and, for $i = 1, \ldots, n-1$, F_{i+1} the extension to F_i described in the monotonicity lemma, then, by induction:

$$F_i : \Sigma_{old} \Rightarrow \Sigma_i, \text{ and especially}$$
$$F_n : \Sigma_{old} \Rightarrow \Sigma_{new}.$$

□

An updating algorithm is, then, a method for constructing a suitably converging sequence of successive states. Calculations of flow values 'on the flight' may be used to determine this sequence — maybe supported by global properties of the syntax tree. An efficient algorithm should visit only those attributes that really need to be re-evaluated — or at least only few other attributes. Hence, an efficient algorithm should include a strategy for throwing large systems of attributes, known somehow to be unaffected, into the growing state.

This section is concluded with an explicit statement of a criterion for whether or not a given attribute actually needs to be re-evaluated.

Definition 14. Assume that

$$\Sigma_n \{v_n := t_n\} \Sigma_{n+1} \text{ and}$$
$$F_n : \Sigma_{old} \Rightarrow \Sigma_n.$$

We say that v_n (or t_n, or the attribute it stands for) is *subject to re-evaluation* whenever

- v_n is unbound in Σ_{old}, (i.e., an entirely new variable), or

- v_n is of structural sort and there exists a variable in t_n whose value in F_n is 'Changed', or

- v_n is of non-structural sort and there exists a variable in t_n whose value in F_n is different from 'Unaffected'.

□

Lemma 6. Assume t_n is an attribute expression which is *not* subject to re-evaluation, then, with notation of definition 14, assuming $\Sigma_n = \langle P_n, h_n \rangle$ and $\Sigma_{n+1} = \langle P_{n+1}, h_{n+1} \rangle$,

$$P_{n+1}(v_n) = P_{old}(v_n)$$

If, furthermore, t_n is a proper pointer expression (def. 5),

$$get(h_{n+1}, p) = get(h_{old}, p)$$

where

$$p = P_{old}(v_n) = P_{n+1}(v_n).$$

□

7 Algorithms

Whenever the shape of a fully attributed syntax tree is altered some new attributes may arise and it may be necessary to re-evaluate a smaller or larger number of 'existing' attributes. An algorithm to perform the necessary attribute evaluations should do so in an appropriate order: When considering a particular attribute, those attributes referred to in its defining expression should either be visited already by the algorithm — or somehow known to be unaffected (or perhaps 'Indirectly-changed' when no dereferencing is needed). In other words, each such attribute should be evaluated in an environment that reflects (enough aspects of) the new state.

For any noncircular attribute grammar, the desired ordering is determined by a topological sorting of the attributes according to the directed acyclic graph described by their mutual dependencies, i.e., the familiar dependency graph, cf. (Knuth, 1968), (Reps, 1984). For circular grammars based on reflexive domains, as discussed earlier on, such orderings may also exist: Circular structures may be updated sequentially since the inserted pointer links make it possible to evaluate their defining expressions with only a partial knowledge of their argument values. However, the subtleties concerning circular attribute grammars have not been investigated and the algorithms considered here refer to the noncircular case only.

Here, I will consider two particular algorithms. The first one applies to grammars satisfying a condition such that the attributes can be evaluated in a depth-first recursive scan of the syntax tree. This illustrates the use of structure sharing and the flow algebra without having to consider any detailed structure of a dependency graph. Furthermore, it naturally covers, as a special case, an algorithm for evaluation of attributes in systems based on top-down parsing. The second algorithm is an enhancement of one of Reps' algorithms, (Reps, 1984), based on my use of structure sharing. In the following, final section, I will discuss the relations to the algorithms described by Hoover, (1986), and Reps, Marceau, and Teitelbaum, (1986). Various possible generalizations and applications of the flow algebra in very efficient algorithms will also be considered.

Left-to-right grammars

An attribute grammar is said to be a *left-to-right* attribute grammar whenever, in any rule, no attribute variable appears in an inherited attribute expression to the left of its defining position. (This class of grammars has also been investigated by Bochmann, (1976), although not in the setting of structure sharing).

The algorithm annotates the attributes with their respective flow values as the updating process proceeds. When referring to the value of the defining expression for a given attribute, the pointer interpretation and an environment of relevant attributes are assumed. It should be emphasized that the term 'defining expression' here refers to the expressions in the filtered attribute descriptor, i.e., with any proper pointer subexpressions factored out; the values of any local attribute expressions are assumed to be stored as local attributes attached to the syntax tree nodes.

The algorithm is described as two recursive procedures, one for updating a particular subtree and one for updating a particular attribute.

Update a tree, T, with root A $\equiv$
{The inherited attributes of A have been updated by the caller}
    For all subtrees, $T_i = T_1, \ldots, T_n$:
        Update the inherited attributes in the root of T_i in sequence,
        Update the tree T_i recursively by this procedure,
    Update the synthesized attributes of A in sequence
{All attributes in T are updated}

Update an attribute, att $\equiv$
    Update any related, local attributes in a suitable order
    using this procedure recursively,
    Annotate att with a flow value found as follows:
        Changed, if att is a new attribute, or otherwise,
        the flow value of att's defining expression,
    If att is subject to re-evaluation {def. 14}, then
        Evaluate att's defining expression to produce a new value,
        Store this value either directly in the tree or
        in an appropriate heap cell {cf. def. 13}.

The correctness of this algorithm follows easily from the corollary to the monotonicity lemma: Each call of the procedure for updating a particular attribute describes a transition between two successive states in the sense of definition 13,

$$\Sigma_i \{v_i := t_i\} \Sigma_{i+1}.$$

The left-to-right restriction on the attribute grammar ensures that each attribute has a correct value wrt. the new state when it is used to determine other attributes. Eventually, the sequence of successive states will cover all attributes in the tree.

The flow values for the attributes of a given node can be represented by two bit-vectors, one for indicating the 'Changed' ones and one for the 'Indirectly-changed'. Hence calculation of flow values can be implemented efficiently by means of a few arithmetic operations and similarly for the decision of whether or not an attribute is subject to re-evaluation.

If a non-structural sort, s, has an efficiently implemented equality test, as for instance is the case for the sort of integer numbers, a drastic speed-up of an update algorithm can be obtained: If the new and old value of an attribute recognized as being 'Changed' are equal, we may fool the algorithm to believe that its flow value is 'Unaffected'. When testing of equality is considered too expensive it may still pay off to search for certain identities: Consider a sort that has a special null value and that the constructors of this sort are strict with respect to the null value. In this case, it is probably worth-while to check whether both the old and new value happen to be the null value.

The time consumed by the algorithm is proportional to the size of the attributed syntax tree when evaluation of attribute expressions is assumed to be of constant time. However, calculations that involve dereferencing may in extreme cases need to trace chains of pointers whose length is comparable to the size of the syntax tree. This indicates that the implementor should be very careful in deciding which attribute sorts should be considered as pointer sorts.

The time consumed by the algorithm is taken up by

- a depth-first traversal of the syntax tree,

- calculation of the flow value for each attribute in the tree, and

- calculation of new values for attributes whose value was left undefined by the editor operation and the attributes whose represented value somehow depends on these.

Since the two first contributions can be implemented rather efficiently, the amount of time used to re-evaluate the attributes may be dominant in the case of small syntax trees. Hence the algorithm, despite its asymptotically disastrous behaviour, may be well-suited for small or highly modularized systems.

The algorithm is also an obvious choice in experimental systems since it is much simpler to implement than the asymptotically more efficient algorithm described below.

The algorithm can be used for evaluation of attributes in a top-down parser, the recursive call trees for the parser and for the evaluation algorithm are isomorphic. Here the flow value of any attribute will be set to 'Changed', any attribute then 'subject to re-evaluation' and hence there is no reason for keeping track of flow values at all. A combined parser and attribute evaluator can take (maybe pointers to) inherited attributes as arguments and return synthesized attributes. The structure sharing will ensure that heap storage is only allocated for proper pointer expressions, i.e., the first occurrence of a given value, and a pointer will be transferred to where that value is used.

Enhancement of Reps' algorithm

Reps, (1984), describes an algorithm for incremental attribute updating that works for any noncircular attribute grammar and whose time complexity is proportional to the number of attributes whose values actually are affected by the process. The optimal behaviour is based on an assumption that attribute values can be evaluated and tested for equality in constant time. Reps has recognized, cf. chapter 8 of (Reps, 1984), that efficient attribute evaluation and equality tests are critical factors and that structure sharing may be a way to achieve this. He uses one efficiently implemented data type based on structure sharing for structured objects, namely 2-3-trees.

However, Reps' use of structure sharing differs essentially from the model suggested in this paper: Reps performs equality tests by comparison of pointers and hence the opportunity for simultaneous updating is lost; even a minor change in the bottom of a structure may cause the entire structure to be re-built.

Here I will show how the approach to structure sharing proposed in the present paper gives rise to an enhanced performance. The flow values are used to suppress re-evaluation and equality tests may be avoided — and for pure structures the change propagation is effectively stopped.

The algorithm performs a traversal of the attributed syntax tree controlled by auxiliary scheduling information derived from the (functional) dependency graph and this extra information must also be maintained incrementally by the editor. The details concerning the scheduling information are of no interest here; it remains unchanged in the re-statement of the algorithm. Interested readers are referred to (Reps, 1984).

The algorithm applies a queue of attributes waiting for being examined and whenever an attribute actually changes it values, all attributes that directly depend on it are entered into the queue. The critical control point in the algorithm is as follows:

> evaluate the value of the attribute of interest;
> if new-value ≠ old-value then
> *propagate the change*
> else
> *forget it*

In the new algorithm, attributes will be annotated with their respective flow value as the updating process proceeds; the initial annotation of any attribute is 'Unaffected' except for the completely new attributes, their flow values are set to 'Changed'. For simplicity, the process is assumed to be started by a separate procedure that evaluates these originally undefined attributes. The critical lines of code are now replaced by the following:

> evaluate the flow value of the defining expression, and
> annotate the attribute with it,
> if the attribute is subject to re-evaluation {def. 14} then
>   evaluate it,
> case ⟨the flow value⟩ of
>   Unaffected: *forget it*
>   Indirectly-changed: *propagate the change*
>   Changed: if the attribute is a pointer
>   or a structure containing a pointer
>   then {test too expensive}
>   *propagate the change*
>   else if new-value ≠ old-value then
>   *propagate the change*
>   else
>   change annotation to Unaffected;
>   *forget it*

Whether or not an equality test should be applied in the case of a 'Changed' attribute can be determined statically from the defining expression for that attribute.

Equality tests for nested structures are replaced by evaluation of flow values. The cases in which the flow value indicates 'Indirectly-changed' but the dereferenced values happen to be equal are probably very rare. The same thing can be said for the cases in which the equality test for attributes originally recognized as 'Changed' are considered too expensive: Any non-accidental equality is presumably caught by equality tests on primitive data object in the deeper levels of the data structures.

The time complexity of the enhanced algorithm is proportional to the number of (directly or indirectly) affected attributes exclusive of pure structures. The time consumed for structural objects that are only indirectly changed is made up by calculations of flow values which can be implemented quite efficiently, cf. the remarks to the left-to-right algorithm. Thus, for syntax trees up to a certain size the time complexity may appear to be proportional to the number of attributes whose represented values are changed.

The only critical factor that remains is the possibility of attributes whose evaluation involves deep levels of dereferencing.

Compared with the original algorithm of Reps whose time complexity is proportional to the number of all affected attributes, the algorithm proposed here is proportional to the number of all affected but the purely structural attributes. If a grammar is characterized by an extensive use of pure structures the new algorithm may, furthermore, turn out to be constant in time whereas the original one is proportional to the height of the tree.

8 Discussion

In this paper, I have described how structure sharing can be utilized in the representation of attributed syntax trees in syntax-oriented editors — inspired by the use of structure sharing in current Prolog implementations, cf. (Warren, 1977). However, attribute grammars concern not only structures but arbitrary objects and functions and hence a throughout use of structure sharing does not make sense. The term filtering and flow algebra serve as a means for switching back and forth between the two modes.

When it comes to efficient attribute updating algorithms, the key is a suitable ordering of the attributes in order to control the sequence of visits to the attributes whose (represented) values need to be re-evaluated:

- Only these attributes should be visited and ideally only once,

- and the (last) visit to an attribute must occur at a moment when the attributes referred to in its defining expression are known to have their consistent value.

Hence an optimal algorithm requires a representation of this desired ordering for controlling the update sequence. But alas, having solved one problem another one of maintaining this represented ordering is introduced.

When no advantage is taken of structure sharing, the attribute ordering is determined — in principle — by a topological sorting of the traditional dependency graph, cf. (Knuth, 1968). Reps (1984) describes a representation of this ordering which can be incrementally maintained. The technique is based on the fact that changes, i.e., the edges in the dependency graph, propagate gradually from node to node in the syntax tree. (A representation of the ordering which, for each tree modification, requires a complete topological sorting of the dependency graph would be in vain.) A drawback of this approach, however, is that moving the editor's current focus from one subtree to another takes time proportional to thier distance in the tree. In section 7 of this paper, it is shown how structure sharing and calculation of flow values give rise to an immediate enhancement of Reps' algorithm although the full potentiality in structure sharing is not employed this way.

Structure sharing implies a decreased number of objects to maintain. In the following discussion, I will refer to these objects as *locations*. There are two kinds of such locations,

- attributes of non-pointer sorts,

- heap cells allocated for proper pointer expressions, cf. definition 5.

I have ignored attributes of pointer sort whose defining expressions consist of singleton variables: The maintenance of these pointers can be made in a separate phase — it concerns the creation of pointers for new proper pointer expressions and the transportation of these pointers via chains of copy attributes, i.e., those whose defining expressions consist of singleton variables. This is intimately related to the creation of new syntax tree nodes and can be performed without any specialized scheduling information.

Whenever a location, ℓ say, has changed its value, an algorithm should ideally skip over all locations whose values are updated automatically via shared structures and only visit those that really depend on the actual contents of ℓ. This concerns the locations whose flow values are 'Changed' whenever ℓ's flow value is 'Changed'. These dependencies give rise to a dependency graph whose edges may stretch over arbitrary distances in the syntax tree. Hence, there is no obvious relation, as in the case without structure sharing, between the shape of the dependency graph and the underlying syntax tree — so there are no direct generalizations of Reps' methods, (Reps, 1984). I have not found any efficiently maintained representation of a topological ordering of the locations in this dependency graph, but, on the other hand, I cannot exclude that such a representation actually may exist. I will return to this subject later.

The work by Hoover, (1986), and aspects of Reps, Marceau, and Teitelbaum's work, (1986), can be seen as attempts to introduce restricted forms of structure sharing and still retain a hold on the ordering implied by the attribute dependencies.

Hoover, (1986), has investigated how chains of attributes that are copies of each other can be utilized in order to optimize the updating process: Only the copies that are actually used, i.e., those who serve other purposes that just passing their value on to the next copy, need to receive a new value. Although it is hard to judge the generality of the method from the paper, (Hoover, 1986), it represents new thinking in that it applies an almost-correct representation of the topological ordering of the attributes: The amount of work for maintaining the represented ordering is reduced at the cost of occasionally having to evaluate certain attributes more than once in an update sequence.

Reps, Marceau, and Teitelbaum, (1986), maintain a totally correct representation of the attribute ordering for a class of attribute grammars extended with so-called remote references, i.e., the defining expression for an attribute expression may contain variables that stand for other attributes than those found in its immediate neighbourhood in the syntax tree. Furthermore, for attribute values recognized as symbol tables, called 'aggregate values' in their paper, there is kept a record, for each entry in the table, of those attributes that refer to exactly that symbol table entry. Consequently, when a declaration of some object is modified only the applications of that object — and not of any other object appearing in the same symbol table — need to be considered for re-evaluation. However, the problem in Reps' original work remains, that the deletion or creation of an entry in a symbol table causes all embedding symbol tables to be re-built from scratch — a problem which disappears with the kind of structure sharing proposed in the present paper. It is hard to compare the work of Reps, Marceau, and Teitelbaum and my approach as their method relies on a set of non-obvious restrictions. However, it seems likely that their method, and this remark goes for Hoovers work as well, could have been formulated clearer if structure sharing and the flow algebra had been used. It should be stressed, though, that the idea of a fine-grained tracing of changes through symbol tables is beyond the flow algebra; an appropriate generalization is discussed later.

Other extensions (than the 'remote dependencies' described above) to the attribute grammar framework have been suggested in order to provide for efficient implementations. Horwitz and Teitelbaum, (1986), have proposed a mixture of attribute grammars and relational data bases such that information can be stored in and retrieved from an external data base system.[1] Demers, Rogers, and Zadeck, (1985), suggest an interesting model based on message passing.

My final remarks concern some algorithmic experiments and possible generalizations of the structure sharing framework. As discussed above, updating of the attributes in a system based on structure sharing has to do with the propagation of changes among a set of locations that represent attributes of non-pointer sorts and heap cells for values of proper pointer expressions. The corresponding dependency graph has an edge from one location, ℓ_1, to another, ℓ_2, whenever,

---

1. In fact, an argument used by the authors for using a relational data base instead of Prolog is the lack of incrementality in current Prolog systems, cf. p. 586 in the referenced paper. Maybe my work provides for the desired, incremental and structure sharing environment.

- ℓ_1 appears in the defining expression for ℓ_2, either directly in the shape of an attribute variable or by a means of a chain of copy attributes or structures, and

- whenever ℓ_1 has the flow value 'Changed' the same thing holds for ℓ_2.

My experimental algorithm decorates each location, ℓ, with the following auxiliary data:

- the edges in the dependency graph that go into ℓ and away from ℓ,

- a topological index which is an integer number describing its position in a linear ordering implied by the dependency graph.

The topological index of a given location, however, is unfortunately a global property of the dependency graph and hence it may be impractical to keep all indices persistently correct. Inspired by Hoover, (1986), my experimental algorithm will keep only an approximation to the correct set of indices: Whenever, in an updating sequence, a given attribute is considered for re-evaluation, it is taken care that its index is at least one greater than the maximum indices of its predecessors in the dependency graph. This relies on a heuristic assumption that the propagation of changes in the topological indices is likely to resemble the propagation pattern for the attributes. Although the algorithm works nicely on particular toy examples, I cannot present any general results yet.

With a little carefulness in the implementation of operations for looking up items in symbol tables (and similar objects) it is possible to achieve an efficient change propagation through symbol tables analogous to what is described by Reps, Marceau, and Teitelbaum, (1986), cf. the discussion above: The operation that finds the contents in the symbol table for a given identifier should return a location for, i.e., a pointer to, this contents instead of the contents itself. Hence there is no reason to propagate the change explicitly from the definition of a symbol table entry to its application — the shared structures imply that the new information is already there!

This optimization fits nicely into the algorithm based on partially correct, topological indices considered above. But still, this is on an ad-hoc level, no generally valid statements can be given yet.

References

Boyer, R.S. and Moore, J.S., The Sharing of Structure in Theorem-Proving Programs, *Machine Intelligence* 7, pp. 101-116, 1972.

Demers, A., Rogers, A., and Zadeck, F.K., Attribute Propagation by Message Passing, *Sigplan Notices*, vol. 20, no. 7, pp. 43-59, 1985.

Deransart, P., Jourdan, M., and Lorho, B., A Survey on Attribute Grammars, Part III: Classified Bibliography, INRIA, *Rapports de Recerce*, no. 417, 1985.

Deransart, P., Jourdan, M., and Lorho, B., A Survey on Attribute Grammars, Part I: Main Results on Attribute Grammars, INRIA, *Rapports de Recerce*, no. 485, 1986a.

Deransart, P., Jourdan, M., and Lorho, B., A Survey on Attribute Grammars, Part II: Review of Existing Systems, INRIA, *Rapports de Recerce*, no. 510, 1986b.

Deransart, P. and Maluszynski, J., Relating Logic Programs and Attribute Grammars. *Journal of Logic Programming*, vol 2, pp. 119-155, 1985.

Ganzinger, H., On Storage Optimization for Automatically Generated Compilers, *Lecture Notes in Computer Science* 67, pp. 132-147, Springer-Verlag, 1979.

Goguen, J.A., Thatcher, J.W., and Wagner, E.G., An Initial Algebra Approach to the Specification, Correctness and Implementation of Abstract Data Types, *Current Trends in Programming Methodology*, vol. IV, ed. R.T. Yeh, Prentice-Hall, 1979.

Hoover, R., Dynamically Bypassing Copy Rule Chains in Attribute Grammars, *Proc. of 13th Annual ACM Symposium on Principles of Programming Languages*, 1986.

Horwitz, S. and Teitelbaum, T., Generating Editing Environments Based on Relations and Attributes, *ACM Transactions on Programming Languages and Systems* 8, pp. 577-608, 1986.

Jespersen, P., Madsen, M., and Riis, H., *New extended attribute systems — NEATS*, Computer Science Department, Aarhus University, 1978.

Kastens, U., Hutt, B., and Zimmermann, E., GAG: A Practical Compiler Generator, *Lecture Notes in Computer Science* 141, 1982.

Knuth, D.E., Semantics of Context-Free Languages, *Mathematical Systems Theory* 2, pp. 127-125, 1968.

Madsen, O.L., On defining semantics by means of extended attribute grammars, *Lecture Notes in Computer Science* 94, pp. 259-299, 1980.

Milne, R. and Strachey, C., *A theory of programming language semantics*, Chapman and Hall, London, 1976.

Mycroft, A., Abstract Interpretation and Optimizing Transformations of Applicative Programs, *Edinburgh University*, CST-15-81, 1981.

Räihä, K.-J., Dynamic Allocation of Space for Attribute Instances in Multi-Pass Evaluators of Attribute Grammars, *Sigplan Notices*, vol. 14, no. 8, pp 26-34, 1979.

Reps, T.W., *Generating Language-Based Environments*, MIT Press, 1984.

Reps, T., Marceau, C., and Teitelbaum, T., Remote Attribute Updating for Language-Based Editors, *Proc. of 13th Annual ACM Symposium on Principles of Programming Languages*, pp. 1-13, 1986.

Sonnenschein, M., Global Storage Cells for Attributes in an Attribute Grammar, *Acta Informatica* 22, pp. 397-420, 1985.

Warren, D.H.D., Implementing Prolog — compiling predicate logic programs, *D.A.I. Research Reports* 39 & 40, Department of Artificial Intelligence, University of Edinburgh, 1977.

Watt, D.A. and Madsen, O.L., Extended Attribute Grammars, *DAIMI PB*-105, Computer Science Department, Aarhus University, 1979.

A Semantic Evaluator Generating System in Prolog

Pedro Rangel Henriques
Computer Science Group, University of Minho
Rua D. Pedro V, 4700 Braga, PORTUGAL

Abstract

This paper describes a semantic evaluator generating system developed with the objective of combining attribute grammars and logic programming.
Both the generator and the attribute based semantic evaluator are Prolog programs. The language to be analysed is specified by a strongly non-circular (SNC) attribute grammar. The parser is of type SLR(1) incorporating error handling (by means of local correction). The evaluator is based on a top-down recursive algorithm computing attributes by dynamic need.

1 Introduction

This paper describes a *semantic evaluator generating system* (SEGS, for short) based on attribute grammars and entirely implemented in Prolog.

By *semantic evaluator* we designate a program that analyses a text (a string of characters) and, if it is a valid sentence of a given language (a string of symbols that complies with the language's syntax and semantic rules) determines its *meaning* .

An *attribute based semantic evaluator* is a semantic evaluator that performs his task by constructing the derivation tree (DT) associated with the source-text and by computing the synthesized attribute occurrences at the root of the DT.

A semantic evaluator *generator* is a program, or collection of programs, that takes a formal definition of a language and automatically produces a semantic evaluator for sentences belonging to that language.

In the SEGS herein presented, both the generator and the evaluator are Prolog programs and the formalism used to describe the language is an attribute grammar (AG). The system processes a very large class of attribute grammars (SNC); The LR technique augmented with error handling (based on a local correction strategy) is used for parsing; and a top-down recursive method implementing a dynamic evaluation by need is employed in the attribute evaluator.

The paper is organized as follows: Section 2 reviews some important contributions on attribute grammars and logic programming to the compiler development problem, giving the motivation for the work here reported. Basic definitions and notations are introduced in section 3. An overview of the system can be found in section 4: system's general strategy is presented and the basic principles of both the semantic evaluator and the generator are discussed. Section 5 is concerned with implementation details: the representation of an AG in Prolog is described; some design decisions which improve the evaluation time and memory usage are analysed; the static analysis of attribute dependencies and the non-circularity test are discussed. Finally, section 6 presents some concluding remarks.

2 Background

In this paper we intend to focus on two problems in the area of compiler development: language analysis— assigning meaning to sentences of a given language; and automatic production of such analysers.

Formal language specification is a basic requirement to solve the second problem and also a very convenient way to approach the first. From the most widespread formalisms for language description — attribute grammars, denotational semantics and algebraic semantics — we shall devote particular attention to attribute grammars (AGs).

Attribute grammars were proposed by Knuth [Knu68] as an extension of context-free grammars with semantic rules defining the value of attributes associated with the symbols of the grammar's vocabulary. Its main purpose is the formal specification of the syntax and semantics of programming languages (although intermediate language or code generation could also be described by means of the so-called *translation* attributes).

AGs are well accepted and widely used by the compilers community. Many front-end compiler generators based on this approach have been developed (see, for instance, [DJL86b]). Most of these systems, implemented in procedural languages, are built upon long programs, difficult to understand, to port and to maintain, requiring long time and hard work to be developed. Moreover, to comply with efficiency requirements coming from real-word applications, they usually impose restrictions on the AG class accepted.

Jourdan proposed [Jou83] some recursive algorithms for evaluation of strongly non-circular AGs (a very broad class, including all the practical cases of programming languages) and implemented, in Lisp, two versions—systems FNC/ERN [Jou85]—reaching powerfull and efficient evaluators. We adopted his method for attribute evaluation, in the SEGS here reported.

The *declarative principle* inherent to AGs intuitively suggests a closed relation to logic programming. Deransart et Maluszynski, in [DM85], studied this problem and presented the relation between logic programs and attribute grammars in a formal context (later on this subject was also studied by Courcelle and Deransart [CD87]). These authors apply some results on AGs to logic programming.

By the same time, Arbab [Arb86] conceived two algorithms for compiling synthesized-only (with recursive definitions) and inherited-synthesized attribute grammars into Prolog. Generally speaking, in his approach, each production and the associated semantic rule is translated to a Prolog clause whose head predicate is the nonterminal on the left hand side (its arguments being the right hand side of the production, and the attribute definitions) and whose body is a sequence of atoms derived from the attribute occurrences appearing in the semantic rule.

Definite Clause Translation Grammars (introduced by Abramson [Abr84]) are also an example of a logical implementation of attribute grammars. In his approach, Abramson makes no difference between inherited and synthesized attributes. This formalism grew up from DCGs but it allows a clear distinction between syntax and semantics specifications. Semantic rules are Horn clauses attached to the nodes of the syntax tree (automatically constructed during parsing) and a special language to define tree manipulation is provided.

Definite Clause Grammars (DCGs) were introduced by Pereira and Warren (see [PW80]) after Colmerauer's Metamorphosis grammars. DCGs are a notation to describe languages that can be translated directly to a parsing program in Prolog (many Prolog implementations handle this translation mechanism as a built-in feature—grammar rules are transformed automatically as they are consulted). The equivalent Prolog program is a top-down, left-to-rigth recursive parser that backtracks if necessary (this allows the processing of conflictuous, or even ambiguous, grammars). DCGs can be seen as a generalization of context-free grammars with Prolog features—the most important extensions are: the addition of arguments to nonterminal symbols and the reference to Prolog goals in the body of grammar rules. Althought the arguments of nonterminals can be thought of as semantic attributes they are used, in the original formalism, without any discipline. However, DGCs can be used to implement an evaluator for the *basic term interpretation* of AGs in the sense of [DM85].

Our approach is different from those above because, in the generated evaluator, syntax and semantics are completely separated—production rules are translated into SLR(1) tables and semantic rules into clauses whose head predicates are attributes.

Other authors also have implemented in Prolog bottom-up algorithms for parsing. For example, the AID system by Nilsson [Nil86] is a translator that produces a SLR(1) parser for a given grammar. The works of Matsumoto et al [MTea83] and Kuniaki Uehara et al [UOea84] are other applications of LR parsing techniques to natural language analysis in Prolog.

3 Definitions

The purpose of this section is to create a formal context which will allow a simple, precise and clear presentation of the implementation details concerning both the evaluator and the generator. As we have followed closely the algebraic approach of Courcelle and Deransart, we refer the reader to their report [CD87] for further details on the basic definitions hereafter omitted.

To develop the SEGS we adopted the definition bellow.

Definition 3.1 (Attribute Grammar) *An attribute grammar is a tuple*

$$G = <N, P, Attr, \Phi, \mathcal{D}>$$

where:

1. *N is a finite set of sorts (the so-called "nonterminal alphabet");*

2. *P is a finite N-signature (a set Pn of operator symbols given with to mappings: $\alpha : Pn \longrightarrow N^*$ the arity; and $\sigma : Pn \longrightarrow N$ the operator sort) –the "derivation" or "production rules".*
   The pair $<N, P>$ is an abstract context free grammar (CFG for short);

3. *Attr is a finite set of attributes, each attribute $a \in Attr$ being the name of a partial relation mapping elements of N into a sort $\sigma(a)$ that belongs to some set of sorts S.*
   $Attr(X)$, for $X \in N$, denotes the set of attributes 'a' such that $a(X)$ is defined.
   So $Attr = \bigcup_{X \in N} Attr(X)$.
   The set Attr is splited in two disjoint sets Inh and Syn (respectively the inherited and the synthesized attributes) — $Attr = Inh \cup Syn$ with $Inh \cap Syn = \emptyset$ — and then we define:

$$Inh(X) = Attr(X) \cap Inh$$
$$Syn(X) = Attr(X) \cap Syn$$

4. *$\Phi = \{\Phi_p\}_{p \text{ in } P}$ is a finite set of formulas (the "semantic rules"), such that Φ_p is a formula associated with production rule p in P of profile $<X_1 \ldots X_n, X_0>$ and belonging to a logical language $<\mathcal{L}, C, \models>$ (C is a class of structures and $\models$ denotes the validity relation, as defined in [CD87]) defined over $(W(p), \mathcal{F}, \mathcal{R})$, where*

   - *$\mathcal{F}$ is an S-signature (recall that S is the set of attribute sorts);*
   - *$\mathcal{R}$ is a set of many-sorted predicate symbols, with arity in S^+ and implicit sort bool (the sort of boolean values <u>true</u> and <u>false</u>);*
   - *$W(p) = \{a(i)\}_{i \in \{0,\ldots,n\}}$ is a set of variables called the set of attribute occurrences of p.*
     Each $a(i)$—an occurrence of attribute a in p—is a new symbol introduced for each $a \in Attr(X_i)$, $i \in \{0,\ldots,n\}$, that denotes the value associated by attribute 'a' to the nonterminal $X \in N$ that occurs at position 'i' of p.
     $W(p)$ is partitioned in two disjoint sets $W_{in}(p)$ and $W_{out}(p)$ (respectively, the input and the output attribute occurrences of p) — $W(p) = W_{in}(p) \cup W_{out}(p)$ with $W_{in}(p) \cap W_{out}(p) = \emptyset$ — defined as follows:

$$W_{in}(p) = \{a(i) \mid a \in Inh(X_0), i = 0 \text{ or } a \in Syn(X_i), 1 \leq i \leq n\}$$
$$W_{out}(p) = \{a(i) \mid a \in Syn(X_0), i = 0 \text{ or } a \in Inh(X_i), 1 \leq i \leq n\}$$

The formula Φ_p is the conjunction of a set of formulas of the form:

$$AND\{\Phi_{p,w} \mid w \in W_{out}(p)\} \tag{1}$$

Each $\Phi_{p,w}$ is a formula associated with an output attribute occurrence, $w \in W_{out}(p)$, of the form

$$OR\{\varphi_j\} \tag{2}$$

with φ_j, $j \geq 1$ being

$$\Gamma_j \Rightarrow w = t_j \tag{3}$$

and Γ_j being the boolean conjunction of atomic formulas (usualy designated by "contextual conditions") constructed with predicate symbols $r \in R$ of the form

$$r(t_1, \ldots, t_n) \text{ or } \underline{not}(r(t_1, \ldots, t_n)) \tag{4}$$

where $t_j, t_i \in W(\mathcal{F}, W_{in}(p))$ are terms of the term-$\mathcal{F}$-algebra generated by variables $W_{in}(p)$ (the grammar is considered in normal form without loss of generality)

5. *D is a structure in C, i.e. an object of the form*

$$D = <(D_s)_{s \in S}, (f_D)_{f \in \mathcal{F}}, (r_D)_{r \in R}>$$

where $<(D_s)_{s \in S}, (f_D)_{f \in \mathcal{F}}>$ is an heterogeneous $\mathcal{F}$-algebra and r_D is a total mapping $D_{s1} \times \cdots \times D_{sn} \longrightarrow \underline{bool}$ for each $r \in R$ of arity $\alpha(r) = s_1 \ldots s_n$.

□

Please note that Γ_j may be omitted in formula (3) if the condition is $\underline{true}$. In this case, if $j = 1$ then formula (2) is simply $w = t$.

In [CD87], the authors introduce three classes of AGs. Definition (3.1) is a combination of the classes *usual attribute grammar* and *conditional attribute grammar* (also called *functional AG* in [DM85]).

Formulas (2) and (3) allow the conditional definition of each output attribute occurrence, i.e. the association of a value that depends on the input attribute occurrences in the context of the same production. This definition also contemplates non-deterministic semantic rules, although it seems of no actual interest in the context of nonambiguous programming languages processing. It is the users' responsability to avoid such situation, by providing mutually exclusive conditions.

A *derivation tree* (DT in the sequel) is an element of W(P), i.e. it is a ground term of the term P-algebra.

In pratice we need to deal with *concrete* grammars and not abstract ones as the above. To comply with this requirement, it is necessary to extend the previous definition as follows.

Definition 3.2 (Concrete AG) *A concrete attribute grammar is an abstract attribute grammar defined as in (3.1) extended with:*

1. A new finite set of symbols T (the "terminal alphabet");

2. A mapping $\mathcal{T} : character^+ \longrightarrow T$ that associates nonempty strings of characters with terminal symbols;

3. A mapping $IntrAttr : T \longrightarrow W(\mathcal{F})$ ("intrinsic attribute") associating terminal symbols with ground terms of any sort $s \in S$.

We now redefine the arity in P as being $\alpha : Pn \longrightarrow (N \cup T)^*$

The definition of formula Φ_p, attached to production p (see item 4, in def. 3.1) is also adapted. For each production p of profile $< X_1, \ldots, X_n, X_0 >$, we introduce new symbols $intra(i)$, $1 \le i \le n$, denoting the intrinsic value associated by $IntrAttr$ to the terminal $X \in T$ occurring at position 'i', which are constants (i.e., elements of $W(\mathcal{F})$).

□

The semantic rules Φ_p introduce dependencies between attribute occurrences in $W(p)$ which induce in p an order of evaluation. The same dependencies hold between attribute occurences associated with the nodes of any DT. So one is faced with the problem of knowing if all the attribute occurrences of all nodes in any DT can be evaluated—if it is always possible the AG is said to be *well-defined* (or *well-formed*). The well-definedness of an AG implies, for every derivation tree t, the noncircularity of the dependency graph $D(t)$ but its test, although solveable statically, is intrinsically exponencial in time and space.

To improve the practical efficiency of attribute based systems, one usually imposes some restrictions on these dependencies. This idea corresponds to the introduction of AG classes. The properties of the dependency relation characterizing each class induce the kind of evaluator that can be built (see [DJL86a]). AG classes are largely discussed in the literature as shown in Räiha [Rai80] or Deransart et al [DJL85] (about this subject refer to [WG84] or [DJL86a]).

The rest of this section is devoted to the definition of the SNC class of AGs, as it was the one choosen for the development of the SEGS.

Definition 3.3 Let $D(p) \subseteq W(p) \times W(p)$ be a binary relation such that $w' D(p) w$ if $w \in W_{out}(p), w' \in W_{in}(p)$ and there is a φ_j in $\Phi_{p,w}$ where w' appears in t_j or Γ_j.

The local dependency graph of p, denoted $D(p)$, is the graph $< W(p), D(p) >$ with set of vertices $W(p)$ and binary relation $D(p)$.

□

Let $t \in W(P)$ be a DT and $w \in \underline{Node}(t)$ a node labelled by production p ($p = \underline{lab}_t(w)$). $w.D(p)$ is a local dependency graph associated with node w with set of vertices $w.W(p) = \{a(wu) \mid a(u) \in W(p)\}$ (the attribute occurrences in p) and relation $\rightarrow_{w,p}$ defined as

$$a(wu) \rightarrow_{w,p} b(wu') \; iff \; (a(u), b(u')) \in D(p)$$

Definition 3.4 *The (global) dependency graph, $D(t)$, of a tree $t \in W(P)$ is a graph with nodes $W(t)$ defined as the union of local dependency graphs $w.D(p)$ for all nodes w of (t)*

$$D(t) = \cup\{w.D(p) \mid w \in \underline{Node}(t), p = \underline{lab}_t(w)\}$$

□

Let $X \in N$ be the sort of p in P and t a tree with root labelled by p $(t \in W(P)_X)$. Then, $sd_t(X)$ denotes the dependency relation induced on $Attr(X)$ by $D^+(t)$ (with edges coming from $Inh(X)$ to $Syn(X)$) and $IO(X) = \cup_t sd_t(X)$ denotes the set of possible dependencies induced on $Attr(X)$ at the root of all trees of sort X.

Definition 3.5 *A dependency indicator D is a mapping associating each $X \in N$ to a set $D(X)$ of binary relations on $Attr(X)$.*

D is non-circular iff, for all production p of profile $< X_1 \ldots X_n, X_0 >$, all $r_i \in D(X_i)$, $i \in \{1, \ldots, n\}$, the graph

$$D(p)[r_1, \ldots, r_n]$$

is cycle-free.
D is closed if, for such p, r_i there exists a $r_0 \in D(X_0)$ such that

$$D(p)_0^+[r_1, \ldots, r_n] \subseteq r_0$$

□

According to [CD87] we can now give a definition for the SNC class of attribute grammars introduced by Courcelle and Franchi-Zannettacci in [CF82].

Definition 3.6 *An AG is strongly non-circular (SNC) iff there exist a closed and non-circular dependency indicator D such that $D(X)$ is singleton for all $X \in N$.*
□

Recalling [DJL86a], this class satisfies two important properties:

- for $X \in N$, $IO(X) \subseteq D(X)$;

- there exists a polynomial algorithm that computes D.

4 System Overview

4.1 General Structure

The SEGS has two components: a *generator*; and an *archetype of a semantic evaluator*.

Given an attribute grammar, the generator produces Prolog code to instanciate this archetype—then, it becomes a specific semantic evaluator for sentences belonging to the language. Given a string of characters, the specific semantic evaluator either gives its meaning—represented by a sequence of pairs $< attribute, value >$, corresponding to the values of synthesized attributes occurrences at the root of the derivation tree—or produces *error messages*, if the text doesn't belong to the language.

The archetype is a set of Prolog clauses which implement the standard evaluation operations (by *operation* we mean a sequence of deductive transformations that infers new facts from a given set of facts and rules), i.e. those operations that are language independent.

To build up a specific semantic evaluator it is necessary to instanciate the archetype with knowledge about the particular language. The operation of instanciation is easily realized in Prolog through the consult() predicate. As the language is described by means of an AG, the required knowledge must obviously be extract from the AG. So, for the purpose of instanciation, we shall define a suitable (adequate to be processed by the standard operations) representation of the grammar.

As it is well known (see, for instance [DF86]) a logic program is a description of the knowledge about a domain (the univers of the problem we want to solve) where objects are represented by *terms* and its properties and relations are stated by *facts* and *rules* (Horn clauses). So, aiming at logic programming-based language description, the input AG must be translated into a set of facts and rules.

Because the AG is a mathematically defined object and because the translation rules are systematic, the refered translation can be carried out automatically—this transformation is, precisely, the task of the generator.

4.2 The Evaluator

The operation of an attribute based semantic evaluator can be decomposed into three subtask, as follows:

- Lexical analysis

- Parsing

- Attribute Evaluation

We can suppose that these tasks are executed sequentially.

Lexical Analysis

Lexical analysis is concerned with the translation of a character string into a string of terminal symbols (elements of T) and the computation of terminals intrinsic value (defined by $IntrAttr$).

SEGS lexical analyser is built upon two operations: getword() and findsymbol().

getword() reads characters from the input stream and gives the next *word* (a string of characters between "separators"). The operation is trivial and essentially language independent—so it is embedded in the generic framework (the evaluator archetype). The central concept is that of *separator*—a character that defines the end of a word. We see it as a property of characters which must be defined for each particular language. The definition is given as a set of facts of the form *separator*("*c*").

The second operation, findsymbol(), determines the terminal associated with a word and simultaneously the intrinsic value associated with this terminal. This operation is language dependent and is defined by the mappings T and *IntrAttr* given with the AG.

Parsing

Parsing is concerned with syntax analysis—given a string of terminals, the parser verifies if the string is derivable from the CFG production rules and, if so, it builds up the derivation tree.

LR method is a well known (see [ASU86] or [WG84]) and powerfull bottom-up strategy for parsing context free languages. This technique is based on a table-driven iterative algorithm. The algorithm is standard and can be included in the archetype. The knowledge about a particular language, necessary to drive the algorithm, is described by the signature P (for each p in Pn it is necessary to know its sort $\sigma(p)$ and its rank $\rho(p) = length(\alpha(p))$) and two mappings—$action : Q \times T \longrightarrow < AT, (Q \cup Pn \cup \bot) >$ and $goto : Q \times N \longrightarrow Q$, where Q is a finite set of states and AT ("action-types") is the sort of the values accept, shift, reduce and error.

Those mappings, describing the so-called *LR deterministic automaton*, can be derived from the CFG in a systematic way. This construction is carried out by the generator.

Concerning the development of the LR parser in Prolog we have adopted an approach quite similar to that proposed in [Nil86], except in what concerns error handling.

The parsing algorithm is implemented through the operation parse(), whose arguments are a string of symbols, a state-stack, a semantic-stack and a tree. parse() calls itself recursively until *action-type* is accept or the input string is empty. If *action-type* is error then a *local error correction strategy* (suggested by Boullier in [Bou84]) is applied. The basic idea can be described as follows: take an input substring envolving the error symbol and try to transform it in a correct one by *insertion, deletion, substitution* or *interchange* of symbols. Then substitute the so-formed correct substring for the erroneous one and go on parsing. The possible transformations are formally defined through "correction models" which also incorporate some confidence criteria and an implicit order of application. The transformations take into account the present parsing state and are validated against the "action" table.

Attribute Evaluation

Attribute evaluation is concerned with *tree decoration*, i.e. with the computation of attribute occurrences attached to the nodes of the derivation tree. In fact this consist on the interpretation of semantic rules Φ_p

under the given structure $\mathcal{D}$.

The main operation, evaluate-tree(), associates with a tree an *assignment* $\upsilon : W(t) \longrightarrow \mathcal{D}$ restricted to the set of attribute occurrences at the root of t (see [CD87]).

evaluate-tree() is a tail-recursive operation that for every $a \in Syn(X)$ (X is the sort of t) calls another operation, svalue() which computes the value associated by a synthesized attribute 'a' with a nonterminal X, according with the principle [CF82]:

> A synthesized attribute occurrence at a node of a tree only depends on: the subtree issued from that node; the inherited attribute occurrences at that node.

As in Jourdan's evaluator, we only use a subset of $Inh(X)$, that on which 'a' actually depends (in [Jou83] that subset is defined by the "argument selector" and in [DJL86a] it is denoted by $Use(X,a)$).

Note that all the attribute occurrences in $W(t)$ but those in $Syn(X)$ (X is the sort of t) are computed only if dynamicaly needed.

In the SEGS the set of inherited attributes on which a synthesized depends is defined by a mapping sDi : $Syn \times N \longrightarrow \underline{setof}(Inh)$ that is computed statically by the generator.

4.3   The Generator

Generator's main job is the translation of the input AG into an adequate Prolog representation (see next section) in order to supply the evaluator with the necessary language dependent information.

Namely, the generator must:

- translate the mappings $\mathcal{T}$ and $IntrAttr$;

- build the parsing tables (mappings $action$ and $goto$);

- translate the semantic rules;

- construct the mapping sDi

The metalanguage for writing the input AG (not detailed in this paper) was conceived with the purpose of simplifying the translation job.

Additionally, and because the user of a generating system wants to be sure that the evaluator will not crash or loop forever when submited to a given input stream, the generator must assure the input AG is well-defined in the sense of the class for which the evaluator is designed—in our case this means that the generator has to test that the AG is *strongly non-circular*. Moreover, it is also necessary to verify that the underlying CFG satisfies the restrictions imposed by the parsing method choosen (to guarantee that it is always possible to build the DT) This test is performed during parsing tables construction and the SNC check is realized after sDi construction.

4.4 Using the System

To end up this section we will summarize the use of the generating system here described.

The *generator* program runs taking as argument the file containing the AG for the language to be processed. If the input AG has no conflicts nor cycles, the *generator* produces a file containing Prolog code representing the lexical information, the SLR(1) parsing tables and the semantic rules. If SLR(1) conflicts, mal-formed semantic rules (not in *normal form*), or cycles are detected, the *generator* informs the user via console—the generation aborts only in the last case.

After a sucessfull generation phase, the standard *evaluator* (the archetype previously refered) can be executed, being necessary to identify the file produced by the generator. The *evaluator* then takes the source-text from the console or from any other file and asserts in the knowledge-base its meaning or reports to the console the errors found.

5 Implementation Details

5.1 Representation of a Concrete AG in Prolog

Taking into account definition (3.2) and the evaluator's requirements, it is possible to define a suitable Prolog representation for a given AG.

5.1.1 Lexical information

The mapping T is represented: by facts, if it defines a fixed terminal (a keyword, for instance); or by rules, if it defines a terminal class (identifiers, integer-constants, string-constants, ...) and a check for class inclusion is needed.

The mapping *IntrAttr* is also represented either by facts (association of a constant value) or by rules (if some term interpretation is necessary).

Actually, we have joined those two mappings in only one relation, term(...), which is represented by rules of the general form

$$term(sc, (ts, ia)) :- body. \tag{5}$$

where sc is a list of characters, ts is the terminal symbol, ia is the intrinsic attribute value and *body* is a sequence, may be empty, of atoms representing class conditions and functions.

Example 5.1 *The fact*

$$term("+", (adop, plus)).$$

states that the character string with only one element '+' is associated with the grammar terminal symbol 'adop' which in turn is associated with the value 'plus' belonging to some enumerated carrier.

The rule

$$term(INT, (int, IV)) :- is\_intconst(INT), intval(INT, IV).$$

states that a variable character string INT is associated to the terminal symbol 'int' if it satisfies the class condition 'is_intconst' and the terminal is associated to an integer value IV given by the function representation 'intval(INT, IV)'.

5.1.2 Context Free Grammar

The three mappings *action*, *goto* and *prods* (associates each production symbol with its sort and rank) are represented in Prolog by facts of the general form bellow:

$$action(q, t, at, ai).$$
$$goto(q, nt, q1).$$
$$prod(p, nt, r).$$

where 'q' and '$q1$' are state symbols in Q; 't' a terminal in T; 'nt' a nonterminal in N; 'p' a production symbol in Pn; 'at' an action type in AT; 'ai' a state if $at = shift$, or a production symbol if $at = \underline{reduce}$ or <u>undefined</u> ($\perp$) otherwise; and $r = \rho(p)$ the rank of p.

Actually, if there are n facts of the form $action(q, t, \underline{reduce}, p)$ which only differ in the terminal symbol, then they are replaced by one rule of the form

$$action(q, T, \underline{reduce}, p) :- member(T, [t_1, \ldots, t_n]).$$

This strategy aims at reducing the size of the generated code.

In order to improve the execution time and the complexity of the reduce operation, the facts $prod(p, nt, r)$ are extended with five extra arguments

$$prod(p, nt, r, \phi, \phi_1, ss, ss_1, tr).$$

ϕ and ϕ_1 (ss and ss_1) define the transformation produced by the "reduction" on the state-stack (semantic-stack); and tr is the new tree whose root is labelled by the production just recognized.

5.1.3 Semantic Rules and Structure

Each semantic rule Φ_p, associated with production p, of form (1) is implemented by a sequence of clauses originated by the translation of each formula $\Phi_{p,w}$.

A formula $\Phi_{p,w}$ corresponding to an output attribute occurrence $a(i) \in W_{out}(p)$ $(a(i) \equiv w)$ of form (2), is represented by a sequence of clauses (one for each φ_j) (note that for a given valuation the *good association* $w = t_j$ is found by "backtracking"; if more than one value could be choosen–two or more conditions hold simultaneously–the first one is always selected) obtained as follows:

1. Every clause has the same head

$$a(p, i, T, I, Vai)$$

   where the predicate symbol 'a' is the attribute name and whose arguments are: the production symbol 'p'; the occurrence position 'i'; a logical variable, say Vai, that denotes the value associated by the attribute to a nonterminal at position i; and two auxiliar variables, T and I, representing respectively the subtree of sort X_0 whose root is labelled by p and a set of inherited values associated with X_0;

2. For each φ_j of form (3), the clause body is a sequence of atoms derived from the representation schema bellow:

   For each term t appearing somewhere in φ_j we introduce a logical variable Vt and define an atom of one of the following kinds:

$$Vt = c$$

   if t is a constant c;

$$f(Vt_1, \ldots, Vt_n, Vt)$$

   if t is a generic term of the form $f(t_1, \ldots, t_n)$;

$$intrvalue(i, T, Vt)$$

   if t is a special constant $intra(i)$;

$$ivalue(a, I, Vt)$$

   if t is a variable $a(k) \in W_{in}(p)$ with $k = 0$ (an inherited attribute of X_0);

$$svalue(a, k, T, I, Vt)$$

   if t is a variable $a(k) \in W_{in}(p)$ with $k > 0$ (a synthesized attribute of X_k).

   Each atom $r(t_1, \ldots, t_n)$ *in* Γ_j is simply translated into an atom of the form

$$r(Vt_1, \ldots, Vt_n)$$

The atoms obtained are ordered in such a way that those defining Vt appear before its use and those corresponding to Γ_j appear first before the atoms derived from t_j.

Example 5.2 *Let p be a production of profile* $< Ab, S >$ *with* $A, S \in N$ *and* $b \in T$. *Let* $Inh(S) = \{x\}$ *and* $Syn(S) = Syn(A) = \{y\}$. *If we consider the formula* φ_1 *in* $\Phi_{p,w}$ $(w \equiv y(0))$ *as:*

$$equal(x(0), 1) \Rightarrow y(0) = f(x(0), y(1), intra(2))$$

This formula will be represented by the following Prolog clause:

```
x(p,0,T,I,Vx) :-
            ivalue(x,I,Vt1),
            Vt2 = 1,
            equal(Vt1,Vt2),
            svalue(y,1,T,I,Vt3),
            intrvalue(2,T,Vt4),
            f(Vt1,Vt3,Vt4,Vx).
```

Definitions for the predicates intrvalue(). svalue() and ivalue() are embedded in the evaluator's archetype—they are language independent but depends on the derivation tree internal representation. The purpose of such operations is to implement the attribute evaluation method: intrvalue() extracts the intrinsec value associated with a specific leaf of the tree; ivalue() extracts from the list of inherited values, the value corresponding to a given attribute; svalue searches for the inheriteds on which a synthesized depends, computes their values, builds an atom with the attribute name and the arguments and calls it.

Given a derivation tree t (of sort X and root labelled by p) and a sequence of clauses (derived from all the semantic rules in Φ in accordance with the above criteria) the evaluation of a synthesized attribute occurrence $a(0)$ is equivalent to compute the answer to the query $a(p, 0, t, [], V)$.

Obviously, this computation is only possible if all the predicates appearing in the body of all those clauses are defined. Those predicates, except intrvalue(). svalue() and ivalue that we consider predefined, correspond to the operators f in $\mathcal{F}$ and predicate symbols $r \in R$. So the statement above requires, precisely, the representation of the structure D (the last element of the AG).

The carriers D_s will not be explicitly defined. The definition of the operations f_D and the relations r_D must be supplied by the user in the form of Prolog clauses. The head of these clauses must agree with the syntatic definition given above for the construction of the atoms in the body of clauses implementing formulas φ_j.

Note that the user may omit definitions of predicates that are alredy defined in its Prolog system.

The SEGS provides means to identify the file containing such definitions and automatically includes them in the evaluator.

5.2 Evaluator Details

The interface between the parser and the attribute evaluator is the derivation tree.

The derivation tree is implemented as linked-lists of nodes, each node pointing to its descendants. The nodes are stored independently in the knowledge-base, as facts of the general form:

$$node(nodeid, sort, label, attrs, descs)$$

where *nodeid* is an identifier (to be referenced by other nodes or operations); *sort* records the *sort* of that node (a nonterminal if it is intermediate, or a terminal if it is a leaf); *label* records the node *label* (a production symbol) if it is an intermediate node; *attrs* is the list of attribute values attached to the node; *desc* is a list of node identifiers (its descendants).

Attribute values (both synthesized and inherited) are stored in the nodes to improve the evaluation time (the time complexity is linear in the size of $W(t)$ [DJL86a]).

With respect to the interaction of its three components, the evaluator, instead of calling them sequentially, behaves as follows: the parser is called by the evaluator with only the first symbol in the list parameter that implements the input string; each time that list is empty, the parser calls the lexical analyser to get the next symbol; the attribute evaluator is called upon by the parser after an action of type _reduce_ whenever the sort of the production recognized is a $X \in N$ for which the predicate evalbu(X) holds.

evalbu is a property of nonterminals, instanciated during the generation phase. We say that $evalbu(X)$ holds $(XinN)$ iff for every $a \in Syn(X), sDi(a, X, \emptyset)$ holds. This means that all the synthesized attributes of a nonterminal don't depend on any inherited—so they can be evaluated during bottom-up tree construction. The importance of that property relies on the following fact: After the evaluation of all the synthesized attribute occurrences attached to the root of a tree, its subtrees are no longer necessary and can be eliminated in order to save memory. This strategy leads to the improvement of memory space required by the evaluator.

5.3 Generator Details

In the SEGS all the operations concerned with attribute dependencies rely on the two basic relations bellow, whose tuples are deduced and asserted during the processing of semantic rules:

$$sD(a, X, ld)$$
$$iD(b, X, ld)$$

where $a \in Syn(X)$, $b \in Inh(X)$ and ld is a list (may be empty) of pairs $< c, Y, p >$, $c \in Attr(Y)$, p in P, representing the attribute occurrences on which a (or b) depends.

Obviously, those two relations are a representation for all the *local dependency graphs* $D(p)$, p in P.

The mapping defined by the facts $sDi(a, X, I_a)$ (where I_a denotes the set of inherited attributes of X on which the synthesized attribute a of the same symbol X depends) is equivalent to the "argument selector" [Jou85] and is used as a representation for $\mathcal{D}(X)$ for every X in N. So, to construct the mapping sDi (infer and assert its tuples) and to perform the non-circularity test we have adapted the algorithms of Jourdan [Jou85] to manipulate the graphs under such a representation.

The construction of $sDi(a, X, I_a)$ is based on the following principle:

Let sD(a,X,ld). An inherited attribute $b \in Inh(X)$ is an element of I_a $(b \in I_a)$ iff

1. there exist a p in P such that
   $< b, X, p >$ is an element of ld; or

2. there exist a p in P of profile $< X_1 \ldots X_n, X_0 >$, a $a_i \in Syn(X_i)$, $b_j \in Inh(X_j)$, $1 \le i, j \le n$
   such that
   $< a_i, X_i, p >$ is in ld and $< b, X, p >$ is in ld_j (with $iD(b_j, X_j, ld_j)$) and
   $i = j$ and $b_j \in I_{a_i}$ or
   there is an indirect path from b_j to a_i through edges in D(p) and $\mathcal{D}(X_k)$, $1 \le k \le n$

To begin the construction process, we use the facts $sD(a, X, ld)$ and assert facts $sDi(a, X, I_a)$ where I_a is initialized with the inherited attributes satisfying item 1 above. Then, using iD and sDi, we proceed applying iteratively the second condition until no more information is added to I_a.

To perform the non-circularity test, we verify, for every $sDi(a, X, I_a)$, if there exist any $b \in I_a$ such that b depends on a.

6   Conclusion

The problem of determining the meaning of sentences belonging to a given language was discussed under the attribute grammars paradigm. We have defined what is an attribute based semantic evaluator and a generator for it. A strategy to represent an AG in Prolog was proposed with the objective of solving that problem implementing the evaluator and the generator in Prolog.

The development of the system has shown the adequacy of logic programming in what concerns the size and understandability of the programs as well as the time and simplicity of development. However, memory limitations, intrinsec to the Prolog interpreter, prevents the processing of real size texts.

So it seems reasonable to conclude that this problem deserves further research to attain real and complete benefit from the integration of logic programming and attribute grammars, two powerfull paradigms for language analysis. One of the approaches to be investigated is the "symbolic evaluation" which seems promissing because of its ability to compute attribute values during parsing and in only one top-down tree-traversal.

Acknowlegdements

Thanks are due to Dr. Pierre Deransart for suggesting and discussing this work. Also I would like to thank all members of "Langages et Traducteurs" project at INRIA, Rocquencourt, for their helpfull comments and informations. I am also indebted to Prof. J.M. Valença, my supervisor at the University of Minho, and Mário Martins for reading drafts of this paper. The visits of the author to INRIA were supported by INIC (the first) and (the others) by Fundação Calouste Gulbenkian, both at Lisbon, Portugal.

References

[Abr84]   Harvey Abramson. Definite clause translation grammars. In *Proc.84 – Int. Symp. on Logic Programming, Atlantic City*, pages 233–240, IEEE, 1984. (University of British Columbia).

[Arb86]   Bijan Arbab. Compiling circular attribute grammars into prolog. *Journal of Research and Development*, 30(3):294–309, May 1986.

[ASU86]   Aho, Sethi, and Ulman. *Compiler Principles Techniques and Tools*. Addison-Wesley, 1986.

[Bou84]   Pierre Boullier. *Contribution à la Construction Automatique d'Analyseur Lexicographiques et Syntaxiques*. PhD thesis, Université d'Orleans, 1984.

[CD87]   B. Courcelle and P. Deransart. *Proofs for Partial Correctness for Attribute Grammars with Applications to Recursive Procedures and Logic Programming*. Technical Report I-8702, Univ. de Bordeaux I, U.E.R. de Mathématiques et Informatiques, January 1987.

[CF82]   B. Courcelle and P. Franchi-Zannettacci. Attribute grammars and recursive program schemes. *Theoretical Computer Science*, 17:163–191 and 235–257, 1982.

[DF86]   P. Deransart and G. Ferrand. *Initiation a Prolog: Concepts de Base*. Support de Cours 86-2, Université d'Orleans, Dep. de Mathématiques et Informatique, June 1986.

[DJL85]   P. Deransart, M. Jourdan, and B. Lorho. *A Survey on Attribute Grammars: Part III Classified Bibliography*. Rapport de Recherche 417, INRIA, Rocquencourt, January 1985.

[DJL86a] P. Deransart, M. Jourdan, and B. Lorho. *A Survey on Attribute Grammars: Part I Main Results*. Rapport de Recherche 485, INRIA, Rocquencourt, January 1986.

[DJL86b] P. Deransart, M. Jourdan, and B. Lorho. *A Survey on Attribute Grammars: Part II Review of Existing Systems*. Rapport de Recherche 510, INRIA, Rocquencourt, January 1986.

[DM85]   P. Deransart and J. Maluszynski. *Relating Logic Programs and Attribute Grammars*. Rapport de Recherche 393, INRIA, Rocquencourt, April 1985.

[Jou83]   Martin Jourdan. *An Efficient Recursive Evaluator for Strongly Non-Circular Attribute Grammars*. Rapport de Recherche 235, INRIA, Rocquencourt, October 1983.

[Jou85]   Martin Jourdan. *Evaluation Récursive des Grammaires Attribuées: Deux Implantations*. Rapport de Recherche 409, INRIA, Rocquencourt, May 1985.

[Knu68]   Donald E. Knuth. Semantics of context-free languages. *Mathematical Systems Theory*, 2(2):127–145, 1968.

[MTea83] Y. Matsumoto, H. Tanaka, and H. Hirakawa et al. BUP: a bottom-up parser embedded in prolog. *New Generation Computing*, 1, 1983.

[Nil86] U. Nilsson. AID: an alternative implementation of DCGs. 1986. Dep. of Computer and Information Science, Linköping University (draft version).

[PW80] F. C. N. Pereira and D. H. D. Warren. Definite clause grammars for language analysis: a survey of the formalism and comparison with augmented transistion networks. *Artificial Intelligence*, 13(3):231–278, 1980.

[Rai80] K. J. Räihä. Bibliography on attribute grammars. *SIGPLAN Notices*, 15(3):35–44, 1980.

[UOea84] Kuniaki Uehara, R. Ochitani, and O. Kakusho et al. A bottom-up parser based on predicate logic: a survey of the formalism and its implementation techique. In *Proc.84 - Int. Symp. on Logic Programming, Atlantic City*, pages 220–227, IEEE, 1984. (Osaka University).

[WG84] William Waite and Gerhard Goos. *Compiler Construction. Texts and Monographs in Computer Science*, Springer-Verlag, 1984.

A GRAMMATICAL VIEW OF LOGIC PROGRAMMING

Pierre Deransart
INRIA
Domaine de Voluceau - B.P. 105
78153 LE CHESNAY Cedex
FRANCE
and
Jan Maluszynski
Linköping University
DCIS
S-58183 LINKÖPING
SWEDEN

Introduction

A pure logic program has a declarative reading and a procedural reading. This paper discusses the idea that these can be complemented by a grammatical reading, where the clauses are considered to be rewrite rules of a grammar. The objective is to show that this point of view facilitates transfer of expertise from logic programming to other research on programming languages and vice versa. Some examples of such transfer are discussed. On the other hand the grammatical view presented justifies some ad hoc extensions to pure logic programming and facilitates development of theoretical foundations for such extensions.

The logical notions of the declarative reading are to be related to their direct counterparts in the grammatical reading. As discussed in our early papers the grammar turns out to be a very special case of W-grammar (van Wijngaarden's two-level grammar). This opens for immediate extensions of the notion of logic program by introducing more general classes of W-grammars than these consisting of logic programs. One of them is the class of definite clause grammars. In our presentation the notion of DCG has a direct grammatical reading, in contrast to its usual understanding as a "syntactic sugar" for a special type of logic program. The construction of this program is now seen as a compilation of DCG.

It is well known that van Wijngaarden grammars are closely related to Knuth attribute grammars (AG's) which have been extensively studied and found many applications. Our previous work relating attribute grammars and logic programs uses as the unifying concept a common notion of decorated tree. This paper summarizes briefly this point of view and relates proof methods for logic programs with proof methods of attribute grammars ; new proof methods for run-time properties and completness of logics programs are presented.

1. Proof trees of definite clause programs.

This section relates the grammatical notion of derivation tree with the notion of proof tree of DCP. It shows that the semantics of logic programs can be expressed in the grammatical terms of proof trees.

One of the important concepts related to grammars is the notion of derivation tree. Let G be a context-free grammar and x a symbol of its alphabet. Then the notion of a derivation tree of G and z can be defined as follows.

Definition 1.1.

A *derivation tree* of G and z is any labeled ordered tree satisfying the following conditions :

1. Its root is labeled by z,

2. If a node labeled x has n immediate descendants labeled $x_1, ..., x_n$

   (where the indices correspond to the ordering)
then each x_i is either in the alphabet of G or $n = 1$ and x_1 is the empty string, and $x \rightarrow x_1 ... x_n$ is a production rule of G.

A *complete derivation tree (a parse tree)* is a derivation tree such that none of its leaf nodes is labeled by a nonterminal of the grammar.

Example 1.1

Let G be the following collection of the production rules written in the BNF notation :

```
<triple>   →    <aseq><bseq><cseq>
<aseq>     →    a l a <aseq>
<bseq>     →    b l b <bseq>
<cseq>     →    c l c <cseq>
```

A parse tree of G and <triple> is shown in Fig. 1.

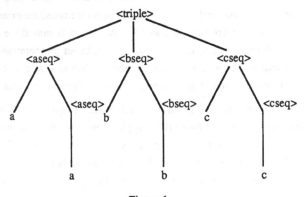

Figure 1

A derivation tree can be seen as a result of pasting together "copies" of the production rules of the grammar. The parse trees of a grammar describe its language and give (possibly ambiguous) structure to every string in the language. Thus a grammar can be considered a specification of a class of parse trees rather than a specification of the language, which is a secondary concept defined in terms of parse trees.

Consider now the notion of definite clause program. Let P be a program and G a goal clause. For simplicity assume that the body of G is one atomic formula a. Following Clark [Cla 79] one can introduce a notion of proof tree. Informally speaking a proof tree is a result of pasting together instances of the clauses of P as stated more precisely by the following definition.

Definition 1.2.

A *proof tree* of P and $\leftarrow a$ is any ordered labeled tree satisfying the following conditions :

1. Its root node is labeled by an instance of a ,

2. If a node of the proof tree is labeled x and the nodes of its direct descendants are labeled $x_1, ..., x_n$ (where the indices reflect the ordering) then $x \leftarrow x_1 .. x_n$ is an instance of a clause of P.

A complete proof tree is a tree whose leaf nodes are instances of the unit clauses (facts) of P.

Example 1.2

Consider the following DCP :

```
triple(X,Y,Z)     ← aseq(X,I), bseq(Y,J), cseq(Z,K).
aseq(a,s(0)).
aseq(a.X, s(I))   ← aseq(X, I).
bseq(b, s(0)).
bseq(b.X, s(J))   ← bseq(X, J).
cseq(c, s(0)).
cseq(c.X, s(K))   ← cseq(X, K).
```

An example of a complete proof tree for P and <- triple(X,Y,Z) is given in Fig. 2.

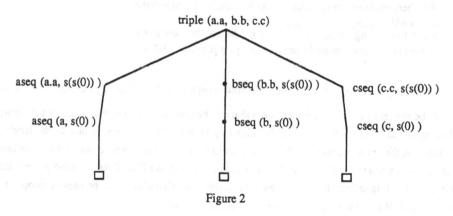

Figure 2

In the sequel we will not distinguish between the trees which are identical up to renaming of the variables in their labels. (Thus, as a matter of fact we deal with equivalence classes of trees and labels).

The concept of a complete proof tree can be used as a basis for a model-theoretic semantics of a logic program. Denote by DEN(P) the set of the root labels of all complete proof trees of P. According to the convention above DEN(P) is determined up to the renaming. It has been proved in [Cla 79] that DEN(P) is the set of all (not-necessarily ground) atomic logical consequences of P. This is connected with the declarative reading of P and can be used for defining the semantics of P as DEN(P).

On the other hand, the definition of proof tree resembles very much the definition of the derivation tree of a context-free grammar. The difference is that the clauses of P usually include variables and because of that may have infinitely many distinct instances, while every instance of a production rule of a CFG is simply its copy. On the other hand the alphabet of a Definite Clause Program does not include terminal symbols in the sense of CFG.

The concept of proof tree is purely declarative. The question arises how to construct proof trees. In particular, for given program P and goal $\leftarrow a$ it may be interesting to find the set T of all complete proof trees t such that the root of t is an instance of a.. The problem can be solved by using the SLD-resolution. Each refutation for P and $\leftarrow a$ via some computation rule corresponds to some proof tree. Now T consists of all instances of all such trees. The well-known result on the independence of the computation rule [Llo 87] shows that the set of complete proof trees corresponding to all refutations of a given goal is the same regardless of the computation rule. This result allows one to define (nondeterministic) operational semantics of a definite clause program. The basis for that is a nondeterministic algorithm that extends proof trees.

Algorithm (Nondeterministic Derivation Algorithm-NDA).

The algorithm transforms an incomplete proof tree into a proof tree of a given definite program P :

For a given incomplete proof tree t
do
  - select one of its leaves labeled by an atom g;
  - take a renamed version of a clause $h \leftarrow b_1,...,b_n$ of P, such that h
    unifies with g ; let μ be the mgu ;
  - extend t by adding the sons $b_1,...,b_n$ to g ; denote this new tree t' ;
  - the result is the tree obtained from t' by applying μ to every label.
od

For a given program P consider all goals of the form $\leftarrow n(X_1, ..., X_q)$, where X_i s are different variables.

Let t(P) be the set of all complete proof trees that can be constructed from that goals by the algorithm NDA. By the independence result t(P) is unique up to renaming of the variables in the labels. Let NDOS(P) be the set of all root labels of the trees in t(P). This set is also unique up to renaming of variables. It characterizes all computed answer substitutions [Llo 87] of P for the most general atomic goals and since it is defined in terms of the nondeterministic algorithm it can be seen as an operational semantics of P. We illustrate this concept by an example program.

Example 1.3

Consider the following program P defining addition on natural integers :

    plus(zero, X, X).

plus(s(X), Y, s(Z)) :- plus(X, Y, Z).

Its denotation DEN(P) contains all atoms of the form $plus(s^n(0), t, s^n(t))$ for any non negative n and any term $t : t = zero, X, s(zero), s(X), ...$ where X is any variable, since the atoms identical up to renaming of the variables are not distinguished.

On the other hand, NDOS(P) contains the atoms :

$plus(s^n(zero), X, s^n(X))$ $n \geq 0$

For a given atomic goal $\leftarrow g$ the set of all computed answer substitutions can be obtained by unifying g with the elements of NDOS(P).

For example the goal

plus(N1, N2, s(zero))

unifies only with the following elements of NDOS(P)

plus(s(zero),X,s(X))

and

plus(zero, X, X)

giving the two expected answer substitutions

N1 ← s(zero), N2 <- zero

and

N1 ← zero, N2 <- s(zero)

This shows also that NDOS(P) is a representation of DEN(P) (i.e. each element of DEN(P) is an instance of an element of NDOS(P)). This result is known as completness of the SLD resolution [Cla 79, Llo 87,see DF 87 for an approach based on the proof trees]). Thus NDOS(P) is empty if and only if DEN(P) is empty.

2. Definite clause programs as a special class of Van Wijngaardens grammars.

This section shows a class of grammars whose derivation trees resemble very much the proof trees of DCP's. These are Van Wijngaarden grammars (W-grammars) introduced in [Wij 65]. The concept is presented informally in the spirit of the formal definition given in [Mal 84].

The idea behind the concept of W-grammar is to enrich nonterminals of a CFG with parameters ranging over some context-free languages. The notion of a production rule extends thus to a parameterized production rule scheme. Every scheme describes possibly infinite number of production rules each of which can be obtained by instantiating parameters of the scheme by arbitrary chosen elements of their domains.

Example 2.1

For the grammar of Example 1.1 the nonterminal <triple> derives the (regular) language L_G(<triple>) = $a^+b^+c^+$.

We now introduce parameters in the production rules so that the language specified by the resulting W-grammar is the subset of L_G(<triple>) consisting of the strings with equal numbers of the symbols a, b and c.

The parameters to be introduced are X, Y, Z and N.

Their domains are defined by the following CFG :

$$X \rightarrow a \mid a.X$$

$$Y \rightarrow b \mid b.Y$$

$$Z \rightarrow c \mid c.Z$$

$$N \rightarrow s(0) \mid s(N)$$

and the parameterized production rules are the following :

<triple(X, Y, Z)> → <aseq(X, N)><bseq(Y, N)><cseq(Z, N)>

<aseq(a,s(0))> → a

<aseq(a.X,s(N))> → a <aseq(X, N)>

<bseq(b,s(0))> → b

<bseq(b.Y,s(N))> → b <bseq(Y, N)>

<cseq(c,s(0))> → c

<cseq(c.Z,s(N))> → c <cseq(Z, N)>

The actual production rules are those which can be obtained from the parameterized production rule schemata by instantiation of the parameters. For example, using the substitution {X/a.a,Y/b.b,Z/c.c,N/s(s(0)} one can construct the following production rules :

<triple(a.a,b.b,c.c)> → <aseq(a.a,s(s(0)))><bseq(b.b,s(s(0)))><cseq(c.c,s(s(0)))>

Similarly, by {X/a,N/s(0)} one gets :

<aseq(a.a,s(s(0)))> → a <aseq(a, s(0))>
and by {Y/b,N/s(0)}

<bseq (b.b, s(s(0)))> → b <bseq (b, s(0))>, etc.

There are infinitely many actual production rules which can be constructed in that way since the domains of X,Y,Z and N are infinite.

The language specified by a W-grammar G and a parameterized nonterminal h consists of all and only those strings which can be derived from any parameter-free instance of h using the rules of W (i.e. the parameter-free instances of rule schemata).

A W-grammar can be seen as a CFG with infinite number of production rules and infinite number of nonterminal symbols. This means that the notion of derivation tree is the same as for CFG's. A derivation tree for the W-grammar of Example 2.1 and for the nonterminal <triple(a.a, b.b, c.c)> is shown in Fig 3. It resembles very much the proof tree of Fig. 2. Both have been obtained by pasting together instances of the rules, in the first case of the DCP, in the other - of the W-grammar. There are, however, important differences between the concept of DCP and the concept of W-grammar which are discussed below.

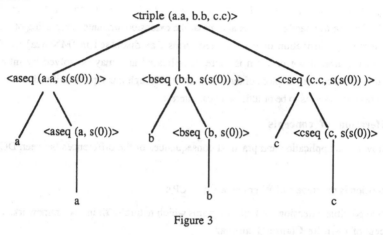

Figure 3

Terminal symbols and the language.

The rule schemata of a W-grammar, and consequently the production rules, may include terminal symbols. The notion of complete derivation tree gives thus a concept of terminal string derivable from a given nonterminal and consequently the notion of the language specified by a given W-grammar and given nonterminal symbol. The language specified by a parameterized nonterminal is the union of all languages specified by its parameter-free instances.

The clauses of a DCP include atoms and no concept of a terminal alphabet in the sense discussed above is introduced.

Domain specifications.

W-grammar includes as its component a finite set of context-free production rules specifying the domains of the parameters, called the *metagrammar*. The parameters are instantiated by the elements of the domains. Thus, the parameters play the role similar to that of variables in the clauses. Similarly the domain elements may be compared with terms. It is worth noticing that for a given finite alphabet of functors the Herbrand universe is a context-free language and can be easily defined by an (unambiguous) context-free grammar. Therefore, a DCP can be viewed as a W-grammar with the empty terminal alphabet, and with the domain of every parameter defined by default to be the Herbrand universe.

Thus the notion of W-grammar is an extension of the notion of DCP which allows many-sorted terms (sorts are the nonterminals of the metagrammar). It opens also for user-defined syntax of terms, where the structure of a term is defined by the parse tree of the string in the metagrammar. This approach brings also certain difficulties since, if the metagrammar is ambiguous, the structure of the string is not unique.

Resolution

The derivation trees of a W-grammar have no parameters in node labels. Thus, considering a DCP program to be a W-grammar one restricts the class of proof trees to ground ones. For a given program P the ground proof trees may be constructed as ground instances of not necessarily ground proof trees obtained by SLD-resolution. This raises the problem whether resolution can be extended for W-grammars. In the case of unambiguous metagrammar the extension amounts to replacing of unification of one-sorted terms by unification of many-sorted terms , as discussed in [MN 82a]. In the case of ambiguous metagrammar the problem is more complicated and may be solved by introduction of unification under associativity in place of term unification. Though this type of unification is decidable [Si 84] this generalization seems to be of little practical interest.

2.1. Proliferation of concepts

We now show some application and practical consequences of the differences between DCP's and W-grammars.

The first question is the impact of W-grammars on DCP's.

There are two possible extensions of logic programs which naturally fit in that framework. The first one is the concept of **Definite Clause Grammar**.

It is obtained by introducing terminal symbols and allowing the clauses to include them. A DCG is then a special type of W-grammar rather than a syntactic sugar for a special class of DCP's [PW 80].

Example 2.2

A simplified version of the W-grammar of Example 2.1 is the following DCG, where the predicates carry the information about the length of the underlying strings, expressed as Prolog numerals.

triple(N) → aseq(N),bseq(N),cseq(N).

aseq(1) → [a].

aseq(N) → [a], aseq(M), {N is M+1}.

bseq(1) → [b].

bseq(N) → [b], bseq(M), {N is M+1}.

cseq(1) → [c].

cseq(N) → [c], cseq(M), {N is M+1}.

This point of view opens for development of alternative implementations of DCG's, like that mentioned in [Nil 86] and based on the LR-parsing techniques.

The second extension is the introduction of many-sorted type discipline and domain declarations in logic programs. This was first suggested in [MN 82a, MN 82b]. The idea of using domain declarations for improving efficiency of the compiled logic programs was explored in [Nil 83].

It appears also in Turbo Prolog [Bor 86]. To illustrate this statement we quote an example Turbo Prolog program from the manual [p. 51].

domains

    title, author = symbol

    pages   =   integer

    publication = book(title, pages)

predicates

      written_by(author, publication)

      long_novel(title)

clauses

      written_by(fleming, book("DR NO", 210).

      written_by(melville, book("MOBY DICK", 600)).

      long_novel(Title) :-written_by(_,book(Title, Length)), Length> 300.

The domain declarations of this program are (non-recursive) context-free production rules, where

    title, author = symbol

is a shorthand for two rules :

    title   → symbol

    author → symbol

The rules include :

    nonterminals : title, author, symbol, integer, publication,

    terminals : book, , , (,)

and refer to the standard domains of integers and symbols for which grammatical rules are not included.

The predicate declarations specify types of the arguments by using nonterminals of the metagrammar. The terms of the clauses have to observe these declarations, i.e. they are sentential forms derived in the full metagrammar (including its standard implicit part). The variables are implicitly typed by parsing of the terms according to the predicate declarations : the variable Title is of type *title*, hence *symbol*, the variable Length is of type *pages*, hence *integer*.

Let us discuss now the impact of DCP's on W-grammars. As pointed out in Section 2.2 the original definition of W-grammar gives no practical possibility for constructing derivations. In [Mal 84] a notion of transparent W-grammar was defined which opens for application of resolution techniques in construction of proof trees. The idea is that the metagrammar should be unambiguous and every parameterized nonterminal should be its sentential form. In this case it has a unique parse tree which can be seen as a term and can be subject of unification. Now the formalism of transparent W-grammars can be used as a logic programming language with many-sorted type discipline and with the operational semantics based on resolution. An experimental implementation of such a language is described in [Näs 87].

3. Definite Clause Programs and Relational Attribute Grammars.

As discussed in Section 1 proof trees of a DCP resemble derivation trees of CFG's but have much more complicated labels. The question arises whether the concept of proof tree can be decomposed into two simpler concepts: a context-free skeleton tree and a labeling mechanism that decorates the skeleton. This idea is not new. It was formalized by Knuth as the notion of Attribute Grammar, which found many applications. Our previous work [DM 85] attempted to relate formally these two notions.

In the rest of this paper we briefly outline some ideas based on that work.

3.1. Relational Attribute Grammars

This section presents a general notion of Relational Attribute Grammar [CD 87] which can be seen as a generalized version of DCG where labeling mechanism is defined separately from the context-free skeleton grammar.

The labeling mechanism is then restricted and refined to the usual more specific notion of AG. Special attention is devoted to comparison of the formalisms to indicate possible transfer of ideas between them.

To facilitate presentation we assume that the set of terminal symbols of the CFG is empty so that the definition presented is an extension of DCP rather than DCG.

Definition 3.1

Relational Attribute Grammar (RAG) is a 5-tuple

$$<N, R, Attr, Phi, Int>$$

where

N   is a finite set of non terminal symbols,

R   is a finite set of context free rules, built with N. R can be viewed as a N-sorted signature of a R-Algebra. Elements of R will be denoted as usual :

$$n_0 \rightarrow n1... , n_k..., n_p \quad p \geq 0$$

Thus N and R give rise to a set of context-free parse trees and the other elements of RAG provide a labeling formalism.

Attr is a finite set of attribute names. Every nonterminal of N has associated a set of attribute names. To simplify presentation it is assumed that these sets are disjoint and linearly ordered. Thus the attributes associated with a non terminal n will be denoted $n_1,..., n_q$, where n_i denotes the ith attribute of n in the ordering. As usual, the labeling mechanism will be specified at the level of grammatical rules. Different occurences of the same non terminal in a rule will lead to different occurences of the same attribute. They will be denoted by additional indices referring to the occurrence number of the non terminal. For example consider the rule

$$n \rightarrow n \ n$$

where n has two attributes n_1 and n_2. The different occurrences of the attribute n_1 will be denoted : n_1 (0), n_1 (1) and n_1 (2), or briefly n_{10}, n_{11}, n_{12}, and those of n_2 : : n_{20}, n_{21}, n_{22}.

Phi is an assignment of a logic formula Phi_r to each production rule r in R. The formula includes attribute occurrences as the variables. Thus for every interpretation it defines some relation between the values of the attribute occurrences in the rule r.

Int is the interpretation of the language used in Phi : it defines the domains, associates functors of the language with functions on the domains and predicate letters with relations.

The formalism defines a set of labeled trees. Each of them has the context-free skeleton defined by the production rules of R. A node of the skeleton with nonterminal n is to be additionally labeled by a k-tuple of values in the domain of Int, where k is the number of attributes of n .

The tree consists of instances of the production rules. Let r be one of them. Then the nodes of r have to be decorated by the tuples of values. Each of the values corresponds to some attribute appearing in the formula Phi_r. It is required that the formula is true in Int with this valuation.

A decorated parse tree such that this condition is satisfied for all its component instances of the production rules is called *valid decorated tree* of the RAG. Thus, the semantics of a RAG is the set of the valid decorated trees or in short valid trees. For a more complete treatment of this definition see [CD 87] or [DM 85].

Example 3.1 : Relational Attribute Grammar for factorial

The following RAG describes the computation of i ! the factorial of i (i.e: 0! = 1 and for i > 0, i !=(i - 1)!* i). A systematic presentation of such constructions is given in [CD 87].

N is { fact },

R is { fact $\rightarrow$e , fact $\rightarrow$ fact }, (e denotes the empty string)

Attr is { fact1, fact2 }, where fact1 denotes the argument and fact2 the results.

Phi is { fact1=0 and fact2 = 1, fact1(1)=fact1(0)-1 and fact2(0)=fact2(1)*fact1(0) }

Int is Nat, the domain of the natural (or non negative) integers together with the usual operations and relations (equality ...).

A valid decorated tree for the given RAG is shown below (Figure 4).

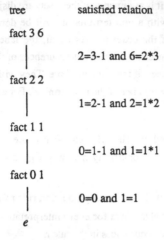

tree	satisfied relation
fact 3 6	
	2=3-1 and 6=2*3
fact 2 2	
	1=2-1 and 2=1*2
fact 1 1	
	0=1-1 and 1=1*1
fact 0 1	
	0=0 and 1=1
e	

Figure 4

End of Example

It is easy to see that every subtree of a valid tree is valid. Thus, the concept of valid tree makes it possible to associate a relation on the domain of Int with every nonterminal n of the grammar. The relation is q-ary, where q is the number of attributes of n. A q-tuple of attribute values is in the relation iff it is a root label of some valid proof tree for n. This relation will be called the *basic relation* and denoted BR_n. The family of the relations $\{BR_n \mid n \text{ in } N\}$ will be denoted BR.

It is easy to see that the relation associated with the nonterminal fac of Example 3.1 is the set of pairs (i ,i !) for $i \geq 0$.

3.2. DCP's as a special class of RAG's.

We now show that a DCP can be viewed as a special kind of RAG. In Section 1 two types of "grammatical" semantics of DCP's have been defined. The first one associates with a DCP P the set of all proof trees, the other deals with the computation trees of the NDA algorithm. The idea is then to construct a RAG whose valid trees are isomorphic to the considered class of proof trees of P.

A general framework for this is as follows.

Let P be a DCP with :

- the alphabet of functors FUNC,

- the alphabet of predicate letters PRED

- and with the set of clauses CLAUSE.

We associate with it a RAG

$G = < N, C, Attr, Phi, Int >$

where

N   is PRED,

C   is CLAUS in which all the arguments have been removed,

Attr is a set of attribute names denoting the arguments of the predicates (the i th argument of the predicate p will be denoted p_i),

Phi will be defined below; for each of the two types of semantics of P a separate definition will be given

Int is the interpretation of the logical language used for defining Phi ; the domain of interpretation are (not necessarily ground) terms constructed from the symbols of FUNCT ; the symbols of FUNCT are interpreted as term constructors. It is called the canonical term interpretation denoted T (V, FUNC) or in short T.

By specifying two different sets Phi we define now two different RAG's :

- RAGD whose valid trees model the proof trees of P, and

- RAGO whose valid trees model the computation trees of the NDA algorithm.

Let

$c : n_0(T_0) :- n_1(T_1) ...n_k(T_k) ...n_p(T_p)$

be a clause of P, where T_i for i=1,...p denote the tuples of terms which are the arguments of the predicates n_i.

The corresponding context-free production rule is :

$c : n_0 \rightarrow n_1, ...,n_k, ..., n_p,$

The associated formula Phi_c of RAGD is

$\exists X$ AND(for all k > 0 and $1 \leq j \leq q_k$) $n_{kj} = t_{kj}(X)$

where = is interpreted in Int as the identity on terms, t_{kj} is the j-th term in the tuple of terms T_k and X are all variables appearing in the clause c.

Notice that n_{kj} are (the only) free variables of Phi_c. Thus, for a given valuation of n_{kj}'s Phi_c is true iff there exists a substitution ß, such that n_{kj} is the instance of t_{kj} under ß.

It is shown in [DM 85, CD 87] that BR for RAGD is exactly DEN(P).

The associated formula Phi_c of RAGO is

AND (for $1 \leq j \leq q_0$) $n_{0j} = \partial(t_{0j})$ (or in short $N_0 = \partial(T_0)$)

where

$$\partial = mgu(<T_1,...T_p>,<N_1,...N_p>) ;$$

N_k is the tuple of attributes n_{kj} for j from 1 to q_k, T_k is the tuple of arguments of the k-th atom in the body of the clause, and the variables of the clause have been renamed away of the variables of the N_k's values.

It is shown in [Der 88c] taht BR for RAGO is exactlly NDOS(P), which corresponds also to the least N-models in [FLM 88].

Example 3.2

Consider the program for addition of Section 1

> plus(zero, X, X).
>
> plus(s(X), Y, s(Z)) :- plus(X, Y, Z).

Its underlying set of production rules is :

plus →

plus → plus

The corresponding formulae of RAGD are

$\exists\, X \ plus_1 = zero \wedge plus_2 = X \wedge plus_3 = X$

$\exists\, X,Y,Z \ plus_{01} = s(X) \wedge plus_{02} = Y \wedge plus_{03} = s(Z) \wedge plus_{11} = X \wedge plus_{12} = Y \wedge plus_{13} = Z.$

The corresponding formulae of RAGO are

$plus_1 = zero \wedge plus_2 = X \wedge plus_3 = X$

$plus_{01} = \partial(s(X)) \wedge plus_{02} = \partial(Y) \wedge plus_{03} = \partial(s(Z))$

where

$$\partial = mgu(<X,\ Y,\ Z>, <plus_{11},\ plus_{12},\ plus_{13}>)$$

assuming that X, Y, Z do not appear in $plus_{11}$, $plus_{12}$ and $plus_{13}$.

Fig. 5 shows one example of valid tree for both RAG's.

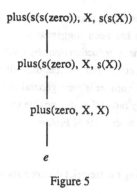

plus(s(s(zero)), X, s(s(X)))

plus(s(zero), X, s(X))

plus(zero, X, X)

e

Figure 5

3.3 Proliferation of ideas

The concept of RAG was first introduced in [DM 85] as a "common denominator" of DCP's and Attribute Grammars. There are two important differences between RAG's and DCP's :

Interpretations

RAG's have explicit concept of interpretation, which is a basis for defining the semantic relations BR. There is no restriction on the type of semantic domains or on the functions associated with the functors of the alphabet. DCP programs refer to the term domain and the functors are always interpreted as term constructors.

Operational Semantics

The relations specified by a DCP can be computed by the resolution techniques. No operational semantics of RAG's has been suggested in [DM 85].

The differences suggest a possibility of a natural extension of the concept of DCP to logic programs with interpreted functors. In practical applications of attribute grammars the interpretation of the functors is provided as the "semantic functions" [Kn 68], which are some external procedures. The formalism of RAG's incorporates such low-level procedures into the high-level and declarative structure of semantic rules. An important feature of the formalism is that it imposes no restrictions on the language of the procedures or their actual form. Now the idea is to use the same approach to incorporate external functional procedures into logic programs. This should give a general method of amalgamation of logic programming with functional programming without being specific about the functional language to be used. Although the Concept of RAG gives the declarative semantics of such amalgamation it provides no direct suggestion for an operational semantics on which a practical implementation could be based. To solve this problem two ways can be suggested.

The first possibility is to modify resolution so that it can handle interpreted terms. If some appropriate axiomatization of the interpretation is available this would amount to logic programming with equality [JLM 84]. But this would also bring all difficulties related to E-unification [Si 85]. However, in the tradition of AG's it is more natural to expect that an implementation of semantic functions is given rather than their axiomatization. If the problem could be solved in this framework it would open for re-usability of the existing functional procedures in logic programs without violation of the declarative semantics. An incomplete solution along this lines has been suggested in [LBM 88] and [BM 88]. The idea is to combine Robinson's unification with term reduction done by calling the external procedures defining the interpretation of the functors. This generalized unification, called S-unification, is an incomplete E-unification. If it produces a unifier, the unifier is most general and unique. If it fails, no E-unifier for the arguments exist. In some cases it may report that it is unable to solve the problem. This resembles run-time errors reported by the arithmetic procedures of Prolog.

Example

For the RAG of Example 3.1 specifying the factorial the corresponding amalgamated program may look as follows :

fac(0,1).

fac(X,Y*X) ← fac(X-1,Y).

where 0,1,* and - are functors interpreted on the domain of nonnegative integers.

Consider the goal

← fac(3, V).

The S-unifier of fac(3,V) and fac(X,Y*X) is {X/3, V/Y*3} and results in the next goal ← fac(2,Y). Eventually the computation succeeds with the answer V = 6.

The second way of giving an operational semantics for amalgamated programs would be transformation of the corresponding RAG into the usual type of AG where some standard attribute evaluation techniques could be used. The construction and its limitations are discussed in [DM 85]. Some comments will be also given in the next section.

3.4. Functional Attribute Grammars and Logic Programs.

The RAG's provide no way of computing the values which can be assigned to the positions of a given tree. Their semantics is purely declarative and can be easily related to the semantics of logic programs as discussed above. However, the formalism of attribute grammars was originally introduced with some additional restrictions which make it possible to compute attribute values of a derivation tree in a deterministic way. These can be expressed as restrictions on the form of formulæ associated with the production rules. The basic concept is splitting of attributes into synthesised and inherited. The splitting is called *direction assignment* since it describes a dependency relation between attributes of any parse tree

It is then required that the formula associated with the production rule is conjunction of the atomic formulae of the form X = t where X is an inherited attribute of a body nonterminal or a synthesised attribute of the head nonterminal of the rule and the only variables of t are inherited attributes of the head or synthesised attributes of the body nonterminals. Furthermore some global well-formedness condition is formulated which excludes circular dependencies between the attributes of parse trees thus making possible unique decoration of any given proof tree. Following [DM 85] such grammars will be called Functional Attribute Grammars (FAG's).

As discussed above RAG's include DCG's (thus also DCP's) as a special subclass. Another subclass are FAG's with the operational semantics defined by the attribute evaluation techniques. The intersection of the subclasses is not empty. The elements of the intersection have a similar declarative semantics based on the concept of decorated tree but different operational semantics: the decorated tree may be constructed either by resolution, where parsing is interleaved with parse tree decoration or by attribute evaluation technique applied to the CF parse tree constructed before hand by some CF parsing algorithm. This opens for transfer of techniqes between AG's and Logic Programs. There have been many attempts in both directions. Let us mention briefly a few areas.

Writing Parsers in Prolog

In implementation of AG's as well as in other applications it is necessary to generate parsers for given CF Grammars. It has been argued that it is rather easy to compile a CFG into a Logic Program that can be used for parsing. The approaches, like [Col 78, PW 83, CH 87] may be useful to write a top down nondeterministic parser, but the resulting program is rather inefficient on big grammars in case of deterministic languages. On the other hand the top down approach can be made deterministic in some cases if the CFG is LL(1) and some more conditions are satisfied [Der 88]. Thus it has been proposed to encode known algorithms for bottom up deterministic parsing [CH 87, Nil 87, MTH 83, Hen 88] are variants of such approach. It seems that the resulting deterministic parsers can be compared favorably with those obtained by traditional methods (assuming the parsers are built automatically). But the only real advantage of using Prolog seems to be the ease of rapid implementation of parser constructors rather than efficiency of the parsers. This point requires further investigation.

Using parsing techniques in logic programming

It seems that the real strength of the logic programming is its ability to handle nondeterministic parsing. Thus suggestions have been made to combine deterministic parsing methods with resolution for restriction of the nondeterminism of execution. For example [UOK 84] is an attempt to restrict the clause selection using bottom up parsing techniques and look ahead. Similarly [Nil 86] extends LR-parsing techniques to nondeterministic parsing and combines this with resolution to give an alternative implementation of DCG's. For some examples this look-ahead technique allows a considerable reduction of the search space.

Implementation of Attribute Grammars in Prolog

Since Functional Attribute Grammars resemble Logic Programs many authors suggested to use Prolog to write them and to execute them. Different implementations of this idea can be found in [Abr 84, Arb 86, Hen 88]. The analogy is particularly clear for FAG schemes, where the interpretation is not given, or for FAG's with the free interpretation, where the functors are interpreted as term constructors. A formal study of this relation was presented in [DM 85]. It has been shown that such a FAG can be transformed into an equivalent logic program where the nonterminals correspond to the predicates, the attributes correspond to the argument positions of the predicates and the production rules to the clauses. In particular, the inherited attributes of the head of a grammatical rule and the synthesized attributes of the body nonterminals are represented as distinct variables in the corresponding clause.

As shown in [DM 85] a pure FAG's can be turned into a logic program in which all input arguments (i.e inherited of the head and synthesized of the body) are simple distinct variables.

A classical example of FAG is that of [Knu 68] describing computation of the decimal value of binary numbers specified by a CFG.

The corresponding logic program is the following DCG :

binnum(V1 plus V2) → num(0, L1, V1), [.], num(minus(L2), L2, V2).

num(R0, s(L1), V1 plus V2) → num(s(R0), L1,V1), digit(R0,V2).

num(R0, 0, 0) → [ ].

digit(R0, 0) → [0].

digit(R0, exp(2,R0)) → [1]

In the original FAG the nonterminal *binum* has one synthesized attribute (the resulting decimal value), *num* one inherited (R, the range of the right most digit of the derived string of digits) and two synthesized (L, the length of the derived string of digits and V the corresponding decimal value), and *digit* has two attributes (R the range of the digit and V its decimal value). These are represented by the variables of the DCG rules.

It is shown in [DM 85] that in such DCG the circularity problem is equivalent to the occur-check problem, i.e. that such program can be (symbolically) evaluated by a Prolog interpreter without occur-check if and only if no cyclic definition of attribute instance may appear in some tree.

The circularity test is decidable (see [DJL 88] for more details and references). The given example satisfies this property and thus it is possible to obtain the symbolic value of the synthesized attribute of the root by executing the corresponding Prolog program. For example, with the string 1.1 we will obtain

$$(0 \text{ plus } exp(2,0)) \text{ plus } (0 \text{ plus } exp(2, minus(1)))$$

This apparently easy correspondence between FAG's and Logic Programs raises the question whether the encoding of a FAG in Prolog will lead to an efficient attribute evaluator. Unfortunatly it is not the case.

First of all the experiments with attribute grammar evaluation show that the decorated trees are so large ([DJL 88]) that available Prolog systems cannot handle efficiently corresponding proof trees. However, the main problem comes from the interpreted operations. The constructed logic program produces only symbolic expressions for attribute values. They quickly become very large and their efficient evaluation is a difficult problem. Thus, for efficiency reasons one should interleave construction of the tree with computation of the attribute values.

Since inherited (resp. synthesized) attributes play the role of input (output) arguments, for some AG's implementation of the interleaving may be easy. It is the case if the input arguments of every predicate in the constructed program are ground at the moment of its call and its output arguments are ground at the success. (For more discussion see [DM 85]. According to [Dr 87] this type of logic programs is quite common.)

For example the second rule of the example DCG may be transformed as follows :

num(R0, L0, V0) → {R1 is R0+1}, num(R1, L1, V1), {L0 is L1+1}, digit(R0, V2), {V0 is V1+V2}.

Such translation is not possible in general. For example in the first rule of the DCG the first argument of the second body literal is *minus(L2)*. It should be translated into *R2 is -L2* . But *L2* is not known; it corresponds to a synthesized attribute and cannot be computed until the subtree is constructed. Thus the method fails.

This problem is well known in the field of attribute grammar where different cathegories of algorithms have been introduced to evaluate attributes. For a complete review of this aspect see [DJL 88]. So the logic programming implementations of attribute grammar are essentially encodings of known algorithms in Prolog [Hen 88]. No strong indication exists until now that the resulting logic programs could be substantially more efficient. However, known AG implementations in Prolog show that this encoding is possible and can lead to rapid prototyping of compilers or metacompilers.

Use of Functional Attribute Grammars to compute proof trees.

It is an interesting problem whether attribute evaluation techniques can be used for giving alternative semantics for some classes of logic programs. For example a well-known class of AG's are L-AG's where all attributes can be computed during top-down parsing. There is a corresponding class of DCG's for which the process of proof tree construction would "simulate" the process of parsing and attribute evaluation. This generalizes the example above explaining incorporation of the attribute evaluation in the second rule of the DCG. The question is whether this approach may improve efficiency of computation of a logic program.

In [DF 85] a category of "data driven" logic programs is defined in which L-AG are used to analyse the data flow in the proof trees and deduce the best strategy depending on the instantiation patterns of the arguments of the goal.

In [AF 88] a special class of logic programs is introduced for which the proof tree construction can be performed by an attribute evaluator.

4. Fixpoint induction in Logic Programming

As discussed in Section 3 DCP's can be seen a special class of RAG's.

This section applies the validation method for RAG presented in [CD 87] for proving properties of Logic Programs. The kind of proved properties depends on the type of semantics considered. For example for the RAG modeling the nondeterministic operational semantic, properties of the computed answer substitutions can be proved. On the other hand, for the RAG modeling the declarative semantics the properties to be proved concern all correct answer substitutions.

The proof method discussed was presented in [CD 87]. It resembles fixpoint induction for algorithmic languages. A similar approach was suggested in [Cla 79] and [Hog 84] but without giving technical details.

4.1 Partial correctness of RAG's.

This section outlines basic concepts of the proof method for RAG's presented in [CD 87].

The notion of partial correctness of a RAG is defined with respect to some specification. Let G be a RAG $<N, R, Attr, Phi, Int>$. Let L be a logical language with an interpretation that extends Int.

A *specification* S for G is a family $\{S_n\}$ of formulas indexed by n in N and such that the only free variables of the formula S_n are the attributes of n. If the number of attributes of n is q then the variables will be denoted $n_1, n_2, ...n_q$.

For example, the following formulas are specifications for the RAG *fact* :

$S1_{fact}(fact_1, fact_2) : fact_1 \geq 0$

$S2_{fact}(fact_1, fact_2) : fact_2 = fact_1!$

Another specification for the same RAG could be.

$S3_{fact}(fact_1, fact_2): \exists\, m\; fact_2 = m!$

A specification is said to be *valid* iff for every q-tuple $<v_1,...,v_q>$ of attribute values which is the root label of a valid tree for n, the formula associated with n is true in Int under the valuation $\{n_1/v_1,...n_q/v_q\}$.

In other words, if S is valid then every element of the basic relation BR_n will also satisfy S_n. Thus, since the interpretation is given, every S_n specifies a relation which is a superset of BR_n. A specification which defines exactly BR is then the strongest valid specification.

It is shown in [CD 87] that BR is not always first order expressible. As the basic relation BR can be unknown or very difficult to express, we need a method to prove the validity of a specification. In [CD 87] the notion of inductive specification is introduced as a basis of a proof method similar to the fixpoint induction.

A specification S is *inductive* iff for every r in R : $n_0 \rightarrow n_1, ..., n_k, ..., n_p$ the formula

$$\text{AND (for k from 1 to p) } S_{nk} \wedge Phi_r \Rightarrow S_{n0}$$

is valid in the interpretation Int.

The formulas S_{nk} are those obtained from S_n by replacing the free variables denoting the attributes by corresponding attribute occurrences, i.e. $n_i(k)$, or in short n_{ik}.

As an example, consider the specification $S1_{fact}$. It is inductive, since the formulas

$$fact_1 = 0 \wedge fact_2 = 1 \Rightarrow fact_1 \geq 0$$

and

$$fact_1(1) \geq 0 \wedge fact_1(1) = fact_1(0) - 1 \wedge fact_2(0) = fact_2(1)*fact_1(0) \Rightarrow fact_1(0) \geq 0$$

are valid under the considered interpretation (as $fact_1(0) = fact_1(1)+1$).

The method of the inductive specification is general as it is shown in [CD 87] that a specification is valid if and only if it is the logical consequence of an inductive specification. It is a consequence of the facts that every inductive specification is valid and that there exists the strongest inductive specification that defines BR.

Notice that a specification can be valid without being inductive.

For example $S3_{fact}$ is not inductive, but it is a logical consequence of $S2_{fact}$.

4.2 Declarative semantics and related properties.

The declarative semantics of a Logic Program P is the set of its proof trees or the set of its proof tree roots denoted DEN(P) (see section 1). As discussed in Section 3.2 it can be modeled by the grammar RAGD whose set of valid trees is isomorphic with the set of proof trees of P.

Now we can transfer all the notions introduced for the RAG's to Logic Programming (it has been done in [CD 87] but we use here slightly different attribute definition).

A specification for a logic program P is a family of logic formulas indexed by the predicate letters. (If a formula associated with some predicate p is the logical constant true then it is omitted). The language of formulae has some fixed interpretation. It is assumed that it defines meaning of all the functional symbols of FUNC. Notice that no restriction is put on the kind of interpretation; it needs not be the term interpretation.

A specification S is valid if for every atom of DEN(P) of the form $n(t_1, ..., t_q)$ the formula $S_n(t_1, ..., t_q)$ is valid in the interpretation considered.

A specification is valid if it is a logical consequence of an inductive specification.

A specification is inductive iff for every rule c

$n_0 \rightarrow n_1, ..., n_k, ..., n_p$ corresponding to the clause $n_0(T_0) :- n_1(T_1), ..., n_k(T_k), ..., n_p(T_p)$

where T_k is $t_{k1}, ..., t_{kj}, ..., t_{kqk}$, the formula

$$\text{AND (for k from 1 to p) } S_{nk} \wedge Phi_c \Rightarrow S_{n0}$$

where

$$Phi_c \text{ is } \exists ..X.. \text{ AND(for k from 1 to p and } 1 \leq j \leq q_k) \ n_{kj} = t_{kj}(..X..)$$

is valid in the interpretation considered.

The formula can be simplified by replacing existential quantifiers in premises by universal quantifiers applied to the whole formula.

Thus :

A specification is inductive if the universal closure of the formula

$$\text{AND (for k from 1 to p) } S_{nk}(...t_{kj}(...X...)...) \Rightarrow S_{n0}(...t_{0i}(...X...)...)$$

is valid in the interpretation.

This gives a simple method for proving partial correctness of a logic program w.r.t. a specification. (In practice its applicability is restricted to small programs. Other proof methods, which can be used for larger programs have been considered in [CD 87]. More developments and justifications are given in [Der 88b]) One important aspect of the method presented is that it allows arbitrary interpretations. Thus it applies also for extensions of logic programs , like amalgamated programs mentioned in Section 3.2. In fact if a specification is proved inductive using a non-term interpretation, then the values of the labels of all proof tree roots will satisfy this specification. The converse is not true (some specification may be inductive even if there is no proof tree at all or few proof trees -see FACT2 below-), but this is of no use here.

We now illustrate the method by some examples.

Example 4.1 program FACT1

fact(zero,s(zero)) .

fact(s(X),mult(s(X),R)) :- fact(X,R) .

interpreted on Nat (natural numbers) with *zero* as 0, p as -1 and *mult* as multiplication.

It is easy to show that the specification S2

$S2_{fact}(fact_1,fact_2) : fact_2 = fact_1!$

is valid, provided that ! is interpreted as the function factorial.

Indeed :

s(zero) = zero!

and

$R = X! \Rightarrow mult(s(X),R) = s(X)!$

what is easy to prove in the intended interpretation :

1 = 0!   ok

$R = X! \rightarrow (X+1)*R = (X+1)!$ ok

Note that we would have exactly the same proof with the following program FACT2 which corresponds to the RAG given in the section 3.2 :

fact(zero,s(zero)).

fact(X, mult(X,R)) :- fact(p(X),R).

Thus the specification $S2_{fact}$ is inductive, but the denotation of this program is reduced to the singleton fact (zero, s(zero)) ; it has few proof trees ! This shows that the proofs of partial correctness say nothing about the existence of proof trees satisfying the specification. For more complete discussion of this problem see [DF 88, Der 88b].

Example 4.2 program linear reverse REV

(naive reverse with difference lists)

rev(nil, L-L).

rev(A.L, R) :- rev(L, Q), concd(Q, A.M-M, R).

concd(L1-L2, L2-L3, L1-L3).

Valid specification : (repr is defined on difference lists only and reverse on lists -i.e all variables appearing in the formulas are universally quantified on difference lists or lists depending on the type of the arguments of repr, reverse or concat)

S_{rev} : repr(rev_2) = reverse(rev_1)

S_{concd} : repr($concd_3$) = concat(repr($concd_1$),repr($concd_2$))

The following formulas hold for lists and difference lists :

repr(L-L) = reverse(nil) (as repr(L-L) = nil=reverse(nil))

and

repr(Q) = reverse(L) $\land$ repr(R) = concat(repr(Q), repr(A.M-M)) $\Rightarrow$ repr(R) = reverse(A.L)

as reverse(A.L) = concat(reverse(L), A.nil) and repr(A.M-M) = A.nil .

It is also easy to show the correctness of the following specification

S_{rev} : list(rev_1) $\land$ difflist(rev_2)

S_{concd} : difflist($concd_1$) $\land$ difflist($concd_2$) $\Rightarrow$ difflist($concd_3$)

where list and difflist are term typing functors ranging respectively on lists and difference lists.

Proofs of this kind are is easy to perform ; many useful (declarative) properties may be inferred very quickly, improving the ability of the programmer to write a logic program.

Another kind of properties which are generally easy to deduce are "modes", i.e. properties of the form : if some arguments are ground then some others are too. For example in the program FACT1 or FACT2 it is easy to deduce (with the term interpretation) that both arguments are always ground.

A more interesting example of specification of this kind concerns the following program PERM, specifying all the permutations of a given list :

perm(nil,nil).

perm(A.L,B.M) :- extract(A.L,B,N), perm(M, N).

extract(A.L, A, L).

extract(A.L, B, A.M) :- extract(L, B, M).

Note the specific construction of the second clause of perm (second atom of the body).

One can show by induction that the following specification is valid :

S_{perm} : $ground(perm_1) \Leftrightarrow ground(perm_2)$

$S_{extract}$: $ground(extract_1) \Leftrightarrow (ground(extract_2) \wedge ground(extract_3))$

This type of properties can be also proved in an automatic way, e.g. by abstract interpretation.

4.3 Non Deterministic Operational Semantics and related properties.

The non deterministic operational semantics of a logic program P is the set of the effectively computed proof trees by the non deterministic algorithm NDA (see section 1) starting with the most general goals.

In Section 3 this semantics was modeled by the relational attribute grammar RAGO. RAGO can be viewed as a functional AG (see section 3.2) in which all attributes are synthesized.

For example consider RAGO for the program plus :

Phi_1 : $plus_1 = zero \wedge plus_2 = X \wedge plus_3 = X$

Phi_2 : $(plus_{01}, plus_{02}, plus_{03}) = \partial((s(X), Y, s(Z)))$

where $\partial = mgu((X, Y, Z), (plus_{11}, plus_{12}, plus_{13}))$

The tree in Fig. 5 (section 3.2) is valid.

It is also a proof tree of the program. However valid trees of RAGO(P) need not be proof trees. For example, the valid tree of Fig. 6 for the RAGO of the program REV (4.2 Example 2) is not a proof tree.

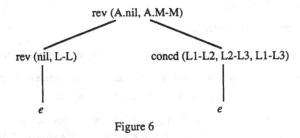

Figure 6

To get the corresponding proof tree it is sufficient to apply recursively in a descendent manner (as the instantiation does not affect roots) all the mgu used in the attribute instances definitions [Der 88c].

For the example above the substitutions produced are

$L \leftarrow A.M$, $N \leftarrow nil$, $Q \leftarrow A.M\text{-}A.M$, $L1 \leftarrow A.M$, $L2 \leftarrow A.M$, $L3 \leftarrow M$, $R \leftarrow A.M\text{-}M$

and the corresponding proof tree is shown on Fig. 7.

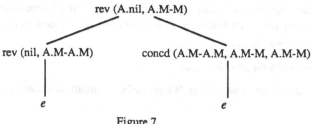

rev (nil, A.M-A.M)   concd (A.M-A.M, A.M-M, A.M-M)

  | |

  e   e

Figure 7

Now a specification is a logical formula interpreted on the canonical term interpretations defined with elements of FUNC, T (section 3.2).

A specification is valid if it is satisfied by all elements of NDOS(P).

A specification is inductive if it satisfies the following formulas on T, the canonical term interpretation :

for every clause c : $n_0(T_0) \leftarrow ..., n_k(T_k), ...$.

AND(for k from 1 to p) $S_k(A_k) \wedge A_0 = mgu((...T_j...), (...A_j...))(T_0) \Rightarrow S_0(A_0)$

Note that only the variables representing attribute occurrences are universally quantified.

Although the RAG constructed for a given program is different from that used in Section 4.2 the same proof method can be still applied: to prove that a specification is valid it suffices to show that it is implied by an inductive one.

We will now consider three applications of this proof method :

- proofs of partial correctness (non deterministic operational properties).

- proofs of completness.

- proofs of run time properties.

4.3.1. Proving properties of the computed answers.

Since RAGO describes the computed answers it is now possible to specify and prove properties of the answers computed for most general atomic goals. In that case the canonical term interpretation is to be used.

Consider for example the program REV (Example 4.2)

rev(nil, L-L).

rev(A.L, R) :- rev(L, Q), concd(Q, A.M-M, R).

concd(L1-L2, L2-L3, L1-L3).

and the specification :

$S2_{rev}$: $\exists n \geq 0$ (rev1 = $A_1.A_2$. ... A_n.nil $\wedge$ rev2 = $A_n.A_{n-1}$. ... A_1.L-L)

$S2_{concd}$: concd1= L1-L2 $\wedge$ concd$_2$ = L2-L3 $\wedge$ concd$_3$ = L1-L3

The specification characterizes expected forms of the computed answers for most general atomic goals (here S2 specifies exactly BR_{rev} of RAGO up to a variable renaming). To show that S2 is valid it suffices to prove that it is inductive in RAGO :

The condition holds trivially for the unit clauses.

It suffices then to examine the second clause. We get (using a partially renamed instance of the second clause) :

$$\partial = mgu((L4,Q,Q, A.M\text{-}M, R), (A_1....A_n.nil,A_n....A_1.L\text{-}L, L1\text{-}L2, L2\text{-}L3, L1\text{-}L3))$$

hence (with $n \geq 0$)

$$\partial = L4 \leftarrow A_1....A_n.nil, Q \leftarrow A_n....A_1.A.M\text{-}A.M, L1 \leftarrow A_n....A_1.A.M, L2 \leftarrow A.M,$$
$$L \leftarrow A.M, L3 \leftarrow M, R \leftarrow A_n....A_1.A.M\text{-}M$$

hence

$$A_0 = \partial((A.L4,R)) = (A.A_1....A_n.nil, A_n....A_1.A.M\text{-}M) \text{ with } n \geq 0$$

and $S2_{rev0}$ is satisfied with $n'= n+1$.

This property does not seem easy to prove manually. However, it appears in practice that simpler properties can be quickly infered using simpler but useful specification. The following property will be used in the sequel (4.3.2) :

$S3_{rev}$: the queue of rev_2 is an uninstantiated variable and does not depend of $rev1$

$$S3_{concd} = S2_{concd}$$

The specification says that in every element of NDOS(REV) the queue of the second argument of rev is always a variable (this result will not depend on the nature of the first one - which by the way is always a list).

We show that S3 is inductive hence valid :

This is obvious for the unit clauses.

For the second clause we have :

$$\partial = mgu((L4,Q,Q, A.M\text{-}M, R),(rev_{11}, rev_{12}, L1\text{-}L2, L2\text{-}L3, L1\text{-}L3))$$

provided that $rev_{12} = ...\text{-}L$, thus $Q = ...\text{-}L$ thus $L2 = ...\text{-}L$ and $L= A.M$,

and thus $L3 = M$ and the queue of R is M, a new variable, which does not depend on A.L4.

This property will be used in the next section to prove completness of REV .

The possibility to prove non deterministic operational properties by this type of inductive method seems to be an attractive feature of logic programming. In some sense the method is simple : only one set of variables (i.e. attributes denoting the argument of a non terminal) is needed. Another approach presented in [DrM 87] requires two sets of variables for proving the same kind of properties.

This nice feature has been also noticed in [FLM 88], where NDOS(P) is called the least N-model. However, it should be noted that a N-model is not a model (in the usual logical sense) and that a N-model has only an operational (i.e. algorithmic) definition equivalent to the definition of RAGO.

4.3.2. Proving completeness

A program will be called *complete* with respect to a specification if there exists a proof tree whose labels satisfy the specification. Recall that the specification is a family of formulae in some logical language indexed by the predicate letters of the program. We assume now that the formulae are interpreted on the canonical term interpretation.

Now we demonstrate on an example that the notion of RAGO may be used to prove completeness.

The method presented here consists in finding a subset of NDOS(P) which covers the family of atoms defined by the formulæ.

For example consider the programs plus (section 3.2)

> plus (zero, X, X)

> plus (s(X), Y, s(Z)) :- plus (X, Y, Z).

We want to prove its completness with regard to the set of atoms : $n, m \geq 0$ plus $(s^n(\text{zero}), s^m(\text{zero}), s^{n+m}(\text{zero}))$.(subset of DEN). Tus we prove by induction on the set of atoms that all atoms $n \geq 0$ plus $(s^n(\text{zero}), X, s^n(X))$ are in NDOS (up to a renaming).

Case : $n = 0$ obvious by the first clause.

Case : $n \geq 0$ suppose plus$(s^n(\text{zero}), X, s^n(X))$ is in NDOS, thus plus $(s^{n+1}(\text{zero}), X, s^{n+1}(X))$ is in NDOS.

         Obvious by the second clause, using RAGO's definition.

As one way observe by this example the proof method consists in showing that it is possible to build valid trees in RAGO provided the existence of valid subtrees.

We illustrate the power of the method on a more sophisticated example in which we want to prove the existential completness. By *existential completeness* we mean that not all arguments are specified by the formulæ, the unspecified being left as different independent variables. Thus we want to prove only that it exists a substitution for these variables such that the resulting atom is in NDOS (thus in DEN).

For example the reverse program of example 4.2 is existentially complete w.r.t. the (sub) set of atoms :

$$n \geq 0 \qquad \text{rev1} = A_1.A_2 \dots \text{nil}$$

Thus we are looking for a substitution σ of R in the atoms   rev$(A_1 \dots A_n.\text{nil}, R)$ such that rev$(A_1. \dots A_n.\text{nil}, \sigma R)$ is in NDOS (thus in DEN).

To perform the proof, we will prove an other property (combining the atom caracterization and S_3 of section 4.3.1), i.e. :

$n \geq 0$ $rev1 = A_1. \ldots A_n.nil$ and $rev2 = ? - V$, V a free variable are in NDOS.

Case : $n = 0$ obvious by the first clause.

Case : $n > 0$ we need to unify : (definition of RAGO) :

L	Q	Q	A.M - M	R
$A_1. \ldots A_n.nil$	$? - V$	$L_1 - L_2$	$L_2 - L_3$	$L_1 - L_3$

The unifier exists (as V is a free variable) and is :

$L \leftarrow A_1 \ldots A_n.nil$, $Q \leftarrow ? - V$, $L_1 \leftarrow ?$, $L_2 \leftarrow A.M$, $V \leftarrow A.M$, $L_3 \leftarrow M$, $R \leftarrow ? - M$, M a new free variable.

Thus the following atom is in NDOS :

$rev_1 = A.A_1 \ldots An.nil$ and $rev_2 = ? - M$, M a new free variable.

Hence the results of (existential) completness (with $n' = n + 1$).

This shows an important aspect of proof of completness : all arguments do not need to be specified to prove completness. But combining partial correctness properties and (existential) completness leads to completness. Note that in this method, we do not need to find a decreasing criterion as in the method which we introduce in the next section. This method is a "bottom-up", when the next one is "top down".

Notice that RAGO may be also used for proving incompleteness : if there is no valid tree in NDOS(P) then there is no corresponding proof tree in DEN(P). For example from the fact that the atoms fact(p(X), R) and fact(zero, s(zero)) are not unifiable one can conclude that there is no valid tree (hence no proof tree) for the predicate fact of the program FACT2 (see 4.2) using the second clause, hence NDOS (fact) is a singleton.

4.3.3. Proving run-time properties and using it to prove completeness

By run-time properties [DrM 87] we mean properties of selected subgoals during the SLD resolution process. (Notice that the first selected subgoal originates from the initial goal so that the run-time properties concern not only the program but also the initial goal). This notion is similar to the concept of Invariant Search Tree Property presented in [DF 88]. It refers to a specific strategy, i.e. a particular computation rule. We will consider here the standard computation rule, that is the left to right depth first construction of the proof trees.

A specification of a run-time property is a family of formulae indexed by predicate letters. The formulae are interpreted on the canonical term interpretation. The free variables of a formula indexed by p represent arguments of the predicate p at call time. A specification is correct iff at every call the corresponding formula is valid under the valuation of the variables by actual arguments of the call.

If we consider now the non deterministic operational semantics RAGO, the roots of the valid trees are decorated by the instances of most general atomic goals under the computed answer substitutions. Thus, for a given atomic goal, its instance under a computed answer substitution can be obtained by unifying it with the root label of a valid tree of RAGO [Der 88c].

Consider an incomplete proof tree obtained at some step of the computational process, as illustrated below (Fig. 9) :

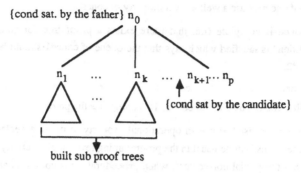

Figure 9

The actual subgoal n_{k+1} originates from a variant of a clause c ; the actual instance of this clause is :

$$n_0 :- n_1...n_k...n_p.$$

The actual form of n_{k+1} (thus any of its properties) is determined by the original form of n_0 at the call time and by the nondeterministic operational semantics of the predicates of $n_1,...,n_k$. Thus to know the form of the subgoal n_{k+1} at call time, it is sufficient to compare n_0 with the current goal (after renaming of the clause c) and to compare the instances of $n_1, ..., n_k$ with their possible non deterministic semantics in NDOS (or some properties). This observation can be used for proving correctness of run-time specifications. It suffices to consider separately each clause of a program, say

$$n_0 :- n_1,...,n_k,...n_p.$$

For every k=1,..., n_p one has to show referring to the nondeterministic operational semantics of the predicates of $n_1,...,n_{k-1}$ that whenever an instance of n_0 satisfies S then the corresponding instance of n_k after solving $n_1...n_{k-1}$ will also satisfy S. Formal presentation of the method is outside of the scope of this paper. The method resembles that of [DrM 87]. The difference is that it refers to the concept of nondeterministic operational semantics, while the other approach requires another type of specification combining description of run-time properties with the description of properties related to nondeterministic operational semantics.

As an example of use of run-time properties, we prove completeness of the program REV w.r.t goals of the form $rev(A_1.A_2....A_n.nil, Y)$ using the specification $S3_{rev}$. The idea of the proof consists in showing that it exists an instance of the goal, i.e. of the variable Y, which is a proof tree root by building a valid tree in RAGD. We use run-time property to build partial proof trees. Thus using the standard computation rule we show that the computation process will always terminate successfully.

Unification of the head rev(A.L,R) with such a goal gives the new goal $rev(A_2....A_n.nil,Q)$ of the same form. Hence the computation will continue preserving the run-time property and it will terminate as the first argument has a strictly decreasing size. Note that failure is not possible since goals of the form $rev(A_1.A_2....A_n.nil,Y)$ with $n \geq 0$ are always unifiable with one of the clause head of rev.

To complete the proof one may use a well-known property of concd.

It is known that concd is complete (i.e. that there exists a proof tree for some given goal) if a "compatibility condition" is satisfied which says that the queue of concd1 should be unifiable with the first element of concd2.

It remains to notice that after having obtained the proof tree for rev the second argument satisfies $S3_{rev}$, hence the compatibility condition holds for concd. This completes the proof.

Remark : one could be surprised to use an operational property to prove a declarative property like existence of proof trees. This is quite usual in the programming (even logic) activity : axiomatic view of the clauses guarantees the partial correctness, when procedural view comes as an help (but not as a complete proof in general) to be convinced of the completness of the clause. This semantical duality serves two different aspects of the logic program correctness. But this appears as a trick and one should not forget that completness as stated here is a declarative property, i.e. a property of the denotation.

Conclusion

We presented a grammatical view of logic programming where logic programs are considered grammars. This gives a natural framework for defining extensions to the concept of logic program. The paper shows that many useful extensions of Horn clauses incorporated in Prolog without theoretical justification correspond to well-established grammatical concepts. In particular the notion of DCG is a special case of W-grammar, modes are related to dependency relation of AG's, domain declarations of Turbo Prolog can be seen as a metagrammar of W-grammar and Prolog arithmetics fits naturally in the framework of RAG's with non-term interpretations. The grammatical point of view shows also a possibility of further extensions, not incorporated in Prolog, like a natural use of external procedures in logic programs. It also opens for the use of "grammatical techniques" like parsing or attribute evaluation in implementation of logic programs. On the other hand, the comparison of the formalisms shows that resolution techniques can be used for some grammars which were considered practically intractable, like RAG's or W-grammars. Last but not least, the grammatical point of view makes it possible to apply in logic programming some proof techniques developed originally for proving correctness of attribute grammars.

BIBLIOGRAPHY

[Abr 84]   Abramson H.: Definite Clause Translation Grammar, International Symposium on Logic Programming, Atlantic City, IEEE, pp 233-240, 1984.

[AF 88]   Attali I., Franchi-Zannettacci P.: Unification-free Execution of TYPOL Programs by Semantic Attribute Evaluation. PLILP'88, Orléans, France, May 16-18, 1988.

[Arb 86]   Arbab B.: Compiling Circular Attribute Grammars into Prolog, Journal of Research Development, 30 3, pp 294-309, May 1986.

[BM 88]   Bonnier S., Maluszynski J.: Toward Clean Amalgamation of Logic Programs with External Procedures, PLILP'88, Orléans, France, May 16-18, 1988.

[Bo 86]   Turbo Prolog Owner's Handbook, Borland Int., Scotts Valley, 1986.

[CD 87]   Courcelle B., Deransart P.: Proofs of Partial Correctness for Attribute Grammars with Application to Recursive Procedures and Logic Programming, RR I-8702, University of Bordeaux (to appear in Information and Computation 1988).

[CH 87]   Cohen J., Hickey T.J.: Parsing and Compiling Using Prolog, ACM Trans. on Progr. Lang. and Systems, 9 2, pp 125-163, April 1987.

[Cla 79]   Clark K.L.: Predicate Logic as a Computational Formalism, Res. Mon. 79/59, TOC, Imperial College, December 1979.

[Col 78]   Colmerauer A.: Metamorphosis Grammar, LNCS 63, pp 133-189, Springer Verlag, (Bolc L. ed.), 1978.

[Der 88]   Deransart P.: PROLOG : Basic Concepts and Methodology : Commented Exercises (french), University of Orléans, to appear, 1988.

[Der 88b]   Deransart P. : Proof of declarative properties of Logic Programs, INRIA report (to appear).

[Der 88c]   Deransart P. : On the Multiplicity of Operational Semantics for Logic Programming and their Modelization by Attribute Grammars. INRIA Report 1988 (to appear).

[DF 87a]   Deransart P., Ferrand G.: Logic Programming with Negation: Formal Presentation (in french), RR 87-3, Laboratoire d'Informatique, University of Orléans, June 1987.

[DF 87b]   Deransart P., Ferrand G.: An Operational Formal Definition of PROLOG, comprehensive version. RR 763, INRIA Rocquencourt, December 1987.

[DF 88]   Deransart P., Ferrand G.: Logic Programming: Methodology and Teaching, 2nd French-Japan Symposium, Cannes, Nov 1987, North-Holland 1988.

[DJL 88]   Deransart P., Jourdan M., Lorho B.: Attribute Grammars: Main Results, Existing Systems and Bibliography. LNCS 323, Springer Verlag, August 1988 (first edition : A Survey on Attribute Grammars, INRIA RR 485, 510, 417).

[DM 84]   Deransart P., Maluszynski J.: Modelling Data Dependencies in Logic Programs by Attribute Schemata, INRIA RR 323, July 1983.

[DM 85]   Deransart P., Maluszynski J.: Relating Logic Programs and Attribute Grammars, J. of Logic Programming 1985,2, pp 119-155.

[Dra 87]   Drabent W. : Do Logic Programs Resemble Programs in Conventional Languages, Proc. of IEEE SLP'87, San Francisco, September 1987.

[DrM 87]   Drabent W., Maluszynski J.: Inductive Assertion Method for Logic Programs. CFLP 87, Pisa, Italy, March 22-27 1987.

[FLM 88]   Falashi M., Levi G., Martelli M., Palamidessi C.: A new Declarative Semantics for Logic Languages. Dipartimento di informatica, University of Pisa, Italy. LP'88, Seattle, August 1988.

[Hen 88]   Henriques P.R.: A Semantic Evaluator Generating System in Prolog, PLILP'88, Orléans, May 16-18, 1988.

[Hog 84]   Hogger C.J.: Introduction to Logic Programming, APIC Studies in Data Processing 21, Academic Press, 1984.

[HS 85]   Hsiang J., Srivas M. : Prolog based Inductive Theorem Proving, LNCS 206, Springer Verlag, pp 129-149, Dec. 85.

[JLM 84]   Jaffar J., Lassez J.L., Maher M.J. : A theory of complete logic programs with equality, Journal of Logic Programming, 1984/3, pp 211-223.

[Kan 86]   Kanamori T. : Soundness and Completness of Extended Execution for Proving Properties of Prolog Programs. TR 175 ICOT, 1986.

[Knu 68]   Knuth, D.E. : Semantics of Context-Free Languages, Math. Systems Theory 2 (1968), pp 127-145.

[LBM 88]   Leszczylowski J., Bonnier S. and Maluszynski J.: Logic Programming with External Procedures : Introducing S-Unification, IPL 27, 1988, pp 159-165.

[Llo 87]   Lloyd J.W.: Foundations of Logic Programming, Springer, 2nd edition, December 1987 (first 1984).

[Mal 84]   Maluszynski J.: Towards a Programming Language based on the Notion of Two-level Grammar, TCS 28 (1984) pp 13-43.

[MN 82a]   Maluszynski J., Nilsson J.F.: Grammatical Unification, IPL 15 (1982), pp 150-158.

[MN 82b]   Maluszynski J., Nilsson J.F.: A Comparison of the Logic Programming Language PROLOG with Two-level Grammars, in : Van Caneghem, ed., First Int. Logic Programming Conf., pp 193-199, Marseille 1982.

[MN 82b]   Maluszynski J., Nilsson J.F.: A Version of PROLOG based on the Notion of Two-Level Grammar, in`: J. Komorowski (ed) PROLOG Programming Environments, Proc. of the Workshop, Linköping University 1982

[MTH 83]   Matsumoto Y., Tanaka H., Hirakawa and al. : BUP : a Bottom Up Parser embedded in Prolog, New generation Computing, 1, 1983.

[Näs 87]   Näslund T.: An experimental implementation of a compiler for two-level grammars, in : Z.W.Ras and M. Zemankova (eds.), Proc. of the 2nd Int. Symposium, Methodologies for Intelligent Systems, pp 424-431, North-Holland 1987.

[Ni 83]   Nilsson J.F.: On the Compilation of a Domain-based Prolog, in : R.E.A. Mason, ed., Information Processing 83, pp 293-298, North-Holland 1983.

[Nil 86]   Nilsson U., AID : an Alternative Implementation of DCG's, New Generation Computing 4, pp 383-399, 1986.

[PW 80]   Pereira F.N.C., Warren D.H.D.: Definite Clause Grammars for Language Analysis : a Survey of the Formalism and Comparison with Augmented Transition Networks. Artificial Intelligence, 13-3, pp 231-278, 1980.

[PW 83]   Pereira F.N.C., Warren D.H.D.: Parsing as Deduction, 21st Annual Meeting of the Ass. for Computational Linguistics (Cambridge, Mass.), pp 137-144, June 1983.

[Sie 85]   Siekmann J.H.: Universal Unification, in Proc. of the 7th Int. Conf. on Automated Deduction, R.E.Shostak, ed., LNCS 169, Springer-Verlag, 1984.

[UOK 84] Uehara K., Ochitani R., Kakusho O., Toyoda J.: A Bottom Up Parser Based on Predicate Logic : a Survey of the Formalism and its Implementation Technique, ISLP, Atlantic City, pp 220-227, 1984.

[Wij 65]   Van Wijngaarden A.: Orthogonal Design and Description of a Formal Language, MR 76, Mathematisch Centrum, Amsterdam, 1965.

COMPILING TYPOL WITH ATTRIBUTE GRAMMARS [1]

Isabelle Attali

INRIA – Sophia-Antipolis
Route des Lucioles
06565 Valbonne Cedex, France
e-mail: ia@trinidad.inria.fr

Abstract

We have shown in a previous paper that TYPOL specifications and Attribute Grammars are strongly related: we presented a general construction to build an Attribute Grammar from a TYPOL program. Thus, it was possible to use AG techniques to replace, during TYPOL specifications execution, run-time unification by semantic attribute evaluation.

We go on now with this transfer of expertise between Logic Programming and Attribute Grammars applying AG techniques to the TYPOL domain. The purpose of this paper is twofold. First, we show that TYPOL can be viewed as a higher-level Attribute Grammar definition language, owing to unification; thus, evaluating TYPOL specifications with an automatically-generated attribute evaluator provides straigthforwardly efficiency in both time and space, and incrementality. Second, we develop a method to partially evaluate TYPOL specifications. This method is based on the abstract interpretation of the dependency graph of semantic attributes associated with TYPOL variables.

1 Introduction

This paper discusses the relationship between TYPOL [14,15], a specialized logic programming language, and Attribute Grammars (AGs) [33], having in mind to find classes of TYPOL programs based on the general classification of AGs. Thus, we deduce for TYPOL programs a specific, optimized, and unification-free resolution strategy based on AG techniques.

TYPOL is a computer formalism for expressing *Natural Semantics* [29]. Such a semantic definition is identified with a logic made of axioms and inference rules: reasoning with the language is proving theorems within that logic. TYPOL is developed as a semantic specification formalism for an interactive language-based editor, CENTAUR [6], at INRIA.

TYPOL is well-suited to specify type-checkers, interpreters, and translators. Natural semantic specifications are expressed in a relational and declarative style, and are straightforwardly executable. A user-friendly environment is now available for TYPOL programmers: a pretty-printer produces inputs for TEX (TYPOL examples shown here are produced using this pretty-printer); a compiler, including a type-checker, produces PROLOG code (executable under MU-Prolog [36]); a convivial debugger allows control of execution.

On the one hand, TYPOL programs, under certain conditions, can be viewed as a generalization of *Primitive Recursive Schemes* introduced by Courcelle and Franchi-Zannettacci [10]. On the other hand, TYPOL programs are merely logic programs manipulating typed terms such as syntactic patterns. Following both approaches, a TYPOL domain can be viewed as a many-sorted algebra.

---

[1]This work is supported by CNRS-GRECO in Programming

As a rule-based system executable with an inference engine, TYPOL may satisfy the requirements of both language designers (readability, expressive power of the specifications) and end-users (friendliness, power and efficiency of the generated tools).

Once the equivalence between certain TYPOL programs and Attribute Grammars is proved, we can from now on consider (and use) TYPOL as a definition language for Attribute Grammars. This approach makes it possible to achieve earlier requirements:

- language designers are relieved of major drawbacks of AGs due to their low-level notations (all attributes have to be named, transfer rules must be given, ...);

- TYPOL specifications are more compact than AG specifications (which seem to frighten people with their tremendous size);

- unification is provided in TYPOL and makes the expressive power higher;

- on the other hand, the language designer is not bothered about standard PROLOG operational semantics (concerning rules order and sequents order in a rule);

- finally, one can automatically generate an efficient and incremental evaluator from TYPOL specifications;

Furthermore, using AG techniques, we propose a method for partially evaluating a TYPOL equation (on an abstract syntax tree) with respect to a TYPOL program (an AG specification). This method is based on the *abstract* or *free interpretation*[2] of auxiliary functions used in semantic definitions of attribute values. For TYPOL programs that have exactly the same power as Attribute Grammars, this method applies directly. For TYPOL programs in a larger subclass to be defined, we need to extend Attribute Grammars to dynamic semantics. Then, given an AG defining an interpreter for the language L, we have a method to partially evaluate an L-program and get a more efficient compiled version of that program.

Section 2 gives necessary notions and results concerning AGs on the one hand, and the TYPOL formalism on the other hand; we present our theoretical construction mapping TYPOL specifications (under certain conditions) to AGs and describe a pragmatic application of this construction, the evaluation of TYPOL programs with an already existing attribute evaluator generator, which requires a translation from TYPOL specifications to an AG definition language. Section 3 develops, according to an AG extention to dynamic semantics, a general partial evaluation method for TYPOL programs based on semantic attribute dependency graph.

2 TYPOL and Attribute Grammars

Studying the relationship between the TYPOL formalism and Attribute Grammars, we wish to address three problems that occur during execution of TYPOL specifications.

1. Gaining the benefits of memory optimization from results in AGs should eliminate the *space explosion* experienced in practice (some variables can be implemented as global variables, or stacks as described in [31,28]).

---

[2]This notion comes here from recent theoretical works on AGs [10,20] but can be related to abstract interpretation in Logic Programming [7].

2. Some AG evaluators provide *incremental* computation (e.g. the FNC-2 system [27] and the Cornell Program Synthesizer Generator [40,11]): changing a subtree in the parse tree leads to a minimal re-computation of the attribute values. The massive use of unification is an obstacle to any incremental facility.

3. Using pre-compiled unification-less strategies during execution (see [5,30,10]) even though an unification is expressed at the TYPOL level should definitively distinguish TYPOL semantics from standard PROLOG semantics (depth-first and left-to-right execution strategy).

After recalling some basic definitions on Attribute Grammars and TYPOL, we present our construction that makes it possible to compile TYPOL specifications into an Attribute Grammar. We give an application for TYPOL implementation: execution of TYPOL specifications by an incremental AG evaluator, the Cornell Program Synthesizer Generator. Finally, we show an example of TYPOL program compiled into a Synthesized Specification Language source.

2.1 Attribute Grammars: some useful notations

Since Knuth's initial paper [33], Attribute Grammars have been widely used in translation, compiler-compiler techniques and definitions of programming languages [30,44]. Let us recall the usual definition of Attribute Grammars and present their semantics in an informal manner.

Definition 1: An *Attribute Grammar G* $= < \mathcal{O}, \text{ATTR}, R, \mathcal{I} >$ is:

- an abstract syntax $\mathcal{O}$ (a $\mathcal{P}$-signature);

- ATTR = INH $\cup$ SYN (two disjoint finite sets of symbols);

  For each phylum $X \in \mathcal{P}$, we associate two disjoint finite sets of symbols: *inherited* (INH(X)) and *synthesized attributes* (SYN(X)).

  For each operator $p \in \mathcal{O}, p : X_0 \rightarrow X_1 \cdots X_n$, we define two disjoint sets INPUT(p) and OUTPUT(p):

    - INPUT(p) = INH$(X_0) \cup$ SYN$(X_i), i = 1, \ldots, n$;
    - OUTPUT(p) = SYN$(X_0) \cup$ INH$(X_i), i = 1, \ldots, n$.

  We note $W(p) = \text{INPUT(p)} \cup \text{OUTPUT(p)}$ the set of all attribute occurrences for p.

- a set R of *semantic definitions*, using a set $\mathcal{F}$ of semantic functions, defined as follows:

  For each operator $p \in \mathcal{O}, p : X_0 \rightarrow X_1 \cdots X_n$, semantic definitions describe *local dependencies* between the values of attribute occurrences to compute OUTPUT(p):

    form 1 INH(X_i) depend on INH(X_0) and SYN(X_i) for $i = 1, \ldots, n$
    form 2 SYN(X_0) depend on INH(X_0) and SYN(X_i), for $i = 1, \ldots, n$;

- $\mathcal{I}$ is an interpretation: the resulting domain reached during the computation of the attributes (i.e. after evaluation of functions in $\mathcal{F}$).

We define a *local dependency relation* on $W(p)$ defined by: $a \Rightarrow a'$ iff a appears in definition of a' (a' depends on a).

Evaluating an AG with respect to a parse tree can be viewed as decorating the nodes in the parse tree with the values of attributes. In other terms, AGs can be viewed as a mean to associate semantic functions (semantic checks, generating functions, ...) to abstract syntax trees. Thus, evaluating an AG can be viewed as a two-step translation:

$$M(\mathcal{O}) \mapsto M(\mathcal{F}) \mapsto \mathcal{I}$$

This intermediate step (*free interpretation* [20,2]) makes it possible to separate, in the evaluation process of attributes, the scheme of function calls and the computation of these functions. The free interpretation of a given abstract syntax tree T, with respect to an AG can be considered as a pre-compilation of T: the free interpretation describes computations that have to be done but are not at free-interpretation time. Lisp hackers should say: free interpretation is a λ-expression that requires an *eval* to produce a result on attributes domains. This *formal translation* from T to the free interpretation makes it possible to prove scheme properties due to the dependency graph on attributes. Scheme properties are valid for any semantic function so they are independent of the following step, the evaluation on attribute domains.

The major area of active research in AGs is the design of automatically-generated efficient attribute evaluators (see [13] for an annotated bibliography). For this purpose, different subclasses (based on partial orders between attributes) have been introduced, and associated membership tests have been developed (e.g. *OAG* [30], *l-ordered* [5], *FNC* [10]). With these (mathematically well-founded) subclasses, efficient (optimized, incremental) evaluators can be automatically generated by computing at generation time an evaluation order on attributes.

Let's focus now on the FNC subclass (Strongly Non-Circular), introduced by [32],[10] and implemented by [26]. As shown in [10], any Attribute Grammar in the FNC subclass can be transformed into a recursive tree-transducer [18] (namely a set of deterministic *Primitive Recursive Schemes*) by a transitive closure algorithm on local dependencies (given by $\Rightarrow$) to compute *potential global dependencies*. Intuitively, each synthesized attribute s is computed by a function taking as arguments any subtree t and inherited attributes that s may depend on.

More formally, we consider a function (named *argument selector*), defined as follows:

$$\gamma : \mathcal{P} \times \text{SYN} \rightarrow \Pi(\text{INH}) \qquad \gamma(X, a) = \emptyset \text{ if } a \notin \text{SYN}(X)$$
$$\gamma(X, a) \subseteq \text{INH}(X) \text{ if } a \in \text{SYN}(X)$$

The transitive closure algorithm computes the *minimal closed* argument selector γ_0 for all operators and synthesized attributes.

The characterization of the FNC subclass is given by the following theorem from [20]:

An AG is *Strongly Non Circular iff* γ_0 is *non circular*.

Primitive Recursive Schemes stand for a functional subclass of logic programs. They are evaluated with a noetherian and confluent rewriting system based on a tree pattern-matching instead of the general unification mechanism [20]. Thus, for any FNC Attribute Grammar:

$$M(\mathcal{O}) \mapsto M(\mathcal{F}) \mapsto \mathcal{I}$$

2.2 TYPOL: some definitions

We recall from [3] some formal definitions about TYPOL programs (see [14,29,15] for a detailed description).

Definition 2: A TYPOL program is a 7-uple $T = < S, \mathcal{O}, P, F, R, \mathcal{D}, E >$ where:

S is a finite set of sequent symbols with assigned arities and types;

$\mathcal{O}$ is an imported abstract syntax;

P is a finite set of predicate symbols with assigned arities and types;

F is a finite set of functor symbols with assigned arities and types;

R is a set of TYPOL rules constructed with S, $\mathcal{O}$, P and F;

$\mathcal{D}$ is a safe direction assignment;

E is an acceptable goal.

The notion of *safe direction assignment* (from [12] and related to the concept of *input-output directionality* in [39]) defines a mapping of the arguments of each sequent symbol into *inherited* and *synthesized* positions. It also provides a *good* dependency flow between different positions within a TYPOL rule. By analogy with Attribute Grammars, we split positions of a TYPOL rule into *input positions* (inherited positions of the conclusion and synthesized positions of the premises) and *output positions* (inherited positions of the premises and synthesized positions of the conclusion). A safe direction assignment ensures that output positions are defined within the TYPOL rule in terms of input positions (or/and constants) while input positions are determined elsewhere, by the outer context.

As TYPOL specifications are oriented, but their execution is not (in PROLOG), we need the additional hypothesis of an *acceptable goal*. An acceptable goal is a TYPOL equation (a sequent) with its subject and inherited positions instantiated to ground terms, and variables at synthesized positions. With acceptable goal, we are now sure the TYPOL program is run with its basic orientation. Thus, TYPOL equations are solved by *structural induction* [8] on a many-sorted algebra, $M(S \cup \mathcal{O} \cup P \cup F)$, using full unification. By analogy with Attribute Grammars, one can distinguish different steps in the resolution process as follows:

$$M(S \cup \mathcal{O}) \mapsto M(S \cup \mathcal{O} \cup P \cup F) \mapsto M(P \cup F) \mapsto \mathcal{I}$$

where $\mathcal{I}$ is the underlying interpretation of predicates of P and functors of F.

In the general case, this resolution relation is not confluent. We give in proposition 1 the sufficient conditions for a TYPOL program to make this resolution relation confluent.

During the execution process, *pattern-matching* on the subjects directs the construction of a *proof tree* for a TYPOL equation. Clearly, every TYPOL program can be straightforwardly simulated by a PROLOG program (and TYPOL equations turned into PROLOG goals). However, executing such programs by the inference engine of PROLOG, we lose a large part of TYPOL semantics, due to both the particular role of the subjects and the relationship between antecedent and consequent parts in a TYPOL sequent (positions dependencies are computed on the fly, at run-time, through the PROLOG unification).

To propose a specific, optimized, and unification-free resolution strategy for each TYPOL program, we have in mind to find subclasses of TYPOL programs based on the general classification of Attribute Grammars. Here are some further definitions for such subclasses in the TYPOL domain.

Definitions 3:
A TYPOL program is *strictly decreasing* if, for each of its inference rules r, subjects of the premises of r are proper subterms of the subject of r.
A TYPOL program is *linear* if, for each of its inference rules r, synthesized positions of premises of r have no common variables.
A TYPOL program is *deterministic* if, at each step of a proof, only one inference rule can apply.
A TYPOL program is *pseudo-deterministic* if all its inference rules have different subjects (this does not exclude non determinism within auxiliary sets).

Remark: These definitions apply only on sequents refering to the local set or program (i.e. named sequents, refering another formal system, are not involved in these definitions).

Definition 4: We call *global argument selector* and we note $\Gamma(X_0)$ the set of all inherited positions of the conclusion of the rule whose subject is p and $p : X_0 \rightarrow X_1 \cdots X_n$.

This definition implies that the global argument selector is *consistent* within a TYPOL program: two distinct abstract syntax operators $p_1 : X_0 \rightarrow X_1 \cdots X_n$ and $p_2 : X_0 \rightarrow Y_1 \cdots Y_n$ (with the same type) have the same global argument selector $\Gamma(X_0)$.

Definition 5: A TYPOL program is *non-circular* if its global argument selector is non circular. Otherwise, it may exist a splitting of its circular global argument selector into non circular minimal ones and the program is said to be *pseudo-circular*. The least fix point computation expressed within the specification is currently solved with an unification process during execution. On the other hand, if such a splitting does not exist, the TYPOL program is said to be *circular*. It expresses a *real* least fix point resolution and is equivalent to schemes with fix point introduced by [8].

Proposition 1: Pseudo-circular strictly decreasing TYPOL programs are equivalent to Strongly Non-Circular AGs. Thus, the resolution relation is noetherian. Moreover, if the TYPOL program is deterministic, this relation is also confluent.

2.3 From TYPOL to Attribute Grammars

We merge into a single construction the two-step construction relating TYPOL programs and AGs presented in [3]. We first need the auxiliary notion of selectors defined in [12]. A *selector* is a partial operation on terms: for a given term t of the form $f(t_1, \cdots, t_n)$ the selector $s_i f(t)$ is defined to be t_i.

Construction : *from TYPOL programs to Attribute Grammars*
Let $T = < S, \mathcal{O}, P, F, R, \mathcal{D}, E >$ be a strictly decreasing pseudo-deterministic and not circular (i.e. pseudo-circular or non-circular) TYPOL program, we construct a AG $G = < \mathcal{O}, \mathcal{A}, \mathcal{R}, \mathcal{I} >$ defined as follows:

1. $\mathcal{O}$ is the abstract syntax imported in T (a $\mathcal{P}$-signature);

2. $\mathcal{A} = \text{ATTR} \cup \text{AUX}$ where:

   - ATTR is the union of inherited and synthesized positions of all phyla in $\mathcal{P}$; the attributes are named from the positions of the arguments in the sequents:
   $$\text{ATTR}(X) = \{X.i/i = 1, \cdots, n\}.$$

   - AUX is the set of auxiliary attributes introduced during **step 2** below.

3. For each rule $r \in R$, semantic definitions of $\mathcal{R}$ are constructed as follows:

   step 1 For each output position a of r, let t_a be the term at this position. For a variable x in t_a let b be an input position including x and t_b the term at this position. Denote by $S_x b$ the set of all composed selectors s such that $s(t_b) = x$. The semantic definition for a is of the form: $\qquad a = \alpha(t_a)$

   where α is a substitution assigning to each variable x in t_a, the term $s(b)$ for some $s \in S_x b$.

   step 2 For each pair of different occurrences of a variable x at input positions b_1 and b_2 of the rule r, it exists a partial order between b_1 and b_2 (since the TYPOL program is not circular). Let b_1 be computed before b_2. We introduce two new attributes x and y for X_j and we construct the following semantic definitions:
   $$x := s_1(b_1)$$
   $$y := \text{fcond}(s_1(b_1) = s_2(b_2), b_2, \perp)$$

   where $\perp$ is the overloaded undefined value on attribute domains, and s_1 and s_2 are the selectors corresponding to the considered occurrences of x in the terms at the positions b_1 and b_2.

4. $\mathcal{I}$ is the underlying interpretation of predicates of P and functors of F, augmented with the interpretation of used selectors and *fcond* function.

Remark : If the input TYPOL program is moreover linear, step 2 is useless.

2.4 Compiling TYPOL into SSL: an example

We present here a straigthforward pragmatic application of our construction. Since certain TYPOL programs are equivalent to AGs, why not use automated AG processors to evaluate such programs ? With this technique, compiling TYPOL specifications into Attribute Grammars means, in a first step, produce an input for an AG evaluator such as GAG [31], FNC-2 [27] or the Cornell Program Synthesizer Generator [40], or any other one, and, in a second step, generate the corresponding evaluator.

Thus, our two major objectives should be reached:

1. keep semantics of TYPOL specifications really independent of standard PROLOG features;

2. provide a specific and optimal evaluator for each TYPOL program instead of the general interpretation process due to the PROLOG engine.

Using an existing AG evaluator is a fruitful way to obtain easily a TYPOL compiler. We just need to implement a translator from TYPOL to a given attribute definition language and automatically generate from this a specific evaluator for our source TYPOL program. Of course, our ultimate goal is to provide, directly from TYPOL specifications, such an evaluator, fully compatible with the syntactic tools of CENTAUR (parsing, unparsing, and the Virtual Tree Processor, VTP [35], an abstract syntax tree manipulation kernel). This should make the TYPOL compiler self-sufficient within the CENTAUR system.

Most existing attribute evaluators directly work on (partially-) decorated attributed trees; they can be considered as tree-to-tree translators. Some of them provide an incremental re-computation of attribute values. When such systems are integrated in structured editors, this leads to syntactical and semantical checks during edition.

Among more than 30 systems which can be considered as AG evaluators, we have chosen the Cornell Program Synthesizer Generator to generate an efficient incremental evaluator from TYPOL specifications, for several reasons:

- The Synthesizer Generator and CENTAUR use, at generation-time, the same tools to build grammar tables (LEX and YACC) for syntactic definitions;

- the accepted AG subclass is very large (non-circular AGs);

- it provides an incremental re-computation of attribute values;

- it uses memory optimization techniques such as structure sharing for large attributes, or reducing the maximum number of attribute values retained at any stage of evaluation;

- it has been widely used to build a variety of experimental editors;

- it is a well-known competitor for CENTAUR !

The definition language for the Synthesizer Generator (Synthesizer Specification Language, SSL) includes concrete and abstract syntax definitions, rules for unparsing and attribution rules for semantics. From a SSL specification, the Synthesizer Generator produces a language-based editor based on an attributed tree manipulation kernel [11] taking its input from the keyboard and checks consistency of the current tree (with an incremental re-evaluation of attributes when needed).

We are only concerned with attribution rules in SSL because we only want to gain from the Synthesizer Generator the ability of an incremental re-computation of attributes values in an abstract syntax tree (and we don't want to generate a whole syntax-directed editor).
On the other hand, we have to handle, when editing a program, syntactic changes in the VTP-tree and pass them to the attributed-tree manipulation kernel that will execute appropriate operations on the current tree.

Such an interface is not satisfactory from a practical point of view, because, when editing, a lot of time is lost in coercions of VTP-subtrees to Cornell-tree changes, even if the incremental re-computation of attributes (obtained for free) results in time gain. The most challenging aspect of such a coupled system was to use TYPOL as a definition language for semantic attributes and thus to demonstrate that running TYPOL specifications with attribute evaluation was possible.

Our TYPOL compiler is now partially implemented in TYPOL. It includes three major components:

- a front-end checks consistency of the given TYPOL program (see definition 4) and determines the subclass it belongs to (see definition 5);

- if the TYPOL program is acceptable, a translator completes our construction (see section 2.3) into an intermediate representation for the resulting Attribute Grammar;

- a back-end generates either SSL source, either directly a Lisp code that handles attribute evaluation; this code works, in an object-oriented manner, on the abstract syntax tree (a VTP-tree), computing attribute values and storing them (when necessary) into local or global variables.

Whenever we decide to compile TYPOL programs with another existing AG evaluator, we just have to produce a new back-end generating, for instance, ALADIN source (for GAG) or OLGA source (for FNC-2).

Here is an example of TYPOL specifications and their corresponding SSL source automatically produced by our TYPOL compiler.

Example 1: *Compiling marked regular expressions into deterministic automata*
This example describes how to build a finite automaton from a regular marked expression (see [1,4] for the detailed algorithm).
The syntax of regular expressions over a set of input symbols is, as usual:

$axiom ::= E\ end$

$E ::= 0 \mid \epsilon \mid I \mid E + E \mid E \cdot E \mid E^*$ where *end* is an endmarker symbol;

Definitions
$L(E)$ denotes the language generated by a regular expression E.
$first(E) = \{a \mid av \in L(E)\}$
$follow_E(a) = \{b \mid uabv \in L(E)\}$
$\delta(E)$ stands for *true* if the empty string belongs to L(E);
otherwise, $\delta(E)$ stands for *false*.

The TYPOL inference rules compute inductively the value δ and two sets simultaneously, the set ρ of pairs of the form $<a, follow_E(a)>$ and the set h, the *first* set of E. These three components define the automaton that recognizes the given regular expression.

program *COMPILE_EXP* **is**
use EXPRESSIONS;
use AUTOMATES;
import $\mapsto, \cdot, \vee, \cup, \wedge$;
ρ, ρ_1, ρ_2 : ARCS ;
s, h, h_1, h_2 : STATES ;
$\delta, \delta_1, \delta_2$: BOOLEAN ;

$$\frac{end \vdash \text{E}:<\rho, h, \delta>}{\vdash \text{axiom}(\text{E}):<\rho, h, \delta>} \tag{1}$$

$$s \vdash \text{I}: \ <\text{I} \mapsto s, \text{I}, false> \tag{2}$$

$$s \vdash \epsilon: <\emptyset, \emptyset, true> \tag{3}$$

$$\frac{s \vdash \text{E}_1 : <\rho_1, h_1, \delta_1> \qquad s \vdash \text{E}_2 : <\rho_2, h_2, \delta_2>}{s \vdash \text{E}_1 + \text{E}_2 : <\rho_1 \cdot \rho_2, h_1 \cdot h_2, \delta_1 \vee \delta_2>} \tag{4}$$

$$\frac{s \vdash \text{E}_2 : <\rho_2, h_2, \delta_2> \qquad h_2 \cup \delta_2 \cdot s \vdash \text{E}_1 : <\rho_1, h_1, \delta_1>}{s \vdash \text{E}_1 \text{E}_2 : <\rho_1 \cdot \rho_2, h_1 \cup \delta_1 \cdot h_2, \delta_1 \wedge \delta_2>} \tag{5}$$

$$\frac{h \cdot s \vdash \text{E} : <\rho, h, \delta>}{s \vdash \text{E}^* : <\rho, h, true>} \tag{6}$$

end *COMPILE_EXP*;

Running this TYPOL program on the following expression:

$$e = (1 \cdot 2 + 3)^* \cdot 4 \cdot 5$$

produces the following automaton:

$$<\{1,3,4\}, \{1 \mapsto \{2\}, 2 \mapsto \{1,3,4\}, 3 \mapsto \{1,3,4\}, \{4 \mapsto \{5\}, \{5 \mapsto \{end\}\}, false>$$

given in Figure 1.

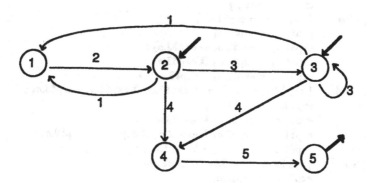

Figure 1

The compile_exp TYPOL program is strictly decreasing, linear, and deterministic.
Its global argument selector for EXP is $\Gamma(\text{EXP}) = \{s\}$. Rule (6) induces a pseudo-circularity and requires an unification during execution in PROLOG.
Splitting Γ for each synthesized position produces a minimal non circular argument selector γ such that:

$$\gamma(\text{EXP}, \rho) = \{s\} \qquad \gamma(\text{EXP}, h) = \emptyset \qquad \gamma(\text{EXP}, \delta) = \emptyset$$

Proposition 1 states this TYPOL program is equivalent to a Strongly Non-Circular AG (without conditions) resulting from our construction. In fact, the resulting AG belongs to the OAG subclass (inside the FNC subclass).

The code produced by our compiler results in the following attribution rules in SSL source (assuming some extra type definitions for ARCS, STATES and used primitives on these types; in the TYPOL program, abstract syntax and auxiliary primitives are defined elsewhere and can be referenced using import and use clauses).

/* attribution rules for compiling a regular expression into a finite automaton */

```
axiom    {synthesized ARC a₁;
         synthesized STATES a₂;
         synthesized BOOL a₃;};
exp      {inherited STATES a₁;
         synthesized ARC a₂;
         synthesized STATES a₃;
         synthesized BOOL a₄; };
axiom  : Exp      { exp.a₁ = end ;
                   axiom.a₁ = exp.a₂ ;
                   axiom.a₂ = exp.a₃ ;
                   axiom.a₃ = exp.a₄ ;};
exp    : Empty    { exp.a₂ = ARCS∅ ;
                   exp.a₃ = STATES∅ ;
                   exp.a₄ = true ; };
       | Int      { exp.a₂ = INT ↦ exp.a₁ ;
                   exp.a₃ = INT ;
                   exp.a₄ = false ; }
       | Plus     { exp$2.a₁ = exp$1.a₁ ;
                   exp$3.a₁ = exp$1.a₁ ;
                   exp$1.a₂ = exp$2.a₂ @ exp$3.a₂ ;
                   exp$1.a₃ = exp$2.a₃ @ exp$3.a₃ ;
                   exp$1.a₄ = exp$2.a₄ || exp$3.a₄ ; }
       | Prod     { exp$2.a₁ = exp$3.a₄ ? exp$3.a₃ @ exp$1.a₁ : exp$3.a₃ ;
                   exp$3.a₁ = exp$1.a₁ ;
                   exp$1.a₂ = exp$2.a₂ @ exp$3.a₂ ;
                   exp$1.a₃ = exp$2.a₄ ? exp$2.a₃ @ exp$3.a₃ : exp$2.a₃ ;
                   exp$1.a₄ = exp$2.a₄ && exp$3.a₄ ; }
       | Star     { exp$2.a₁ = exp$2.a₃ @ exp$1.a₁ ;
                   exp$1.a₂ = exp$2.a₂ ;
                   exp$1.a₃ = exp$2.a₃ ;
                   exp$1.a₄ = true ; };
```

Considering the TYPOL formalism as an AG definition language, the reader should appreciate the high-level expressive power, the readability and the compactness of the TYPOL program compared to the low-level notations of the SSL AG definition. On the other hand, the implementation of this TYPOL program, via Attribute Grammars paradigm, provides, at evaluation-time, efficiency, incrementality and a small memory size.

3 Partial evaluation of TYPOL with AGs

The main idea of *partial evaluation*, in any language, is to evaluate a program with some of its inputs known. This gives a new program, that, given the remaining inputs, is equivalent to the starting program [19,21,25]. Applying this idea to an interpreter, where the only known input is a program to interpret, results in a program-tailored compiler. L. Hascoët adapted this definition to Logic Programming and proposed a method to partially evaluate TYPOL programs [23]. First, we present his technique based on the Logic Programming behavior of TYPOL programs. We next define what is a partial evaluation of TYPOL programs in terms of Attribute Grammars and we discuss the equivalence of these two methods. However, partially evaluate programs with standard AGs that can only express static semantics (translations, type-checkers, ...) is not very exciting. Partial evaluation is more useful for compilation when applied on interpreters. Thus, we propose an AG extension that can handle dynamic semantics. This extension can be viewed as a subclass of circular AGs. We explain how we can implement such Attribute Grammars with non-circular AG techniques. Finally, we show as an example a TYPOL program partially evaluated with a TYPOL interpreter.

3.1 Logic partial evaluation

Considering the TYPOL formalism as a Logic Programming language, the execution of a TYPOL program can be represented by a proof tree [29]: running a TYPOL program on a TYPOL equation means building a completely solved proof tree from the starting goal (with partial proof trees yielding intermediate steps during execution).

With this approach, Hascoët gives an operational definition for *logic partial evaluation* with TYPOL [23]. To partially evaluate a TYPOL equation, with a given TYPOL program, means: from a partially instantiated goal, prove all sequents that can be proved, and then obtain a new TYPOL program. The result of the total evaluation is the execution of this new TYPOL program on the remaining input, given by another goal.

A logic partial evaluator is implemented in TYPOL, based on a proof-tree builder working with specific tactics to unfold calls. Roughly speaking, for an unsolved goal in the current proof tree, when only one rule can apply, the proof tree is expanded; if more than one rule can apply, the set of proof trees is split into as many subsets as there are applicable rules (the reader could refer to [23] for more details about these tactics).

Thus, with this method, given a program **P** in some language **L**, and a set **R** of TYPOL rules expressing the dynamic semantics of **L**, one can instantiate a new set R_P of TYPOL rules expressing the dynamic semantics of **P**, completely independent from the source language **L**, and, of course, with better performances in time and space than with **P** (the evaluation of **R(P)**).

3.2 Partial evaluation using Attribute Grammars

We propose here another method for partial evaluation of TYPOL programs. As Hascoët privileges the Logic Programming aspect of the TYPOL formalism (using proof trees), we focus on the Attribute Grammar specification resulting from our construction (section 2.3) (using attributed syntax trees). In this context, we give another operational definition for partial evaluation of TYPOL programs and we discuss the equivalence with logic partial evaluation.

Let **R** be a strictly decreasing, not circular and pseudo-deterministic TYPOL program and let **G** be the equivalent Attribute Grammar obtained with our construction. Let **E(T)** be a TYPOL equation with **T** as subject. To partially evaluate **E(T)** with **R** means: compute, on the syntax tree **T**, with respect to semantic definitions of **G**, all attributes that can be computed. The result is a compiled version of **R**, a term of $M(\mathcal{F} \cup \mathcal{I})$: a sequence of semantic function calls applied to already computed values (dealing, for instance, with store management and input/output operations). The result of the total evaluation is the execution of this sequence of semantic functions calls.

To check the correctness of our method, we just have to prove the following proposition, provided the equivalence between the starting TYPOL program **R** and the AG **G** (proved in [3]).

Proposition 2: The computation of the partial evaluation of **T** with respect to **G** is equivalent to the interpretation of **T** with respect to **G** (the total evaluation).
In other terms,

$$T \in M(\mathcal{O}) \mapsto F_i \in M(\mathcal{F}) \mapsto P_e \in M(\mathcal{F} \cup \mathcal{I}) \mapsto \mathcal{V} \in \mathcal{I}$$

F_i is an unevaluated tree on $M(\mathcal{F})$, the free interpretation. P_e is a first step in the computation on attribute domains, the partial evaluation.
The proof is based on formal properties of the resolution relation. This relation is confluent if the starting TYPOL program is determistic (Proposition 1).

So, we can apply our partial evaluation technique on all strictly decreasing, not circular (i.e. pseudo-circular or non-circular) and deterministic TYPOL programs.

We describe now the relationship between the two partial evaluation techniques (one with TYPOL rules, the other with Attribute Grammars).

Given **R** a strictly decreasing, not circular and deterministic TYPOL program and **E(T)** a TYPOL equation (with **T** as subject); given **R'** the result of the partial evaluation of **E(T)** with **R**, by logic partial evaluation; let **G** be the equivalent Attribute Grammar obtained with our construction on **R**.

(i) **R'** is equivalent to the partial evaluation of **T** with respect to **G**;

(ii) the proof tree obtained by executing **R'** with the remaining equation **E'(T)** is equivalent to the interpretation of **T** with respect to **G**.

This relationship can be sketched in Figure 2.

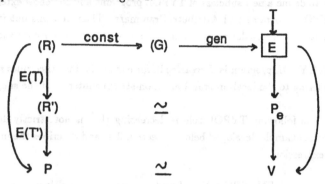

Figure 2

The left part of the diagram is proved in [23], the right part comes from proposition 2 and the lower part is proved is [3].

The remaining proof (equivalence between **R'** and P_e) is based on some specific properties of the resulting TYPOL program **R'**. Due to two steps in logic partial evaluation (simplification and syntax elimination), **R'** is a relational version of P_e: each sequent maps to a subtree of P_e and each evaluable predicate maps to a semantic function call. In other words, **R'** can be viewed as a simplified AG working on a very simple abstract syntax (abstract syntax of **T**). We are still studying properties of these resulting TYPOL programs.

To implement our technique, we work on the dependency graph of attribute values within the given abstract syntax tree (w.r.t. the AG). Given an abstract syntax tree, this dependency graph is independent of remaining unknown inputs (property of the free interpretation). We split this graph into layers yielding what can be computed in a same instant. Introducing time in such a data-flow system provides an ordered sequence of operations.

More formally, let T be an abstract syntax tree and a an attribute occurrence, we note $L(a)$ the *attribute layer* for a defined as follows:

- $L_0 = \{a \in \text{ATTR}(T) \mid a = constant\}$;

- $L_{n+1} = \{a \in \text{ATTR}(T) \mid \max_{b \Rightarrow a} L(b) = n\}$.

Then, with register allocation techniques [41,42], we produce from this resulting graph an optimized code in Lisp with local and global variables. This code expresses the partial evaluation of the given abstract syntax tree, with respect to the AG.

3.3 Extending AGs to Dynamic Semantics

Our technique, compared to logic partial evaluation, lacks generality. It applies only on a subclass of TYPOL programs: strictly decreasing, not circular and deterministic TYPOL programs. We explain here the trick that makes it possible to extend our technique to a larger class of TYPOL programs expressing dynamic semantics.

We first have to define a new subclass of TYPOL programs and somehow extend our construction relating TYPOL programs and Attribute Grammars. Then, it turns out it is necessary to handle the computation of circular semantic definitions produced by our construction.

Definition 6: A TYPOL program is *decreasing* if, for each of its inference rules r, subjects of the premises of r (refering to the local program) are (non-strict) subterms of the subject of r.

Example 2.1: The following TYPOL rule is decreasing (but is not strictly decreasing). This rule comes from the example developed below in section 3.4. and describes the interpretation of a regular marked expression.

$$\frac{\mathrm{MEMBER}(l, s_1) \qquad l, end \overset{\mathrm{follow}}{\vdash} \mathrm{E} : s_2 \qquad w, s_2 \vdash \mathrm{E}}{l \cdot w, s_1 \vdash \mathrm{E}}$$

Let $\mathcal{A}$ the automaton that recognizes the expression E. This rule simply says that a word $l.w$, given a current state s_1 in $\mathcal{A}$, belongs to $L(E)$ if the first letter l is acceptable in this state, produces a new state s_2, and if w, given this new state s_2, is recognized by $\mathcal{A}$. In fact, the rule deals with the expression instead of the automaton because the automaton is computed on the fly with *follow* sets that denote the current state of the automaton. Note another rule is necessary to handle the end of the recursion (empty word or/and termination state). Furthermore, note the computation of *follow* sets requires another set of inference rules to describe a right-to-left traversal in the whole expression.

In our construction, the strictly decreasing TYPOL rules produce the same semantic definitions while the other ones produce circular semantic definitions.

Example 2.2: The following semantic definitions are produced by our construction.

$E.3 = car(E.1);$
$E.4 = end;$
/* $E.2$ is the current state in the automaton */
/* $E.5$ is the **follow** attribute computed by another set of rules (see section 3.4.) */
/* $E.6$ is the new current state derived from $E.3$ */
$E.6 = if(member(E.3, E.2), E.5);$
/* inducing a circularity : stops when length(E.1) = 0 or E.2 = *end* */
$E.2 = E.6;$
$E.1 = cdr(E.1);$

Such semantic definitions can not be evaluated by classical evaluators, because of circularity. Our trick to evaluate these attributes is to implement them not as *circular* attributes but as *duplicate* attributes (at each new step, we assign a new *tuple* of attribute values). This is possible because synthesized attributes of step n are only used to compute inherited attributes of step $n+1$.

The duplication process may not terminate to precisely express dynamic semantics of loops, for instance. The number of attributes is then potentially infinite. The formalization of such an extension of Attribute Grammars is currently in progress. Roughly speaking, we can see on our example that, even if the evaluation process computes an infinite number of duplicate attributes, the number of registers needed for the computation is constant.

In our example, the duplication process ends with the end of the word or a termination state so the number of attributes is not infinite. We simply implement such an evaluation (in Lisp, for instance) with assignment of global variables denoting the duplicate attributes.

Example 2.3: The following Lisp code is produced by our TYPOL compiler (assuming a renaming of variables for clarity).

```
(de interpret (exp word state)
   (setq letter (car word))
   (tag stop
      (while (and (neq (length word) 0) (nequal state end))
         (if (member letter state)
            (progn
               (setq state (follow exp end letter))
               (setq word (cdr word))
               (setq letter (car word)))
            (exit stop ()))))))
```

This AG extension (duplicate attributes) does not affect our partial evaluation algorithm. We still have a dependency graph on attribute values within a given abstract syntax tree, even if the number of attributes is infinite. Splitting the graph into layers handles the computation of the great (possibly infinite) number of attributes.

Extending Attribute Grammars to dynamics semantics makes it possible to treat a larger class of TYPOL programs: both to provide an attribute evaluation technique to implement them and to partially evaluate them with attribute grammars paradigm. Then, the most famous application of partial evaluation can be applied with our method: partially evaluate a TYPOL interpreter, where the only known input is a program to interpret, automatically generates a program-tailored compiler. We have applied our partial evaluation to typical examples. One of them is a regular marked expression partially executed by a TYPOL interpreter for regular marked expressions.

3.4 Application to a given interpreter

Given a regular marked expression **E**, the following TYPOL program describes how to interpret the corresponding automaton (that can recognize any word belonging to **L(E)**), according to a given symbol. Such a program simulates the behavior of an automaton, after it should have been computed from a regular expression with example 1 (see section 2.4.). Intuitively, simulating an automaton means, with a given state (in the automaton) and a given symbol (a transition) produce a new state. States are simulated by *follow* sets since the expression is marked and the automaton is deterministic. This process can be iterated for all symbols of a word to answer the question: "does this word belong to the language generated by this regular marked expression ?"

Example 3.1: *Interpreting marked regular expressions in TYPOL*

program *INTERP_EXP* is
use EXPRESSIONS;
use AUTOMATES;
use WORDS;
e : EXP;
s, s_1, s_2 : STATES ;
l : SYMBOL;
w : WORD;

$$\frac{\overset{\text{first}}{\vdash} \text{E} : s \qquad w, s \vdash \text{E}}{w \vdash \text{E}} \tag{1}$$

$$\epsilon, end \vdash \text{E} \tag{2}$$

$$\frac{\text{MEMBER}(l, s_1) \qquad l, end \overset{\text{follow}}{\vdash} \text{E} : s_2 \qquad w, s_2 \vdash \text{E}}{l \cdot w, s_1 \vdash \text{E}} \qquad (s_1 \neq end) \tag{3}$$

set **FOLLOW** is
– computes the **follow** set for l in the whole expression
end **FOLLOW**;

set **FIRST** is
– computes the **first** set of the whole expression (as in example 1)
end **FIRST**;
end *INTERP_EXP*;

The interp_exp TYPOL program is decreasing, linear, and deterministic. As shown in previous section, the equivalent AG is circular.

To partially evaluate a regular marked expression, given this TYPOL program, we need to construct the dependency graph of attribute values. This dependency graph provides some features:

- the initial state of the automaton can be computed at partial evaluation time with the **first** attribute;

- **follow** sets are computed in a right-to-left manner; computing the **follow** set of a symbol l may require the computation of the **follow** set of other symbols. Such computations don't need to be redone (if the results are stored). Extending this idea, one can pre-compute all **follow** sets, store them (just for symbol leaves), and just load them when needed, to compute a new state.

The partial evaluation of our TYPOL program, given the following expression:

$$e = (1 \cdot 2 + 3)^* \cdot 4 \cdot 5$$

produces the following optimized free-Lisp code (with global variables), that is in fact a compiled version of our starting program.

Example 3.2: *The partial evaluation of e with the interpreter given in Example 3.1.*

```
(defvar letter ())
(defvar first {1 3 4})                              ; the first set for the expression
(defvar follows (vector {2} {1 3 4} {1 3 4} {5} {end}))   ; the follow sets for all symbols

(de follow (l)
   (vref follows (differ l 1)))

(de interpret (word)
   (setq state first)
   (setq letter (car word))
   (tag stop
      (while (and (neq (length word) 0) (nequal state {end}))
         (if (member letter state)
            (progn
               (setq state (follow exp end letter))
               (setq word (cdr word))
               (setq letter (car word)))
            (exit stop ()))))
      (and (eq (length word) 0) (equal state {end})))))
```

As a comparison with the work of Hascoët [23], we admit that our partial evaluation method via Attribute Grammars applies only on a subclass of TYPOL programs, compared to the general evaluation method with proof trees. However, it seems that, on TYPOL programs in this subclass, formal properties due to abstract interpretation of auxiliary functions in the equivalent Attribute Grammar make our technique more powerful than logic partial evaluation. With our technique, the dependency graph on variables (attributes) is computed at partial evaluation time; with the logic resolution process, this graph is not kwown before the total evaluation (on the remaining inputs). As a matter of fact, a partial evaluation with the TYPOL interpreter of marked regular expressions required some adjustments in Hascoët's partial evaluator.

References

[1] Aho A., Sethi R., & Ullman J. "Compilers: Principles, Techniques, and Tools" Addison-Wesley, Reading, Mass., 1986

[2] Attali I. & Franchi-Zannettacci P. "Prolog-like schemes for Ada static semantics" Ada UK news, 6, 2, 1985

[3] Attali I. & Franchi-Zannettaci P. "Unification-free Execution of TYPOL Programs by Semantic Attribute Evaluation", Proceedings Fifth International Conference Symposium on Logic Programming, Seattle, August 1988, MIT Press.

[4] Berry G. & Sethi R. "From regular expressions to deterministic automata" TCS 48, 1, 1986

[5] Bochmann G. "Semantic evaluation from left to right" CACM 19, 2, 55-62, 1976

[6] Borras P., Clément D., Despeyroux T., Incerpi J., Kahn G., Lang B., & Pascual V. "CENTAUR: the system" INRIA research report 777, 1987. To be published in proc. of SIGSOFT'88, Third Annual Symposium on Software Development Environments, Boston, 1988

[7] Bruynooghe M. " A Framework for the abstract interpretation of logic programs" Katholoeke Universiteit Leuven, Report CW 62, 1987

[8] Chirica L. & Martin D. "An order algebraic definition of Knuthian semantics" Math. Systems Theory 13, 1979

[9] Clément D., Despeyroux J., Despeyroux T., & Kahn G. "A simple applicative language: Mini-ml" Symp. on Functional Programming Languages and Computer Architecture, 1986

[10] Courcelle B. & Franchi-Zannettacci P. "Attribute Grammars and Recursive Program Schemes" TCS 17, 163, 1980

[11] Demers A., Reps T. & Teitelbaum T. "Incremental evaluation for attribute grammars with application to syntax-directed editors" in Conference Record of the 8th ACM Symposium on Principles of Programming Languages, Williamsburg, Va, 1981

[12] Deransart P. & Maluszynski J. "Relating Logic Programs and Attribute Grammars" J. Logic Programming 2:119-155, 1985

[13] Deransart P., Jourdan M., & Lorho B. "Attribute Grammars: Definitions, Systems and Bibliography" LNCS 323, Spinger Verlag, 1988

[14] Despeyroux T. "Executable Specification of static semantics" Semantics of Data Types, LNCS 173, 1984

[15] Despeyroux T. "TYPOL: a formalism to implement Natural Semantics" INRIA research report 94, 1988

[16] Donzeau-Gouge V., Kahn G., & Lang B. "A complete machine checked definition of a simple programming language using denotational semantics" INRIA research report 330, 1978

[17] Drabent W. "Do logic programs resemble programs in conventional languages ?" 1987 IEEE Symp. on Logic Programming, San Francisco, 1987

[18] Engelfriet J. & File G. "The formal power of one-visit attribute grammars" Proc. of the seventh ICALP, LNCS 85, 1980

[19] Ershov A. P. "On the partial computation principle" Information Processing Letters, 6-2, 1977

[20] Franchi-Zannettacci P. "Attributs sémantiques et schémas de programmes" Thèse d'Etat, Univ. of Bordeaux I, 1982

[21] Fumatura Y. "Generalised Partial Computation" Proc. workshop on Partial Evaluation and Mixed Computation, Denmark, Oct 1987. Also New Generation Computing Journal, Vol. 6, N°s 2 & 3, 1988.

[22] Ganzinger H. & Hanus M. "Modular Logic Programming of Compilers" Proc. Symp. on Logic Programming, Boston, Massachusetts, 242-253, 1985

[23] Hascoët L. "Partial evaluation with inference rules" Proc. workshop on Partial Evaluation and Mixed Computation, Denmark, Oct 1987. Also New Generation Computing Journal, Vol. 6, N°s 2 & 3, 1988.

[24] Johnsson T. "Attribute Grammars as a Functional Programming Paradigm" Symp. on Functional Programming Languages and Computer Architecture LNCS 274, Portland, 1987

[25] Jones N. D., Setsoft P. & Sondergaard H. "MIX: a self-applicable partial evaluator for experiments in compiler generation", report 87/8, DIKU, University of Copenhagen, 1987

[26] Jourdan M. "Strongly Non-Circular Attribute Grammars and their recursive evaluation" ACM Sigplan Symp. on Compiler Construction, Montreal Sigplan Notices 19, 6, 1984

[27] Jourdan M. & Parigot D. "The FNC-2 system : advances in Attribute Grammar Technology" INRIA research report to be published, 1988

[28] Julié C. "Optimisation de l'espace mémoire pour les compilateurs générés selon la méthode d'évaluation OAG: Etude des travaux de Kastens et propositions d'améliorations" Rapport de DEA, Univ. of Orléans, 1986

[29] Kahn G. "Natural Semantics" Proc. of Symp on Theoretical Aspects of Computer Science, Passau, Germany, LNCS 247, 1987

[30] Kastens U. "Ordered Attribute Grammars" Acta Informatica 13, 1980

[31] Kastens U. "The GAG-system - A Tool for Compiler Construction" in *Methods and Tools for Compiler Construction*, ed B. Lorho, 165-182, Cambridge University Press, 1984

[32] Kennedy K. & Warren S. K. "Automatic generation of efficient evaluators for Attribute Grammars" Proc. of the 3rd ACM Conf on Principle of Programming Languages, Atlanta, 1976

[33] Knuth D. E. "Semantics of Context-Free Languages" Math. Syst. Theory 2, 1968

[34] Komorowski H. J. & Maluszynski J. "Unification-free execution of logic programs" 1985 IEEE Symp. on Logic Programming, Boston, 1985

[35] Lang B. "The Virtual Tree Processor" in Generation of Interactive Programming Environments, Intermediate Report, J. Heering, J. Sidi, A. Verhoog (Eds), CWI Report CS-R8620, Amsterdam, May 1986

[36] Naish L. "Negation and Control in Prolog" LNCS 238, 1986

[37] Plotkin G. D. "A structural approach to operational semantics" Report DAIMI FN-19, Computer Science Dpt, Aarhus Univ., Aarhus, Denmark, 1981

[38] Prawitz D. "Ideas and results in proof theory" Proc. of the Second Scandinavian Logic Symposium, North Holland, 1971

[39] Reddy U. S. "On the relationship between logic and functional languages" in Logic Programming: Functions, Relations and Equations, DeGroot D., Lindstrom G. eds., Prentice Hall, 1986

[40] Reps T. "Generating Language based Environments" M.I.T. Press, Cambridge, Mass, 1984

[41] Sethi R. "Complete Register Allocation problems" SIAM J. Comp 4, 1975

[42] Sethi R. & Ullman J. "The generation of optimal code for arithmetic expressions" JACM 17, 4, 1970

[43] Tavernini V. E. "Translating Natural Semantic Specifications to Attribute Grammars" Master's Thesis, University of Illinois, Urbana-Champaign, 1987

[44] Uhl J., Drossopoulou S., Persch G., Goos G., Dausmann M., & Winterstein G. "An Attribute Grammar for the semantic analysis of Ada" LNCS 149, 1982

Formal Specification of a Prolog Compiler

Michael Hanus

Fachbereich Informatik, Universität Dortmund

D-4600 Dortmund 50, W. Germany

(uucp: michael@unidoi5)

This paper presents an outline of a formal specification of a compiler and a virtual machine for the programming language Prolog. The specification of the compiler can be transformed into an equivalent Prolog program. The specification of the virtual machine is the basis of an implementation of the virtual machine as an interpreter written in a low-level language. Moreover, the specification may be used for correctness proofs of a Prolog system.

1 Introduction

Many compilers for the programming language Prolog are based on the so-called "Warren Abstract Machine" (WAM) presented in [Warren 83]. The WAM is a virtual machine with specific operations for executing logic programs (unify operations, indexing for clauses etc.). The execution of a Prolog program is done in two steps in a WAM-based implementation:

1. Compilation of the program into a sequence of WAM instructions.

2. Execution of the WAM program by an interpreter or compilation of the WAM program into another language, e.g., machine language.

Although there are several formal descriptions of the operational semantics of Prolog and Prolog interpreters [Arbab/Berry 87] [Debray/Mishra 88] [Deransart/Ferrand 87] [Jones/Mycroft 84] [Nilsson 84], there is no formal specification of the translation of Prolog programs into WAM programs and the semantics of the WAM. [Warren 83] is a good foundation for the implementation of the compiler and the WAM. But there are many problems if we go into details, because it is only a proposal for the implementation of pure Prolog (without cut, disjunction and non-logical predicates) based on an informal description. From a practical point of view a formal specification is very useful for an implementation of a Prolog compiler, because it is a precise description of the implementor's tasks and the interfaces between different modules. On the other hand, it is necessary for a correctness proof of the Prolog implementation. [Kursawe 86] has shown that the unify instructions of a WAM program can be derived from the source program by partial evaluation, but his method covers only a small part of the WAM.

In the following we present an outline of a full specification of the translation of Prolog programs into WAM programs and the operational semantics of the WAM. These specifications are the basis of a Prolog system developed at the University of Dortmund (see [ProCom 87]). We assume the reader is familiar with the basic concepts of the WAM (for details, the reader is referred to [Warren 83]).

2 Specification of the Prolog compiler

The compilation of Prolog programs into WAM programs is a complex task [Van Roy 84] and therefore it is desirable to divide the specification into several subtasks. We use the ideas of attribute coupled grammars [Ganzinger/Giegerich 84] and specify the compilation as the composition of translations between abstract syntax trees:

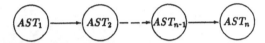

AST_1 is the abstract syntax tree corresponding to the given clauses of a predicate and AST_n is the abstract syntax tree corresponding to the translated WAM program. The signatures of the intermediate trees $AST_2, ..., AST_{n-1}$ are enriched with informations that are computed in a preceding translation step and may be used in a subsequent translation step. We give some examples from the compiler specification.

The signature of the abstract syntax of Prolog programs is specified in the following way:

sorts: *Prog, Clauses, Clause, Terms, Term, String*

operations:

prog:	*Clauses*	→	*Prog*
csequ:	*Clause, Clauses*	→	*Clauses*
empty_csequ:		→	*Clauses*
clause:	*Term, Term*	→	*Clause*
tsequ:	*Term, Terms*	→	*Terms*
empty_tsequ:		→	*Terms*
var:	*String*	→	*Term*
structure:	*String, Terms*	→	*Term*

A Prolog program is a list of clauses. A clause is a pair of terms consisting of the head and the body of the clause. A term is either a variable or a structure with a (possibly empty) list of subterms. The sort *String* is assumed to be a basic sort. Note that the subdivision of a clause body into disjunction and conjunction of literals is done in subsequent translation steps. The term corresponding to the clauses

```
append([],L,L).
append([E|R],L,[E|RL]) :- append(R,L,RL).
```

for the predicate **append** is

```
prog([
        clause(append([],var(L),var(L)) , true),
        clause(append([var(E)|var(R)],var(L),[var(E)|var(RL)]) ,
               append(var(R),var(L),var(RL))
      ])
```

(We use the usual Prolog notations for lists of clauses and structured terms [Clocksin/Mellish 81] and omit operators like "**structure**", "**csequ**" etc.)

In the first translation step a term of sort *Prog* will be enriched with the following informations:

- Is there a cut in one clause? This will be used for generating instructions for handling the cut.

- Name and arity of the predicate which is defined by the clauses.

- Number of the clauses.

- List of the first arguments in each clause. This will be used to generate the indexing instructions.

The signature of the abstract syntax tree after the first translation step is the following:

sorts: *Prog2, Clauses, Clause, Terms, Term, Args, Arg, String, Nat, Bool*

operations:

prog2:	*Bool, String, Nat, Nat, Args, Clauses*	$\rightarrow$	*Prog2*
var_arg:	*String*	$\rightarrow$	*Arg*
struct_arg:	*String, Terms*	$\rightarrow$	*Arg*
asequ:	*Arg, Args*	$\rightarrow$	*Args*
empty_asequ:		$\rightarrow$	*Args*
csequ:	*Clause, Clauses*	$\rightarrow$	*Clauses*
empty_csequ:		$\rightarrow$	*Clauses*
clause:	*Term, Term*	$\rightarrow$	*Clause*
tsequ:	*Term, Terms*	$\rightarrow$	*Terms*
empty_tsequ:		$\rightarrow$	*Terms*
var:	*String*	$\rightarrow$	*Term*
structure:	*String, Terms*	$\rightarrow$	*Term*

If there is a term of the form

$$prog2(C, F, A, N, As, Cs)$$

then the following conditions holds after the first translation step:

- C is true iff the clauses Cs contain a cut.

- F is the name and A the arity of the predicate defined by the clauses Cs.

- N is the number of elements in the clause list Cs.

- As is the list of the first arguments in the heads of Cs.

Hence the term corresponding to the clauses of append is translated into the term

```
prog2(false, append, 3, 2,
        [ struct_arg([]) , struct_arg([var(E)|var(R)]) ],
        [
         clause(append([],var(L),var(L)) , true),
         clause(append([var(E)|var(R)],var(L),[var(E)|var(RL)]) ,
                append(var(R),var(L),var(RL))
        ])
```

in the first translation step. In subsequent translation steps program terms are enriched with the following informations:

- Classification of cuts in the clauses.

- Elimination of disjunctions by introducing new predicates.

- Numbering of the literals in each clause.

- Numbering of the arguments in each literal.

- Classification of arguments: Subargument or head argument (this is important for generating unify, get and put instructions).

- Classification of variables (permanent or temporary).

With this information it is possible to generate the WAM code for each clause. The complete code for all clauses consists of the code for each clause and an indexing scheme which filters out a subset of clauses that could match a given procedure call. The creation of this indexing scheme can also be specified by several translation steps. The last translation step of the specification merges the code for the indexing scheme with the code for each clause.

Each translation step is formally specified as a mapping from terms of the preceding signature into terms of the next signature. For the description of these mappings we use no specific formalism as in [Ganzinger/Giegerich 84], but the mappings are inductively defined on the structure of the terms using usual mathematical notations.

This description of the compiler has several advantages:

- All details of the compilation are described. It is clear how to translate a given Prolog program into a WAM program.

- It can be proofed that a WAM program is the translation of a Prolog program.

- The complexity of the compilation is divided into several simple translation steps.

- The description is a good basis for implementing a Prolog compiler. Several authors have shown the advantages of logic programming for compiler writing ([Warren 80] [Ganzinger/Hanus 85], among others) and therefore we have used Prolog as an implementation language of the compiler: The abstract syntax trees are Prolog terms and the implementation of the translation steps is a simple coding of the specification into Prolog. The performance of the compiler is acceptable (it translates approximate 30 clauses per second on a Sun-3).

3 Specification of the Warren abstract machine

We give an operational semantics of the WAM. The WAM is defined as an abstract interpreter for WAM instructions. The interpreter has an initial state and each interpretation of a WAM instruction maps a state into a new state. The state of the WAM interpreter consists of the values of all registers and the contents of the memory (code area, heap, local stack and trail stack). For example, the heap contains all terms created during a computation of a program. Hence we model a particular state of the heap as a function from the domain of heap addresses into the domain of terms.

In detail, the following domains are defined:

$Code\_address$ = <an infinite denumerable set with a linear ordering, i.e. there exists a successor $succ(e)$ for each element e and there exists a predecessor $pred(e)$ for each element e except for the least element $min(Code\_address)$ >

$Heap\_address$ = <similar definition as $Code\_address$ >
$Local\_stack\_address$ = <similar definition as $Code\_address$ >
$Trail\_address$ = <similar definition as $Code\_address$ >

The Y-, X-, and A-registers of the WAM are addressed by natural numbers (the first components are used for disjunctive unions of the register domains):

$Y\_register$ = $reg : \{Y\} \times nr : Nat$
$X\_register$ = $reg : \{X\} \times nr : Nat$
$A\_register$ = $reg : \{A\} \times nr : Nat$

We use cartesian products with a tag for each component. This allows us to identify a component by dot notation: If r is an element of type $X\_register$, then $r.reg$ denotes the first and $r.nr$ the second component of that element.

If we denote by "+" the disjunctive union, we can define the domain of terms as

$$
\begin{aligned}
Term \quad = \quad & tag : \{int\} \times cont : Integer \\
& + \; tag : \{atom\} \times cont : (Atom + func : Atom \times ar : Nat) \\
& + \; Trail\_element \\
& + \; tag : \{var\} \times (adr : Heap\_address + \\
& \qquad\qquad\qquad\qquad\quad eadr : Local\_stack\_address \times ereg : Nat) \\
& + \; tag : \{structure\} \times adr : Heap\_address \\
& + \; tag : \{list\} \times adr : Heap\_address
\end{aligned}
$$

($Atom$ is the domain of all Prolog atoms), where a $Trail\_element$ represents an unbound variable:

$$
\begin{aligned}
Trail\_element \quad = \quad & tag : \{undef\} \times \quad (adr : Heap\_address + \\
& \qquad\qquad\qquad\qquad eadr : Local\_stack\_address \times ereg : Nat)
\end{aligned}
$$

Hence a term is either an integer value, an atom or functor (atoms have arity zero whereas functors have an arity greater than zero), an unbound variable, a variable bound to a term on the heap or local stack, or a reference to a structure or list stored on the heap.

The local stack of the WAM contains two kinds of objects: environments and backtrack points. "An **environment** consists of a vector of value cells for variables occuring in the body of some clause, together with a continuation comprising a pointer into the body of another clause and its associated environment" [Warren 83]. Therefore the domain of environments is defined as

$$
Environment = ee : Local\_stack\_address \times ecp : Code\_address \times y : [Nat \rightarrow Term]
$$

($[A \rightarrow B]$ denotes the domain of all functions from domain A into domain B). A **backtrack point** "contains all the information necessary to restore an earlier state of computation in the event of backtracking" [Warren 83]. Thus a backtrack point consists of the values of the relevant registers of the WAM (see below) and a reference to alternative clauses (component bp):

$$
\begin{aligned}
Backtrackpoint \quad = \quad & ba \;\; : \; [Nat \rightarrow Term] \times \\
& bce : Local\_stack\_address \times \\
& bcp : Code\_address \times \\
& bb \;\; : \; Local\_stack\_address \times \\
& bp \;\; : \; Code\_address \times \\
& btr : Trail\_address \times \\
& bh \;\; : \; Heap\_address \times \\
& nr \;\; : \; Nat
\end{aligned}
$$

For example, if b is an element of $Backtrackpoint$, then $b.ba$ denotes the contents of all A-registers stored in b and $b.ba[0]$ is the contents of the first A-register stored in b. The component nr contains the arity of the predicate in which the backtrack point is created. Now it is easy to define the memory areas of the WAM:

$$
\begin{aligned}
Local\_stack\_element \; &= \; Environment + Backtrackpoint \\
Local\_stack \; &= \; [Local\_stack\_address \rightarrow Local\_stack\_element] \\
Heap \; &= \; [Heap\_address \rightarrow Term] \\
Trail \; &= \; [Trail\_address \rightarrow Trail\_element] \\
Code\_area \; &= \; [Code\_address \rightarrow Instructions]
\end{aligned}
$$

Instructions is the domain of all instructions with appropiate parameters. We omit the necessary definitions here. A **state of the WAM interpreter** contains the following components:

Name	Type	Comment
p	$Code\_address$	program pointer
cp	$Code\_address$	continutation pointer
e	$Local\_stack\_address$	environment pointer
b	$Local\_stack\_address$	backtrack pointer
t	$Trail\_address$	trail pointer
h	$Heap\_address$	heap pointer
s	$Heap\_address$	structure pointer
rw	$\{read, write\}$	read/write register
$error$	$Boolean$	error register for predefined predicates
$occur\_check$	$Boolean$	occur check register
a	$[Nat \rightarrow Term]$	A-registers
x	$[Nat \rightarrow Term]$	X-registers
ca	$Code\_area$	code area
hp	$Heap$	heap
ls	$Local\_stack$	local stack
trl	$Trail$	trail

There are several restrictions on a well-defined state, e.g., $ls(e)$ must be an element of *Environment*, $ls(b)$ must be an element of *Backtrackpoint* and so on. The state transitions of the WAM must preserve these restrictions. The component *error* of the state is set to true if there is a run-time error in some predefined predicate, e.g., arithmetic errors, file errors etc. If the component *occur_check* is set to true then the unification of two terms is done with the occur check (cf. [Lloyd 87]). In the **initial state** all memory areas are undefined (contains no elements) and the values of cp, e, t, h and s are the least addresses of the address domains. The **terminal state** is defined as the state with $error = true$ or $ca(p)$ is a "stop" instruction.

The main part of the WAM specification is the description of the state transition corresponding to an interpretation of a particular WAM instruction. We omit the full description here but present the specification of three WAM instructions. We denote the modification of a component x of a state by

$$ x \; \leftarrow \; <newvalue> $$

If f is an element of the domain $[A \rightarrow B]$, then $f[x \leftarrow y]$ denotes the element of $[A \rightarrow B]$ which is identical to f but has the value y for the argument x. If x is a component of a state, then $'x$ denotes the old value of x before the interpretation of the instruction. Only changes of the WAM state are listed in the specification of a WAM instruction. Components of the WAM state that are not mentioned in the instruction specification are not changed by that instruction.

Examples: The WAM instruction "execute(x)" calls the last goal in a clause body. The program pointer is set to the code address of the predicate in the last goal:

instruction execute(x)
x: *Code_address*
Transformation:
  $p \leftarrow x$

The instruction "put_nil(v)" puts the constant representing an empty list into A-register v:

instruction put_nil(v)
v: *A_register*
Transformation:
  $a \leftarrow {'a}[v.nr \leftarrow (atom, nil)]$

The instruction "put_value(u,v)" puts the value of variable u into A-register v. If u is an A- or X-register, we have direct access to the value of u. If u is a Y-register, the value of u can be found in the actual environment and therefore we need a reference to the actual environment:

instruction put_value(u, v)
u: $(X\_register + A\_register + Y\_register)$
v: *A_register*
Transformation:
  if $u.reg = X$
    then $a \leftarrow {'a}[v.nr \leftarrow x(u.nr)]$
    else if $u.reg = A$
        then $a \leftarrow {'a}[v.nr \leftarrow {'a}(u.nr)]$
        else $a \leftarrow {'a}[v.nr \leftarrow (ls(e).y)(u.nr)]$

The full specification of the WAM can be found in [ProCom 87].

This specification is the basis of a 68000-based WAM implementation at the University of Dortmund. The specified state is mapped into memory and machine registers and the transformations are mapped into sequences of machine code. The complete system is shown in the following picture.

"pass1" is the implementation of the Prolog compiler described in chapter 2 and "pass2" translates every WAM instruction into a sequence of machine instructions. Our implementation is a direct realization of the WAM specification without any optimizations. The performance of our system is approximate 40 Klips on a Sun-3 for the naive reverse example, which is comparable with other Prolog implementations.

4 Correctness proofs

There are at least two reasons for the formal specification of a Prolog system:

1. It is the foundation of an implementation. The specification decreases the problems in coordinating several people working on the project.

2. It makes it possible to prove the correctness of the complete system or some translated programs.

The first reason was very important to our project, whereas the second point is a task for the future. Actually, we are working on correctness proofs for particular programs. [Kursawe 86] has shown that it is possible to derive specific WAM instructions from the source program by partial evaluation. We want to refine the interpreters that define the operational semantics of Prolog (cf. [Debray/Mishra 88], [Jones/Mycroft 84]) in a way that makes it possible to compare these interpreters with the operational semantics of the WAM.

5 Conclusions

We have presented an outline of a formal specification of a Prolog compiler and the Warren abstract machine. The specification is a good basis for a direct implementation of a Prolog system with an acceptable performance. Further work includes a more efficient implementation of the specification and correctness proofs for particular programs.

Acknowledgements

The author is grateful to Jörg Süggel, Jörg Petersen and the members of the project group "ProCom" for their work on the Prolog system.

References

[Arbab/Berry 87]
  B. Arbab and D.M. Berry. Operational and Denotational Semantics of Prolog. *Journal of Logic Programming (4)*, pp. 309–329, 1987.

[Clocksin/Mellish 81]
  W.F. Clocksin and C.S. Mellish. *Programming in Prolog*. Springer, 1981.

[Debray/Mishra 88]

S.K. Debray and P. Mishra. Denotational and Operational Semantics for Prolog. *Journal of Logic Programming (5)*, pp. 61–91, 1988.

[Deransart/Ferrand 87]

P. Deransart and G. Ferrand. An Operational Formal Definition of PROLOG. In *Proc. 4th IEEE Internat. Symposium on Logic Programming*, pp. 162–172, San Francisco, 1987.

[Ganzinger/Giegerich 84]

H. Ganzinger and R. Giegerich. Attribute Coupled Grammars. In *Proceedings of the SIG-PLAN '84 Symposium on Compiler Construction*, pp. 157–170, Montreal, 1984.

[Ganzinger/Hanus 85]

H. Ganzinger and M. Hanus. Modular Logic Programming of Compilers. In *Proc. IEEE Internat. Symposium on Logic Programming*, pp. 242–253, Boston, 1985.

[Jones/Mycroft 84]

N.D. Jones and A. Mycroft. Stepwise Development of Operational and Denotational Semantics for Prolog. In *Proc. IEEE Internat. Symposium on Logic Programming*, pp. 281–288, Atlantic City, 1984.

[Kursawe 86]

P. Kursawe. How to invent a Prolog machine. In *Proc. Third International Conference on Logic Programming (London)*, pp. 134–148. Springer LNCS 225, 1986.

[Lloyd 87]

J.W. Lloyd. *Foundations of Logic Programming*. Springer, second, extended edition, 1987.

[Nilsson 84]

J.F. Nilsson. Formal Vienna-Definition-Method models of Prolog. In J.A. Campbell, editor, *Implementations of Prolog*, pp. 281–308. Ellis Horwood, 1984.

[ProCom 87]

Projektgruppe ProCom. Zwischen- und Abschlußbericht der Projektgruppe ProCom (Prolog Compiler). Univ. Dortmund, 1987.

[Van Roy 84]

P. Van Roy. A Prolog Compiler for the PLM. Report No. UCB/CSD 84/203, Univ. of California, Berkeley, 1984.

[Warren 80]

D.H.D. Warren. Logic Programming and Compiler Writing. *Software - Practice and Experience*, Vol. 10, pp. 97–125, 1980.

[Warren 83]

D.H.D. Warren. An Abstract Prolog Instruction Set. Technical Note 309, SRI International, Stanford, 1983.

Formal Specification of Interactive Languages

Using Definite Clause Grammars *

Weidong DANG

LRI, U.A.410 CNRS
Bât.490, Université de Paris-sud
91405 Orsay, FRANCE
Mail: dang!lri!inria!fr

CRIL S.A.
146, Bd de Valmy
92700 Colombes, FRANCE

ABSTRACT

Modelling human-computer interaction in interactive computer systems through languages is one the of main approaches for the construction of human-computer interfaces. The work presented here describes first how Definite Clause Grammars can be used to formally specify this type of languages. Compared with previous work using BNF etc, this formalism has more expressive power and is easier for rapid prototyping. With this modelling, the user-machine dialogue design becomes a DCG specification process, and the dialogue management becomes a parsing problem. Detailed examples and our experiences are given to demonstrate the interest of such a modelling.

1. Introduction

Modelling human-computer interaction in interactive computer systems through languages is one of the main approaches for the construction of user interfaces, which has become a major topic of research given the growing spread of modern computer systems with graphic output and pointing devices. In this approach, user actions are considered as the terminals of a set of syntax rules which specifies a language. The role of this type of language is to manage the human-computer communication, i.e. to capture a correct user input sequence and then invoke the corresponding procedure of application programs in order to produce and then display outputs.

* Work partially supported by EEC Esprit ALPES project (No.973): Advanced Logic Programming Environments.

Since 1981, formal methods have been used to specify this type of language for different purposes. Reisner was the first to use BNF to formally specify two interactive graphic systems and to evaluate them [Reisner 81]. Soon after, different systems were specified by means of this approach [Browne 86, Jacob 83, Roach 83]. The techniques used include BNF, Command Language Grammars, State Transition Diagram etc. Several software engineering tools, grouped under the name User Interface Management System (UIMS), provide not only a set of powerful graphic primitives as run-time support, but also a series of tools for specification, rapid prototyping, debugging and evaluation of interactive languages [Buxton 83, Green 85, Oslen 83, Sibert 86].

Formal specification allows the interface designer to describe precisely at a very high level the external behavior of a system without specifying its internal implementation. Usually these specifications enable rapid prototyping, easy modifications and even the automatic generation of final interface programs. Modelling human-computer interaction through a language permits also the utilization of traditional language implementation techniques to realize the interface construction.

In modelling human-computer interactions, it is difficult to specify both the user and computer actions, i.e, the entire dialogue [Green 85]. The formalisms used for traditional language specifications have to be modified for this purpose [Jacob 83]. In this paper we present the use of Definite Clause Grammars (DCG) [Pereira 80] in specifying this type of language. The distinguishing features of this formalism lie in its expressive power in describing not only user actions but also, due to the presence of a command part and the shared variables as a communication channel, the entire human-computer dialogue.

2. Dialogue Modelling in DCG

A Definite Clause Grammar rule could contain three components on the right hand side: terminals, non-terminals and commands. In this paper, we follow the syntax of Prolog [Clocksin 81], but to distinguish the DCG used here and the ones used in Prolog for natural language processing, we use ==> instead of --> as separator as follows.

non-terminal ==> [terminal],{commands},non-terminals.

In modelling man-machine interaction, user actions are considered as terminals, which are the tokens returned by the lexical analyser constructed for user input capture. In the specification, the terminals can contain variables in order to reduce the number of syntax rules. For example, a click in a menu, named "main_menu" which contains several entries, can be represented by [menu(main_menu,Item)], the variable "Item" will be the menu entry that you have clicked and this variable should be bound at the lexical analysis level.

Computer actions are considered as the semantics part of interactive languages. They correspond often to procedure calls of application programs (the programs to be interfaced). The procedure calls and the system outputs can be specified by the command part of DCG.

Several commands can be grouped in one pair of brackets. The communication between the interface part and the semantic part is accomplished by shared variables of two parts.

In an interactive language, the computer processing is carried out at various points during the input, and the outputs are produced in order to enhance communication, by prompting, echoing or displaying of results. The user and the computer actions are interleaved, constituing a dialogue. So the syntax specification describes on the one hand, the legal streams of user inputs, and on the other hand how the computer reacts at each point of an input stream. We present here a simple example of a login session to illustrate how a dialogue can be specified by DCG.

Example: A login session specification.

English specification: in a login session, the system print first a message "Enter user name". The user enters a user name, then the password and finally the security level. The system checks first if the user name has been recorded in the system, if so it prints "Enter password", if not "user name not exist, reenter user name". If the password entered by the user is not correct, a message "password not correct" will be displayed and the system restarts the login session. If the password correct, the output message will be "Enter security level". The security level entered by the user must be less than or equal to the authorized level for the user, if not, the user can reenter the security level.

DCG specification: in the following, the predicates "print", "create_session", "exist", "passwd" and "level" are system procedure calls.

```
login ==> { print('Enter user name:')},
        get_user_name(UserName), get_passwd(UserName), get_level(UserName),
        {create_session(UserName)}.

get_user_name(UserName) ==> [read_keyboard(UserNameX)],
        test_user_name(UserNameX,UserName).
test_user_name(UserNameX,UserName) ==> {exist(UserNameX),UserName==UserNameX}.
test_user_name(UserNameX,UserName) ==> {not exist(UserNameX),
        print('User name not exist, Reenter user name:')},
        get_user_name(UserName).

get_passwd(UserName) ==> {print('Enter password:')},
        [read_keyboard(Passwd)],
        test_passwd(UserName,Passwd).
test_passwd(UserName,Passwd) ==> { passwd(UserName,Passwd)}.
test_passwd(UserName,Passwd) ==> { not passwd(UserName,Passwd), print('password not correct')},
        login.

get_level(UserName) ==> { print('Enter security level:')},
        [read_keyboard(Level)],
        test_level(UserName,Level).
test_level(UserName,Level) ==> {level(UserName,MaxLevel),MaxLevel>=Level}.
```

test_level(UserName,Level) ==> {level(UserName,MaxLevel),MaxLevel<Level,print('Level too high')},
get_level(UserName).

3. From Specification to Execution

One of the main advantages using DCG specification is that it is almost executable by a logic programming system such as Prolog, though this formalism can be used in systems other than a logic programming one. To make the DCG specification executable is a problem of parser construction for the language specified. This section deals with several problems concerning the parser in logic programming.

3.1. User input capture

The traditional input technique is the "read" primitive in programming languages. In a graphic environment (i.e. PHIGS), both the synchronous and asynchronous input modes are available. These facilities are very useful in constructing user interface with user initiated and mixed interaction modes. An interface between a standard graphic system and a logic programming language can make the different graphic and input primitives available in the language. Considering the current state of logic programming, we introduce only the synchronous primitives, i.e. user input will not have effect until the user is explicitly asked. This is due on the one hand to semantics and implementation reasons, and on the other hand to the simplicity of error handling.

Since we use only synchrounous input primitives, any user action will be preceded by a primitive which asks the user to act. So these input primitives, considered as computer actions, must be explicitly specified in the command part of DCG rules, and for ergonomic reasons, they are often used with promots or guides to help the user. Once the user acts, we must know how to generate the token for syntactic analysis. Tokens are abstract input entities produced by input primitives. We have defined, in a graphic environment, four types of predefined tokens listed in the following, and their corresponding primitives.

- Input a Prolog term by keyboard: [read_term(T)]::read_keyboard(T)

- A choice from a menu:
  [menu(Name,Choice)]::menu(Name,Item_list,Attributs,Choice)

- Indicate a point on the screen: [point(X,Y)]::inq_mouse_click(Button,X,Y)

- Choose a picture on the screen:
  [picture(Picture_name)]::pick(Valid_choices,Picture_name)

Nevertheless, one can define a token and its corresponding procedure when necessary. For example, to indicate by the mouse the coordinates of two points, the token and its procedure can be defined by the user as follows:

```
[two_points(X1,Y1,X2,Y2)]::get_twopoints(X1,Y1,X2,Y2)
get_twopoints(X,Y,U,V) :-
    inq_mouse_click(Button,X,Y),
    inq_mouse_click(Button,U,V).
```

3.2. The parser

The interactive language we have specified has some fundamental differences in its features compared with traditional static languages. In a static language, the entire text is considered available before any processing begins or any output is produced. For example, a compiler generates an executable program after reading the entire source program. But in interactive languages, the user actions and the computer actions are interleaved, the computer actions are carried out at various points in the input stream and they often contain side effect primitives. This means that when we use only synchronous interactive primitives, the DCG rules must be specified so that after each token is captured, the parser has to decide, in the case of rule choice, which rule is to be used. This constraint is very similar to that of LL(1) grammar, every token can determine one and only one rule during the reduction process. As a consequence, a top-down determinist algorithm is sufficient for the parser.

We have written a meta-interpreter in ASH-Prolog to interpret the DCG specification. The ASH-Prolog [Michard 86] is a C-Prolog system enhanced by interfacing it with ASH window manager of Brown university Workstation Environment [Pato 84]. The ASH-Prolog provides run-time support for graphic output and interactive input. The meta-interpreter traverses the DCG rules in a top down manner with backtracking, as the Prolog interpreter does. The input tokens are produced by an input events manager which corresponds to the lexical analyser of traditional compilers or interpreters. This meta-interpreter is used as tool for rapid prototyping of user interfaces.

The final interface programs could be generated from a specification in DCG. For a logic programming system, the partial evaluation technique can be used to merge the meta-interpreter and the specification into a more efficient program [Takeuchi 86]. Another way is to translate the DCG specification directly into logic code. The translation is very straightforward in replacing "==>" by ":-", changing the [T] with "match_input(T)" built-in predicate, and adding to each input primitive a "push_stack" command by considering the lexical specification for token generation.

4. A Graphic Interface Specification for a Prolog Program Browser

In this section we present the interface specification for a Prolog program browser (browser hereafter). The browser is a tool aimed at providing users with some information and reports related to a Prolog program. Broser makes the user have a global view of a Prolog program without going into the detail. Some typical commands of browser are "find the definition of a predicate", "show the predicates which call a given one", "show the predicates used but not defined in a file" etc [Bergère 88]. We describe here a session of browser and the corresponding specification. Through this example, we show in a graphic computer system environment, how the complicated human-computer interactions can be specified very precisely and netly by DCG.

Figure 1 presents the beginning of the session. The user is asked to choose a context in which the information would be first generated from the source program files and then retrieved according to the subsequent user requests. The rules 1 to 4 describe these actions.

Assuming that the user chooses "local_context", which means the user interests in a single file, after entering the file name, the system proposes a permanent menu containing different available commands. Figure 2 shows the user clicked in "graph" item and a popup menu appears on the screen. These actions are specified by the rules 5 to 7.

In figure 3, we suppose that the user would want to know what predicates have been used in the definition of a predicate, for example "grandfather", he selected "called(p)" request and then typed "grandfather". The browser executes the command "browser_cmd(called,grandfather,List)", and produces a graphic output in a display window. The subsequent user input could be the move of the tree in the display window, click in the "end" entry to return to main_menu or a click in the popup menu to continue the "called" request with the predicates proposed by the system. The dialogue described here is specified by the rules 8 to 12.

```
1) browser ==> { menu(menu_context,[workspace,local_context,global_context],popup)},
        context_choice,
        main_loop.
2) context_choice ==> [menu(menu_context,workspace)],... ...
3) context_choice ==> [menu(menu_context,global_context)],... ...
4) context_choice ==> [menu(menu_context,local_context)],
        {prompt("Which file"), read_keyboard(File_name)},
        [read_term(File_name)], {browser_cmd(local,File_name)}.
5) main_loop ==> {menu(main_menu, [new_context,predicate,file,graph,stop],permanent)},
        level_1_commands, main_loop.
6) level_1_commands ==> graph.        # The other level_1_commands are omitted
7) graph ==> [menu(main_menu,graph)],
        { menu(menu_graph,[called(p),calling(p),zoom(p)],pop_up)},
        graph_inq.
8) graph_inq ==> [menu(menu_graph,Your_CMD)],
        {prompt("Which predicate"), read_keyboard(Predicate_name)},
        [read_keyboard(Predicate_Name)],
        { browser_cmd(Your_CMD,Predicate_Name,L), display_tree(Predicate_name,L)},
        select(Your_CMD,L).
9) select(CMD,List) ==>
```

```
        { menu(menu_new,[end|List],pop_up_with_4_dir)}
        choice(CMD,List).
10) choice(CMD,List) ==> [menu(menu_new,click_to_move(Direction))],
        {move(Direction), menu(menu_new,[end|List],pop_up_with_4_dir)},
        choice(CMD,List).
11) choice(CMD,List) ==> [menu(menu_new,entry(end))].
12) choice(CMD,List) ==> [menu(menu_new,entry(Your_Predicate))],
        { Your_Predicate =!= end, browser_cmd(CMD,Your_Predicate,L),
         display_tree(Your_Predicate,L)},
        select(CMD,L).
```

It is well known that user interface construction, especially in a graphic environment, is very time-consumming; the formal specification method is expected to facilitate design and development. We have used the DCG specification, in the context of Esprit ALPES project [Dang 88], to construct the user interfaces of two application programs in Prolog. The first one is the browser described above, another one is a Prolog program analyser which detects the potential loops in a Prolog program and transforms certain looped programs into non-looped ones [Pelhat 87]. Our experiences clearly demonstrate that this economizes time in interface design and development and so convince us of the usefulness of this approach.

5. Conclusion and future work

We have presented how the Definite Clause Grammars can be used for formally specifying interactive languages, and how the specification could be executed by a logic programming system through meta-interpreting technique or by generation of a Prolog program from DCG rules. Compared with the other formalisms used, the DCG can specify entire dialogues in a natural way. User actions are modelled as terminals, the legal stream of user input is described by syntax rules. The computer actions at each point of an input stream are specified by the command part. The shared variables constitute a communication channel between the interface part and the semantic part of a system.

Generally speaking, a formal specification formalism is the base of a set of tools for dialogue design in UIMS. We are currently designing and implementing a logic programming environment. The graphic interactive primitives are obtained by interfacing X-window manager with C-prolog interpreter. Around the DCG formalism, different tools will be constructed for user interface development: rapid prototyping, visualization, debugging and final program generation.

Another interesting work is to use DCG with asynchronous interactive primitives. In this case, grammars more complicated than LL(1) will be necessary and the potential power of DCG could be totally exploited in the field of human-machine dialogue specification.

6. Acknowledgements

This work has benefitted from the discussions with my colleagues on the ALPES project: J.Hentinger, H.Perdrix, N.Preston, V.Adrian, S.Pelhat of CRIL S.A.; C.Gresse, M.Bergère, M.Teguia of University of Orléans. I would also like to thank A.Michard of INRIA who provided us with his ASH-Prolog, making this experiment possible.

7. Bibliography

[Bergère 88] Bergère M., C. Gresse, M. Teguia, W. Dang, "Browser for logic Programming Environment", 4th international conference on software engineering, Toulouse, France, December, 1988.

[Browne 86] Browne D.P; "The formal Specification of Adaptive User Interfaces Using Command Language Grammar", Proc. of CHI'86 Conf., Boston, April 1986.

[Buxton 83] Buxton W., Lamb M.R., Sherman D., Smith K.C.; "Towards a comprehensive user interface management system". Computer Graphics, 17, 3, 1983, pp 35-42

[Clocksin 81] Clocksin W.F., C.S. Mellish, "Programming in Prolog", Springer Verlag, 1981.

[Dang 88] Dang W. and Hentinger J., "Advanced logic programming environment", Proceedings of 1988 European Conference and exposition of Sun user, March 1988, Versailles, France.

[Green 85] Green M.; "The University of Alberta User Interface Management System", SIGGRAPH 85 Conference Proceedings, San Fransisco July 22-26, Computer Graphics, 19, 3, 1985, pp 205-213

[Jacob 83] Jacob R.J.K.; "Using Foraml Specification in the Design of a Human-Computer Interface", CACM Vol. 26, No.4, April 1983.

[Michard 86] Michard A.; "Le Système Graphique ASH-Prolog et son Utilisation Pour le Prototypage Rapide d'Interface Homme-Machine", RT-076 INRIA, 1986.

[Olsen 83] Olsen D.R.; Dempsey E.P; "SYNGRAPH: A Graphical User Interface Generator", Computer Graphics, 17,3,1983, pp 43-50

[Pato 84] Pato J.N., Reiss S.P., Brown M.H.; "The Brown Workstation Environment", Dept of Comp. Sc., Brown University, Providence, 1984

[Pelhat 87] Pelhat S.; "Analyse de l'inférence récursive en Prolog: le système d'aide à la détection et au controle de boucles", Thèse de Doctorat 3ème cycle, Université de Paris sud, Oct. 1987.

[Peraira 80] Pereira F.C.N., Wareen D.H.D.; "Definite Clause Grammars for Language Analysis - A survey of Formalism and a Comparison with Augmented Transition Networks", Artificial Intelligence, 13, 1980, pp231-278.

[Reisner 81] Reisner P.; "Formal Grammar and Human Factors Design of an Interactive Graphics System", IEEE Tran. on Soft. Engi., Vol. SE-7, No.2, March 1981.

[Roach 83] Roach, J.W., Nickson M.; "Formal Specification For Modelling And Developing Human-Computer Interfaces", Proc. CHI'83 Conf. Boston, Dec. 1983.

[Sibert 86] Sibert J.L. et al.; "An Object-Oriented User Interface Management System", Siggraph'86, Vol.20, No.4, Dallas, August 1986, pp259-268.

[Takeuchi 86] Takeuchi A., Furukawa K.; "Partial Evaluation of Prolog Prolgrams And Its Application To Meta Programming", IFIP, 1986, pp415-420.

Use keyboard to respond: Which file?

workspace
local context
global context

Figure 1

Use keyboard to respond: Which predicate ?

Predicate	file	graph	stop

calling(p)
called(p)
zoom(p)

Figure 2

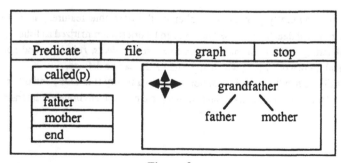

Predicate	file	graph	stop

called(p)

father
mother
end

grandfather
father   mother

Figure 3

Using Logic Databases in Software Development Environments

Patrizia Asirelli *and* Paola Inverardi

IEI-CNR - PISA, ITALY

1. Introduction

The paper discusses a role that logic programming can play in programming development environments. In particular, the suitability of logic databases to handle a specific programming development activity, notably configuration, is presented according to the experience gained while using a prototype logic database to support Ada-like configuration facilities [Asirelli 87a] and a Unix-like make facility [Asirelli 87b].

The work reported in the paper is part of a more general project whose aim is to propose logic data bases as effective tools to be used as project databases. To this respect it is useful to point out that the relations induced on modules by the configuration activity are typical examples of relations that must be dealt with by a project database.

Project Data Bases (PDB) play a central role in the process of software development acting as the repository of all information throughout the life cycle of a software product. PDB's are the heart of integrated development environments by means of which all tools can interact and/or exchange information. Unfortunately, given the high number of relations involved (rather than data) in a PDB, there is no general agreement on which is the best data model for it [Oberndorf 84], neither it has been definitely established which are the desirable functionalities a PDB should provide. On the other hand, attempts to standardization [CAIS1 85], show the need for simplification and formalization, of concepts and mechanisms.

A Logic Data Base (LDB) is essentially a (Horn clause) logic program plus a set of integrity constraints formulas, which define properties to be possessed by the logic program.

An LDB approach is proposed with respect to traditional relational (or entity-relationship) data bases partly because of the capabilities that logic brings to relational data bases, i.e. the ability to make deductions (deduce new facts from existing ones by means of rules), and also the ability to prove properties (integrity constraints) of the theory as logic program properties [Kowalski 78-79, Gallaire 84].

Furthermore, LDBs seem to naturally provide a number of the desirable features, according to [Oberndorf 84], of an environment data base. These features can be briefly summarized as follows:
• LDBs provide a formal setting and a uniform language to express *objects, relations,* and *updates,* thus they offer a bare logical framework within which any data model can be defined;
• evolving theories can easily be handled. The interaction between a theory (the LDB) and other meta-theories operating on it, can formally be described thus allowing the external environment interaction as

well as the concept of different views to be modelled; this means that LDBs are particularly suitable for dealing with advanced programming environments supporting requirements such as open-endness. In fact, the insertion of a new tool in the environment may require the specification of new relations among existing objects, and/or the creation of new objects. In addition, the use of updating operations (transactions) permits a complete integration between the logic data base system and the supporting environment;

• LDBs make it possible to directly address configuration issues. Configuration refers to the activity that *links* smaller components into a system. This should be performed at different stages in the life cycle of a software system, with various objectives, i.e. it should be possible to express, within a uniform and consistent framework, managerial requirements and design decisions as well as any application language constraints defining compilation, recompilation and linking in terms of the components and the relations among them.

• LDBs permits a theory of objects and their relations to be expressed, declaratively, thus providing a formal setting within which configurations can be designed and evaluated. By using SLD it is possible to validate the configurations , e.g. system specifications against user requirements, etc.

To summarize LDBs provide a uniform mechanism to *define* and to *run* configurations.

In the following, we will briefly discuss the logical structure of the EDBLOG system. The system is implemented in Quintus Prolog, extended in order to be integrated with the X-window system [Scheifler 86] to support the graphic interface and it runs on a Sun 3 workstation under Unix 4.2.

A sketch of the two configuration environments that we have considered, is used to discuss the suitability of our approach.

2. Logical components of the system

Our approach considers a data base as a logic program plus a set of formulas expressing integrity constraints. In order to guarantee the termination of the query evaluation process and the evaluation of negative queries the class of logic programs is, at present, restricted to hierarchical program definitions which, in particular, do not allow recursive definitions. The formulas that express the integrity constraints must be proved to be true in the minimal model of the program, thus ensuring the correctness of the data base with respect to the integrity constraints. At present an integrity checking algorithm, based on [Asirelli 85] is supported, but the system is open-ended with respect to the introduction of different algorithms [Asirelli 88b, Lloyd et al. 87].

The logic database management system EDBLOG considers the data base as consisting of three parts:

i) a logic program where *the set of facts*, unit Horn clauses, are considered to be the extensional component of the DB (EDB) and *the set of deductive rules*, definite Horn clauses, which are considered to be the intensional component of the DB (IDB);

ii) two kinds of integrity constraint formulas: *a set of Integrity Constraints* (*IC*), which are formulas of the form $A_k \rightarrow B_1,..., B_s$ that can be interpreted informally as whenever A_k is true then B_1 and...and B_s must also be true; *a set of Controls formulas* which are more general formulas $A_1,..., A_m \rightarrow B_1,...,B_n$ with $n,m \geq 0$ whose informal interpretation is that whenever A_1 and ... and A_m are true then B_1 and ... and B_n must also be true.

iii) a set of clauses that define compound updating operations (*transactions*); such clauses are either definite clauses or *trans* $\leftarrow$ **prec** | *trans* $_1$,..., *trans* $_n$ | **post**.

The two forms of *Integrity Constraints* and *Controls* formulas are used by EDBLOG in two different ways. IC are used to modify facts and rules of the data base so that only those facts which satisfy IC will be derivable from the data base theory, i.e. the semantics of the resulting DB is given by all facts that can be deduced from the data base and which satisfy IC. The second form of constraints, the *Controls*, are used periodically (at user request), to check that changes to the data base have preserved consistency with respect to this sort of constraints.

The language used to express transactions syntactically resembles Concurrent Prolog. The informal interpretation is that to execute the operation *trans*, the precondition (**prec**) must be first verified, and then the clause containing this precondition must be committed, the body executed and the corresponding postcondition verified. As in Concurrent Prolog, the commit operation is a way of expressing the behaviour of the Prolog cut operator. Preconditions and postconditions in the definitions of transactions will operate as controls which must be checked before/after the execution of the set of operations (body of the transaction), and thus they consent to separate global DB controls (*Controls*) from those related to particular transactions, thus reducing the number of necessary global *Controls* formulas.

The operational interpretation of these transaction definitions is the standard Prolog resolution of clauses where clauses are tried in the order they appear in the program. Thus, the *commitment* will be to the first clause whose precondition part succeeds. The successful evaluation of a goal which contains transaction causes the *Controls* formulas to be checked. The required transaction operations are aborted if the *Controls* checking fails. Abortion is also started upon failure of postconditions or of some operations of the body. The abortion of a transaction is handled by maintaining a *transition log* that is also useful in case of system crashes to restore the previous state.

A set of elementary updating operations is provided by the system as a meta-theory with respect to the DB. Such operations also allow *IC*, *Controls* formulas and transactions to be added and deleted.

3 Configuration issues and EDBLOG

Essentially, configuration concerns two distinct but related aspects:

   i) **Knowledge representation**, that is *what* is the relevant information and *which* is the most adequate representation for it. Usually, this aspect is handled by providing a model of the structure of the software under development, sometimes called system model [Marzullo 86]. It may include notions of versions, variants, subsystems etc. [Tichy 88], [Winkler 87]. Problems with this approach concern the flexibility of the model i.e. how easy it is to extend and/or modify such structures according to requirements for the specific software under development. It is not clear at all, in fact, which model can be considered *the most general,* and our experience is that configuration is difficult to be categorized since various kind of constraints can apply, ranging from hardware to managerial and user requirements, as well as application language constraints, thus affecting the knowledge granularity.

   ii) **Search strategies**, that is the ability to get a complete system out of several components following some search pattern. In particular, with respect to configuration issues, search strategies permit to collect together pieces of knowledge in a search space, according to some strategy.

To this respect the automatization of software configuration shares many points with the more general problem of automatizing the process of software development [Barstow 87].

Hence a kernel configuration system strongly demands for *flexibility* both in i) and in ii), that is neither a fixed structuring of the software nor configuration policies (e.g. automatic recompilation) should be mandatory but a model which is powerful and easy to be extended should be provided.

In DB terminology facts, rules, and constraints provide a description of the *concrete and abstract knowledge*, while updating operations and transactions permit to describe the *procedural knowledge and system dynamics*, thus, Horn Clause Logic plus updating operations and transactions represent the conceptual language of our system EDBLOG.

Referring to i) it is possible to define, by using EDBLOG, any system model .

With respect to ii) the context of logic programming offers a search strategy by means of the deduction (resolution) mechanism of the interpreter. Thus, in EDBLOG such mechanism is for granted, with respect to querying the database. Resolution also provides for integrity checking both on the knowledge (units and their relations), and on updatings. Furthermore, different strategies to collect together pieces of knowledge can be obtained, either by simply using the deduction capability of the querying mechanism of EDBLOG, or else by defining transactions which can retrieve and collect modules, according to the chosen strategy.

An important side effect in using EDBLOG is that the use of a uniform formalism both to express knowledge and the configuration facilities permits a powerful and simple interaction with the user. As a consequence, extensibility and modifiability are easily achievable: it is possible to extend relations as well as to modify existing ones, safely with respect to the established integrity constraints which can be checked upon updatings of the DB.

In our experimented examples we have, so far, paid more attention to the process of defining search strategies, point ii) above, than to that of knowledge representation, point i). This was mainly because we used EDBLOG as a kernel database management system in which it is possible to define every classical data model, e.g. relational [Kowalski 78] or entity relationship, [Giannini 86, Asirelli 88a]; in this way the resulting logic data base exhibits the same interface of a classical one, but augmented with the deductional and proof power. This design strategy was used [Giannini 86] in order to compare our approach to a classical one in the contest of a real kernel programming environment [ESP. 85].

In the following we discuss the two examples we have been experimenting, i.e. a project database for an Ada-like supporting environment and a Unix-make-like facility.

The two configuration environments we have treated are interesting because they are in some sense complementary. In fact, the Ada environment concentrates on linguistic aspects and to this respect our approach can be seen, beside a realization of the Ada configuration facilities, as an attempt to formalize notions and concepts which, although deeply related to the language, are not formally part of it. The second one is, instead, related to a more general environment thus trying to perform an integration with the Unix world providing a sort of automatizated version of the make-facilities.

4. An overview of the examples

The two working examples exhibit the same general schema that can be summarized as follows.

The *knowledge* in the PDB is given by:

-*facts* and *rules* that provides the description of the objects in the PDB; relations among objects can be modified via the simple updating operations that EDBLOG provides. E.g. the **insert_f** operation manipulates the database inserting a new fact in the theory.

- *constraints* that can be seen as a mean to enrich the semantics of objects and/or, in general, as a mean to express invariant properties that the objects involved in the constraints have to posses, in every state of the PDB. I.e. upon updating, new objects can be inserted, thus constraints checking will ensure that the update is correct with respect to the stated properties. In this way it is also possible to express constraints on configurations, e.g. implementation constraints or language constraints, that a configuration must satisfy.

The *strategies* are defined by means of *transactions*, e.g. several compilation strategies can be defined.
In the Ada example, the compilation operation that we have defined is the standard one. The user is not forced to use this strategy, he/she can easily define another policy and use it. Actually, in [Asirelli 87a] an automatic compilation strategy is defined too, such that , when called on a module M, it checks that all the modules, on which M depends, are compiled, and if they are not, it forces their compilation. In the Unix example, the search strategy we have implemented is the usual one, i.e it is based on the date and time in which a file was last modified.

The integration with the external environment is achieved by the meta level predicates *comp_Ada* and *exec* that respectively are: the call to the Ada compiler; and the call to the Unix environment (Shell) to execute commands.

A sketch of the Ada-like configuration environment example

knowledge representation

•*Facts and Rules*

...
```
subp_decl (unit (a, null))
subp_body (unit (d, 1))
subp_body (unit (a, 1))
...
sub_unit (unit (fd, 1))
child_of (unit (d, 1), unit (fd, 1))
with_clause (unit (d, 1), (unit (a, null).unit(b, null).nil))
main (unit (X, Y)) ← subp_body (unit (X,Y))
lib_unit (X) ← decl (X)
lib_unit (X) ← main (X)
sec_unit (X) ←body (X)
sec_unit (X) ←sub_unit (X)
has_decl_part (unit(X,Y)) ← Y≠ "null", subp_decl (unit (X,null) )
....
```

•*Constraints*

```
main(unit(X,Y)) →not (has_decl_part (unit(X, Y)) ), Y = 1
sec_unit (unit(X,Y)), sec_unit (unit(X,Z)) → Y ≠ Z
body (unit(X,Y)), not (main(unit(X,Y))) →decl ( unit(X,Y))
```

search strategies

Transactions for compilation

compile (X) ←sec_unit(X), compilable_sec(X) | *comp_Ada* (X),**insert_f** (compiled_sec(X))

compile (X) ← lib_unit(X), compilable_lib(X) | *comp_Ada* (X), **insert_f** (compiled_lib(X))

Make-like facility

• *Facts and Rules*

file(name(a,c))
file(name(f,p))
...
date(name(a,c), (2 10 (11 30)))
date(name(f,p), (2 10 (11 40)))
implicit_dependency(name(X,o), (name(X,p).nil)) ← file(name(X,p))
implicit_body (name(X,o), body(pc -c X.p)) ← file(name(X,p))
...
inconsistent_date (Name, X) ← date (Name, D1), date (X, D2), min (D1,D2)

• *Constraints* :

explicit_dependency (Name,W), W ≠ **nil** → explicit_ body (Name,Y) , Y≠nil

• *Transactions:*

make_file (Name, Dep_list, Body) ← | **insert** (explicit_dependency (Name, Dep_list)),
insert (explicit_body(Name,body (Body)))
...
make (Name) ← implicit_dependency(Name,W) | *check_all_consistency* (Name,W)
make (Name) ← explicit_dependency(Name,W) |*check_consistency* (Name,W,expl)
make (Name) ← explicit_body(Name, body(B)) | *exec* (B).

As it can be seen from the examples, facts and rules are used to model the knowledge that is inherent to the application domain, that is: in the case of Ada, we have modelled the typical objects that constitute the Ada library; in the Unix-make example we have instead modelled the information generally contained in the Unix file system.

With respect to the latter, facts defined by the first two relations state the implicit dependency relation between the object code and the source code. The implicit_dependency predicate defines the built-in knowledge assumed by the Unix Make facility. The inconsistent_date is a predicate which is used to detect whether the creation/modification date between two files is in the right order or not. It is worthwhile noticing that, by this approach, it is possible to handle any kind of dependency relation and to extend the built-in knowledge by adding or removing any kind of implicit dependency relations

With respect to integrity constraints the Ada example is more interesting. In that case, in fact, they are used in two different ways, that is the first two controls integrates the definition of a what a *main* is, while the last one states a global consistency condition on the program library.

The above transactions for Ada implement the compilation operation in fact, according to Ada, it is possible to compile a module iff all the modules it depends on (i.e. *father*, *with clauses*) are compiled. The relations compilable_lib and compilable_sec act as pre-conditions that have to be verified by the database, before calling the Ada compiler which is no more supposed to do any check on the compilability of the unit to be compiled;

The transaction *make_file*, is activated by the user to introduce new dependency relations between files. It has the same purpose of the makefile (of Unix).
The *make* transaction corresponds to the make command, i.e. when issued as a goal in the transaction theory, it checks whether dependency relations exist for the named file, and, if so, it performs all the necessary checks and related commands.
In this case two separate transactions are used in order to update the DB and to interface with the external environment.

5. Conclusions and future developments

As a general remark note that, according to this approach, we have provided the PDB with functionalities that are traditionally part of the tool level. For example, in PCTE [ESP. 85], the Project DB manager, called OMS, provides a set of primitives to interface with the tools that stand at a higher level, without providing more complex functionalities. That is, OMS provides for a set of low level primitives that can be used to implement various management strategies. This is because OMS is thought as a kernel for programming environments and as such it has to be as flexible as possible, with respect to the software that a user might define at a higher level. The cost for such a flexibility is, of course, the primitivity of the functionalities offered by OMS. On the other hand, building a project data base with a logic data base permits the definition of a higher level of basic functionalities with respect to the one offered by traditional databases. To adopt Ada terminology, using a logic database allows the mixture of parts of the functionalities usually offered by the two environment levels KAPSE and MAPSE without loss of generality. Such major power is not payed in term of flexibility and it essentially derives from the deduction and proof checking capabilities that LDBs offer.

Future developments mainly go into two directions, one is more foundational and concerns problems of LDB's views handling, integrity checking optimization and, more generally, problems related to properties preservation upon updatings. The other research line goes towards the use of EDBLOG in practical applications, notably Configuration Environments, and it concerns its suitability as a general purpose configuration kernel. Thus, problems related to knowledge representation methodology have to be faced. To this respect, we are concentrating on the definition, using EDBLOG, of a configuration model which has to balance between maintaining a certain flexibility of the system while providing the user with non primitive configuration capabilities.
The definition of a configuration model is not a trivial problem, as it clearly came out from the discussion and from the papers presented at a recent workshop on Configuration management [WSVCC 88]. We believe that the use a tool that forces formalization will give a valid contribution to the area.

REFERENCES

[Asirelli 85] **Asirelli, P., De Santis, M., Martelli, M.,** Integrity Constraints in Logic Data Bases, *Journal of Logic Programming*, Vol. 2, no. 3, Oct. 1985.

[Asirelli 87a] Asirelli, P., Inverardi, P., A Logic Database to support Configuration Management in Ada, *Proc.1987 Ada EUROPE Conference on Ada COMPONENTS: Libraries and Tools*, Stockholm, 26-28 May, 1987, The Ada Companion Series, Cambridge University Press.

[Asirelli 87b] Asirelli, P., Inverardi, P., Ehnancing configuration facilities in software development: A logic approach, *Proc.ESEC'87 1st European Software Engineering Conference*, Strasbourg, 9-11 September, 1987, LNCS 289.

[Asirelli 88a] Asirelli, P., Inverardi, P., EDBLOG: a kernel for configuration environments, *in* [WSVCC 88].

[Asirelli 88b] Asirelli, P., Inverardi, P., Mustaro, A. Improving Integrity Constraint Checking in Deductive Databases *Proc. Int. Conference on Database Theory*, Brugge Belgium, Sep., 1988, LNCS 326.

[Barstow 87] Barstow, D., Artificial Intelligence and Software Engineering, *Proc. 9th Annual International Conference on SOFTWARE ENGINEERING*, Monterey, California, March 30-April 2, 1987.

[CAIS1 85] CAIS1 Military Standard, Common APSE Interface Set, AJPO, 3rd version, 31st January, 1985.

[ESP. 85] ESPRIT, PCTE:A Basis for a Portable Common Tool Environment. Functional Specification. Third Edition 1985.

[Gallaire 84] Gallaire, H., Minker, J., Nicolas, J., Logic and Databases: a Deductive Approach, *Computing Surveys*, 16, (2), pp. 153-185, 1984.

[Giannini 86] Giannini, F., Grifoni, E., Programmazione Logica in Ambiente di Sviluppo Software : Data Base Logici come Data Base di Progetto, *Tesi di laurea, Corso di Laurea in Scienza dell'Informazione*, Pisa 1986.

[Lloyd et al. 87] Lloyd, J. W., Sonenberg, E.,A., Topor, R. W., Integrity Constraint Checking in Stratified Databases, *J. Logic Programming* 4 (4): 331-343, 1987.

[Kowalski 78] Kowalski, R. A., Logic for Data Description, in *Logic and Databases* (Gallaire, H. and Minker, J. Eds), Plenum Press, 1978.

[Kowalski 79] Kowalski, R.A., *Logic for Problem Solving*, North Holland, Artificial Intelligence Series, N.J. Nilsson (Ed.), 1979.

[Marzullo 86] Marzullo,K.,Wiebe,D., Jasmine:A Software System Modelling Facility, *Proc. ACM SIGSOFT/SIGPLAN Software Engeneering Symp. on Pract. Soft. Devel. Env.*, Palo Alto, CA, December 9-11, 1986.

[Oberndorf 84] Oberndorf, P.A., Penedo, M.H., Summary of Project Database Working Group Discussions , *Proc. ACM AdaTEC Future Ada Environment Workshop*, Santa Barbara, California, 17-20 Sept., 1984, *ACM Ada Letters*, Vol. IV, no. 5, 1985.

[Scheifler 86] Scheifler, R.W.and Gettys J. , The X Window System, *ACM Trans. on Graphics*, 5,(2), pp. 79-109, 1986.

[Winkler 87] Winkler, J.F.H., Version Control in Families of Large Programs, *Proc. 9th Annual Inte.Conf.on SOFT. ENG.*, Monterey, California, March 30-April 2, 1987.

[WSVCC 88] *Proc. Int. Workshop on Software Version and Configuration Control*, Grassau (Munich), 27-29 Jan., J.F.H. Winkler (ed.), German Chap. ACM, Berichte 30, Teubner, 1988.

[Tichy 88] Tichy,W., Tools for Software Configuration Management, in [WSVCC 88].

Lecture Notes in Computer Science

Vol. 245: H.F. de Groote, Lectures on the Complexity of Bilinear Problems. V, 135 pages. 1987.

Vol. 246: Graph-Theoretic Concepts in Computer Science. Proceedings, 1986. Edited by G. Tinhofer and G. Schmidt. VII, 307 pages. 1987.

Vol. 247: STACS 87. Proceedings, 1987. Edited by F.J. Brandenburg, G. Vidal-Naquet and M. Wirsing. X, 484 pages. 1987.

Vol. 248: Networking in Open Systems. Proceedings, 1986. Edited by G. Müller and R.P. Blanc. VI, 441 pages. 1987.

Vol. 249: TAPSOFT '87. Volume 1. Proceedings, 1987. Edited by H. Ehrig, R. Kowalski, G. Levi and U. Montanari. XIV, 289 pages. 1987.

Vol. 250: TAPSOFT '87. Volume 2. Proceedings, 1987. Edited by H. Ehrig, R. Kowalski, G. Levi and U. Montanari. XIV, 336 pages. 1987.

Vol. 251: V. Akman, Unobstructed Shortest Paths in Polyhedral Environments. VII, 103 pages. 1987.

Vol. 252: VDM '87. VDM – A Formal Method at Work. Proceedings, 1987. Edited by D. Bjørner, C.B. Jones, M. Mac an Airchinnigh and E.J. Neuhold. IX, 422 pages. 1987.

Vol. 253: J.D. Becker, I. Eisele (Eds.), WOPPLOT 86. Parallel Processing: Logic, Organization, and Technology. Proceedings, 1986. V, 226 pages. 1987.

Vol. 254: Petri Nets: Central Models and Their Properties. Advances in Petri Nets 1986, Part I. Proceedings, 1986. Edited by W. Brauer, W. Reisig and G. Rozenberg. X, 480 pages. 1987.

Vol. 255: Petri Nets: Applications and Relationships to Other Models of Concurrency. Advances in Petri Nets 1986, Part II. Proceedings, 1986. Edited by W. Brauer, W. Reisig and G. Rozenberg. X, 516 pages. 1987.

Vol. 256: Rewriting Techniques and Applications. Proceedings, 1987. Edited by P. Lescanne. VI, 285 pages. 1987.

Vol. 257: Database Machine Performance: Modeling Methodologies and Evaluation Strategies. Edited by F. Cesarini and S. Salza. X, 250 pages. 1987.

Vol. 258: PARLE, Parallel Architectures and Languages Europe. Volume I. Proceedings, 1987. Edited by J.W. de Bakker, A.J. Nijman and P.C. Treleaven. XII, 480 pages. 1987.

Vol. 259: PARLE, Parallel Architectures and Languages Europe. Volume II. Proceedings, 1987. Edited by J.W. de Bakker, A.J. Nijman and P.C. Treleaven. XII, 464 pages. 1987.

Vol. 260: D.C. Luckham, F.W. von Henke, B. Krieg-Brückner, O. Owe, ANNA, A Language for Annotating Ada Programs. V, 143 pages. 1987.

Vol. 261: J. Ch. Freytag, Translating Relational Queries into Iterative Programs. XI, 131 pages. 1987.

Vol. 262: A. Burns, A.M. Lister, A.J. Wellings, A Review of Ada Tasking. VIII, 141 pages. 1987.

Vol. 263: A.M. Odlyzko (Ed.), Advances in Cryptology – CRYPTO '86. Proceedings. XI, 489 pages. 1987.

Vol. 264: E. Wada (Ed.), Logic Programming '86. Proceedings, 1986. VI, 179 pages. 1987.

Vol. 265: K.P. Jantke (Ed.), Analogical and Inductive Inference. Proceedings, 1986. VI, 227 pages. 1987.

Vol. 266: G. Rozenberg (Ed.), Advances in Petri Nets 1987. VI, 451 pages. 1987.

Vol. 267: Th. Ottmann (Ed.), Automata, Languages and Programming. Proceedings, 1987. X, 565 pages. 1987.

Vol. 268: P.M. Pardalos, J.B. Rosen, Constrained Global Optimization: Algorithms and Applications. VII, 143 pages. 1987.

Vol. 269: A. Albrecht, H. Jung, K. Mehlhorn (Eds.), Parallel Algorithms and Architectures. Proceedings, 1987. Approx. 205 pages. 1987.

Vol. 270: E. Börger (Ed.), Computation Theory and Logic. IX, 442 pages. 1987.

Vol. 271: D. Snyers, A. Thayse, From Logic Design to Logic Programming. IV, 125 pages. 1987.

Vol. 272: P. Treleaven, M. Vanneschi (Eds.), Future Parallel Computers. Proceedings, 1986. V, 492 pages. 1987.

Vol. 273: J.S. Royer, A Connotational Theory of Program Structure. V, 186 pages. 1987.

Vol. 274: G. Kahn (Ed.), Functional Programming Languages and Computer Architecture. Proceedings. VI, 470 pages. 1987.

Vol. 275: A.N. Habermann, U. Montanari (Eds.), System Development and Ada. Proceedings, 1986. V, 305 pages. 1987.

Vol. 276: J. Bézivin, J.-M. Hullot, P. Cointe, H. Lieberman (Eds.), ECOOP '87. European Conference on Object-Oriented Programming. Proceedings. VI, 273 pages. 1987.

Vol. 277: B. Benninghofen, S. Kemmerich, M.M. Richter, Systems of Reductions. X, 265 pages. 1987.

Vol. 278: L. Budach, R.G. Bukharajev, O.B. Lupanov (Eds.), Fundamentals of Computation Theory. Proceedings, 1987. XIV, 505 pages. 1987.

Vol. 279: J.H. Fasel, R.M. Keller (Eds.), Graph Reduction. Proceedings, 1986. XVI, 450 pages. 1987.

Vol. 280: M. Venturini Zilli (Ed.), Mathematical Models for the Semantics of Parallelism. Proceedings, 1986. V, 231 pages. 1987.

Vol. 281: A. Kelemenová, J. Kelemen (Eds.), Trends, Techniques, and Problems in Theoretical Computer Science. Proceedings, 1986. VI, 213 pages. 1987.

Vol. 282: P. Gorny, M.J. Tauber (Eds.), Visualization in Programming. Proceedings, 1986. VII, 210 pages. 1987.

Vol. 283: D.H. Pitt, A. Poigné, D.E. Rydeheard (Eds.), Category Theory and Computer Science. Proceedings, 1987. V, 300 pages. 1987.

Vol. 284: A. Kündig, R.E. Bührer, J. Dähler (Eds.), Embedded Systems. Proceedings, 1986. V, 207 pages. 1987.

Vol. 285: C. Delgado Kloos, Semantics of Digital Circuits. IX, 124 pages. 1987.

Vol. 286: B. Bouchon, R.R. Yager (Eds.), Uncertainty in Knowledge-Based Systems. Proceedings, 1986. VII, 405 pages. 1987.

Vol. 287: K.V. Nori (Ed.), Foundations of Software Technology and Theoretical Computer Science. Proceedings, 1987. IX, 540 pages. 1987.

Vol. 288: A. Blikle, MetaSoft Primer. XIII, 140 pages. 1987.

Vol. 289: H.K. Nichols, D. Simpson (Eds.), ESEC '87. 1st European Software Engineering Conference. Proceedings, 1987. XII, 404 pages. 1987.

Vol. 290: T.X. Bui, Co-oP A Group Decision Support System for Cooperative Multiple Criteria Group Decision Making. XIII, 250 pages. 1987.

Vol. 291: H. Ehrig, M. Nagl, G. Rozenberg, A. Rosenfeld (Eds.), Graph-Grammars and Their Application to Computer Science. VIII, 609 pages. 1987.

Vol. 292: The Munich Project CIP. Volume II: The Program Transformation System CIP-S. By the CIP System Group. VIII, 522 pages. 1987.

Vol. 293: C. Pomerance (Ed.), Advances in Cryptology — CRYPTO '87. Proceedings. X, 463 pages. 1988.

Vol. 294: R. Cori, M. Wirsing (Eds.), STACS 88. Proceedings, 1988. IX, 404 pages. 1988.

Vol. 295: R. Dierstein, D. Müller-Wichards, H.-M. Wacker (Eds.), Parallel Computing in Science and Engineering. Proceedings, 1987. V, 185 pages. 1988.